Proselytism and
Orthodoxy in Russia

Religion and Human Rights Series

Series Editors
John Witte Jr.
Abdullahi Ahmed An-Na'im
Emory University

Board of Advisors
Azizah al-Hibri, University of Richmond
Donna Arzt, Syracuse University
Irwin Cotler, McGill University
Frances Deng, The Brookings Institution
Jean Bethke Elshtain, University of Chicago
David Little, United States Institute of Peace
Ann Elizabeth Mayer, University of Pennsylvania
José Míguez Bonino, Facultad Evangélica, ISEDET, Buenos Aires
Chandra Muzzafar, University of Malaysia
John T. Noonan Jr., U.S. Court of Appeals
Kusumita Pedersen, St. Francis College
Lamin Sanneh, Yale University
Max Stackhouse, Princeton Theological Seminary
M. Thomas Thangaraj, Emory University

Other Books Published in the Series

Proselytization and Self-Determination in Africa
    Abdullahi Ahmed An-Na'im, editor
Religious Freedom and Evangelization in Latin America: The Challenge of Religious Pluralism
    Paul E. Sigmund, editor

RELIGION & HUMAN RIGHTS SERIES

Proselytism and Orthodoxy in Russia

The New War for Souls

John Witte Jr.
Michael Bourdeaux
Editors

ORBIS BOOKS

Maryknoll, New York 10545

The Catholic Foreign Mission Society of America (Maryknoll) recruits and trains people for overseas missionary service. Through Orbis Books, Maryknoll aims to foster the international dialogue that is essential to mission. The books published, however, reflect the opinions of their authors and are not meant to represent the official position of the Society. To obtain more information about Maryknoll and Orbis Books, please visit our website at www.maryknoll.org.

Copyright © 1999 by John Witte Jr. and Michael Bourdeaux

Published by Orbis Books, Maryknoll, New York, U.S.A.

Manufactured in the United States of America.

Copy editing and typesetting by Joan Weber Laflamme.

Library of Congress Cataloging-in-Publication Data

Proselytism and orthodoxy in Russia : the new war for souls / John
    Witte, Jr., Michael Bourdeaux, editors.
        p. cm. — (Religion & human rights series)
    Includes bibliographical references and index.
    ISBN 1-57075-262-1 (alk. paper)
    1. Evangelistic work—Russia (Federation) 2. Russia (Federation)—
Church history. 3. Russkaia pravoslavnaia tserkov'—History.
4. Orthodox Eastern Church—Russia (Federation)—History.
    I. Witte, John, 1959– . II. Bourdeaux, Michael. III. Series.
    BX493.P76 1999
    274.7'0829—dc21
                                                            99-21682
                                                            CIP

To the memory of
Jane Ellis
Fellow Worker in the Vineyard

Contents

PART TWO
LEGAL PERSPECTIVES

PART THREE
SIGNPOSTS FOR A NEW WAY

THE RELIGION AND HUMAN RIGHTS
SERIES PREFACE

The relationship between religion and human rights is both problematic and unavoidable in all parts of the world. Religion, broadly defined to include various traditional, cultural, and customary institutions and practices, is unquestionably a formidable force for violence, repression, and chauvinism of untold dimensions. But religion is also a natural and necessary ally in the global struggle for human rights. For human rights norms are inherently abstract ideals—universal statements of the good life and the good society. They depend upon the visions and values of human communities to give them content, coherence, and concrete manifestation. Religion is an inherent condition of human lives and human communities. Religion invariably provides the sources and scales of dignity and responsibility, shame and respect, restitution and reconciliation that a human rights regime needs to survive and to flourish.

This book Series explores the interaction of religious ideas and institutions with human rights principles and practices. It seeks to discover the religious sources of human rights—both their cultivation and their corruption in the discourse of sacred texts, the activism of religious organizations, and the practices of religious polities. It seeks to uncover the legal sources of human rights—both their protection and their abridgment in international human rights instruments and in domestic constitutions, statutes, and cases. It seeks to address some of the cutting edge issues of religion and human rights in theory and practice.

This Series is made possible, in part, by the generous funding of The Pew Charitable Trusts, Inc. and the Ford Foundation. Pew's support came through its funding of a three-year project on "Soul Wars: The Problem and Promise of Proselytism in the New World Order." Ford's support came through its funding of a three-year project on "Cultural Transformation in Africa: Legal, Religious, and Human Rights Perspectives." Several of the early volumes in this Series are parts and products of these two projects. They provide pilots and prototypes for the type of rigorous interdisciplinary and interreligious analysis that the subject of religion and human rights requires.

We wish to express our gratitude to our friends at the two foundations for their generous support of this effort. We also wish to thank the Maryknoll

Fathers and Brothers and Bill Burrows and Bernadette Price of Orbis for their sage stewardship of this Series.

— JOHN WITTE JR.
ABDULLAHI AHMED AN-NA'IM
EMORY UNIVERSITY, ATLANTA

PREFACE

In a series of projects conducted over the past decade, the Law and Religion Program at Emory University has explored the religious and cultural sources and dimensions of human rights and democracy. These projects have sought to uncover the contributions of Christianity, Judaism, Islam, and other faiths to the cultivation—and abridgement—of ideas and institutions of human rights and democracy. These projects have also sought to uncover, within these religious cultures, sources and sanctions for an emerging global understanding and practice of human rights, democracy, and rule of law.

The obvious premise of these projects is that a regime of law, human rights, and democracy is indispensable to the establishment of local and world order. The less obvious premise is that religion is a vital dimension of any such regime. Democratic norms and human rights laws are inherently abstract ideals—universal statements of the good life and the good society. They depend upon the visions and values of human communities and cultures to give them content and coherence. Religion is an ineradicable condition of human persons and communities. Religions invariably provide universal sources and scales of values by which many persons and communities govern and measure themselves. Religions invariably suffuse the cultural, ethnic, and national identity of a person and a people. Religions must thus be seen as indispensable allies in the modern struggle for human rights and democratization. Their faith and works, their cultural and ethnic symbols and structures must be adduced to give meaning and measure to the abstract claims of democratic and human rights norms.

Our first project, *Christianity and Democracy in Global Context* (1989-92), was designed to review the past and potential contributions of Christianity to the precocious rise of democratic movements in various parts of the world. Our second project, *Religious Human Rights in Global Perspective* (1992-96), analyzed the positive and negative contributions that Christianity, Judaism, and Islam had made and could make to the theory and law of religious rights and liberties in the international community and in the Atlantic continents. In both these projects, we came upon a growing paradox of the modern human rights and democratic revolution. In the 1990s, the world seems to have entered something of a "Dickensian era" (in Irwin Cotler's apt phrase). We have some of the best human rights and democratic polities on the books, but some of the worst human rights abuses and autocratic policies on the ground. Religious groups—in all their theological, cultural, and ethnic diversity—have emerged as both leading villains and leading victims in this Dickensian drama.

Our current project, *The Problem of Proselytism in the New World Order,* is focused on one dimension of this emerging global problem of religious conflict—the growing clash within and between indigenous faiths and foreign faiths over proselytism and conversion. This conflict has taken on a variety of forms in the newly transformed (sometimes democratized) polities of the world. On the one hand, religious, ethnic, and cultural rivals, previously kept at bay by a common oppressor, have renewed their hostilities, sometimes with catastrophic results. In some communities, such as the former Yugoslavia, these local rivals have converted their new liberties into licenses to renew ancient hostilities—featuring mass murder and rape, ethnic cleansing and genocide, violent iconoclasm, forced baptisms, and coerced conversions. In other communities, such as the Sudan and Rwanda, ethnic nationalism and religious extremism have conspired to bring violent dislocation or death to thousands of religious believers each year, and false imprisonment, forced starvation, and other savage abuses to tens of thousands of others. In still other communities, most notably in Western Europe and North America, political secularism and resurgent nationalism have combined to threaten a sort of civil denial and death to many minority believers, particularly those of high religious temperature or of low cultural conformity.

On the other hand, in Russia, and parts of Eastern Europe, Subsaharan Africa, and Latin America, the human rights and democratic revolution has brought on a new war for souls between indigenous and foreign religious groups. This is the most recent, and the most ironic, chapter in the Dickensian drama of human rights. With the political transformations of these regions in the past two decades, foreign religious groups were granted rights to enter these regions for the first time in generations. In the past decade, they have come in increasing numbers to preach their faiths, to offer their services, to convert new souls. Initially, local religious groups welcomed these foreigners. Today, they have come to resent these foreign religions, particularly those from North America and Western Europe who assume a democratic human rights ethic. Local religious groups resent the participation in the marketplace of religious ideas that democracy assumes. They resent the toxic waves of materialism and individualism that democracy inflicts. They resent the massive expansion of religious pluralism that democracy encourages. They resent the extravagant forms of religious speech, press, and assembly that democracy protects. A new war for souls has thus broken out in these regions—a fight to reclaim the traditional cultural and moral souls of these new societies and a fight to retain adherents and adherence to the indigenous faiths.

The goal of our current project has been to assess this emerging problem through empirical and normative studies and, where possible, seek to assuage the most acute forms of conflict through the cultivation of theological and human rights solutions. We have sought through this process to try to parse and police the line between legitimate and illegitimate forms of exercise, enhancement, and extension of religious, cultural, and ethnic traditions.

This exercise has required us to open some difficult theoretical issues and to explore them in various cultural and religious contexts. In Christian theological terms, the dialectic is between the Great Commission and the Golden Rule: how does a person or community abide simultaneously with the callings to "go forth into the world and make disciples of all nations," and to "do unto others as you would have them do unto you"? In human rights terms, the dialectic is between free exercise and liberty of conscience: how does a community balance its own right to expand the faith, and another person's or community's right to be left alone? In sociological terms, the dialectic is among sharply competing understandings of conversion: how does one craft a general rule to govern Christians, who have easy conversion into and out of the faith; Jews, who have difficult conversion into and out of the faith; and Muslims, who have easy conversion into the faith but allow for no conversion out of it? Neither conventional missiology nor current human rights jurisprudence has as yet developed a coherent methodology to resolve these dialectics. This project, and its publications, are taking tentative steps to that end.

This volume on Russia—together with other regional studies on Africa and Latin America, and comparative studies on the theology and law of proselytism and conversion—will be among the first titles in a new book series, "Religion and Human Rights." This book series is a joint venture between Orbis Books and the Law and Religion Program.

It was a special privilege for the Law and Religion Program to form a joint venture with Keston Institute, Oxford, for this study of proselytism in Russia. Founded in 1969, Keston Institute has emerged as the leading institution of the world devoted to the study of religion in Russia and other Communist and former Communist lands. Keston reports on all denominations and faiths, with special emphasis on the protections of religious liberty. It reports its findings in a regular wire news service, a monthly magazine, and a scholarly quarterly; and sponsors lectures, conferences, and educational programs throughout the former Soviet bloc and beyond. It also houses a unique archive of tens of thousands of documents and publications, many produced clandestinely by believers under Communist rule. Keston is currently engaged in a major project, sponsored by The Pew Charitable Trusts, Inc., in mapping and analyzing the religious landscape of Russia.

I owe an enormous debt of thanks to the Rev. Dr. Canon Michael Bourdeaux, the founder and director of Keston Institute, who co-directed this Russian project with me and has co-edited this volume. A leading scholar of Russian religion and winner of the prestigious Templeton Prize, Canon Bourdeaux has devoted his career to protecting and promoting the cause of religious liberty for believers throughout Russia and beyond. In the grimmest days of Soviet religious purges and propaganda, he was one of the few voices bold enough and strong enough to name the persecutors, to expose the propaganda, and to seek the liberty of Christian, Jewish, and other Russian believers. In the days of *glasnost, perestroika,* and *demokratizatsiia,* he has been a visionary leader in sponsoring new understanding and dialogue among rival religious groups within Russia. Michael Bourdeaux's sterling volume, *Gorbachev, Glasnost, and the Gospel* (1990), will long endure as a classic.

From among our other Keston friends, I would like to thank Dr. Philip Walters, Keston's head of research, and Dr. Lawrence A. Uzzell, Keston's Moscow correspondent, for their expert counsel in selecting the contributors to this project, and in making their own valuable contributions to this volume. I would like to thank Ms. Lorna Bourdeaux, Ms. Xenia Dennen, and Mr. Malcolm Walker for their valuable contributions to our research and deliberations. Most special thanks are due to Ms. Erika Cuneo, who administered Keston's involvement in this joint venture, and who organized two major conferences at Oxford in 1996 and 1997 on the topic.

From among our Emory colleagues, I would like to thank my colleagues and friends, Professors Abdullahi A. An-Na'im, Michael J. Broyde, and Johan D. Van der Vyver, for their invaluable collaboration with me on this proselytism project. I would like especially to thank Mr. Joel Nichols and Ms. Louise Jackson for their dedicated work in the editing and production of this volume. I would like to thank Ms. Eliza Ellison and Ms. Anita Mann for their sage administration and fiscal management of the entire proselytism project, and Ms. Elaine Justice and the continued good offices of the Emory news and information center. I would also wish to thank Mssrs. John Ferguson, Luke Andrews, Matthew Miller, and Jason Waite, and Ms. Meaghan Hogan, for commissioning and editing the special issue of the *Emory International Law Review* 12 (1998): 1-737 on the 1997 Russian law on freedom of conscience, and permitting us to reprint updated excerpts from four of the articles herein.

This project and publication on Russia—and the larger project on proselytism of which it is a part—were made possible by a generous grant from The Pew Charitable Trusts, Inc., in Philadelphia, Pennsylvania. On behalf of the Law and Religion Program and Keston Institute, we wish to offer our warmest thanks to the Trusts, particularly President Rebecca M. Rimel, and Dr. Luis Lugo and his predecessor, Dr. Joel Carpenter, of the Religion Division, for their continued solicitude for this vital work.

This volume is dedicated to the memory of Jane Ellis, a long-time member of Keston Institute and a leading scholar of the Russian Orthodox Church. Her untimely death in June 1998 is a great loss to her family and friends in the United Kingdom and abroad, and to the broader community of Russian scholars to which she had made such valuable contributions.

— JOHN WITTE JR.

INTRODUCTION

———————◆———————

John Witte Jr.

It is our obligation to battle [for] people's souls by all legal means available, rather than allowing them to perish. [We must] react to the continuing intensive proselytizing activity by some Catholic circles and various Protestant groups . . . [and] to the growing activity of sects, including those of a totalitarian nature . . . for it is largely our own brothers and sisters who fall victim to these sects.
—PATRIARCH ALEKSII II, DECEMBER 26, 1996[1]

A new war for souls has broken out in Russia—a war to reclaim the traditional spiritual and moral soul of the Russian people, and a war to retain adherence and adherents to the Russian Orthodox Church. In part, this is a *theological* war—as the Moscow Patriarchate of the Russian Orthodox Church has sought to reestablish itself as the spiritual leader of the Russian people, and as rival religious communities from Russia and abroad have begun actively to defame and demonize each other. The ecumenical spirit of the previous decades is giving way to sharp new forms of religious balkanization and rivalry in Russia. In part, this is a *legal* war—as local and national legislatures have passed laws severely restricting the rights of many religious persons and peoples of Russia. Beneath its shiny constitutional veneer of religious freedom and equality for all, Russia is developing a new legal culture of overt religious favoritism for some and overt religious repression of others.

This volume analyzes this new war for souls in Russia—its religious sources and dimensions, its legal modes and measures, its enduring challenges and promises. Metropolitan Kirill of Smolensk and Kaliningrad, the leading voice

---

[1] Aleksii II, Patriarch of Moscow and All Russia, "Address of the Patriarch to the Councils of the Moscow Parishes at the Episcopal Gathering, 12 December 1996," *Tsekovno-obschestvennyi Vestnik* 6 (December 26, 1996): 7, col. 1 [hereafter "Address of the Patriarch"].

1

of the Moscow Patriarchate after Aleksii II, offers a powerful manifesto on the classic Russian Orthodox understanding of the relationship of Gospel and culture and of Church and state in Russia—which views Philip Walters, and Firuz Kazemzadeh place in long historical perspective. James Billington and Michael Bourdeaux recount the vital roles of Orthodox and other religious groups in the transformation of the Soviet state, and in the great awakening of Russian religions. Sergei Filatov, Mikhail Kulakov, Alexsandr Shchipkov, Yuriy Tabak, and Lyudmila Vorontsova provide insiders' accounts of representative religious groups and movements in Russia—and the historical and contemporary rivalries among them. Harold Berman, Jeremy Gunn, Lauren Homer, and Lawrence Uzzell provide firsthand accounts of the machinations surrounding recent provincial and national laws on religion, and their flagrant violations of basic constitutional and human rights. Mark Elliott and Anita Deyneka recount the rise of Western missionaries in Russia. Donna Arzt recounts the plight of the burgeoning population of Russian Muslims. In a concluding section, Deyneka and Uzzell offer guidelines of greater prudence and mutual understanding among foreign mission groups and among local religious and political leaders in Russia.

This Introduction provides a brief overview of some of the main themes that emerge from these chapters. The first part summarizes the remarkable transformation of Russia from a regime that a decade ago guaranteed religious liberty for all, to a regime that today grants full religious rights only to the Russian Orthodox Church. The second part explores some of the "ontological differences" between Russian Orthodoxy and Western Christianity that lie at the heart both of this new war for souls and of any attempted assuagement of it.

FROM GLASNOST TO SOUL WARS

GLASNOST AND THE GREAT AWAKENING

A decade ago, Russia embraced religious liberty for all. President Mikhail Gorbachev's revolutionary ideals of *glasnost* and *perestroika* broke the harsh establishment of Marxist-Leninist atheism, and awakened the sundry traditional faiths of Russia. The late 1980s saw the revival not only of Russian Orthodoxy, but also of an array of traditional Adventist, Armenian Apostolic, Baptist, Buddhist, Georgian Orthodox, Greek Catholic, Jewish, Lutheran, Roman Catholic, Shi'ite and Sunni Muslim, Ukrainian Autocephalous Orthodox, and other groups.[2] Many of these religious groups had been driven underground by Communist purges and reprisals, and kept alive through count-

---

[2] See chapters in this volume by Donna E. Arzt, Sergei Filatov, Sergei Filatov and Lyudmila Vorontsova, Mikhail M. Kulakov, Alexsandr Shchipkov, and Yuriy Tabak. See also Igor Troyanovsky, *Religion in the Soviet Republics: A Guide to Christianity, Judaism, Islam, Buddhism, and Other Religions* (San Francisco, 1991).

less sacrifices and martyrdoms of four generations of the faithful.[3] Gorbachev established an ambitious campaign of restitution for those religious groups, particularly the Orthodox, that had suffered massive losses of clergy, property, literature, and art since the 1917 Bolshevik Revolution.[4] These groups, in turn, provided moral and material support to the tender movements of *glasnost* and *perestroika*.[5] Foreign religious groups—particularly Protestants and Catholics from Europe and North America—began to receive visas to enter Russia in order to reconvene with their co-religionists, to offer their charity, and to spread their faiths.[6] Russian Jews, Christians, and Muslims, in turn, were granted visas to travel to holy sites in Jerusalem, Rome, Mecca, and elsewhere.[7]

These favorable policies toward religion were soon translated into strong legal terms. On October 1, 1990, Gorbachev signed a comprehensive new law, "On Freedom of Conscience and on Religious Organizations" for the USSR.[8] On October 25, 1990, The Russian Soviet Federative Socialist Republic (RSFSR) passed its own law, "Freedom of Worship," which repeated and strengthened many of the provisions of the USSR law, and which survived the breakup of the USSR in December 1991.[9] Both the USSR and RSFSR laws set forth sweeping guarantees of liberty of conscience and freedom of exercise for all citizens. Both laws included strong prohibitions against religious discrimination, stigmatizing, abuse, and coercion.[10] The RSFSR law insisted that "freedom of worship is an inalienable right of the citizens of the RSFSR, guaranteed by the Constitution and international obligations of the RSFSR" and includes "the right to select and hold religious beliefs and to freely change them."[11]

The 1990 laws guaranteed the religious liberty not only of individuals but also of properly registered groups. "All religions and denominations shall be

---

[3] See chapter in this volume by James H. Billington.

[4] See chapters in this volume by Philip Walters and Harold J. Berman, and further Philip Walters, "A Survey of Soviet Religious Policy," in Sabrina P. Ramet, ed., *Religious Policy in the Soviet Union* (Cambridge, 1993), 17ff., and Sabrina P. Ramet, *Nihil Obstat: Religion, Politics, and Change in East-Central Europe and Russia* (Durham, N.C., 1998), 21ff., 229ff.

[5] See chapters in this volume by Billington, Michael Bourdeaux, and Mark Elliott and Anita Deyneka. See also Metropolitan Kirill, "The Church and Perestroika," in Troyanovsky, *Religion in the Soviet Republics*, 82-90; Michael Bourdeaux, *Gorbachev, Glasnost and the Gospel* (London, 1990).

[6] See chapters in this volume by Bourdeaux, and Elliott and Deyneka.

[7] See chapters in this volume by Arzt and Tabak.

[8] Translated in Troyanovsky, *Religion in the Soviet Republics*, at 23-30 [hereafter "USSR Law"], with analysis in chapters in this volume by Berman and T. Jeremy Gunn and further in Kent Hill, *The Soviet Union on the Brink: An Inside Look at Christianity and Glasnost* (Portland, Ore., 1991).

[9] Translated in Troyanovsky, *Religion in the Soviet Republics*, 31-37 [hereafter "RSFSR Law"].

[10] USSR Law, arts. 1-4; RSFSR Law, arts. 1-7, 17, 22, 25, 29.

[11] RSFSR Law, preamble, and elaborated in arts. 3-5, 13, 16.

equal before the law," reads the USSR law. "The institution of any form of privileges or restrictions for one religion or denomination in comparison to others shall be prohibited."[12] Both 1990 laws insisted that state and religious organizations be as separate as possible. Religious groups were not to finance, staff, or interfere in state elections, secular public education, or other political affairs. The state, in turn, was not to finance, tax, control, or interfere in the worship, order, festivals, discipline, education, or charity of religious groups. The RSFSR law included within the "inalienable right to freedom of worship" the right to "establish and maintain international communication and direct contacts" with co-religionists outside Russia.[13] It also included the "right to promotion of a faith," defined as the right to "dissemination of one's beliefs in society directly or via the mass media, missionary work, acts of compassion and charity, religious instruction and education."[14]

These statutory guarantees for religious liberty were confirmed by the Russian Constitution of 1993. Article 14 of the Constitution provides: "1. The Russian Federation shall be a secular state. No religion may be instituted as [a] state-sponsored or mandatory religion. 2. Religious associations shall be separated from the state, and shall be equal before the law." Article 19 states that "[a]ll people shall be equal before the law and in the court of law" and further that "[t]he state shall guarantee the equality of rights and liberties regardless of . . . [a person's] attitude to religion [or] convictions." Article 28 provides: "Everyone shall be guaranteed the right to freedom of conscience, to freedom of religious worship, including the right to profess, individually or jointly with others, any religion, or to profess no religion, to choose freely, possess and disseminate religious or other beliefs, and to act in conformity with them." Russia had incorporated some of the most advanced international human rights norms governing religious liberty, proselytism, and change of religion.[15]

These strong legal guarantees helped to usher in what Mikhail Gorbachev proudly proclaimed to be "a golden age of religious liberty" in Russia.[16] Various indigenous Orthodox, Catholic, and Protestant churches, seminaries, schools, and charities began to be restored or rebuilt—sometimes with the material support of local political leaders. Muslim mosques, Buddhist temples, and Jewish synagogues also began to be restored, together with a few of their schools, charities, and publishing houses.[17] Particularly Russian Orthodox re-

---

[12] USSR Law, art. 5; see parallels in RSFSR Law, arts. 8-10, 16-19, 23-25.

[13] RSFSR Law, art. 25.

[14] RSFSR Law, art. 17. See also USSR Law, art. 23.

[15] Konstitutsiia RF (Constitution of the Russian Federation) (1993), translated in Vladimir V. Belyakov and Walter J. Raymond, eds., *Constitution of the Russian Federation* (Lawrenceville, Va., 1994). See analysis in chapter in this volume by Gunn, and further Natan Lerner, "Proselytism, Change of Religion, and International Human Rights," *Emory International Law Review* 12 (1998): 477-562.

[16] Commencement Address, Emory University (May 11, 1992).

[17] See chapters in this volume by Arzt and Tabak, and the collection of documents in Troyanovksy, *Religion in the Soviet Republics*.

ligious literature, artwork, icons, candles, vestments, and other materials for worship were imported en masse and, later, produced locally.[18] A host of long-dormant Russian animist groups, goddess religions, personality cults, and oc-cultist groups began to revive, especially outside the main cities. Even more startling was the rapid growth of several exotic and well-organized indigenous religions such as the Great White Brotherhood, the Center of the Mother of God, and the Church of the Last Testament.[19]

This religious awakening of Russia came not only from within, but also from without. Already in the wake of the 1986 Chernobyl disaster, and the scourge of ominous accidents, earthquakes, and droughts that followed, for-eign religious groups had begun to trickle into Russia to offer charitable relief and longer-term care.[20] After passage of the 1990 laws, these foreign religious groups came to Russia in greater numbers. From the West, these included various Evangelicals, Pentecostals, mainline Protestants, Roman Catholics, Mormons, Moonies, Scientologists, and others.[21] From the Middle East, they included Shi'ite, Sunni, and Sufi Muslims, together with some Baha'is.[22] From the East, they included Presbyterians and Methodists from Korea; Hindus, Hare Krishnas, Rastafarians, and Buddhists from the Indian subcontinent; members of the Aum Association, Shri Chinmoy, the Rerikh Movement, and other groups from Japan. Many of these groups preached their beliefs and activities on the streets and door to door as well as through distribution of sermons, pamphlets, and texts. Other groups organized crusades, tent meet-ings, billboard advertising, and mass-media events, or rented out stadiums, theaters, and community halls for religious festivals. Many of these groups also began to establish schools, hospitals, charities, youth groups, old age homes, and other social services.[23]

The few reliable demographic studies available suggest that these foreign religious groups have to date made rather modest gains against the Russian Orthodox Church and other local Russian groups. Mark Elliott and Anita Deyneka show that in 1997 the Protestant missionary force in the entire former Soviet Union of over 280 million persons stood at a mere 5,606 persons di-vided among 561 groups.[24] To be sure, as Alexsandr Shchipkov shows, Rus-sian Protestant churches, indigenous and foreign, have more than doubled in number—from a total of 1,002 registered groups in 1993 to 2,280 in 1996.[25] But indigenous Orthodox and Catholic churches in Russia experienced nearly

---

[18] See chapter in this volume by Billington.
[19] See chapters in this volume by Filatov and Shchipkov; see also Ramet, *Nihil Obstat*, 308-40.
[20] See chapter in this volume by Bourdeaux.
[21] See chapters in this volume by Elliott and Deyneka, and Filatov.
[22] See chapter in this volume by Arzt.
[23] See chapters in this volume by Elliott and Deyneka, and Lawrence A. Uzzell.
[24] See chapter in this volume by Elliott and Deyneka.
[25] See chapter in this volume by Shchipkov.

comparable growth, and their absolute numbers dwarf those of Protestants—from a total of 4,815 registered groups in 1993 to 7,666 in 1996. Indeed, in 1996, there were more registered Muslim groups in Russia (2,494) than all Protestant groups combined (2,280).[26]

The rate of growth of *new* religious groups in Russia in this same period was more impressive, but their absolute numbers remained very small. The plight of the Unification Church in Russia is a case in point. According to Sergei Filatov, the Unification Church had already begun secretly to enter the Soviet Union in the early 1980s, using tourist and business visas. It was among the first foreign groups to begin actively proselytizing in Russia in the mid-1980s. After Rev. Moon met with President Gorbachev in 1990, the Unification Church sponsored an aggressive campaign of conferences, seminars, textbook distribution, study trips, and the like aimed especially at political leaders and at lower school and university students and their teachers. "Tens of thousands" of Russians participated in these activities, and by 1994 more than 2,000 state schools used the "moral textbooks" furnished gratis by the Unification Church. Despite this massive effort and expense, the Unification Church in Russia at its peak in 1994 attracted only 5,000 full members; by late 1997, the movement claimed fewer than 3,000 members, with numbers projected only to decline.[27] Indeed, the three largest "totalitarian cults," as they are called in Russia—the Moonies, the Hare Krishnas, and the Jehovah's Witnesses—collectively had 248 registered groups in all Russia in 1996.[28]

Storm Signals

Whatever their real numbers and growth rates, the noisy arrival of these foreign religious groups eventually bred considerable resentment in Russia. Russian Protestant and Catholic groups began to resent the linguistic deficiencies and the fiscal leveraging of some of their Western and Korean co-religionists.[29] Russian Catholics and Protestants also resented the criticisms from afar of the doctrinal, liturgical, and ecclesiological innovations that they had introduced during their decades of brutal isolation—a resentment doubly acute for Greek Catholics, who had suffered savage abuses in the bitter political struggles between Constantinople and Rome for jurisdiction over them.[30] Russian Muslim leaders, as well as political officials, expressed increasing concern about the politicization of some Muslim groups inspired by "the Ayatollah Khomeni's Iranian messianism and Afghan *mujaheddin* agitation and propaganda." A number of clashes also broke out between competing schools of jurisprudence

---

[26] See ibid. and chapter in this volume by Arzt.

[27] See chapter in this volume by Filatov.

[28] See chapter in this volume by Shchipkov.

[29] See chapters in this volume by Anita Deyneka, Filatov and Vorontsova, Kulakov, and Uzzell.

[30] See chapters in this volume by Billington, Uzzell, and Walters.

within and among Shi'ite, Sunni, and Sufi groups—tensions sometimes exacerbated by the sharp ethnic, racial, and linguistic diversity within the Russian Muslim population.[31]

By far the greatest expressions of concern, however, came from the Moscow Patriarchate of the Russian Orthodox Church. Already in 1991, Moscow Patriarch Aleksii II expressed dismay at the "massive influx" of foreign missionaries, both religious and economic, that competed for souls in the new marketplace of religious ideas in Russia.[32] Initially, the Patriarchate's resentment was focused on missionary mavericks. These were culturally and linguistically inept missionaries, inclined toward "a free-spirited 'Lone Ranger' approach to ministry" that resulted in "'hit-and-run evangelism,' producing neglect of discipline for new believers and inattention to respectful partnerships with existing churches."[33] At the same time, officials within the Moscow Patriarchate singled out for special criticism the "totalitarian sects," charging that these groups used "illegitimate material inducements" to win new converts and then turned their converts against "their Russian families, faiths, and cultures."[34]

By 1993, the Moscow Patriarchate's resentment was directed more generally at all "well-organized and well-financed" mission groups, particularly from the West. Unwelcome "foreign proselytizing faiths" now included various Roman Catholics, mainline Protestants, and Western Evangelicals, alongside religious mavericks and totalitarian cults.[35] Members of the Patriarchate often came to regard these groups collectively, and issued three charges against them. First, all these foreign proselytizing groups were forcing an impoverished and understaffed Russian Orthodox Church into an unfair competition for souls— not only lost souls on the Russian streets, but also saved souls within the Russian churches.[36] Second, many Western proselytizing groups seemed bent

---

[31] See chapters in this volume by Arzt and Shchipkov.

[32] See chapters in this volume by Berman, Metropolitan Kirill, and Walters.

[33] See chapters in this volume by Elliott and Deyneka, and Uzzell.

[34] Comments of Alexandr Dvorkin, member of the Moscow Patriarchate Department of External Church Relations, at a conference at Oxford, May 29, 1996. When I asked him to elaborate, Dvorkin defined "illegitimate material inducements" to include the furnishing of humanitarian aid, English lessons, education, and employment; the inculcation of the public school curriculum with religious texts and rituals; the use of television, newspapers, and other mass media to propagate the faith; and the organization of "loud and insensitive crusading carnivals."

[35] Comments by Alexandr Dvorkin at the same conference, who listed among "proselytizing faiths": (1) Roman Catholics "who established dioceses, parishes, and monasteries without Orthodox approval"; (2) "traditional Protestant denominations," including those who are members of the World Council of Churches (Methodists, Finnish and German Lutherans, Free Evangelicals, and Korean Protestants); and (3) "new religious movements" (Hare Krishnas, Bah'ais, Moonies, and Jehovah's Witnesses especially). See further discussion in chapters by Berman, Billington, Gunn, Kirill, and Uzzell.

[36] See chapters in this volume by Berman, Billington, and Walters.

on breaking the soul of the Russian people—by inundating them with a toxic wave of Western materialism, individualism, and pluralism for which Russia was not, and could not be, prepared.[37] Third, many of these foreign proselytizing groups were simply dangerous to the Russian people and to social order—by breaking up families; encouraging civil disobedience; extorting property and money; administering drugs and mind controls; committing battery, rape, and other offenses against recalcitrant members; and even inducing homicide, suicide, and insurrection as acts of faith.[38]

Such charges against foreign proselytizing groups can be seen in dozens of statements issued by the Moscow Patriarchate in the period after 1993.[39] In 1993, Metropolitan Kirill complained of the "dishonorable" actions of "missionaries [who] are making use of . . . the spiritual vacuum" of post-Soviet Russia.[40] In his chapter in this volume, he elaborates his criticism:

> As soon as freedom for mission work was allowed, a crusade began against the Russian Church even as it began recovering from a prolonged disease, standing on its feet with weakened muscles. Hordes of missionaries dashed in, believing the former Soviet Union to be a vast missionary territory. They behaved as though no local churches existed, no Gospel was being proclaimed. They began preaching without even making an effort to familiarize themselves with the Russian cultural heritage or to learn the Russian language. In most cases the intention was not to preach Christ and the Gospel, but to tear the faithful away from their traditional churches and recruit them into their own communities. Perhaps these missionaries sincerely believed that they were dealing with non-Christian or atheistic communist people, not suspecting that our culture was formed by Christianity and that our Christianity survived through the blood of martyrs and confessors, through the courage of bishops, theologians, and laypeople asserting their faith.
>
> Missionaries from abroad came with dollars, buying people with so-called humanitarian aid and promises to send them abroad for study or rest. We expected that our fellow Christians would support and help us in our own missionary service. In reality, however, they have started fighting with our church. . . . All this has led to an almost complete rupture of the ecumenical relations developed during the previous decades. An overwhelming majority of the population refused to accept this activity, which

---

[37] See chapter in this volume by Uzzell.

[38] See chapters in this volume by Gunn and Kirill.

[39] See samples in V. Polosin and G. Yakunin, "Federal Authorities and Freedom of Conscience," unpublished manuscript, November 1996, 16-38, and Jane Ellis, "The Moscow Patriarchate's Attitude to Protestant Missionaries: A Decade of Misunderstanding," unpublished manuscript, June 1998, 2-7.

[40] Interview in *Nezavisimaya gazeta* (June 5, 1993), quoted by Ellis, "The Moscow Patriarchate's Attitude," 2-3. See also Kirill, "The Church and Perestroika."

offends people's national and religious sentiments by ignoring their spiritual and cultural tradition. Indeed, given the lack of religious education, people tend to make no distinctions between the militant missionaries we are speaking about and ordinary people of their own faiths or confessions. For many of Russia today, "non-Orthodox" means those who have come to destroy the spiritual unity of the people and the Orthodox faith—spiritual colonizers who by fair means or foul try to tear the people away from the Church.[41]

Patriarch Aleksii II complained of the corrosive values of liberalism that Western missionaries had fostered within the Russian Orthodox Church itself:

Orthodox consciousness is currently being eroded by extreme liberalism, capable of leading to tragic consequences for the Church—to schism, division in the Church, the undermining of Orthodox beliefs and to ultimate destruction. We must stand against this destructive process by our constancy in faith and belief in the traditions and living Orthodox religious experience of Christian love and concern for each individual believer and for Russia as a whole.[42]

The Council of Bishops meeting in Moscow made an even more pointed charge against foreign missionaries:

We express our concern in connection with the continuing proselytizing activity of Protestant false missionaries in Russia [and] the growth of organized pseudo-Christian and pseudo-religious sects, of neo-pagan communities, occultists and devil worshippers in the CIS and the Baltic States. The Council is extremely troubled by the anti-Orthodox campaign which is being waged by the followers of these pseudo-religious organizations and their protectors. The members of the Council call on the entire Church to confront this false missionary activity and sectarianism through religious education and apologetics, by educating both Orthodox parishioners and society as a whole. We acknowledge that the right of each person to freedom of conscience and religion should be respected, but the leaders of these totalitarian sects are in fact depriving their followers of these rights and reacting to any criticism of their activity. Those who attempt to oppose them are subjected to cruel persecution by the sect leaders and their highly-placed protectors, including intimidation, psychological pressure, the gathering of incriminating information, slanders, and repeated searches of their property.[43]

---

[41] See chapter in this volume by Kirill.

[42] "Address of the Patriarch."

[43] Resolution of the Council of Bishops in Moscow, February 18-23, 1997, Article No. 35, in *Pravoslavnaya Moskva* 7 (103) (March 1997): 11.

These were not idle words. Officials of the Moscow Patriarchate several times requested restraint, even a one-generation moratorium, on foreign mission activities in Russia.[44] This would allow indigenous churches to recover from their Communist plight, and enable them to compete fairly.[45] Orthodox theologians, from Russia and abroad, pressed this case with increasing urgency at various ecumenical conferences on mission.[46] Orthodox clergy that fell out of line with these official sentiments faced firm discipline—defrocking and excommunication in extreme cases.[47]

When such diplomatic and ecumenical entreaties failed, the Moscow Patriarchate turned to the law of the state for its protection. Already in 1993, the Moscow Patriarchate joined with various nationalist groups to pressure the Russian Parliament to amend the 1990 RSFSR law.[48] The proposed amendments gave special protections, subsidies, and rights to "those religious organizations, the activity of which maintains and develops historical traditions and customs, national and cultural originality, art and other cultural heritage of the peoples of the Russian federation—that is, the traditional confessions of the Russian Federation." The proposed law stated categorically that foreign religious groups "have no right of religious-missionary activity in the Russian Federation." And it instituted a series of cumbersome new registration and property regulations designed to deter and obstruct foreign mission groups already in place. Under severe pressure from indigenous and foreign religious and political groups, the Russian Parliament did not pass this proposed law in 1993, nor a variant on the same proposed in 1995.[49]

While, initially, the Russian Parliament did little to assuage the problem of proselytism in Russia, a number of local legislatures did. From 1993 to 1997, Lauren Homer and Lawrence Uzzell write, "more than one third of Russia's eighty-nine provincial governments adopted laws or executive decrees shrinking the rights of foreign religious organizations and religious minorities, and even major religious organizations."[50] These local laws, often passed under strong orchestration by the Russian Orthodox clergy, imposed various regis-

---

[44] See chapter in this volume by Elliot and Deyneka.

[45] See quotes in ibid.; see also "Declaration of the Holy Synod of the Russian Orthodox Church, 3 April 1990," in Troyanovsky, *Religion in the Soviet Republics*, 66-72.

[46] See Joel A. Nichols, "Mission, Evangelism, and Proselytism in Christianity: Mainline Conceptions as Reflected in Church Documents," *Emory International Law Review* 12 (1998): 563-652, at 622-52.

[47] See chapters in this volume by Walters and Billington; see also Polosin and Yakunin, "Federal Authorities."

[48] See details in W. Cole Durham, Lauren B. Homer, Pieter van Dijk, and John Witte Jr., "The Future of Religious Liberty in Russia: Report of the DeBurght Conference on Pending Russian Legislation Restricting Religious Liberty," *Emory International Law Review* 8 (1994): 1-66, at 3-11.

[49] See ibid. and chapter in this volume by Berman.

[50] See chapter in this volume by Lauren B. Homer and Lawrence A. Uzzell.

tration and accreditation requirements as a condition for any religious activity of the non-Orthodox, particularly those who were not Russian citizens. These local laws monitored, restricted, and discriminated against the religious speech, literature, and associations of non-Orthodox believers and groups. They placed limits on the access of non-Orthodox to public forums and media, and restricted their ability to hold corporate property, build religious structures, or to gain permits to build and maintain religious schools, charities, and other ministries.[51] A number of Lutheran, Catholic, Pentecostal, Jewish, and Adventist groups have suffered miserably under these laws.[52]

Not all local governments were so repressive, and not all local officials were so cooperative in the repression. Dozens of provincial and municipal legislatures maintained more open policies toward religious outsiders. Occasionally, strong local officials and advocates also blocked efforts to impose anti-proselytism legislation. For example, in early 1997, the governor of St. Petersburg twice vetoed harsh anti-proselytism laws issued by the city council.[53] Moreover, in a remarkable case, issued on March 5, 1997, the Supreme Court of the Udmurt Republic struck down a Udmurtian religious registration law as unconstitutional—the first such case in Russia of successful judicial review of these anti-proselytism laws. The Udmurt law, which encumbered and fined the missionary activities of several Russian Pentecostal groups, was found to violate a number of religious liberty provisions of the 1993 Russian constitution and the Udmurt provincial constitution, as well as Russia's obligations under prevailing international human rights laws.[54] These isolated local cases held the promise that a federalist system of government might provide some protection for religious liberty—regardless of what took place in Moscow.

THE 1997 LAW ON FREEDOM OF CONSCIENCE AND ON RELIGIOUS ASSOCIATIONS

The promises of Russia's "golden age of religious liberty" ended on September 26, 1997, the day Russian President Boris Yeltsin signed a new law, "On Free-

---

[51] See ibid. and Polosin and Yakunin, "Federal Authorities." For samples of these provincial and municipal laws in English translation, see Appendices B-E, *Emory International Law Review* 12 (1998): 681-714.

[52] See Lawrence A. Uzzell, "Concrete Effects of Russia's New Religious Law: An Overview," unpublished manuscript, April 23, 1998; id., "Khakasskian Authorities Seek to Disestablish Lutheran Mission," *KI Frontier* 2 (1998): 10-11; Felix Corley, "Uzbek Pastor Sentenced to Two Years' Hard Labor," *Human Rights without Frontiers* (January 27, 1998): 18; id., "Further Legal Setback for Moldovian Church," *Human Rights without Frontiers* (January 27, 1998): 10.

[53] See chapter in this volume by Homer and Uzzell.

[54] The case is analyzed in ibid. An English translation of the opinion is included in Appendix F, *Emory International Law Review* 12 (1998): 715-38. The Udmurt law that the court struck down is translated by Felix Corley as Appendix E, *Emory International Law Review* 12 (1998): 703-14.

dom of Conscience and on Religious Associations."[55] This new law—passed
after four years of open advocacy and four months of secret machinations by
the Moscow Patriarchate and various nationalist groups within Russia—institutes a Soviet-style system of severe state registration and restrictions on religion. The 1997 law supersedes the 1990 RSFSR law. It preempts all provincial
and municipal laws on religion to the contrary.[56] New administrative regulations, issued in the spring of 1998, have ensured the rapid execution of the
1997 law.[57] These same regulations also exacerbate some of its harshest provisions—for example, by imposing a new registration fee on all foreign religious
organizations of "fifty times the minimum monthly wage established by the
laws of the Russian federation."[58]

The 1997 law effectively establishes three classes of religions in Russia: (1)
the Russian Orthodox Church and its members, which receive full legal protection and various state benefits; (2) various "traditional" Christians, Muslims, Jews, and Buddhist groups and persons, which receive full legal protection, but fewer state benefits; and (3) all other religious groups and persons,
which receive only a pro forma guarantee of freedom of worship and liberty of
conscience.

This tripartite classification of religious groups is adumbrated in the preamble to the 1997 law. The preamble "recogniz[es] the special contribution of
Orthodoxy to the history of Russia and to the establishment and development
of Russia's spirituality and culture." It further "respect[s] Christianity, Islam,
Buddhism, Judaism, and other religions and creeds which constitute an inseparable part of the historical heritage of Russia's peoples." For the rest, the
preamble provides only that it "consider[s] it important to promote the achievement of mutual understanding, tolerance, and respect in questions of freedom
of conscience and freedom of creed."

This tripartite classification is elaborated in the eighteen articles on religious associations set out in the 1997 law—and the 1998 regulations in amplification of the same. The 1997 law defines a religious association as a "voluntary association of citizens of the Russian federation and other persons
permanently and legally residing [therein] formed with the goals of joint confession and possessing features corresponding to that goal: a creed, the performance of worship services, religious rituals, and ceremonies; the teaching of
religion and religious upbringing of its followers."[59]

---

[55] Federal Law No. 125-FZ (September 26, 1997), translated by Lawrence A.
Uzzell as Appendix A, *Emory International Law Review* 12 (1998): 657-80 [hereaf-
ter "1997 Law"].

[56] Ibid., arts 27.6, 2.2.

[57] See analysis in chapter by Gunn in this volume.

[58] Resolution on the Procedure for Opening the Missions of Foreign Religious
Organizations in the Russian Federation (1998), item no. 5 [hereafter "1998 Regulations"].

[59] 1997 Law, art. 6.1.

Religious *associations* are differentiated into (1) religious *organizations*, which receive a wide array of protections and benefits; and (2) religious *groups*, which receive only minimal protections. Religious *organizations*, in turn, are divided into (a) favored *centralized* groups (notably, the Russian Orthodox Church); and (b) less favored *local* groups (mostly other "traditional" Russian religions).

Religious organizations receive "juridical personality"—the basic right to exist as a licit group, from which a number of other rights automatically follow. "Religious organizations can own buildings, plots of land, objects for the purpose of production and for social, charitable, educational, and other purposes, articles of religious significance, financial means and other property which is essential for their activity including that necessary for historical and cultural monuments." Religious organizations can acquire property by purchase or donation and devote it to multiple uses—worship, pilgrimage, hospitals, cemeteries, children's homes, charities, cultural-educational institutions, seminaries, and "business undertakings." Such properties are generally held free from state taxation, and those properties devoted to worship are immune from "proceedings by creditors."[60]

Religious organizations are also assured of various affirmative rights. They have the right to undertake charitable activities, including the administration of chaplaincy and other religious services in state hospitals and "places of detention." "Religious organizations have the right to produce, acquire, export, and distribute religious literature, printed, audio and video material and other articles of religious significance. Religious organizations have the exclusive right to institute enterprises for producing liturgical literature and articles for religious services." Religious organizations have the right to establish and maintain contacts with co-religionists abroad, and have "the exclusive right to invite foreign citizens for professional purposes, including preaching and religious activity in the said organizations."[61]

Religious organizations are also entitled to certain direct benefits from the state. They have "the right to use for their own needs plots of land, buildings and property provided by state, municipal, social and other organizations . . . free of charge." Moreover, the state "is to provide financial, material, and other aid to religious organizations in the restoration, maintenance, and protection of buildings and objects which are monuments of history and culture, and also in providing instruction in general educational subjects in educational institutions created by religious organizations."[62]

A religious organization's panoply of rights and benefits does not come automatically. Only properly registered religious associations are classified as "religious organizations" and entitled to these rights and benefits. It is here that the 1997 law works its greatest injustice. And it is here that the law in

[60] Ibid., arts. 4.3, 7.1; 16; 18; 21; 23.
[61] Ibid., arts. 16.2-3, 17.1-2; 18.1; 20.1-2.
[62] Ibid., arts. 4.3, 22.1-2.

effect establishes what Michael Bourdeaux calls "another Council for Religious Affairs (the name of the hated body which oversaw and controlled the persecution of the Churches, in the days of Communism)."[63]

The law distinguishes between "local" and "centralized" registered groups. *Local* religious organizations must consist of "ten or more participants who are at least 18 years of age and who are permanently residing in one locality or in one urban or rural settlement." *Centralized* religious organizations must consist "in accordance with its charter of no fewer than three local religious organizations." Once a religious organization is deemed "centralized," as is the case with the hierarchical Russian Orthodox Church, every new local unit created thereafter is automatically registered as a religious organization. If a religious organization is only "localized," however, as in the case of many Protestant, Mormon, Jewish, and other congregationally organized religious communities, each new local unit must be registered separately.[64]

Only "*centralized* religious organizations which have been active [in Russia] *on a legal basis* for no fewer than 50 years" may use the term "Russian" in their title.[65] In practice, the Russian Orthodox Church is the only group that qualifies. Other traditional religions of Russia, such as Muslims, Jews, and Buddhists, were "illegal" after 1917 and before 1905. And while they were "legal" briefly between 1905 and 1917, they were not "centralized." The Orthodox Church's right to use the term "Russian" is more than honorary. In practice, this is the only religious organization that receives the promised governmental subsidies for the "restoration, maintenance, and protection of buildings and objects which are monuments of history and culture."[66]

Centralized or local religious communities that "existed" in Russia "no less than 15 years" must register only once to be categorized as "religious organizations."[67] Once registered, they are thereafter automatically entitled to the full range of rights and benefits set forth above—save the direct benefits reserved to the Russian Orthodox Church alone. In reality, this "15 year" provision covers only a few "traditional" Russian groups—Muslims, Jews, and some Christians. As Lawrence Uzzell explains:

> These provisions discriminate in favor of those religious organizations that were legally registered under the Soviet state fifteen years ago and against those that were founded more recently or that existed only illegally or semi-legally during the Soviet years. Thus, for example, the favored category included many Baptist congregations—those which were willing during the pre-glasnost era to make the compromises needed to

---

[63] Michael Bourdeaux, "Religious Freedom Russian-style," *The Tablet* (September 27, 1997): 1216.

[64] 1997 Law, arts. 8.1-6; 9.1-2.

[65] Ibid., art. 8.5 (emphasis added).

[66] Ibid., arts. 4.3; 22.1.

[67] Ibid., art. 9.1.

get official registration. . . . [But] the [Roman] Catholics have only two parishes in all of the Russian Federation that were legally registered or functioning fifteen years ago.

The other 160 Roman Catholic parishes in Russia, the diocesan administrations in Moscow and Novosibirsk, the Catholic seminary in St. Petersburg, the dozens of Jesuit orders, publishing houses, charities, and other groups affiliated with Rome have "now been reduced to second-class status."[68]

This "second-class status" is occupied by all religious communities in Russia that do not meet either the "50 year" or the "15 year" registration provisions. The 1997 law categorizes all these as "new" religions—regardless of their real vintage. "New" religions are required to register with local and/or centralized authorities—annually. The registration procedures are cumbersome, fraught with delay and discretion, and expensive. Applicants for local religious organization status must submit an application form; a list of all members' names, addresses, and dates of birth; their minutes and religious charters (which must include detailed statements about their organization and its finances, activities, purposes, and "other information relevant to the peculiarities of their activities"). Applicants must also submit a fee of "fifty times the minimum monthly wage established by the laws of the Russian federation." A "new" religious community once properly registered is categorized as "a religious organization" with all attendant rights and benefits—but only for a year. After a year, the community must register anew.[69]

Registration can be denied, or a registered group can be dissolved, on any number of stated grounds. Some of the grounds set forth in the 1997 law are reasonable enough—"by decision of their founders"; because of the group's "creation of armed units"; or "in the case of frequent and gross infringement of the norms of the Constitution . . . or federal law."[70] But vaguer, and more expansive, grounds for denial of registration or dissolution of a religious organization have been smuggled into the new regulations implementing this law. These include: "if the founder(s) of the religious organization is (are) incompetent"; if "the organization being established is not recognized as a religious one"; and "on the grounds of a judicial ruling in cases established by law."[71]

Those religious communities that cannot—or for religious or political reasons will not—register themselves are categorized as *religious groups*. Religious groups "have the right to carry out worship services, religious rituals, and ceremonies, and also the teaching of religion and religious upbringing of

---

[68] Lawrence A. Uzzell, "Letter from Moscow," *First Things* 79 (January 1998): 17-19.

[69] 1997 Law, arts. 10.2; 11.5.

[70] Ibid., art. 14.1. But see 1998 Regulations, no. 24, which softens the last provision into "the objectives and activities of the religious organizations are at variance with the Constitution of the Russian Federation and legislation in force."

[71] 1998 Regulations, items 24 and 31.

their followers."[72] But nothing more. Religious groups are subject to a number of explicit restrictions and disabilities. Such groups have no right of juridical personality, no right to hold collective property, and no access to state material benefits to religion. Their clergy and members are denied conscientious objection status to military participation. They cannot create or own schools, seminaries, or other educational institutions, nor have their faith taught in local state schools. They may not have "a representative body of a foreign religious organization" in place in Russia. They may not carry out religious rites or services, or furnish chaplain services in hospitals, health centers, children's homes, homes for the aged or handicapped, or prisons. They may not produce, acquire, export, import, or distribute religious literature, videos, and other articles of religious significance, nor establish local institutions for the production of the same. They may not invite foreign citizens into Russia to preach or carry on religious activities.[73]

This entire law on religious association contradicts the guarantees of individual and corporate religious liberty set forth elsewhere in the 1997 law. The preamble to the 1997 law, for example, confirms "the right of each to freedom of conscience and freedom of creed, and also to equality before the law regardless of his attitude to religion and his convictions." Article 2.3 states boldly that "[n]othing in the law . . . may be interpreted in such a way as to diminish or limit the rights of man and citizen to freedom of conscience and freedom of creed." Article 4 provides familiar guarantees of freedom of all from discrimination, abuse, coercion, or other deprivations on religious grounds. It further guarantees to all persons "the right to confess, individually or jointly with others, any religion or not to confess any, and the freedom to choose, change, possess or disseminate religious or other convictions and to act in accordance with them." The 1997 law guarantees that "the Russian federation is a secular state. No religion may be established as a state or compulsory religion. Religious associations are separate from the state and are equal before the law." In amplification of this guarantee, the 1997 law repeats a number of the provisions of the 1990 law on separation of church and state.[74] Even the most skillful casuistry cannot explain the blatant contradictions between these guarantees of religious liberty for all and the discriminatory regulations on religious associations.

The 1997 law is not only blatantly self-contradictory but also violates a number of the most basic human rights guarantees. As Jeremy Gunn demonstrates, the 1997 law must respect the human rights norms of the 1993 Russian Constitution, the 1966 International Covenant on Civil and Political Rights, and the 1950 European Convention of Human Rights, all of which are formally binding on Russia. The 1997 law defies these norms openly and without

---

[72] 1997 Law, art. 7.2.
[73] Ibid., art. 27.3, read with arts. 3.4, 5.3, 5.4, 13.5, 16.3, 17.1, 17.2, 18.1, 18.2, 19.
[74] Ibid., arts. 3.1-3.7, 4.1-4.2.

justification. It violates the rights of equality between citizens and noncitizens, and the prohibitions against nondiscrimination on grounds of religion. It tramples on basic rights of freedom of thought, religion, and belief, freedom of expression, and freedom of association.[75]

The injustice of the 1997 law was not lost on Russia's political and religious leaders when they were crafting it. Many religious groups and human rights advocates in Russia formally protested earlier drafts of the bill—the Baptist Union, the Pentecostal Union, the Seventh-day Adventists, the Union of Councils for Soviet Jews, the Roman Catholic Church, the Russian Orthodox Free Church, the Russian Orthodox Church Abroad, and the Old Believers. Pope John Paul II sent a personal letter to President Yeltsin protesting the bill. Several Western European heads of state and the Council of Europe registered their stern objections with President Yeltsin, with members of his Cabinet, and with members of the Russian Parliament. Presidents Clinton and Carter did likewise, together with 160 senators and representatives in the U.S. Congress. Human rights organizations and religious liberty experts from around the world issued a torrent of detailed and devastating criticisms of draft bills, many of which came into the hands of members of the Russian Parliament.[76]

Indeed, the best summary critique of the 1997 law was provided by President Boris Yeltsin himself in his veto of a July draft of the law—all of whose most objectionable provisions remained in the September draft which he signed.[77] In a long veto letter of July 23, 1997, Yeltsin wrote that the law "contradicts the foundations of the constitutional structure of the Russian federation and generally recognized principles and norms of international law." The law "characterizes the Russian federation as a secular state, but . . . it introduces discriminatory rules of registration and reregistration of religious organizations." The law states its adherence to principles of religious freedom and equality, but many of its provisions "are deliberately aimed at the restrictions of the rights of citizens of the Russian federation." "Still more seriously infringed are the rights of foreign citizens and persons without citizenship [since] they do not have the right to profess and disseminate belief corporately and they can meet their religious needs only on an individual basis." Moreover, Yeltsin wrote, "[t]here is a serious unconstitutional provision in the federal law in the absence of a principle of equality of religious associations before the law." The requirement that "foreign religious organization may be [represented] only under Russian organizations" improperly renders foreign groups "directly dependent on the attitude of Russian religious organizations." It also renders Russian religious groups effective "agencies of state authority"—

[75] See analysis in chapter in this volume by Gunn.

[76] See Derek Davis, "Editorial: Russia's New Law on Religion: Progress or Regress," *Journal of Church and State* 39 (1997): 643, 647-48.

[77] Letter from the president of the Russian Federation, Boris Nikolaevich Yeltsin, to the president of the State Duma, G. N. Seleznev, and president of the Federation Council, E. S. Stroev (July 23, 1997), available at <www.stetson.edu/~psteeves/relnews/yeltsinveto2207.html>.

a violation of "the principle of the separation of religious associations and the state." Yeltsin took particular umbrage that "local administrative units" could make the decision "about the existence of a centralized religious organization"—thundering that "the President of the Russian Federation already has expressed frequently" his disdain of such an "unconstitutional practice," "specifically twice by refusing to sign such a law."

President Yeltsin also objected to the "constitutional inequality" of privileging the Russian Orthodox Church "as an integral part of the all-Russian historical, spiritual, and cultural heritage." It was likewise "impermissible" to render the status of other religious groups dependent on an artificial fifteen-year registration period. Yeltsin found it unconstitutional and inequitable to allow the state "to give financial, material, and other aid to religious organizations" for religious education. After citing several other inconsistencies and unconstitutional provisions in the law, Yeltsin concluded his veto letter thus:

> In order to secure the full participation of the Russian federation in the integrative processes not only in Europe but also in the whole world, in light of the multiconfessional nature of the population of the Russian federation, the problem of securing the guarantees of human and civil rights and freedoms in the area of freedom of religious profession, the choice and dissemination of religious convictions, and the equality of religious associations before the law has exceptionally great importance. In order to avoid international isolation of the traditional Russian confessions and to prevent conflicts on religious bases within the country and to avoid charges against the Russian federation of persecution for convictions, . . . to bring the federal law . . . into conformity with the constitution of the Russian federation, with international legal norms, with other laws of the Russian federation, and also to remove the internal contradictions of the law, I submit that it is necessary to make substantial revisions.

No such substantial revisions were made. Every one of the offensive provisions in the July draft law which Yeltsin vetoed remained in place in the September draft which he signed into law. As Yeltsin predicted, "traditional Russian confessions," particularly the Russian Orthodox Church, have experienced considerable "international isolation." Even worse, Russia now faces massive "conflicts on religious bases" and many "charges against the Russian federation of persecution for convictions."

Today, as Cole Durham and Lauren Homer have demonstrated, the best hope seems to lie not in the continuation of diplomatic bombast or imposition of economic sanctions by foreign governments, but in the gentle cultivation of a more prudential jurisprudence.[78] The religious association laws on the books

---

[78] See W. Cole Durham Jr. and Lauren B. Homer, "Russia's 1997 Law on Freedom of Conscience and Religious Associations: An Analytical Appraisal," *Emory International Law Review* 12 (1998): 101-246.

need not necessarily be applied in their fullest vigor, once their purpose of granting Russian religions some temporary relief has been achieved. Moreover, the Russian constitution and provincial constitutions provide ample means for judicial review and renunciation of the more odious and otiose parts of the 1997 law and parallel provincial laws. Given the failure of high-level political attachés to avert passage of the 1997 law, academic, religious, and human rights groups must now take the lead in identifying and cultivating local sources and resources to temper, and eventually perhaps to overturn, the 1997 law.

ONTOLOGICAL DIFFERENCES

Russia has moved from *glasnost* to soul wars—from the open embrace of religious rights for everyone to tight restrictions on everyone's rights, save those of the Russian Orthodox Church. Today in Russia, the Russian Orthodox Church is free and favored by the state. Other indigenous Russian Christians, Muslims, Jews, and Buddhists are largely free, but on their own. Foreign religions, particularly from the West, are neither free nor welcome. None of this religious line-drawing has been done in secret or in ignorance of Russia's human rights obligations. Russian leaders have telegraphed their protectionist intentions for the whole world to see, and have calculated their religious discrimination so carefully that no religious person or group can be confused about where it stands.

There is more at stake in the current war for souls than temporary concerns over unfair religious competition, unsafe religious practices, or unruly religious policies in the provinces. If this were all that was at stake, surely a diplomatic solution could be crafted. Surely, these warring parties could agree more easily to a ten-, fifteen-, or twenty-year moratorium on further foreign missions to Russia, for example—with the interim period used for intense interreligious dialogue and education, for policing of the more belligerent and dangerous groups in Russia, for multilateral negotiations on future Russian visa and import controls that affect religious groups, for aggressive affirmative-action programs to shore up beleaguered Russian religions, and the like.

But there are deeper sources of this war for souls in Russia. Orthodox Ecumenical Patriarch Bartholomew of Constantinople hinted at these sources repeatedly during his lecture tour in the United States in the fall of 1997. Responding to American Church overtures for greater cooperation with the Orthodox Churches, and greater respect among them for human rights values, the patriarch replied: "The Orthodox Christian does not live in a place of theoretical and conceptual conversations but rather in a place of an essential and empirical lifestyle and reality as confirmed by grace in the heart."[79] "The

---

[79] Address of His All Holiness Ecumenical Patriarch Bartholomew "*Phos Hilaron* (Joyful Light)," Georgetown University, Washington, D.C., October 21, 1997, available at <ww2.goarch.org/patriarchate/us-visit/speeches/Fwd_Address_at_Georgeto.htm> [hereafter "Georgetown Address"].

Orthodox Church is not a museum church. . . . It is a living church which, although keeping the old traditions from the very beginning, nevertheless understands very well the message of every new era, and it knows how to adapt itself to the conditions of every period of human history."[80] The Orthodox Church's adaptations in matters of theology, polity, and law over the centuries have differed from those of Western Christianity. "The divergence between us [on these points] continually increases," the patriarch stated, "and the end points to which our courses are taking us, foreseeably, are indeed different." But the heart of our difference is "something deeper and more substantive. The manner in which we exist has become *ontologically different*."[81]

Western Christianity exists under "the shadow of the Enlightenment," the patriarch explained. Orthodox Christianity does not. The Enlightenment provides too little room for faith and too much room for freedom. "Since the Enlightenment, the spiritual bedrock of Western civilization has been eroded and undermined. Intelligent, well intentioned people sincerely believed that the wonders of science could replace the miracles of faith. But these great minds missed one vital truth—that faith is not a garment to be slipped on and off; it is a quality of the human spirit, from which it is inseparable."[82] "There are a few things America [and the rest of the West] can learn from the Orthodox Church," the patriarch declared. Foremost is the lesson "that, paradoxically, faith can endure without freedom, but freedom cannot long abide without faith."[83] A balance must be struck between freedom and faith, as the transplanted Orthodox churches of the West have only recently come to realize. "Orthodox Christians, who live in a country where full religious freedom reigns and where adherents of various religions live side by side, . . . constantly see various ways of living and are in danger of being beguiled by certain of them, without examining if their way is consonant with the Orthodox Faith. Already, many of the old and new Orthodox . . . are stressing different, existing deviations from correct Orthodox lives."[84]

Ontological differences between the Orthodox and the non-Orthodox, between the East and the West: These are deep, and often intractable, sources of the current war for souls in Russia. The Russian people, the Russian Church, and the Russian state are fundamentally different from their counterparts in the West—in their traditions and experiences, in their anthropology and psychology, in their world views and visions. These fundamental differences have led to intense mutual misunderstanding between East and West, and between Orthodox and Western Christians, in the past few years. They warn against any attempts to craft simple legal, political, or diplomatic solutions to the current war for souls.

---

[80] *Washington Post*, October 25, 1997, H12.

[81] Georgetown Address (emphasis added).

[82] Quoted in *Washington Post,* October 25, 1997, H12.

[83] Ibid.

[84] Quoted in *The Jupiter Courier*, November 16, 1997, A17.

CHANGE OF RELIGION, MISSION, AND PROSELYTISM

These ontological differences between Orthodoxy and Western Christianity are evident in competing understandings of evangelism and proselytism. Natan Lerner puts the matter sagely: "What constitutes the sacred duty of evangelization for one group is seen by another group as improper proselytizing. Some groups would consider a given act a normal exercise of freedom of expression and freedom of teaching or propagating a religion or belief; others would view this same act as an illegitimate intrusion into their intimacy, their group identity, and a violation of their freedom of conscience."[85] This problem of perspective, which Lerner parses carefully in human rights terms, must also be parsed in theological terms.

Russian Orthodox and Western Evangelicals, in particular, have fundamentally different theologies of mission. Some of these missiological differences reflect more general differences in theological emphasis. Russian Orthodox tend to emphasize the altar over the pulpit, the liturgy over the homily, the mystery of faith over rational disputation on faith, the priestly office of the clergy over the devotional tasks of the laity.[86] Western Evangelicals generally reverse these priorities—and sometimes accuse the Orthodox of idolatry, introversion, and invasion of the believer's personal relationship with God.[87] And, even without such accusations and prejudicial actions taken upon them, it is these rational, homiletic, and plastic qualities of non-Orthodox faith that sometimes attract converts to Protestantism, as well as to Catholicism, Adventism, and other faiths.[88]

These differences in theological emphasis are exacerbated by conflicting theologies of the nature and purpose of mission. Evangelicals assume that, in order to be saved, every person must make a personal, conscious commitment to Christ—to be born again, to convert. Any person who has not been born again, or who once reborn now leads a nominal Christian life, is a legitimate object of evangelism—regardless of whether the person has already been baptized. The principal means of reaching that person is through proclamation of the Gospel, rational demonstration of its truth, and personal exemplification of its efficacy. Any region of the world that has not been open to the Gospel is a legitimate "mission field"—regardless of whether the region might have another Christian church in place. Under this definition of mission, Russia and its people are prime targets for Evangelical witness.[89]

---

[85] Lerner, "Proselytism," 488.

[86] See chapters in this volume by Berman and Billington.

[87] See chapter in this volume by Elliott and Deyneka. See further Fr. Leonid Kishkovsky, "The Mission of the Russian Orthodox Church after Communism," *East-West Church and Ministry Report* 1 (Summer 1993): 1-2; Mark Elliott, "For Christians Ignorance Is Not Bliss," *East-West Church and Ministry Report* 1 (Summer 1993): 5-6; Don Fairbairn, "Eastern Orthodox: Five Protestant Perspectives," *East-West Church and Ministry Report* 1 (Spring 1995): 5-7.

[88] See chapters in this volume by Billington, Filatov and Vorontsova, and Kulakov.

[89] See chapter in this volume by Elliott and Deyneka.

The Russian Orthodox Church, too, believes that each person must come into a personal relationship with Christ in order to be saved. But such a relationship comes more through birth than rebirth, and more through regular sacramental living than a one-time conversion. A person who is born into the Church has, by definition, started *"theosis"*—the process of becoming "acceptable to God" and ultimately coming into eternal communion with him. Through infant baptism, and later through the mass, the Eucharist, the icons, and other services of the Church, a person slowly comes into fuller realization of this divine communion.[90] Proclamation of the Gospel is certainly a legitimate means of aiding the process of *theosis*—and is especially effective in reaching those not born into the Russian Orthodox Church. But, for the Russian Orthodox, Joel Nichols writes, "mission does not aim primarily at transmission of moral and intellectual convictions and truths, but at the incorporation of persons into the communion that exists in God and in the Church."[91]

This theology leads the Russian Orthodox Church to a quite different understanding of the proper venue and object of evangelism. The territory of Russia is hardly an open "mission field" which Evangelicals are free to harvest. To the contrary, much of the territory and population of Russia is under the "spiritual protectorate" of the Russian Orthodox Church. Any person who has been baptized into the Russian Orthodox Church is no longer a legitimate object of evangelism—regardless of whether that person leads only a nominal Christian life. Indeed, according to some Orthodox, any person who is born in the territory of Russia can at first be evangelized by the Russian Orthodox Church alone; only if he or she actively spurns the Orthodox Church is that party open to the evangelism of others.

This is the theological source of the Patriarchate's repeated complaints about "the proselytizing activity of many Protestant churches, missionary organizations, and individual preachers . . . on the historical territory of our Church."[92] The Patriarchate is not only complaining about *improper methods* of evangelism—the bribery, blackmail, coercion, and material inducements used by some groups; the garish carnivals, billboards, and media blitzes used by others. The Patriarchate is also complaining about the *improper presence* of missionaries—those who have come not to aid the Orthodox Church in its mission, but to compete with the Orthodox Church for its own souls on its own territory. "The Patriarch has quoted, in this connection, the Epistle of St. Paul to the Romans, where the Apostle said: 'It is my ambition to bring the gospel to places where the very name of Christ has not been heard, for I do not want to build on another man's foundation' (Rom. 15:20). . . . [T]he Moscow Patri-

---

[90] See chapters in this volume by Elliott and Deyneka.

[91] Nichols, "Mission, Evangelism, and Proselytism," 624.

[92] Aleksii II, Patriarch of Moscow and All Russia, "The Report to the Bishops Council in Moscow, 18-23 February 1997, Section 11: Interconfessional and Interfaith Relations; Participation in the Activity of International Christian Organizations," *Pravoslavnaya Moskva* 7 (103) (March 1997): 4.

arch welcomes friendly visits by Russian Christians of other denominations from other countries, but opposes their proselytism of Russian Christians."[93]

Human rights norms alone will ultimately do little to resolve this fundamental theological difference between Russian Orthodox and Western Christians. "In seeking to limit the incursion of missionary activity we often are accused of violating the right to freedom of conscience and the restriction of individual rights," Patriarch Aleksii explained. "But freedom does not mean general license. The truth of Christ which sets us free (John 8:32) also places upon us a great responsibility, to respect and preserve the freedom of others. However, the aggressive imposition by foreign missionaries of views and principles which come from a religious and cultural environment which is strange to us, is in fact a violation of both [our] religious and civil rights."[94] The Russian Orthodox Church must be as free in the exercise of its missiology as Western Evangelicals wish to be. Both groups' rights, when fully exercised, will inevitably clash.

Harold Berman, James Billington, Michael Bourdeaux, Anita Deyneka, and Lawrence Uzzell thus all properly urge a theological resolution of the war for souls, as much as a human rights resolution. Interreligious dialogue, education, and cooperation sound like tried-and-tired remedies, but these are essential first steps.[95] Self-imposed guidelines of prudential mission are essential steps as well: know and appreciate Russian history, culture, and language; avoid Westernization of the Gospel and First Amendmentization of politics; deal honestly and respectfully with theological and liturgical differences; respect and advocate the religious rights of all peoples; be Good Samaritans before good preachers; proclaim the Gospel in word and deed.[96] Such steps will slowly bring current antagonists beyond caricatures into a greater mutual understanding, and a greater unity in diversity.

Western Christians, in particular, have much to learn from Orthodox worship—the passion of the liturgy, the pathos of the icons, the power of the silent spirit, the paths of pilgrimage of the soul toward God and the angels. Western Christian Churches also have much to learn from Orthodox Church life—the distinctive balancing between hierarchy and congregationalism through autocephaly, between uniform worship and liturgical freedom through use of the vernacular rites, between community and individuality through a trinitarian communalism, centered on the parish and the home.[97]

Orthodox Christians, in turn, have much to learn from their Western co-religionists—the emphasis on personal moral responsibility, stewardship, and vocation; the importance of daily devotion, regular penance, and individual spiritual growth; the cultivation of homiletics, apologetics, and disputation;

---

[93] See chapter in this volume by Berman.
[94] Aleksii II, "The Report to the Bishops Council."
[95] See chapters in this volume by Elliott and Deyneka, and Uzzell.
[96] See ibid. and also chapters in this volume by Bourdeaux and Deyneka.
[97] See chapter in this volume by Billington.

the insistence on the continued nurture and inherent plasticity of the Christian tradition. As Jaroslav Pelikan reminds us: "Tradition is the living faith of the dead; traditionalism is the dead faith of the living"—an adage equally appropriate for individual and corporate Christianity.[98]

The ultimate theological guide to resolve the deeper conflict over mission and conversion, however, must be a more careful balancing of the Great Commission and the Golden Rule.[99] Christ called his followers to mission: "Go therefore and make disciples of all nations, baptizing them in the name of the Father and of the Son and of the Holy Ghost, teaching them to observe all that I have commanded you" (Mt 28:19-20, *RSV*). But Christ also called his followers to restraint and respect: "Do unto others, as you would have done unto you" (Mt 7:12, *KJV*). If both sides in the current war for souls would strive to hold these principles in better balance, their dogmatism might be tempered and their conflicts assuaged.

CHURCH, STATE, AND NATION

A related, and deeper, ontological difference is reflected in the Russian Orthodox Church's attitude toward the state. The Russian Orthodox Church has no concept akin to the Western dualistic constructions of church and state—no Augustinian division between the City of God and the City of Man, no medieval Catholic doctrine of two powers or two swords, no Protestant understandings of two kingdoms or two realms, no American understanding of a wall of separation between church and state.[100] In Russian Orthodoxy—as in many parts of the Orthodox world rooted in the ancient Byzantine Empire—church and state are viewed as part of an organic religious and political community, united by blood and by soil.[101] Throughout Russian history, there was always a "close connection between the Russian people, the *narod*, the nation, on the one hand, and Russian Orthodox Christianity, on the other."[102] At the same time, there was always a "symbiosis of Church and State."[103] President Boris Yeltsin captured this belief in his 1998 Christmas Eve message:

> For more than 1000 years the Russian Orthodox Church has fulfilled its sacred mission, affirming spiritual and moral values on Russian soil. . . . The Church is an inalienable part of the history of our country and our

---

[98] Jaroslav Pelikan, *The Vindication of Tradition* (New Haven, 1984), 68. See also chapters by Billington, Bourdeaux, Elliott and Deyneka, Filatov and Vorontsova, Kulakov, and Walters.

[99] See chapter in this volume by Billington.

[100] See Noel B. Reynolds and W. Cole Durham Jr., eds., *Religious Liberty in Western Thought* (Atlanta, 1996).

[101] See chapters in this volume by Berman, Billington, and Walters.

[102] See chapter in this volume by Berman.

[103] See chapter in this volume by Firuz Kazemzadeh.

people. Its selfless activities have deservedly earned [the state's] gratitude and respect.[104]

This organic unity of church, state, and nation gave the Russian Orthodox clergy a unique spiritual and moral voice among the Russian people, and unique access to the power and privileges of the Russian state. It allowed the Orthodox clergy to lead Russia in times of great crisis, such as the Napoleonic Wars and World War I. It allowed the Orthodox clergy to teach Russia, through its schools and monasteries, its literature and preaching. It also allowed the Orthodox clergy to nourish Russia through the power and pathos of its liturgy, icons, prayers, and music.[105]

But this organic unity also subjected the Russian Orthodox Church to substantial state control over its polities and properties, and substantial restrictions on its religious ministry and prophecy. Particularly during and after the reign of Tsar Peter the Great at the turn of the eighteenth century, the Church was effectively reduced to an "arm of the State, teaching obedience to the government, glorifying absolutism, and serving as spiritual police" of the Russian people. The "tripartite formula of Orthodoxy, Autocracy, and Nationality was eagerly embraced by the tsars [and patriarchs alike] and became a central element of the Russian official ideology at least until 1905."[106]

In return for their subservience, the Russian Orthodox clergy could turn to the state to protect them against religious outsiders and competition. A poignant and prescient illustration of this is offered by Joachim, the Patriarch of Moscow at the turn of the eighteenth century. In a 1690 testament, for example, the Patriarch implored co-Tsars Ivan and Peter "never to allow any Orthodox Christians in their realm to entertain any close friendly relations with heretics and dissenters—with Latins, Lutherans, Calvinists, and godless Tatars." He further urged the tsars to pass a decree "that men of foreign creeds who come here to this pious realm shall under no circumstances preach their religion, disparage our faith in any conversations, or introduce their alien cus-

---

[104] Boris Yeltsin, Christmas Eve Message (6 January 1998), quoted in Gareth Jones, "Yeltsin Lauds Orthodoxy on Russian Christmas Eve," available at <www.stetson.edu/ ~psteeves/relnews>. See also the statement from the meeting of the Russian Orthodox Church's Council of Bishops in Moscow in March 1997: "The Russian Orthodox Church has for a thousand years of Russian history formed the spiritual and moral outlook of the Russian people, and . . . the overwhelming majority of religious believers belong to the Russian Orthodox Church" (reprinted in *Pravoslavnaya Moskva* 7 [103] [March 1997]: 12).

[105] See chapters in this volume by Berman and Billington. See also Harold J. Berman, "The Challenge of Christianity and Democracy in the Soviet Union," in *Christianity and Democracy in Global Context*, ed. John Witte Jr. (Boulder/San Francisco, 1993), 287ff.

[106] See chapter in this volume by Kazemzadeh. See also chapters by Berman, Billington, Bourdeaux, Tabak, and Walters.

toms derived from their heresies for the temptation of Christians."[107] "Such was the position of the Muscovite Church at the close of the seventeenth century," Firuz Kazemzadeh concludes, "and such, in essence, it has remained."[108]

To be sure, Russia has, since the days of Peter and Joachim, occasionally experimented with Western ideas of liberalism and religious liberty—only to have the state crush these experiments. In the later nineteenth century, for example, Russian elites trained in the West or exposed to Enlightenment literature began pressing for cultural, political, and legal reforms of all kinds. One of the products of this liberal agitation was the Russian Law on Tolerance, signed by the tsar immediately after the 1905 Revolution. The 1905 law gave new rights to Old Believers (who reject the authority of the Moscow Patriarchate) as well as to Christian sects (from within and beyond Russia) to worship, to hold property, to build churches and schools, and to train children in their faith. The 1905 law also gave parties the right to leave the Russian Orthodox Church, even if they were born and baptized in it.[109] The Bolshevik Revolution of 1917 crushed this experiment. And the Communist Party ultimately outlawed all churches, besides the Russian Orthodox Church, and all religious expression, save Orthodox worship services. Again, in the heady days of Gorbachev's democratic revolution of the late 1980s, the USSR and Russia in 1990 passed visionary statutes of religious freedom for all. The 1997 law crushes this experiment, again in favor of the Russian Orthodox Church.

We can easily read current developments as the inevitable next act in this Russian drama of church-state relations. For seven centuries, the Russian tsars ruled and protected the Orthodox Church—sometimes benignly, occasionally belligerently; often restricting other religions, sometimes tolerating them. For the next seven decades, the Communist Party ruled the Orthodox Church—following the same pattern, albeit more harshly. For the last seven years, a "constitutional government" has ruled the Orthodox Church—again following the same patterns, but now at an accelerated pace. The Russian state has always indulged and occasionally protected the Orthodox Church, in return for the Church's support and allegiance. The Russian state has always restricted and occasionally crushed non-Orthodox faiths, in response to the Church's needs and requests. In this light, the 1997 law comes as no surprise.[110]

We can also treat current developments as the birth pangs of a new political and legal order struggling to come forth in Russia. Great legal revolutions, Harold Berman reminds us, always pass through phases of radicality and retrenchment before settling down.[111] The 1990 laws reflect the radical phase of

---

[107] Quoted in chapter in this volume by Kazemzadeh.

[108] Ibid.

[109] See chapters in this volume by Berman and Walters.

[110] See chapters in this volume by Kazemzadeh and Walters.

[111] Harold J. Berman, *Law and Revolution: The Formation of the Western Legal Tradition* (Cambridge, Mass., 1983). See also James H. Billington, *Russia Transformed: Breakthrough to Hope, Moscow, 1991* (New York, 1991).

this revolution; the 1997 law reflects the retrenchment phase. Both phases are part of a greater revolutionary soul-searching of Russia for a new vision, indeed a new ontology.

It is often said that Russia did not experience the Enlightenment, and that this is one reason for its fundamental differences from the West. But the reality is that Russia and the West drew different lessons from the same Enlightenment, which visions Russia is now struggling mightily to integrate. The 1917 Bolshevik Revolution had drawn one lesson from the Enlightenment—that of totalitarian fascism. The 1987 Gorbachevian Revolution drew a second lesson from the same Enlightenment—that of "totalitarian democracy."[112] Neither course has worked in Russia. Ultimately, Russia will settle somewhere between these extremes, or it will direct its collective genius to the creation of a wholly new understanding of church, state, and nation. A new religious liberty law will follow in this course—settling somewhere between the extremes of 1990 and 1997, or cast into a wholly new ensemble.

---

[112] See J. L. Talmon, *The Origins of Totalitarian Democracy* (New York, 1955).

Part One

RELIGIOUS PERSPECTIVES

1.

THE RUSSIAN ORTHODOX CHURCH AND FOREIGN CHRISTIANITY

The Legacy of the Past[1]

———————— ◆ ————————

Philip Walters

The Russian Orthodox Church which in 1988 emerged battered but triumphant into the environment of contemporary religious liberty was a strange creature. It had kept open the passage to and from heaven for millions of humble believers throughout seventy years of atheist Soviet rule, and its clergy had become skilled in dealing with antireligious maneuvers, mendaciousness, and violence, accommodating to them or resisting them. But the Church in 1988 remained in many respects exactly as it had been in 1917; and in 1917 it had been in many respects exactly as it had been in 1721 when Peter the Great had made it into a department of State.[2] In this chapter I shall look at the

---

[1] Some of the material in this chapter first appeared in the chapter by Philip Walters in Adrian Hastings, ed., *A World History of Christianity* (London, 1999), and is used with permission of Cassell.

[2] Useful books covering the history of the Russian Orthodox Church include John Fennell, *A History of the Russian Church to 1448* (London and New York, 1995); Paul Meyendorff, *Russia, Ritual and Reform* (New York, 1991); James Cracraft, *The Church Reform of Peter the Great* (Stanford, 1971); Robert L. Nichols and Theofanis G. Stavrou, eds., *Russian Orthodoxy under the Old Regime* (Minneapolis, 1978); John Shelton Curtiss, *Church and State in Russia: The Last Years of Empire 1900-1917* (New York, 1940); Walter Kolarz, *Religion in the Soviet Union* (London, 1961); William C. Fletcher, *A Study in Survival: The Church in Russia, 1927-1943* (London, 1965); Nikita Struve, *Christians in Contemporary Russia* (London, 1967); Gerhard Simon, *Church, State, and Opposition in the USSR* (London, 1974); Sabrina Petra Ramet, ed., *Religious Policy in the Soviet Union* (Cambridge, 1993); Michael

nature and implications of this continuity as far as the attitude of today's Russian Orthodox Church toward foreign churches and their missionary activity is concerned.

At the end of the nineteenth century the Russian Orthodox Church at once enjoyed extensive privileges and suffered from serious restrictions, both consequent on its legal status as the established religion of the empire. It was supported financially by the government and was defended by law against its religious rivals; it alone had the right to proselytize. Until 1905 defection from the Church by an Orthodox Christian was a punishable offense. The secular authorities welcomed the help of the Church in combatting the influence of non-Orthodox denominations. The Church ran an effective system of parish primary schools throughout the empire. Restrictions on it, however, were manifold. It was encumbered with an inefficient bureaucracy. Parish priests, the "white" or married clergy as opposed to the "black" or monastic clergy from whose ranks the bishops were appointed, suffered from lack of contact with their bishops, who were moved around too frequently to become effective leaders in their dioceses. Priests were also burdened with financial poverty and a large number of secular administrative duties. There was widespread anticlericalism in society, particularly among the intelligentsia, where atheism or positivism had been characteristic for decades before being further encouraged by the Marxism which took hold in the later 1890s. Lenin was a typical member of the nineteenth-century Russian intelligentsia in his profound hatred of institutionalized religion. In the villages, priests were the butt of mockery and frequently despised because their duties to the State included violating the secrecy of the confessional when matters which might be of interest to the organs of State security were involved; bishops were reviled as distant figures revelling in opulent corruption. At the same time, Orthodox traditions imbued every aspect of the peasant's life; the liturgy and religious festivals rendered it tolerable; Orthodoxy was embedded in folk culture; and for all the failings of his clergy, the obduracy of his bureaucrats, and the viciousness of his policemen, the "Little Father," the Tsar, the peasants knew, had the good of his Orthodox people close to his heart. Meanwhile saintly men and women

Bourdeaux, *Patriarch and Prophets: Persecution of the Russian Orthodox Church Today* (London, 1969); Dimitry Pospielovsky, *The Russian Church under the Soviet Regime 1917-1982*, 2 vols. (Crestwood, N.Y., 1984); Jane Ellis, *The Russian Orthodox Church: A Contemporary History* (London, 1986); Pedro Ramet, ed., *Eastern Christianity and Politics in the Twentieth Century* (Durham and London, 1988); Nathaniel Davis, *A Long Walk to Church: A Contemporary History of Russian Orthodoxy* (Boulder, Colo., 1995); and Jane Ellis, *The Russian Orthodox Church: Triumphalism and Defensiveness* (Basingstoke, 1996).

both dead and alive were at hand all over Russia to bring comfort and wise counsel.[3]

The Russian Orthodox Church, then, was at the same time both protected and compromised. This state of affairs was in large part the result of the policies of Peter the Great (1682-1725). He was one of the great "Westernizers" of Russian history. It is ironical that it was Peter's determination to open up Russia ruthlessly to winds of change blowing from the West that in important ways disabled the Russian Orthodox Church.

The head of the Russian Orthodox Church had received the title of Patriarch in 1589. Tsar and Patriarch were theoretically equal, the joint heads of one Christian kingdom. The balance shifted under Patriarch Nikon (1652-58), whose aim to reform the Church involved the novel proposal that the Patriarch rather than the tsar should exercise the leading authority in the State. It was Peter's father, Tsar Aleksei Romanov, who had borne the brunt of Nikon's ambitions. As autocrat, Peter resolved thoroughly to subordinate Church to State so that this kind of interlude would not occur again. When Patriarch Adrian died in 1700 Peter allowed the post to remain vacant for twenty-one years, until with his *Dukhovny reglament* (*Church Regulations*) he abolished it altogether.

As part of his policy of Westernization, Peter put the leadership of the Russian Orthodox Church in the hands of clergy from Ukraine who were already well versed in Western traditions and influenced by developments in the Catholic and Protestant churches. More than three centuries before Peter, Ukraine—the area from which Kievan Christianity originally spread to Russia—had come under the control of Lithuania. In 1386 Lithuania was dynastically united with Poland; one of the conditions was that the Lithuanian Grand Duke Jogaila should convert to Roman Catholicism and that this should become the official religion of the new State. Russian Orthodox living in Lithuania and Ukraine were not at first put under pressure to change their religion, but this changed after 1569 when Poland and Lithuania concluded a much closer union at Lublin. In the climate of the Counter-Reformation, Catholicism was promoted with

---

[3] Useful introductions to the teachings, spirituality, and worship of the Orthodox Church include Vladimir Lossky, *The Mystical Theology of the Eastern Church* (London, 1955); Nicholas Arseniev, *Mysticism and the Eastern Church* (Crestwood, N.Y., 1979); John Meyendorff, *The Orthodox Church* (London, 1962); and Timothy Ware, *The Orthodox Church*, rev. ed. (London, 1993). Books specifically on the history of Russian Orthodoxy theology and spirituality include Georges Florovsky, *Ways of Russian Theology* in *The Collected Works of Georges Florovsky* (Belmont, Mass., and Vaduz, Liechtenstein, 1979); G. P. Fedotov, *The Russian Religious Mind,* 2 vols. (Belmont, Mass., 1975); Nicholas Arseniev, *Russian Piety* (London, 1964); and Nadejda Gorodetsky, *The Humiliated Christ in Modern Russian Thought* (London, 1938).

new energy. The Orthodox, particularly in Belorussia and Ukraine, were induced to accept union with Rome. The "Union of Brest-Litovsk" of 1596 created the "Uniate" Church in the Polish-Lithuanian Commonwealth. Those Orthodox who refused to accept the Union were outlawed and deprived of their bishops, priests, and churches. During the Time of Troubles (1598-1613), as Polish armies penetrated as far as Moscow, their plight seemed hopeless. However, the Cossacks in eastern Ukraine took up their cause, and soon the Theological Academy in Kiev became the center of resistance to Roman Catholicism.

The Kiev Theological Academy understood that it was no longer sufficient simply to train men for the priesthood; they had to be intellectually equipped to contend with the Uniates. This task was addressed under the leadership of Peter Mogila (1596-1647), elected Metropolitan of Kiev in 1633. Educated at the Sorbonne, he realized that those who knew only Old Church Slavonic and Greek had no access to contemporary literature. He therefore made Latin the language of instruction at the academy and put Western texts in the curriculum. This exposure to Western Catholic culture produced more sophisticated clergy, but it also inevitably led to some modification of traditional Orthodox practices and doctrines.

War between Russia and Poland lasted until 1667, and in the eventual compromise peace Ukraine was divided. The eastern part, including Kiev and its theological academy, came under Russian control. A body of scholars trained in sophisticated Western debate and familiar with Western textbooks was thus incorporated into the Russian Church.[4]

From Kiev, Peter the Great summoned the churchman Feofan Prokopovich to draw up the new *Dukhovny reglament*. Prokopovich had had some training in Lutheran traditions. The Patriarch was replaced as head of the Church by a new collegiate body, the Holy Synod, modeled on Protestant synodal bodies, under a chief procurator, who was a layman appointed by the tsar. Originally the function of the procurator was to communicate the tsar's wishes to the synod and to make sure the synod's decisions did not violate the laws of the land. By the end of the nineteenth century, however, he had become the de facto ruler of the Church.

The "Westernization" of the structures of the Russian Orthodox Church by Peter the Great might have been expected to lead to increased contact between Orthodoxy and Western Christianity and to progressive cross-fertilization between the two. It did not in fact do so, for two reasons. First, as noted above, the new administrative structure for the Church meant that it became a subordinate part of a modern autocratic regime which modeled itself now on French Enlightenment, now on Prussian militarism, but had little in common

---

[4] See William K. Medlin and Christos G. Patrinelis, *Renaissance Influences and Religious Reforms in Russia: Western and Post-Byzantine Impacts on Culture and Education* (Geneva, 1971).

with Muscovy in its heyday (the fifteenth and sixteenth centuries) in which Patriarch and emperor had enjoyed complementary but equal status. The second factor was that in this objective situation of thrall to the State those traditions came to predominate within the Church which were suspicious of and hostile to the ways of Western Christianity.

In order to identify the source of those traditions, we need to look further back into the history of the Russian Orthodox Church. In 1240 Mongol invaders from the East destroyed Kiev. Before the Mongol conquest, Kievan Rus' had formed the northeastern edge of Christendom; politically and socially part of Europe, it had been intimately involved in shaping Europe's early medieval Christian history. For the next 150 years, however, virtually all the Russian lands were to be under Mongol control, and increasingly nominal Mongol rule persisted until the late fifteenth century. While Western Europe experienced the Renaissance and the Reformation, then, the Russian lands were isolated from the rest of Europe. They received a compulsory new identity as the Western edge of an Asiatic empire; the Russian princes had to travel to central Asia to pay tribute to their rulers. At the end of this period, Russia reemerged as an independent State under the leadership of Moscow, four hundred miles north-northeast of Kiev.

In 1472 the Muscovite Grand Prince Ivan III (1462-1505) married Zoe Palaiolog [in a Palaiologina], the niece of the last Byzantine emperor; he proceeded to use the title tsar (emperor) and adopted the Byzantine two-headed eagle. The capture of Constantinople by the Turks in 1453, it was argued in Moscow, showed God's displeasure with the Greeks. The belief was promoted in Moscow that God would now need to choose another nation to further his purposes and that Moscow and its ruler were the natural heirs to the Byzantine legacy. The doctrine of "Moscow the Third Rome" was expounded in a letter written in 1510 by Abbot Filofei to Tsar Vassili III (1505-33). The Church in Rome, argued Filofei, fell to heresy, and the Church in Constantinople to the infidel. The Church in Muscovy, however, would, like the sun, illumine the entire world, and moreover would last forever: two Romes had fallen, and the third was now in existence; a fourth Rome there would never be.[5]

The reign of Ivan IV, the Terrible (1533-84), coincided with the period of the Henrician breach with Rome, the birth of the Church of England, the Marian Counter-Reformation, and the development of Anglicanism in the first half of the reign of Elizabeth. There was no Reformation in Russia; on the contrary, the Muscovy of the second half of the sixteenth century was compared by foreign visitors to one vast religious house in which Church canons were as binding on all citizens as the laws of the State. The 1556 book

---

[5] For a recent short summary of the context in which this doctrine arose see Emmanuel Lanne, "The Three Romes," in *The Holy Russian Church and Western Christianity,* ed. Giuseppe Alberigo and Oscar Beozzo, Concilium no. 6 (London and Maryknoll, 1996), 10-18.

Domostroi (*Household Management*) by the monk Silvestr gave detailed instructions on how a Muscovite should run his life and household: the themes were ritualism, formalism, piety, and patriarchalism.

In the course of the seventeenth century "High Muscovy" was destroyed, and Russians were brought back into contact with the rest of Europe. This process, which was repeatedly traumatic, was catalyzed by three periods of particular crisis: the Time of Troubles (1598-1613); the Great Schism (1653-67); and the reign of Peter the Great (1682-1725). The Time of Troubles was a long period of political turmoil during which Muscovy was invaded by foreign armies in support of various pretenders to the throne. These foreigners were predominantly Poles, and Catholics. Having missed participation in the more creative periods of the Renaissance and Reformation, Muscovy was now suddenly embroiled in the destructive European religious conflicts which from the mid-sixteenth to the mid-seventeenth centuries accompanied the Counter-Reformation. Old suspicions of the Roman Catholics as secular and predatory were violently confirmed. The Great Schism, which involved controversy over whether and how the Orthodox Church was to be reformed in the wake of its reexposure to the West, resulted in the birth of the Old Believers and a still unhealed rift in the body of the Church.[6] It weakened it both spiritually and institutionally and left it helpless in the face of the aggressive policies of Peter the Great.

The eighteenth century saw the Russian Orthodox Church severely compromised. The synod was subject to all the vicissitudes of court politics. Bishops, who were always monks, were controlled by the synod; they were regularly nominated without consideration of the interests of the Church and were moved from one diocese to another, promoted and demoted on political rather than spiritual grounds. Meanwhile the parish clergy, who were married men and in whose family the job of priest tended to become hereditary, remained completely dependent on the decisions of remote bishops, often unknown to them, who nevertheless appointed and dismissed them. Under new legislation parishioners no longer had any say in appointing their own pastors. However, the upkeep of a parish priest and his assistants remained, as in the old days, a parish responsibility. This often led to friction and discontent and sowed the seeds of later widespread anticlericalism. Catherine the Great (1762-76), a German who became empress through marriage, was baptized a Lutheran, entered the Orthodox Church, but espoused the rationalism of Voltaire. She saw her role in Russia as that of an enlightened and benevolent autocrat; for her the Orthodox Church was steeped in superstition, a vehicle for keeping a backward people in ignorance. The procurators she appointed reflected her views.

---

[6] For the history of the Russian Church to the Schism and the origin of Russian sects see Albert F. Heard, *The Russian Church and Russian Dissent* (London, 1887).

Nevertheless, Orthodoxy was vigorously enlisted in the pursuit of Russia's political aims. In the eighteenth century, Russia intensified its contacts with the representative bodies of Orthodox populations in other parts of Europe, and eventually assumed the role of self-styled protector of Orthodoxy wherever it was threatened. The Russian Church was, of course, not only much larger numerically than all other Orthodox Churches put together, but it was the recognized spiritual arm of a secular power at a time when all other Orthodox were either within the Ottoman Empire or divided among small states. It was in the treaty concluding the Russo-Turkish war of 1768-74, the Russians were later to claim, that the Turkish authorities had conceded them a general right of protection over all the Orthodox Christians in the Ottoman Empire.

The reign of Catherine the Great saw further extension of the Western boundary of the Russian Empire. The three partitions of Poland (1772, 1793, and 1795) brought with them large populations of Orthodox Ukrainians and Belorussians as well as territories inhabited by Jews, Roman Catholic Poles, and Greek Catholics. The political, social, and religious structure of the empire grew more complex. For four decades after the partitions, the Russian government suppressed the Greek Catholic dioceses in the newly acquired territories, and in 1839 all Greek Catholics in the Russian Empire were aggregated to the Russian Orthodox Church. For the next century and a half, under the Imperial Russian and then Soviet governments, Greek Catholicism was both illegal and officially nonexistent.

Russia experienced a period of national revival during the campaign against Napoleon (1812-14). Tsar Alexander I (1801-25) was attracted to German pietism and mysticism and in the early part of his reign had liberalizing inclinations. He was open to non-Orthodox initiatives: in 1814 the Russian Bible Society was founded on a Protestant model. There were great hopes of political reform. However, before long Alexander drew back, disconcerted by the Europe-wide unleashing of forces apparently seeking to overthrow legitimate authority. When the Greeks revolted against Turkish rule in 1821 and the Ottoman authorities responded by executing the ecumenical Patriarch, the Russians confined themselves to withdrawing their ambassador from Constantinople.

Under Alexander's successor Nicholas I (1825-55) the pendulum swung decisively back from enlightenment and reform to discipline and reaction. Nicholas I wanted to close Russia's windows on the West. As a department of State, the Russian Orthodox Church had no room to dissent from this policy. The stream of Western ideas could not now be stopped, however; the flow was simply diverted into side channels unconnected with the official life of State and Church. From now on philosophy, history, and literature became the vehicles for Russian cultural development, replacing politics and religion, both of which were increasingly identified with the establishment status quo.

During this period of institutional eclipse, the Church nevertheless continued to nurture men of great spiritual stature. St. Tikhon Zadonsky (1724-83) lived as a simple monk at the service of all in need of help and advice, and wrote books of devotion. He was venerated as a holy man and canonized in 1861. One of the most beloved saints of the Russians is St. Serafim of Sarov (1759-1832), an ascetic who devoted himself to the service of others as a healer and seer. Paisi Velichkovsky (1722-94), from his monastery in Moldavia, translated into Russian the Greek classics on asceticism and contemplation and helped revive Orthodox monastic traditions, which by the eighteenth century had fallen into decay in many parts of the Eastern world. His disciples brought his revived ascetic tradition to Russia and established monastic communities. The monastery of Optina Pustyn near Tula was to become famous in the nineteenth century as a place where Westernized intellectuals in search of genuine Christian teaching and practice could meet monks maintaining the authentic patristic traditions of Eastern Orthodoxy.[7]

The Russian Orthodox Church had, from the very beginning, been a missionary church. Geography and history dictated, however, that this missionary effort would be directed north and east: away from Europe; into unknown lands inhabited by tribesmen; into territories which would naturally form part of an expanding Russia. It thus did not impinge on Western Christendom. St. Sergi of Radonezh (1314-92) founded the Holy Trinity Monastery in what became Sergiyev Posad (Sergi's Settlement) near Moscow in 1337. (In communist times it was called Zagorsk.) In the following century Sergi's successors founded some 150 new monasteries in one of the most remarkable missionary movements in Christian history. By 1397, with the founding of the Monastery of St. Cyril on the White Lake, monastic communities were three hundred miles north of Moscow, and by 1436, they were another three hundred miles north, with the founding of the Solovetsky Monastery in the White Sea, still the most northerly monastery in the world. (In communist times it became one of the earliest and most notorious political prisons, before being virtually destroyed; it is now in the process of restoration, and a monastic community is living there again.)

The mid-nineteenth century saw renewed missionary activity on the part of the Russian Orthodox Church. Missionaries went to Siberia, to Alaska (part of the Russian Empire until 1864), to the Muslim tribes in the Volga and Ural regions, and even to Japan. Father Ioann Veniaminov, who for forty-four years devoted himself to missionary work, became Metropolitan of Moscow in 1868.

---

[7] The writers Gogol, Dostoyevsky, and Tolstoy visited Optina Pustyn, as did the philosophers Solovev and Rozanov. Ivan Kireyevsky and Konstantin Leontev made it their permanent home. They found there holy men, *startsy* or elders, saintly figures who embodied and continued the hesychast tradition and who stood outside the all-too-compromised hierarchy of the Church. A powerful portrayal of a *starets* is that of Fr. Zosima in Dostoyevsky's novel *The Brothers Karamazov*. See Nadejda Gorodetsky, *Saint Tikhon Zadonsky: Inspirer of Dostoevsky* (London 1951); John B. Dunlop, *Staretz Amvrosy: Model for Dostoevsky's Staretz Zossima* (Belmont, Mass., 1972); and Donald Nicholl, *Triumphs of the Spirit of Russia* (London, 1997).

He founded the Orthodox Missionary Society, which continued its activities up to the Revolution of 1917. In 1899 the Russian Church had twenty missions inside the empire and five foreign missions in Alaska, Korea, China, Japan, and Persia.[8]

By the nineteenth century, then, despite its institutional dependence on an autocratic State, the Russian Orthodox Church had developed a liturgical and spiritual life of immense distinctiveness and richness; but generally speaking its encounters with Western Christianity had been either of a negative nature in themselves (as in the Time of Troubles), or short-lived, their potential development blighted for political reasons (as with the Russian Bible Society under Alexander I, which was closed down after only a few years of existence). There were always clergy and theologians within the Orthodox Church who were interested in Western traditions—German theology and philosophy, for instance, were heavily influential on the development of Russian Orthodox theology in the nineteenth century—but the force of political gravity was increasingly to pull the Church as an institution back into a nationalist and eventually chauvinist and isolationist orientation. Meanwhile "Western" ideas in the public sphere came to be associated either with the institutions of an autocratic State or, conversely, with secular revolutionary thinking culminating, of course, in the spread of positivism and finally of Marxism.

From the beginning of the nineteenth century, small circles within the Russian intelligentsia devoted themselves to the development of social and political ideas derived from what they believed to be the true doctrines of Russian Orthodoxy. Central was the concept of *sobornost*, which they understood to define "community" as "individual diversity in free unity" and to represent a Russian Orthodox alternative to inappropriate social models derived from Western Enlightenment individualism. These "Slavophiles" (as opposed to the "Westernizers") included the Kireyevsky brothers Ivan (1806-56) and Petr (1808-56), the Aksakov brothers Konstantin (1816-60) and Ivan (1823-86), and Aleksei Khomyakov (1804-60).[9]

When hopes for the introduction of liberal, Western-inspired reforms in Russia began to fade after 1825, the imperial government adopted a program which bore some external resemblance to the Slavophile program but was designed to consolidate the autocracy. It was summarized in 1832 by Count

---

[8] See Paul D. Garrett, *St. Innocent: Apostle to America* (Crestwood, N.Y., 1979). For a general overview of Orthodox mission see James J. Stamoolis, *Eastern Orthodox Mission Theology Today* (Maryknoll, 1986). See also Vyacheslav Maiyer, "Russian Orthodox Missions to the East," *Religion, State, and Society: The Keston Journal* [*RSS* hereafter] 25(4) (December 1997): 369-79.

[9] See Andrzej Walicki, *The Slavophile Controversy: History of a Conservative Utopia in Nineteenth-Century Russian Thought* (Oxford, 1975); Peter K. Christoff, *An Introduction to Nineteenth-Century Russian Slavophilism*, 2 vols. (The Hague, 1961 and 1972); Aleksi I. Osipov, "The Theological Conceptions of the Slavophiles," in Alberigo and Beozzi, *Holy Russian Church*, 33-48.

Uvarov as "Orthodoxy, Autocracy, and Nationality" and guided the policies of the last two Russian tsars and of Konstantin Pobedonostsev, procurator of the Holy Synod from 1880 to 1905 and a dedicated conservative. Creative Christian thinking was thus coopted by the secular arm and adapted as underpinning for the status quo.

Meanwhile the Christianized minority among the Russian intelligentsia continued to contribute to the intensifying political debate. Their most important product was the collection of essays *Vekhi* (*Signposts*) of 1909. The central message was an urgent call to the Russian intelligentsia to repent; a spiritual reorientation was needed if Russia were not to head for self-destruction wrought by maximalist egoism. The unfamiliar message obviously touched a nerve: *Vekhi* aroused intense controversy. The proposed solutions were ineffective, however. Some of the same authors came together in the collection *Iz glubiny* (*From the Depths*), published in 1918, where the lament was that it was now too late.[10]

It was in this climate that a movement took shape to reform the Church, to free it from the suffocating embrace of the State, and to equip it as an institution able to tackle contemporary challenges. The movement was supported not only by members of the intelligentsia but by bishops, ordinary clergy, and lay believers. In order to restore canonical self-government to the Church the reformers planned to convoke a National Council (*Pomestny sobor*), traditionally the supreme ecclesiastical organ. There was serious discussion within the Church of the different models of Church-State relations which had developed historically in East and West. A brief interlude of political liberalization (1905-6) saw religious concessions, including the edict of April 17, 1905, which granted religious freedom to non-Orthodox denominations. This development meant that reform of the Orthodox Church was now urgent; it needed institutional independence in order to join the other newly legalized denominations on equal terms.

However, renewed reaction (1906-17) spelled an end to the reformers' hopes, and it was only after the February revolution in 1917 that the Church was able to convene a National Council in Moscow and elect a Patriarch, Tikhon—the first since 1721. The council continued its reform deliberations until September, but by then the Bolsheviks were in Moscow. The only one of its decisions the council was able to put into effect was the decision to restore the Patriarchate.[11]

At the turn of the century, and increasingly as religious toleration became official tsarist policy, Western and particularly American missionaries began to

---

[10] See Nicolas Zernov, *The Russian Religious Renaissance of the Twentieth Century* (London, 1963); George F. Putnam, *Russian Alternatives to Marxism: Christian Socialism and Idealistic Liberalism in Twentiety-Century Russia* (Knoxville, 1977); Alexander Schmemann, ed., *Ultimate Questions: An Anthology of Modern Russian Religious Thought* (New York, 1965); Christopher Read, *Religion, Revolution, and the Russian Intelligentsia, 1900-1912: The "Vekhi" Debate and Its Intellectual Background* (London, 1979).

[11] See James W. Cunningham, *A Vanquished Hope: The Movement for Church Renewal in Russia 1905-1906* (New York, 1981).

target the Russian lands. The experiences of those times show many features which were to be typical of the 1990s, and nobody who has examined this missionary endeavor of the early twentieth century ought to be surprised by the recent developments that are partly the subject of this present book. In 1908 a Methodist missionary enthusiastically reported that "the Greek Orthodox Church has lost her grip upon the people," and explained, "The Russo Greek Church does not preach. Hers is a religion of male singing, ritual and image-worship. Like other branches of paganized Christianity, she offers a stone to those who are hungering for the Bread of Life." Frequently, the Western missionary efforts were linked with the aim of introducing Western-style democracy and capitalism to Russia, and the expectation was that they would be financially rewarding. The missions were conceived of in business terms: expecting "ample returns from our outlay," missionaries were typically confident that (in the words of one of them) "from a business point of view this thing will not be a fizzle." Small wonder that the Russian Orthodox Church experienced severe disorientation and dismay, and that in the last period of political reaction in Russia it should make strenuous efforts to defend itself. Typical was a pamphlet published in 1911 featuring a cartoon depicting rival faiths as agents of the devil attempting to steal lambs from Christ's flock, and identifying Adventists and Baptists as two of the most dangerous and aggressive of these faiths.[12]

For seventy years the Communist Party of the Soviet Union sustained an offensive against religion on a scale unprecedented in history.[13] The Russian Orthodox Church was naturally the first target. Priests and bishops were put on trial; open season was declared on the Church's wealth and possessions. Most of the leading figures in the "Russian religious renaissance of the twentieth century," those associated with *Vekhi* and *Iz glubiny*, were sent into exile. It was their fate to bear fruit in the West. Men like Sergei Bulgakov (1871-1944), Semen Frank (1877-1950), Nikolai Lossky (1903-58), and Nikolai Berdyayev (1874-1948) were centrally involved in the development of Russian Orthodox philosophy and theology in the West during the Soviet period; and Berdyayev in particular was to have significant influence on existentialist philosophers as well as Christian theologians in non-Orthodox traditions. This encounter was promoted in centers like the Institut St. Serge in Paris; ecumenical societies like the Fellowship of St. Alban and St. Sergius[14] were to nurture

---

[12] David S. Foglesong, "Redeeming Russia? American Missionaries and Tsarist Russia, 1886-1917," *RSS* 25(4) (December 1997): 353-68.

[13] See Philip Walters, "A Survey of Soviet Religious Policy," in Ramet, *Religious Policy in the Soviet Union*, 3-30.

[14] Contacts between the Anglican Church and the Russian Orthodox Church began in the seventeenth century, and were renewed with particular vigor after 1917 when the Russian Orthodox Church was in desperate need of contacts in the world outside the Soviet Union. Conferences between the two churches in 1923, 1927, and 1928 led to the founding of the Fellowship of St. Alban and St. Sergius.

relations between the Orthodox and Western churches over the crucial decades to come.

The Russian Orthodox–Western encounter, however, was definitely not going to continue to involve the Moscow Patriarchate and the Church within the Soviet Union, which by the end of the 1920s was fighting for its very existence. Patriarch Tikhon died in 1925, and once again the office lapsed. The 1929 Law on Religious Associations meant that from now on the only legally permissible religious activity was meeting for an act of worship in a registered building; and soon it would become practically impossible for most believers to exercise even this right. There was savage and prolonged persecution throughout the 1930s. By 1939 the Orthodox Church had virtually ceased to exist as an institution: in the territory under Soviet control from 1919 to 1939 no more than a few hundred churches remained open out of a prerevolutionary total of some forty-six thousand; clergy and laypeople were in labor camps; only four bishops remained at liberty.

The situation for the Church changed dramatically upon the outbreak of the Second World War. The partition of Poland between Hitler and Stalin in 1939 increased the number of open churches by 40 percent. For the first time Stalin made use of the Church, allowing it to organize Church life in the annexed territories. In 1941, in a further dramatic development, Hitler violated the Nazi-Soviet pact and invaded the Soviet Union. Metropolitan Sergi responded before Stalin did, calling on the faithful to defend the Motherland. Meanwhile a remarkable revival of Church life was taking place in those areas of the Soviet Union now under Nazi control.[15]

In September 1943, Stalin summoned Metropolitan Sergi to the Kremlin; four days later he was elected Patriarch after an interregnum of eighteen years. The government then set up a council to deal directly with the Church hierarchy, a move which amounted to de facto recognition of the Church as an institution. The new policy continued after the war. Churches were reopened, the number of clergy and bishops grew, theological schools and monasteries began to function again, and the Church was allowed to publish a journal. There was, however, no change in the law of 1929, and the new liberties had no legal status.

During the war Stalin realized that the Church could be of positive help to the State in mobilizing public support for the defense of the Motherland. It was soon clear, moreover, that it would continue to be of help in furthering the Soviet State's postwar political agenda. Between 1945 and 1948 the Soviet authorities encouraged the Church to extend its authority over the Orthodox Churches in the countries of Eastern Europe now coming under Soviet politi-

---

[15] See Wassilij Alexeev and Theofanis G. Stavrou, *The Great Revival: The Russian Church under German Occupation* (Minneapolis, Minn., 1976).

cal control. When Western Ukraine was again incorporated into the Soviet Union, the Greek Catholic Church there was suppressed (in 1946) and declared aggregated to the Russian Orthodox Church.

Those deemed reliable enough by State and Church to represent the Church officially were soon providing valuable service in building up the Soviet State's diplomatic relations with the world at large, and spreading a favorable Soviet image abroad. After 1948 Church representatives were regularly to be found promoting the Soviet concept of peace in international gatherings. In 1961 the Russian Orthodox Church became a member of the World Council of Churches; it could not have done so without the consent of the Soviet authorities.

From 1961 to 1991 the World Council of Churches believed that it was fostering a genuine ecumenical encounter between Orthodoxy and Protestantism. Representatives of Protestant churches from the First and Third Worlds (the latter ever increasing in number) were in the vast majority in the WCC. Some Orthodox leaders were genuinely interested in encounter between the major faiths; but the inclination even of these was to seek such encounter with those churches which on the face of it seemed most congenial to Orthodoxy: the Church of England and the Roman Catholic Church (which was not a member of the WCC). The outstanding figure in Russian Orthodox–Roman Catholic relations was Metropolitan Nikodim of Leningrad, who died in the presence of Pope John Paul II in the Vatican in 1988. As far as the WCC is concerned, however, it is now clear that the minority Orthodox delegates by and large did not understand, and were disconcerted by, the multifarious and often exotic Protestant denominations on display at WCC gatherings, and were out of sympathy with their preoccupations, which the Orthodox tended to regard as essentially secular concerns having nothing to do with true spirituality. The Orthodox delegates were present in the WCC for complex political reasons. The Soviet authorities wanted them there to demonstrate that there was religious freedom in the USSR and to promote Soviet interests where appropriate; the Moscow Patriarchate wanted them there to guarantee a toehold in the international arena as a safeguard against the ever-present possibility of repression at home. Meanwhile, the Orthodox delegates would maintain an attitude of hearty bonhomie toward their Protestant hosts, on whom they depended for facilities and material assistance, while secretly growing ever more confirmed in their view that these so-called Christian denominations were essentially heretical.[16]

---

[16] For discussion of the policy of the World Council of Churches toward the churches in communist countries see Michael Bourdeaux, "The Russian Church, Religious Liberty, and the World Council of Churches," *Religion in Communist Lands* [*RCL* hereafter] 13(1) (1985):4-27. Hans Hebly, "Liberty or Liberation—the Dilemma of the WCC," *RCL* 13(2) (1985): 131-51; and materials in *RSS* 25(1) (March 1997) and 26(2) (June 1998).

It was ironical that one of the tasks of Russian Orthodox representatives in the WCC was to deny that there were any restrictions on religious freedom in the Soviet Union. At the very time the Russian Orthodox Church joined the WCC a massive and unexpected new antireligious campaign was being launched by Nikita Khrushchev. The campaign lasted from 1959 to 1964 and led to the closure of two-thirds of the twenty thousand legally operating churches. The total of some seven thousand churches still open in the mid-1960s was to remain more or less unchanged until the later 1980s, and the total had still not been reconstituted by the late 1990s.

The trauma of the Khrushchev years of persecution gave way to the "years of stagnation" under Brezhnev and his successors. For ordinary churchgoers this meant that if they confined themselves to attending services of worship in registered buildings and did not attempt to comment on or interfere in political or social matters from a Christian perspective they would be left in peace. As in the eighteenth and nineteenth centuries, bishops were appointed and removed on political rather than spiritual grounds; they were remote from the parish clergy; perforce they had a close relationship with the organs of State security. The Church was allowed a limited institutional existence, able to train some clergy in a small number of theological educational establishments, to publish limited numbers of official journals and calendars, and to produce very small print runs of the Bible. The average believer received no spiritual nourishment beyond attendance at the liturgy; Sunday schools, discussion groups, charitable activity, parish newsletters were all prohibited in a society in which the official ideology continued its systematic occupation of the public space.

In their isolation, the churches in communist countries were, generally speaking, unable to inform themselves systematically about developments in the world at large, including developments within the churches in other countries—remaining, for example, ignorant of the details of even such important events as the Second Vatican Council. This was especially true of the Russian Orthodox Church, both because of its traditional suspicion of Western Christianity and because of the particular harshness of the Soviet regime. This alienation was compounded by the fact that Christians in the Soviet Union came to view with suspicion many apparently progressive concepts which were tainted as a result of their exploitation by the communist authorities: not only words such as *peace* and *democracy* became suspect, but also such purely ecclesiastical concepts as *ecumenism,* which was perceived as a politically motivated process through which churches were compelled to go as the price for being allowed to continue to function. In colloquial Russian today the word *ecumenism* is often mispronounced as "e-communism" or "economism."[17]

---

[17] See Vladimir Fedorov, "Barriers to Ecumenism: An Orthodox View from Russia," *RSS* 26(2) (June 1998): 129-43.

Mikhail Gorbachev came to power in 1985, and soon *glasnost* and *perestroika* had become household words. Gorbachev himself believed the Soviet system could be reformed, but with the active cooperation of "all citizens of goodwill"—and this soon came to include religious believers. The Millennium celebrations in 1988 for the thousandth anniversary of the acceptance of Christianity in Kiev were already marked by cautious triumphalism on the part of the Church; and in the next two years religious freedom became once again a reality.[18]

While welcoming the new freedoms, the Church was nevertheless seriously shaken as an institution by the events of the late 1980s. The basic certainties inherent in the status of second-class servant of the State which the Russian Orthodox Church had had since the Second World War were abruptly destroyed. In 1989, for example, the Soviet government suddenly relegalized the Ukrainian Catholic Church, and immediately millions of nominal Orthodox in Western Ukraine revealed their true allegiance. It might even be argued that the emerging Ukrainian Catholic Church played a key role in the referendum on whether Ukraine should secede from the Soviet Union, which in turn led to the latter's disintegration. Since the collapse of the Soviet Union the Ukrainian Catholic Church has become one of the major denominations in independent Ukraine, and its revival has been one of the major causes for the precipitous deterioration in relations between the Moscow Patriarchate and the Vatican, a deterioration exacerbated by Orthodox suspicions about Catholic plans to engage in systematic missionary work in the Russian lands.

In 1990, both the Soviet Union and the Russian Federation passed new laws on freedom of conscience, at last replacing the harsh Stalinist law of 1929. After decades of persecution, all denominations found themselves legally among the freest in the world: free to reopen churches, monasteries, and theological academies; to publish; to engage in mission, social work, and political activity. State persecution was, however, soon replaced by a whole range of different problems.

Many of these problems were inherent in Russian Orthodox Church life in the late nineteenth century, carried over in deep freeze, and are now reemerging, often exacerbated by the unique conditions in which the Church had to survive the Soviet period. Other problems are specific to the Soviet period itself, a result of the experience of totalitarianism. In all cases they have been rendered more serious by the speed of the transition to postcommunism. Developments which have taken decades in the West have been forced through in only a few years in the successor states of the USSR.

---

[18] See the special millennium issue of *RCL* 15(3) (1987); and Helen Bell and Jane Ellis, "The Millennium Celebrations of 1988 in the USSR," *RCL* 16(4) (1988): 292-328.

A fundamental problem for the Church has been the internal split which has developed between "progressives" and "conservatives." While some among the clergy and laity are struggling to maintain openness to the West and ecumenical dialogue, now that this is genuinely possible for the first time for decades, and to promote spiritual renewal and a commitment to social and even political involvement, loud voices have begun to champion chauvinist programs and stress the need to return to the traditional teachings and disciplines of the Church. The area in which the Russian Orthodox Church has been most successful in rebuilding its activity in the postcommunist period has arguably been in the sphere of theological education, yet even the dozens of new seminaries and academies tend to be divided into "progressive" and "conservative."[19]

The split reaches into the hierarchy itself, and the Church thus finds itself unable to speak with one voice on important issues of the day. Within the hierarchy the conservatives undoubtedly predominate, and are doing so increasingly. This tendency is exacerbated by the all-pervasive authoritarianism within the Russian Orthodox Church today. This is in part a legacy of the tsarist period, but possibly to a larger extent of the Soviet period. The Russian Orthodox Church is in fact the only national Soviet institution still surviving in Russia today, in that its leadership remains largely unchanged from Soviet times. Canonically the highest authority in the Orthodox Church is a National Council, bringing together bishops, priests, and laypeople, but there are no signs that the current Church leadership is planning to summon one, and many key issues are thus unlikely to be submitted to open debate by representatives of the whole Church membership.

The progressive Russian Orthodox priest Father Veniamin Novik writes that "if one had to describe the spiritual condition of Russia in one word, that word would be 'schism.'"[20] As we have seen, schism was the response of the Church in the seventeenth century to newly presented challenges from the modern world. Within the Russian Orthodox Church today the splits seem to be growing more profound rather than healing.

The tendency toward schism is exacerbated by particular aspects of the Soviet legacy. Immediately after the end of communism a fundamental problem within the Russian Orthodox Church (and generally in churches throughout Eastern Europe) was that of achieving reconciliation between two groups now divided by bitterness and distrust: those who had "compromised" or "collaborated" with the secular authorities and those who had "resisted" and had been persecuted or discriminated against as a result. The picture was, moreover, complicated by a further consideration. It soon became clear that a

---

[19] See materials on religious education in Russia in *RSS* 22(2) (1994); see also Dimitry Pospielovsky, "Impressions of the Contemporary Russian Orthodox Church: Its Problems and Its Theological Education," *RSS* 23(3) (September 1995): 249-62.

[20] Fr. Veniamin Novik, "Russia—Between Past and Future," *RSS* 22(2) (1994): 183.

basic question needed to be asked about any religious believer who had resisted the communist system: had he or she done so because that system was *totalitarian* or because it was *atheist*? An individual in the former category would now, in the postcommunist period, very likely be found in the camp promoting democratization, pluralism, and freedom of conscience for all. An individual in the latter category, by contrast, would in the postcommunist period tend to be defensive of the "truth," conservative, triumphalist, and intolerant of innovations in the spiritual sphere. During the communist period both Father Gleb Yakunin (a priest of the Russian Orthodox Church) and Bishop Ioann (later to become Metropolitan Ioann of St. Petersburg) were a thorn in the side of the secular authorities. Father Gleb continues his democratic political activity to this day, and has been defrocked for his pains; from 1991 until his death in 1995, by contrast, Metropolitan Ioann spoke out against the "Jewish conspiracy" against Russia and called for laws against the activities of "pseudo-Christian" Western non-Orthodox denominations on what he saw as the canonical territory of the Russian Orthodox Church. There has thus been an increasing estrangement between those who had been on the same "side" in the communist period.[21]

A further exacerbating factor is the post-totalitarian mentality. This comprises contradictory elements. On the one hand, it includes the tendency to expect solutions from strong leaders rather than from personal initiative, and the tendency to dramatize oneself as the impotent victim of uncontrollable circumstances ("learned helplessness"). On the other hand, the individual may see himself or herself as the measure of all things, showing a tendency to seek maximalist solutions and to regard compromise as suspect and dishonorable— "if you disagree with me you are not only mistaken but a scoundrel"—and a tendency to identify personal opinion with absolute truth. The contradictory elements in the post-totalitarian mentality tend toward polarization among those who are faced with the message the churches are trying to bring. While some are extremely skeptical and suspicious of any attempt to replace the old compulsory truths with a new set, however different in content these may be, others eagerly embrace the Christian message as a new set of truths to be adhered to as unquestioningly as the old communist ideology. Many enthusiastic new converts to Orthodoxy used to be active members of communist youth movements. These neophytes are often among the most xenophobic and isolationist of Church members, bringing over wholesale into their new faith the conviction nurtured in them in communist times that they were surrounded by enemies and needed constantly to be vigilant and unmask them.

In resisting communism, the churches in Eastern Europe were in fact doing something different from what they thought they were doing. "In opposing its own conception of totality to that which the official system was attempting to impose," writes Patrick Michel, "the church, whether it knew it or not, was in

---

[21] See materials on reconciliation in *RSS* 21(3/4) (1993).

fact defending the relative"—an environment of pluralism and democracy. "Everything seems to indicate that this will be a challenge much more difficult to meet than that which was posed by the Soviet system."[22]

What should be the role of a church in a pluralist society? This basic question facing the churches in the postcommunist countries is one which has also been facing the churches in the West. Like other challenges, however, this one is presenting itself in a particularly acute form in the postcommunist world because the transition to pluralism has been so sudden and extreme.

Jürgen Moltmann argues that in a pluralistic society Christians do not have the right to speak on behalf of all citizens, but that all citizens nevertheless have the right to hear what Christians have to say. Those who follow this line tend to believe that the only meaningful way in which Christians can respond to a situation of moral dissonance is to accept that situation and contribute vigorously to the debate. Polish theologian Father Józef Tischner has taken a rather different view. He has argued that after its confrontation with communism Christianity is now likely to have to enter into a confrontation with liberalism. For some, then, the primary challenge to the Church will be whether it can now rise to the opportunity of entering the debating chamber on equal terms with all other partners; but for others, the primary challenge to the Church will be specifically to combat the obviously deplorable consequences of "pluralism," such as unrestrained individualism and self-seeking, exacerbated in the context of the new free-market economy.[23]

Metropolitan Kirill clearly believes that the Russian Orthodox Church should be free to reevangelize the traditional Orthodox believers on its own "canonical territory."[24] A central problem here, however, is the failure of the Russian Orthodox Church in postcommunist times to rise to the challenge of effective witness to its own nominal flock. It is arguably this failure, as much as the aggressive "proselytizing" activities of non-Orthodox denominations, which gives Orthodox denunciations of "sheep-stealing" their strident character.

Like virtually all the churches in postcommunist countries, the Russian Orthodox Church faces the challenge of reestablishing itself as a properly functioning social organism. In communist times it was severely restricted in its witness, and its infrastructure was dismantled; parish life ceased to exist. The Church was rich, with nothing to spend its money on except international travel for privileged hierarchs. It was critically short of equipment, literature, and material resources of all kinds, which were taken for granted by denominations in the West; but the lack was without consequence since it would not have been permitted to use them in any case. In the postcommunist period the

---

[22] See Patrick Michel, "Religious Renewal or Political Deficiency: Religion and Democracy in Central Europe," *RSS* 20(3/4) (1992): 339-44.

[23] See various articles in ibid.

[24] See chapter 3 in this volume.

opportunities for witness to society have suddenly become almost infinite. All churches in postcommunist countries are suffering from a lack of resources and experience; for a church with canonical claims on the scale of those of the Russian Orthodox Church, the chasm between potential and reality is correspondingly exceptionally wide.

One fundamental problem for the churches in postcommunist countries is that of finding a language in which to communicate with their nominal flock and even more so with those who have never had contact with a church. This problem is particularly acute for the Russian Orthodox Church. Communism, with its atheist educational system and secularized discourse, was in power for seventy years rather than forty in Eastern Europe, that is, for two generations rather than one. Moreover, the liturgy is conducted in Old Church Slavonic rather than modern Russian; bitter dispute within the Church revolves around modernizing the form and language of the liturgy to make it accessible to newcomers, and "progressive" priests can expect harsh disciplinary reprisals from the hierarchy. The whole problem of vigorous mission into society is compounded by the fact that it is not only the ordinary people who are ignorant; by and large the clergy have had inadequate theological education and pastoral training, or none at all.

The bitterness of the dispute over liturgy reflects the fact that for the Orthodox Church it is the liturgy itself which is in fact at the heart of its spirituality. The Orthodox tradition is that in the beauty of the timeless liturgy conducted among the body of the believers, both living and dead (the latter present in the icons), the transcendent realm is mediated to the faithful, who in turn participate in the process of the transfiguration of creation, a cooperative process involving both God and humanity. Throughout the Tsarist and Soviet periods the priority of the Russian Orthodox Church was always to maintain the liturgy. Solzhenitsyn has written movingly of the cupolas of the churches rising like flames out of the lowly Russian landscape. Certainly in Soviet times the churches were islands of beauty and love in a harsh and colorless environment; the people flocked to them. Because of their Soviet past, as Kent Hill has remarked, Russians are much more aware than Westerners of the consequences if those with political power start seriously trying to put non-transcendent views into systematic operation. This is one of the reasons why Christians in Eastern and Central Europe are genuinely shocked by the excesses, as they see them, to which liberalizing tendencies have led in some Western churches. They often see these as symptoms of that Western secularism which has so traumatically been revealed to them in the postcommunist period, the spiritual and moral effects of which look uncannily similar to those of Marxist atheism.

The French Jesuit Philippe de Régis, who died in 1954, looked forward to the time when it would be possible for missionary work to begin again in Russia. He was firmly opposed to all who would set out to "conquer" Russia for Roman Catholicism. His words were accurately prophetic:

When Russia opens up there will be a great temptation for us to rush into this vast mission field as though it were virgin land to be brought under cultivation. We will burn with the desire to "convert" these people, and this will provoke a violently hostile reaction from Orthodox circles. The clergy will feel themselves under threat and will start looking out for "wolves in sheep's clothing"; and so a rift will open up between the two halves of Christendom, which ought to be brought into unity rather than set against each other. There will be only one way to achieve this unity: impartial fraternal collaboration with the Russian Orthodox Church in the task of education and spiritual formation among the people.[25]

The only major Orthodox Church which did not have to endure communism is the Greek Orthodox Church. The Orthodox Churches of the postcommunist countries soon began showing interest in the legal status of religion in Greece and the pattern of Greek Church-State relations as it has developed during the twentieth century. A perennial question is whether the Greek Orthodox Church has a monopoly on the "truth." The Church has a history of resistance to liturgical or scriptural change. The new Greek constitution of 1975 now allows missionary activity by "recognized" non-Orthodox denominations, thus moving toward recognition of religious pluralism, but Orthodoxy is still recognized as the "dominant" religion. Until the end of communism the Orthodox Church in Greece was in a unique category in the Orthodox world, but it is now likely that other Orthodox Churches in postcommunist countries will be interested in achieving a similar status. The new legislation on religion passed in Russia in 1997 may later be seen as the first step on the road to the reestablishment of Orthodoxy as the "national" faith of the Russian people.

[25] Quoted in Constantin Simon, "How Russians See Us: Jesuit-Russian Relations Then and Now," *RSS* 23(4) (December 1995): 343-57, at 350-51 (translation in ibid., 315-16).

2.

ORTHODOX CHRISTIANITY AND THE RUSSIAN TRANSFORMATION

————————◆————————

James H. Billington

Very possibly, the most important single political event of the late-twentieth century was the almost instantaneous implosion of Communism, collapse of the Soviet Empire, and sudden end to the Cold War at the beginning of the last decade of the twentieth century. The overthrow of Communism has been written about largely as the result of the intrusion of Western values and ideas. But it was produced in almost equal part by a recovery of the half-forgotten spiritual substratum of a deeply Orthodox Christian culture.

Christianity played a central role in the overthrow of the world's first political system designed systematically to supplant all belief in God. In particular, the rooting of Solidarity, a working-class movement, in traditional Catholic culture introduced into the largest Soviet satellite of Poland the kind of challenge to which a Leninist system could never respond. Arnold Toynbee's monumental *Study of History* suggests that all imperial systems collapse when they meet a challenge to which they are inherently incapable of dealing with.[1] The bottom-up movement in Poland was something that even martial law could not repress, and its religious underpinnings provided a legitimacy that was not amenable to the usual techniques of political manipulation. Haltingly, often only subliminally, Eastern Europe began to rediscover a Christian vocabulary amid the disintegration of the world's first large-scale effort to link

Portions of this paper were originally presented as the Twenty-Fourth Thomas Verner Moore Lecture, "The Role of Eastern Orthodoxy in Christianity Today," given at The Catholic University of America, September 30, 1997, here reproduced with permission of St. Anselm's Abbey, co-sponsor of the lecture and copyright holder.
    [1] See Arnold J. Toynbee, *A Study of History,* 12 vols. (London, 1935-61).

the exercise of power systematically with the destruction of religion. And the Christian recovery proved to be as ecumenical as the earlier persecution. Important roles were played by the Catholic Church in Poland, the Protestant Church in East Germany, and the Orthodox Church in Russia.

CHRISTIANITY AND THE COUP OF AUGUST 1991

Communism in the Soviet Union would not have collapsed and broken up if there had not been the amazing events of forty-eight hours in Moscow in August 1991, which I was privileged to witness firsthand.[2] Nothing could have seemed more unlikely than that a mere 150 armed people, holed up in a single building at the very heart of the world's most vast and long-lived land empire, could face down the largest armed force of the modern era. *Chudo*, a miracle, was the word used by almost everyone in the motley crowd of resisters around the White House at dawn of the third day to describe their unexpected victory. Tanks that had driven massively into Moscow forty-eight hours earlier were now leaving covered with flowers, and the instant television documentaries that celebrated Russia's newfound freedom spoke in the half-forgotten, Old Testament language of the ancient Russian chronicles, in which victory was almost always the result of a divine miracle.

Western commentators, meanwhile, fumbling to explain an event that they had previously deemed impossible, called it a revolution. But modern revolutions have generally been violent, militantly secular, led by politicized intellectuals, and focused on a utopian ideal. Russia and Eastern Europe had produced instead what Czech President Vaclav Havel called "velvet revolutions"—largely nonviolent and unled, focused on the anti-utopian aim of creating what they simply called a "normal society," and deeply tinged with Christian idealism.

For the small righteous remnant that had kept Russian Orthodox Christianity alive during what they called the Babylonian captivity of Soviet rule, it seemed providential that the August 1991 coup began on the Feast of the Transfiguration, commemorating Christ's transfigured appearance to his disciples on Mount Tabor. In the pictorial theology of Orthodoxy, the icon for this feast centers on a Christ robed in a many-layered white garment used only to depict direct divine intrusion into human life. The Patriarch of Moscow was celebrating a morning liturgy before this icon within the Kremlin Cathedral of the Assumption at precisely the time when tanks supporting the coup could be heard rumbling into nearby Red Square. Many went directly from the church service to help defend the center of resistance that was spontaneously forming at the building of the Russian government popularly called the White House, where the color white seemed itself to play a galvanizing role. Moscow, the "whitestoned" Christian redoubt of medieval legend, suddenly

---

[2] See a full account in James H. Billington, *Russia Transformed: Breakthrough to Hope* (New York, 1992) and summary in "Russia's Fever Break," *Wilson Quarterly* (Autumn 1991): 58-65.

had a new locus of legitimacy: a white building containing a white-haired Yeltsin surrounded by the whiteness of a shirt-sleeved crowd. And the first and most persistent new emblem to appear in that crowd was pictures of St. George slaying the dragon: an image dominated in Russian icons by the whiteness of the horse.

In Eastern Christian (as in Buddhist) art, the hands and face signal the spiritual message of a holy figure. These were generally the only parts of a body painted as flesh in Russian icons and left uncovered by metal casings. Two radically different images of a face and hands clarified (even amid all the confusion and disinformation of the first day) the essential nature of the struggle: on the one hand, the widely reproduced picture of Yeltsin atop a tank with a confident smile and raised fist; on the other, the televised leader of the coup, Genady Yanaev, with trembling hands and shifting eyes at the junta's only press conference.

In a society where speech had so long been corrupted, pictures seemed to provide more dependable guideposts. The defenders rallied to the White House in response not to anyone's articulated appeal or program, but to remembered televised images from the recent past: of Lithuanians forming a human wall to defend their government building, and of that lone figure in Tiananmen Square who turned away a tank.

In this time of uncertainty, Russians seemed to recover not just guiding images from their pictorial theology but also the moral conscience embedded in their great literature. Nothing had been more debilitating about totalitarian rule than its total dismissal of personal moral responsibility. The Soviet mantra had always been, "It doesn't depend on me"—a rationalization used by every bureaucracy, which was, however, taken to unprecedented extremes in the Soviet state. Having long functioned in a system where survival depended on avoiding decisions, Russians were now suddenly forced to make decisions for themselves. When the outcome was still uncertain, they had to decide whether and how to speak up; whether to go to the White House; and, for soldiers, whether to sign, or to obey, an order. Russians, on both sides of the barricades, were not only discovering freedom but recovering responsibility, the Siamese twin of any freedom that endures.

Four unlikely groups played key roles in the improbable recovery of freedom with responsibility during those three days in August 1991. First were the ten or so young priests who conducted almost nonstop counseling, baptisms, hymn singing, and improvised communion services. Particularly remarkable was the distribution of two thousand New Testaments to the young would-be attackers and another two thousand to the defenders of the White House by Father Alexander Borisov, who re-founded the Russian Bible Society. Such actions blurred the distinction between the opposing groups and suggested that there might be something deeper to which both sides might rally.

A second group were the Siberians, fortuitously present in Moscow in large numbers for an unprecedented Congress of Compatriots, which opened on the day of the coup attempt in an effort to bring Russian émigrés together with

Russians from the deep interior for the rediscovery of their common heritage. Many came from Siberia, Yeltsin's original political base, which had long been saddled with concentration camps. As the Siberians around the White House described their lives to me during the long standoff, I realized that these were very often the sons and daughters of those who had perished in the camps. They had returned to reclaim their heritage, bringing with them the special aura of those who have suffered but never surrendered.

A third group were the Afghan veterans, victims of that terrible, terminal misadventure of Soviet imperialism, who were determined on both sides of the face-off to avoid another senseless bloodletting. Particularly important were the roles of the war heroes Alexander Lebed and Alexander Rutskoi, the latter Yeltsin's vice-president. Rutskoi later opposed Yeltsin, and Lebed may in the next election. But Lebed's unit was one of the first to go over to the resistance; and Rutskoi, on the day before the coup, had joined the Patriarch in the ritual reburial of the remains of Tikhon, the one great Patriarch who had consistently resisted Soviet authority, in the Moscow monastery dedicated to Our Lady of the Don. The image of that all-protective Virgin, who was credited with turning back the Mongols on the Don river in the fourteenth century, was summoned up anew by the Patriarch in his intercessory prayer broadcast from the White House just after midnight on the second night of the coup attempt, when everyone expected the junta to storm the White House.

How could a motley resistance prevail against preponderant force? How could a largely cynical people who had long been morally anesthetized and historically submissive suddenly come alive so dramatically? The answer to that question may be even more astonishing than the outcome of the crisis. Because, at least for the devout Orthodox, men can come alive on earth at any moment in time because a woman found rest in heaven for all time.

The Assumption of the Mother of God has always represented the ultimate security policy for the Christian East. She had been the protectress of Constantinople; and, after that "second Rome" fell, the famous icon of the Vladimir Mother of God had come from Constantinople through Kiev and Vladimir to Moscow, and was credited with saving the "third Rome" from both Eastern and Western invaders.

The Patriarch's prayer anathematizing fraternal bloodshed, just after the first and only blood of the August coup was shed, took the form of a prayer for the Virgin's protection during the fast before the Feast of the Assumption. There was probably more praying done in Moscow that night than at any other time since the Communist Revolution. Prayers during the fast of the Assumption were followed by a commemorative service in the Cathedral of the Assumption for the three young men who died. A few days later another liturgy in the same Cathedral of the Assumption on the Feast of the Assumption itself opened up the first post-Communist parliamentary session and thus Russia's fragile experiment with democracy.

The fourth group impelling the August miracle was the most seemingly implausible of all—old women. I happened to be meeting with a group of them—apolitical librarians—early on the second night when martial law and a curfew were proclaimed. Spontaneously and without discussion, they all left to join the young men on the barricades and other elderly women who had been rebuking soldiers in the tanks. Lacking clear orders from their military superiors, these young men were now getting moral commands from a rival authority—their mothers.

What could otherwise have escalated into macho violence between the crew cuts in the tanks and their pony-tailed cousins on the barricades was headed off by precisely those "old women in church" that Western observers no less than Soviet propagandists had so long patronizingly dismissed as symbolizing the impending death of religion in the USSR. Now here they were—shaming potential attackers, feeding the resisters, and refusing to leave when the faintly chauvinist Afghan veterans insisted they go because fighting was near. Perhaps prayers did matter by these silent surrogates of that other lady in whose heavenly rest lay both the ultimate assurance of protection and the imminent possibility of miracles.

Orthodox Christians are inclined to believe that we live in liturgical time. Boris Pasternak's *Dr. Zhivago* saw the Communist Revolution as a kind of late winter reenactment of Holy Week.[3] The summer overthrow of Communism occurred quite literally in the nine days between the Feast of the Transfiguration and the Feast of the Assumption.

The funeral procession for the three young defenders of the White House who were semi-accidentally killed seemed to celebrate both unity and pluralism. Sounds of the Orthodox "Eternal Memory" mixed with those of the Kaddish in honor of one of the victims, who was Jewish. Orators repeatedly echoed the Judeo-Christian theme of the redemptive value of innocent suffering. The three boys were unconsciously likened to the first Russian saints, Boris and Gleb, the young sons of Russia's first Christian leader who voluntarily accepted death at an early age in order to overcome the divisions of their people.

The high point of the procession through Moscow came when Boris Yeltsin emerged from the White House, went directly to the parents of the three young men, and said: "Forgive me, your president, that I was unable to defend and save your sons." "Forgive me" is what one Russian often says to whomever is next to him before taking communion and what that other Boris, Tsar Boris Godunov, said to all the Russian people in the last words of the greatest of all Russian operas. Power was being relegitimized morally. Someone not to blame was assuming responsibility in a society where no one in power had ever accepted responsibility for anything.[4]

Of course, the Old Testament repeatedly reminds us that God's miraculous deliverance from evil does not assure humanity's subsequent adherence to good.

---

[3] See Boris Pasternak, *Doctor Zhivago* (New York, 1958), 509ff.

[4] See further Billington, *Russia Transformed*, 122-38.

Since those exhilarating August days, Russians have in many ways been spiraling down into economic insecurity, crime, and corruption—seemingly stuck with the worst of both worlds: the authoritarian habits of their former totalitarian system and the disorder and indulgences of their new freedom.

But Russia has, in fact, experienced a revolution in the older sense that the word was used in the American Revolution—a "revolving back" from a temporary tyranny to a more normal, preexisting condition. The trouble is that the normal condition that preexisted Communism throughout Eastern Europe was nothing like that of thirteen self-governing colonies living under common English law but rather that of combat between fascist-type nationalism and fragile democratic experiments. In releasing Russians and other Soviet nationalities from an ostensibly denationalized Union of Soviet Socialist Republics, the events of August 1991 paved the way for reviving in Russia a vicious version of this omnipresent East European struggle between ethnic authoritarianism and pluralistic democracy. Whereas democracy generally seems to be winning in Poland, the Czech Republic, and Hungary, authoritarian nationalism seems to be prevailing in the former Yugoslavia, and gaining ground in the former Soviet Union.

THE PROMISES OF ORTHODOXY
IN THIS TIME OF TROUBLES

Russians today are living through what they call a "time of troubles," when one form of legitimacy has been rejected, but no new form has yet been fully accepted.[5] In such a time, Russian Christianity, especially Russian Orthodoxy, brings with it the special authority of having survived its targeted extinction under the Soviet system and having provided a previously flagging faith with what Russians call the "new martyrs," perhaps the greatest number of Christians persecuted or killed for their faith in modern times.

The Russian Orthodox Church had an extraordinary revival as the Soviet Union was imploding. The number of churches, monasteries, seminaries, and parishes increased geometrically. Russia and Ukraine have been the site of one of the largest mass conversions to Christianity of the twentieth century. Indeed, Orthodoxy, at least in the physical sense, is alive and well in Russia and Ukraine—and, in many ways, fulfilling the ideological void left by the collapse of Communism. An American polling study found that 30 percent of Russians under 25 converted from atheism. The number of functioning churches in Moscow alone rose from 50 to 250 between 1988 and 1993.

Unfortunately, the Russian Orthodox Church, like any contingent national institution, reflects secular conflicts in its own society and is torn between its own authoritarian and reformist factions. How the Russian Church resolves this internal conflict could be decisive in resolving the broader society's search

---

[5] Ibid., 145-61.

for a post-Communist legitimacy. The reformers no less than the authoritarians tend to be theologically conservative (almost unanimously opposed, for instance, to the ordination of women) and devoted to an elaborate, essentially unchanging, liturgy as the key to salvation: the pearl of great price that enabled faith to survive when teaching and, in effect, even preaching were not permitted.

The authoritarian nationalists within the Church, however, want to build on the moderately privileged position that Russian Orthodoxy obtained in the late Soviet period to become again a fully established state church, featuring social discipline from the top down. For them, Russia itself is a martyred nation victimized by a series of materialistic Western ideas—liberalism in the Tsarist period, Marxism in the Soviet era, and now market economics. Some are decent, pious people simply seeking a restoration of the monarchy. But many favor an almost Nazi-type ethnic Orthodoxy that would reconquer most of the former Soviet Union, assert racial superiority abroad (particularly against Muslims), purge "impurities" at home (mostly Jewish), and limit the incursions of foreign sects (Pentecostals, Evangelicals, Seventh-day Adventists, Mormons, and others). Authoritarians attach extraordinary importance to venerating the physical remains of newly exhumed past saints and to maintaining the liturgy in majestic but unintelligible Church Slavonic.

By contrast, the rival and usually younger reformers in the Church want an internal, moral renewal of Orthodoxy and a total catharsis of the Soviet legacy. They see past hierarchical collaboration with Soviet repression as arguing not so much for a selective purge of Church leaders as for some kind of corporate repentance by the Church as a whole. They are working for a parish-based renewal of Russian society independent of the government and aided by a revived Christian pedagogy centered on the vernacular Bible, to which Russians now have massive access for the first time in their history, and a liturgy translated into modern Russian.

Patriarch Aleksii II was an outstanding parish priest, and he has made an unprecedented number of visits to the grass-roots parishes that are multiplying all over Russia and developing Christian responsibility from the bottom up. One model for the reformers is the last great "new martyr" from the Soviet era, Father Alexander Men. He was exiled by the authoritarians to an obscure parish on the far outskirts of Moscow where he became the most admired Christian teacher of his generation before being murdered by a person wielding an ax early one Sunday in September 1990. Another model is Father Zinon, a saintly thirty-seven-year-old monk who revived icon painting as a disciplined religious art. He wrote that Russian Orthodoxy is at a crossroads and will either become once again a state religion or leaven civil society with a new life of prayer, hard work, and Christian education that will renew local communities in which both human and property rights will be respected. His vision is not merely compatible with, but probably indispensable for, democracy in Russia. More and more thoughtful Russians are coming to believe that, in their present damaged economic and psychological state, they will never succeed in building democracy on a continental scale unless they reconstitute their people's moral fiber with the transforming power of faith.[6]

In this, as in other respects, Russians are, in effect, reconstituting on Europe's eastern frontier the experiment that America launched two centuries ago on Europe's western frontier. A devout Episcopalian, George Washington, noted in a circular letter to the states at the conclusion of the war in 1783 that America "would never be a happy nation . . . without an humble imitation . . . of that charity, humility and pacific temper of mind that were the characteristics of the divine author of our blessed religion."[7] And in his farewell to the entire nation upon leaving the presidency thirteen years later, he warned that our fragile, balanced system for governing a vast region depended on a moral people to survive and that morality could not be sustained without religious faith.[8]

Some Christians in Russia have left the Orthodox Church altogether and converted to Catholicism, Pentecostalism, or, more often, Protestant fundamentalism. But the Orthodox Church remains one of only two institutions (along with the army) that still has some popular support throughout Russia. While Western efforts to convert Russians to other denominations should be defended against current xenophobic measures at restriction, aggressive proselytizing risks further offending an already psychologically bruised people. Most Russians need to recover a positive heritage of their own in order to resist the temptation to recover self-respect through a destructive imperial nationalism.

Behind the tradition of being an established church closely linked with the state, there is an internal tradition of deep spirituality within Orthodoxy, which is still little known to the West and may have unexpected relevance for the future of Russia. Four distinctive characteristics of the Orthodox tradition seem to me to have unusual potential for the constructive, democratic reformation of Russia today—and also for inter-confessional dialogue in the broader Christian world.[9]

First, the basic beliefs of Orthodoxy were taken as the finished product of the first seven ecumenical councils. As a result, the Orthodox have always felt that they can largely avoid the verbal theological disputation that began in the West in the High Middle Ages of the twelfth century and was intensified during the Reformation and Counter Reformation of the sixteenth. Russian Orthodoxy, therefore, is an expression of joy at seeing the world through the eyes of the Resurrection, sharing the joy that comes with "right praising," the literal meaning of *orthodoxy,* and above all attempting to beautify rather than analyze the act of worship and the objects of faith. Eastern Christendom did

---

[6] See further James H. Billington, "The Case for Orthodoxy," *The New Republic* (May 30, 1994): 24-27.

[7] George Washington, "Circular to States (June 6, 1783)," in *Basic Writings of George Washington,* ed. Saxe Cummins (New York, 1948), 488-98.

[8] "Farewell Address (September 19, 1796)," in ibid., 627-44.

[9] See Billington, "The Case for Orthodoxy," and more fully James H. Billington, *The Icon and the Axe* (New York, 1966).

not develop as much verbal theology as the Western Christian world in the second Christian millennium. As Bishop Kallistos Ware, an Orthodox convert, has said: "Orthodoxy stands outside the circle of ideas in which Western Christians have moved for the past eight centuries and lives in that older tradition of the fathers which so many in the West now desire to recover." In an age where attempts at theological modernism and accommodation with contemporary trends almost invariably lead to the weakening of faith and loss of members, the Orthodox effort to go behind the verbal disputation of the High Middle Ages, no less than the modern world, might have fresh appeal as a unifying restarting point for Christian commitment.

Second, the liturgy has always been absolutely central to the life of the Orthodox world, where it justifies its literal meaning of "common work." The focus on certain central feast days on which the community comes together in the liturgy has been actually reinforced by the long period of bondage and periodic frontal assault in the Soviet era. Soviet regulations permitted only liturgical worship and sought to prevent all broader teaching of the faith or even reading of the Bible in the hopes that Christianity would die by becoming simply a theatrical artifact. On the contrary, the intensity of devotion invested in the liturgy became even greater, since there was no other point of contact with the Church. And the Orthodox liturgy, which had always been particularly valued in Russia, became the pearl of great price which kept alive a continued sense of Christian community.

The intense, liturgically centered life of the Orthodox is something that many Western churches appreciate now more than in the past. There has been a returning to an earlier, purer form of the liturgy in many Western churches. The liturgy provides a dramatic structure full of entries and exits, incense, and procession, usually punctuated by interludes of prayer that an individual programs for himself or herself. If liturgy is to play a central role in the future of the broader Christian church as in the past, none is more ornate and compelling than the multimedial theater of total participation in the Orthodox Church.

Third, the broader Orthodox tradition also provides a model for political decentralization. The Orthodox world was not—except in the early years of the Byzantine Empire—unified either by some overall imperial structure or uniform vernacular language. Greek, Syrian, and Georgian from the very beginning and Church Slavic soon thereafter became languages of the liturgy long before Western Christendom tolerated vernacular liturgies. Orthodoxy provided a model of independent or autocephalous national churches, which many of them see as a middle ground between authoritarian centralism of Tridentine Roman Catholicism and the stand-alone independence of Protestantism.

The authority of synods and councils is at least as strong as the principle of patriarchal authority in Eastern Christianity; and the inclination to accept autocephaly and at times intercommunion with other liturgically based Eastern churches, such as the Armenian and the Coptic, indicates an interesting combination of local autonomy with conservative doctrine and liturgy. This linkage assures deeper cultural unity even across political and linguistic borders. This blending of tradition and decentralized conciliar forms of rule suggests greater compatibility with democratic forms than people have generally been inclined to think who focus solely on the Orthodox Church as a hierarchical political instrument of the Byzantine Empire.

Fourth, and perhaps most important, at the core of Orthodox theology is a clear belief in what I can only call the omnipresence of the vertical dimension in life. The Orthodox have a historical rather than a rational theology, believing that they live in the last days when it is important to celebrate and beautify rather than to articulate or argue. Orthodoxy generated one of the most intense inwardly directed forms of mystical theology in all of Christian history. The phenomenon called Hesychasm argued that it was even possible for a human to attain a measure of transformation into Godly company by an intense life of repetitive inner prayer. This movement slowly germinated in the great monastic complex at Mount Athos, which psychologically replaced the political centers of Constantinople, Serbia, and Bulgaria as the true capital of Orthodoxy as they all crumbled before the Muslim Turks. Hesychasm inspired the explosion of monasticism in fourteenth- and fifteenth-century Russia, as it became the new political center of the Orthodox world.

In the process of developing the monastic life, which began in Egypt and Palestine in the fourth and fifth centuries, the Orthodox world struck on a balanced middle way of ordering its clergy, which no one seems yet to have discovered for Western Christendom. The so-called white or parish clergy should be married, presumably to provide a model as well as a sense of identity with ordinary family life. At the same time, bishops who exercised authority over property, money, and appointments in the higher realms of the Church had to come from the monastic or so-called black clergy—again recognizing, perhaps, that only those with no familial attachments could truly make disinterested decisions about such matters.

The intense preoccupation with silence and the uninterrupted rhythmic prayer of the heart led people out into what they called the desert outposts (*pustyni*) in the forests and frozen wastelands of the north just as the first monks had fled to the scorching deserts of Egypt. But, far from leading to quietism, this monastic flight led to an intensely energetic life of clearing, colonizing, and civilizing the hitherto unpenetrated northeastern frontier of Europe and Asian Siberia. It is rather like Max Weber's famous paradox that the intense sense of predestined election in Calvinism led them not to rest fatalistically on their laurels but to engage in frantic entrepreneurial activity. The distinctive Hesychast belief that humanity was capable of being infused not with the "essence," but what they called the "energies" of God, led to an enormous release of human energy, enabling the colonizing monks to accomplish incredible things. Cases in point are three monks from the Russian north all canonized as saints for their extraordinary work in journeying across Siberia and educating Alaskan natives in the late eighteenth and nineteenth centuries. When one of them, who lived on an Aleutian island virtually alone for decades, was asked if he felt lonely, he responded, "How could I here in the constant presence of angels and archangels and all the company of heaven?" All places, after all, are equidistant from eternity, as the great historian Leopold von Ranke once wrote. However harsh the external, horizontal circumstances stretching out across the tundra and taiga, the internal, vertical dimension of reaching in and up to God was always there, and it inspired the Orthodox to great feats. One Russian word for a hero (which is the same as the one often used for saints) is *podvizhnik*. It literally means a mover. Only as one attains the inner peace that comes from personal isolation, silence, and self-purification can one find the strength to be a genuine *podvizhnik*, like the *bogatyrs* of Russian epics and the saints of their hagiography.

THE ROLE OF RUSSIAN ORTHODOXY IN CHRISTIANITY TODAY

The survival and revival of Orthodoxy of an essentially premodern Russian Church may very well have something important to say to postmodern Western churches as well. A church which, in effect, is still rooted in the patristic era may have a distinctive role to play in the third Christian millennium.

Whether the Russian Church will, in fact, be able to play such a role in this, its second millennium, is, of course, an open one. It is by no means clear that the Russian Church will be able to break its long tradition of subservience to the state, or that the Russian people, having almost to a man and woman redefined themselves vaguely as Christian since the fall of Communism, will so strongly identify with Orthodoxy. But what is important for our purposes is not so much predicting the future, which is the province of God, or passing judgment on it, which is the temptation of humans. What is important especially for Christians is to understand more deeply what those who have suffered for their faith in the East might bring to Christians in the West who have generally suffered and sacrificed less for their faith.

First is the spiritual value of beautifying rather than analyzing the ritual reenactment of the mass. For the Russians, the liturgy has always been a total multimedial theater in which there are no spectators, but only participants who are never simply sitting and watching. The rising audiovisually trained generation throughout the world is vaguely seeking spiritual meaning in the midst of the rampant consumerism and materialism of our time. Can anything be more important than recentering life on the beauty-out-of-ugliness of Christ's saving sacrifice, the resurrection-out-of-crucifixion that provides the ultimate destination for all our stumbling vertical strivings?

The Orthodox, like the first Slavic pope, also believe passionately in the all-encompassing protection of the Mother who gave God earthly birth and stands as the protectress and queen of heaven. For the Orthodox, meaning comes from penetration rather than analysis of these mysteries, from a sanctity which integrates rather than a scholasticism that disintegrates the act of knowing.

The Orthodox believe not just in the special majesty but in the ultimate pedagogic power of the liturgy—as potentially the most effective instrument of evangelization in a world surfeited with words and argument.

A second contribution of Orthodoxy, particularly in its Russian form, is its ideal of community. The national icon of Russia is Andrei Rublev's icon of the Holy Trinity, which shows the visitation of the three angels to Sarah and Abraham, the beginning of God's bestowal of special selection on the people of Israel. The Rublevian form follows the patristic model of interpreting an Old Testament event as a symbolic anticipation of an otherwise mysterious Christian doctrine. It represents three persons in one God through three circles defined by three angels; three pools of color engaged in the mutual contemplation of one another—all indicating the total and perfect community that exists within God. This is the ideal model of community which has in one way or another enabled Russians to survive all kinds of authoritarianism at the high levels and retain not merely sanity but sanctity in small groups.

The Russian tradition of maintaining human intimacy and close interdependence in small groups is, of course, a counter to the impersonality of large bureaucracy and distant authority. To compensate for the coldness of both the bureaucracy and the weather, Russians have developed unusual warmth in small circles of friends and in the family nest, usually centered on the *babushka* or grandmother, who brings up the children and anchors the home while both parents work. Only in small circles throughout most of Russian history have people felt able to discuss honestly and openly many of the things that were most important but which the public culture would not tolerate.

Since the fall of Communism and the disintegration of many of the macrosystems that traditionally supported local services like education and health, local communities and parishes have developed rapidly and have often assumed new responsibilities for some levels of health care and education. This has expanded the concept of the parish and the parish system itself (never terribly strong in Russia, which was entirely outside the Roman Empire, the Russian Empire did not inherit the diocesan structures present in both Eastern and Western Roman Empires), for parishes were not always well integrated into the community since the priest was simply appointed as a government official up until 1917, and lacked the organic connection with their parishes that they generally now have.

It may be that only people who have survived a highly centralized totalitarian state can fully appreciate how good it is to have things done locally at the face-to-face communal level. The growth of parishes amid the current disintegration of central structures in Russia and Ukraine may provide an opportunity to rediscover and reclaim for the local level many responsibilities previously assumed centrally—and in the process extend the concept of the smaller community to the larger cooperative efforts of the kind Alexis de Tocqueville spoke about.

Third, the Russian Church has something deep and uniquely spiritual to share with the rest of Christendom in an area that modern Western humanity seems to have sanitized out of the Christian consciousness—the dark subject of martyrdom. It is true that, particularly in the last quarter-century of Soviet rule, there was relatively little direct suffering and perhaps an excess of subservience to the state. Many believed that compromises were needed for the Church to survive at all. But others believed that even the compromises of the late 1920s, the so-called Sergius concessions, were excessive. At least then there was the excuse of a totally repressive regime. More recent collaboration with the state was more deeply corrupting to the Church. But this fact has been allowed in some ways to obscure the fact that more parish priests and believers as a whole in Russia were executed for their faith than in probably any other community of Christians in the twentieth century.

Martyrology has generally played a more important role in Eastern Orthodoxy than in Western Christianity; and many stories of heroic semi-anonymous martyrs are now slowly being gathered, largely at the local level, in Russia. Perhaps only those who have lived under a committed atheist state determined to wipe out religion as such can know how deep and important religion is in ordinary life. There is so much taken for granted in the modern West that the concept of sacrifice for one's faith and, indeed, accepting martyrdom because of its ultimately redemptive value are lost, but these are ideals that tend to be as intimate to the devout Orthodox today as they are foreign to Western Christians. Areas of Africa, Latin America, and other parts of the world have also had their twentieth-century martyrs, but the systematic, vicious, and often sadistic murder and humiliation of priests and believers at the local level in the Soviet era is a story that has yet to be told. I predict that, when it is more fully recorded (as it is rapidly now becoming in Russia) and is digested spiritually by believers everywhere, it will soon overshadow the story of collaboration with state power at higher levels that has so far been the greater focus of outside attention. And the Russia case is only part of the major martyrdom suffered in this century by other Eastern Christian churches: the Ukraine (both Catholic and Orthodox), Greek Orthodox and Armenians at the hands of the Turks, Egyptian Copts at the hands of Muslim extremists, and Ethiopians at the hands of a particularly grotesque Communist-type rule.

Finally, and most important of all, is the rediscovery of the inner life of withdrawal and prayer as the prerequisite for meaningful action in the world. This was the paradoxical result of Hesychasm in the fourteenth and fifteenth centuries, when withdrawing into the countryside and within oneself released energies that colonized much of Russia. This tradition was revived in the nineteenth century; and perhaps the three greatest Russian prose writers of all time—Gogol, Dostoyevsky, and Tolstoy—were frequent visitors to Optina Pustyn, the great Hesychast monastery where elders served as spiritual mentors and advisors to laymen as well as novice monks. The regeneration of Russian monasticism today generally follows this tradition.

The tradition of interior spirituality has a long history that goes back to that of the trans-Volga elders or non-possessors in the fifteenth century, who sought to concentrate on inner spiritual development rather than external ecclesiastical growth. This tradition is revered by Russian society as a whole and sought after by a number of the young people going into monastic life after having been exposed to permissive freedom now as well as to Soviet repression earlier.

If the Russian Church can rediscover the interior life and the divine energies that it can release, there could be a new basis for ecumenism in a two-way learning process. The West could share certain organizational skills and social-service traditions, while the East could enrich the Western search for spiritual renewal with the still largely buried riches of the Church Fathers. A return to roots could help us transcend some of the denominational and doctrinal schisms that have divided the branches of Christianity in the West. One hopes that the Eastern Orthodox Church, particularly in its Russian form, will stay in ecumenical bodies like the World Council of Churches, even though there are powerful forces urging it to pull back and to use the new law on religion to stamp out other forms of Christianity that have been growing recently inside Russia. But, at the same time, one hopes that the Orthodox will not merely communicate with others at the lowest common denominator of platitude. We hope that they will share something of the deep interior spirituality that has attracted so many of us in the West over the years. And, at that level, there is a meeting yet to be held between the Moscow Patriarch and the first Slavic pope, whose fascination with the concept of coredemption makes him already a soulmate of the Orthodox.

CONCLUSIONS

The miraculous fall of Communism represents the victory of a story not yet completed over a finished theory that was put into practice with terrifying results. The reformers are finding fresh guidance in the greatest of all stories: the biblical record of how the people of ancient Israel intruded the idea of seeking justice in time into a world of empires content with exercising power in space.

The Siberians who helped launch Russian's new chapter of hope have a legend that the savage bear was originally just an ordinary person. But, when denied the simple bread and salt of human hospitality by his neighbor, he retreated in humiliation into the forest . . . and later returned unexpectedly in a transformed state to take his revenge.

Right now, Russians should fill us not with fear but with hope—a hope that draws on a faith as relentlessly centered on Easter as any in Christendom; a new hope at the end of a long nightmare, which saw perhaps fifty million people killed by unnatural causes in the last eighty years—half in two world wars, half through internal repression.

One of the old women on the barricades said to me as the tanks were leaving Moscow in August 1991: "We kept alive faith and love all those years; now we have hope." It is the hope given to them—and to us—by Mother

Maria, an emigrant Russian who substituted herself for a young Jewish mother in a Nazi death camp; a hope revived in a Soviet death camp by the anonymous women who, when told they could have an Easter service only if they conducted it waist deep in a slowly freezing lake, sang out, "Christ is Risen. . . . In truth he is risen," and went on with the service. It is the hope that another group of women found when there was not even a body left in a tomb. As Luke tells it, they "were afraid and bowed down their faces to the earth." Then came the unexpected joy of the voice that said, "Why seek ye the living among the dead? He is not here, he is risen."

The word for "living" in the liturgical Slavonic version of that text is *zhivago*, the title of a great testament to Christian hope—written just as the last great systemic campaign to stamp out religion was being launched in the USSR in the late 1950s. Pasternak's novel ends with a poetic view of history that blends the image of Christ's resurrection with that of the ships on the Volga, the "mother river" of Russia and the artery into its deep interior Christianity:

> You see, the passing of years is like a parable
> Which can, at any time, ignite along the way.
> In the name of its terrible majesty
> I go down, a voluntary victim, to my grave.
> I go into my grave, and on the third day rise
> And, like little boats spread across a river,
> Towards me to judgment, like a caravan of barges
> The centuries flow forward out of darkness.

3.

GOSPEL AND CULTURE

———————◆———————

Metropolitan Kirill
of Smolensk and Kaliningrad

I greet all the participants in this Conference on World Mission and Evangelism devoted to the theme "Called to One Hope—The Gospel in Diverse Cultures."

The theme of "one hope" selected for this last world mission conference of the second millennium is profoundly symbolic. We have come close to the juncture between two centuries, summing up the one ending and looking with anxiety and hope to the one to come. We look to it with anxiety because we cannot help but see how many unresolved problems humanity faces today, in what a hopeless situation—both spiritual and material—millions of people live. The world is faced, on the one hand, with an aggressive globalizing monoculture which tries to impose itself everywhere, dominating and assimilating other cultural and national identities and, on the other, with nationalistic upheavals, tribalization, and disintegration of the human family. Yet in the midst of contemporary hopelessness and despair, as Christians we live with hope in the eschatological expectation of *parousia*—the coming of Christ—and Christ's ultimate triumph over the forces of evil. For this reason, it is important to address the "one hope" to which Christians are called, in the light and from the perspective of the one Gospel as it is expressed through and lived in diverse cultures.

Two thousand years ago, our Lord Jesus Christ gave this commandment to his disciples and all succeeding generations of Christians: "Go therefore and

Text of speech "Called to One Hope—The Gospel in Diverse Cultures," presented at World Conference of Churches Conference on World Mission and Evangelism, November 1996, Salvador, Bahia, Brazil, and forthcoming in a conference report published by the World Council of Churches. Reprinted with permission of author and the World Council of Churches, Geneva.

make disciples of all nations, baptizing them in the name of the Father and of the Son and of the Holy Spirit, and teaching them to obey everything that I have commanded you" (Matt. 28:19-20). Has this mission been fulfilled today? This conference is an opportunity for us to assess the missionary situation at the end of the twentieth century and to look forward toward a renewed mission in the twenty-first century.

The second facet of the theme of this conference—"the Gospel in diverse cultures"—poses a set of questions concerning primarily the need for dialogue so strongly felt by Christian churches in the twentieth century. To what extent should Christian mission be a dialogue with non-Christian traditions? How can the proclamation of the Gospel interact with various cultures? What is inculturation of the Gospel? What is culture at all? Is it alien and dangerous to church mission? Is it an altogether external reality that should be radically transformed, or rather can culture itself become a bearer of the Gospel where the voice of church missionaries has grown weak?

THE MISSION OF THE CHURCH IN TODAY'S WORLD

Before sharing with you my ideas on these issues, I would like to say a few words about the situation in which humanity finds itself today. For long decades the world was divided into two zones of confrontation. During the Cold War a billion dollars were spent daily on armaments, and the accumulated arsenal of weapons was large enough to destroy the whole world many times over. Many people in the West believed that once the "Soviet threat" ended, evil itself would perish from the face of the earth and an age of universal prosperity, peace, and harmony would come. They thought that stopping the arms race would solve all problems.

Then the "iron curtain" collapsed before our very eyes and the "Soviet threat" perished, together with the need to spend the billion dollars on armaments. And what happened? Have people become happier? Has the longed-for peace come? No, it has not! On the contrary, we are horrified to see the chaos into which Europe has been plunged and the fratricidal wars waged in the former Yugoslavia, Chechnya, and the republics of the former Soviet Union.

The military and political crisis has been accompanied by economic collapse as whole regions have found themselves below the poverty line. In this situation we are not surprised to see a growing nostalgia for the socialist past felt by people in the former Soviet Union. They may have lived a miserable life deprived of many civil rights and liberties. But they did have their bread, a roof over their heads, and a certain social security. Nowadays many are starving. Criminality is growing at a disastrous pace. Many feel powerless and defenseless in the face of the evil that has fallen upon them so suddenly and forcefully.

Moreover, severe political and economic problems have affected many regions in the world. The disparity between North and South continues to increase, as does the gap between rich and poor. The infant mortality rate in

Asia, Africa, and Latin America remains high. Millions of people have become infected with HIV/AIDS. For more than forty years now, humanity has been struggling to improve the military, political, and economic situation in the world, but paradoxically the situation has not improved.

The ideal of a super-consumer society characteristic of Western civilization has led to global devastation. Christian churches are deeply concerned about the pollution of the environment that has reached a catastrophic level, the contamination of water and air by chemical wastes, the deforestation and depletion of other natural resources, and the exploitation of flora and fauna, which have all resulted in global climatic changes with unpredictable consequences. What then has caused the present crisis of human civilization? It is my profound conviction that the crisis has been caused primarily by a global crisis of personality. Human survival depends today not so much on military-political changes, economic forces, efforts to overthrow totalitarian regimes, or improvements of the existing social system, as on the spiritual and moral state of the human person. Jesus Christ as revealed to us in the Gospels was not primarily a social reformer, but rather a great reformer of the human spirit. That is why he did not call his contemporaries to overthrow Roman rule, to eliminate slavery, to redistribute material resources, but spoke of a spiritual transformation and moral rebirth of every person and all humanity. I do not want at all to say that Christian churches should reconcile themselves to social injustices or refuse to struggle for civil rights and liberties. But I would like to stress that the spiritual and moral rebirth of humanity should be a priority for the churches if they are to remain faithful to the spirit of the Gospel of Christ.

Therefore, mission as a witness to the spiritual and ethical heritage of Christianity becomes the number one task for the churches. For fifty years the World Council of Churches has spoken about concrete matters such as overcoming the consequences of the Second World War, liberation from social oppression, disarmament, and the elimination of racial discrimination and sexism. We have to acknowledge that it is vital for Christians to address these issues, as they are common concerns for the whole human community. But are these not the effects of certain more profound causes of a spiritual and ethical nature? And has the time not come to clarify the causes instead of being fixed on their consequences? Has the time not come to address a human person, to return to the Gospel's message: "Repent, for the kingdom of heaven has come near" (Matt. 3:2, 4:17)? Expressed in these words of John the Baptist and Christ is the quintessence of Christian morality.

We are living at a time when the human person suffers profound moral decay. Human vocabulary seems to have lost the notion of personal sin and personal responsibility before God. "If there is no God, then everything is permissible," says one of Dostoyevsky's characters. We seem to have reached the climax of moral permissiveness. In Russia, just as in many countries in the West, the mass media have been involved in the broadest possible propaganda of lust, debauchery, and violence. Alcoholism and drug addiction have become chronic diseases for entire generations. Who will raise a voice against this moral decay if not the church?

The present crisis of the missionary and ecumenical movement is largely the result of the fact that it has lost this personal dimension. Perhaps the old contradiction between mission and dialogue can be resolved by common efforts of churches to save the person. I am strongly convinced that only morality will save human civilization today. The churches should thus join their efforts to win and transform the human heart and to witness in common to the Christian moral ideal. Only then will our mission succeed, only then will our voice be strong and prophetic, and only then will the world hear our voice.

CULTURE AS A BEARER OF THE GOSPEL OF CHRIST

Let us move on to the second part of the theme of our meeting: the interaction between the Gospel and culture.

Since the middle of this century, especially since Vatican II, it has increasingly been heard in Christian churches that for mission to succeed Christians should use local culture so that Christianity may be understood by people in a given time and place. According to the 1973 world mission conference in Bangkok, "culture shapes the human voice that responds to the voice of Christ." A conclusion drawn from that statement is that Christianity everywhere should take on aspects of the local culture.

Some participants in the ecumenical movement who support in principle the idea of interaction between Christian mission and local cultures have warned from the very beginning against the danger of theological syncretism and have reacted strongly to its manifestations.

The contemporary sporadic tendency to identify inculturation with syncretism seems to be rooted in the theological understanding of culture. No doubt "the wind blows where it chooses" (John 3:8). This means that the Spirit can speak the languages of various cultures. The message of the Gospel is always embodied and conveyed to people in a certain cultural framework. Therefore culture can become a carrier of the Gospel—when the Gospel is preached to the people in their own language and within their own cultural patterns, they will be able to understand it better and to grasp new and deeper spiritual meanings. To reach that stage, however, cultures need to be deeply transformed and transfigured in their encounter with the Gospel. Although the Holy Spirit blows and is present in all cultures, not all aspects of these cultures are necessarily its voice.

Christian acceptance or non-acceptance of a particular culture should be based on certain criteria. For the Orthodox it is the living Tradition of the universal church which guards the scriptural mystery of the incarnation against the invasion of "other gospels." If we reject this protection or ignore this criterion, do we not become vulnerable to "other gods," to "the spiritual forces of evil in the heavenly places" (Eph. 6:12)? These forces are lying dormant in many cultures of our contemporary world, ready to awaken and come into the ecumenical field.

Without entering into polemics regarding extreme practices of inculturation, I will try to offer a vision of the interaction between the Gospel and culture from a slightly different perspective.

I recall my visit in 1975 to the old monastery of St. Cyril of White Lake. During Soviet times it was turned into a museum and kept in good order by the state so that tourists might be attracted. Yet there was not a single soul within its walls. There was neither prayer nor eucharist nor sermon.

I joined an excursion group at the monastery's cathedral. The guide explained the architecture and the icons. Apparently she did not even think about preaching Christianity. Rather, she tried to persuade the group that the magnificence of the church was created not because of but in spite of Christianity, which she maintained did not allow architects and icon painters to express themselves fully. But speaking about the architecture and icons, she willy-nilly spoke about the Gospel, and what she said and the icons and architecture themselves came out as a witness to Christ—and that witness was much more powerful than the scum of the so-called scientific atheism!

In the '70s the communists, apparently, were no longer worried about the revival of religion in Russia because it had been systematically eradicated during nearly seventy years. The mass execution of the clergy in the '20s and '30s actually decapitated the church. While there were about three hundred bishops before the 1917 revolution, by 1939 only five diocesan bishops remained. Most of the priests had been executed and most of the churches destroyed. Some eight thousand churches were closed in 1937 alone, and only one hundred churches remained throughout Russia by the end of 1939. After a brief respite in the last years of Stalin's regime, a new persecution fell upon the remnants of the church under Khrushchev in the '60s, accompanied by a grand eloquence about democracy. It was at that time that the chief communist of the country promised the people that the last remaining priest would be exhibited at a museum twenty years hence.

In 1988, however, when the millennium of the baptism of Russia was celebrated, Christianity escaped from the confinement of the churches into the streets and squares. The celebrations united the intelligentsia and the church and showed that Christian faith was still alive among the people. All this overwhelmed and scared the civil authorities, who in their shock could not understand from which moon it had fallen. They had done everything possible to eliminate Christianity. They had had three generations of people brought up on communist ideology making a caricature of the church. Now it turned out suddenly that Christian faith was still very much alive.

I remember a conversation I had with the mayor of the small Russian town of Vyazma. I asked him to put the town stadium at our disposal for the millennium celebrations. He asked, "Why do you want the stadium if you will not be able to gather even a thousand believers?" But when forty thousand took part in the festive procession, it became a spiritual rebirth for many, including the mayor himself.

Why did state godlessness, which had been imposed on three generations for seventy years to eradicate almost completely traditional religious education in families, suffer such a shattering defeat? True, an important part in all this was played by social processes, including international processes, which brought pressure to bear on the authorities. Still, the crucial factor lay elsewhere.

A unique situation had developed in Russia. At a time when the voice of the church itself was hardly heard, the Gospel was preached not through priests or missionaries or ecclesiastical literature, but through culture, which became a bearer of the Gospel message. This is not surprising, because Russian culture was shaped under the influence of Christianity. Pre-Christian culture absorbed the spiritual power of the Gospel through the church, its worldview and moral message, and gave it back to the people when the church was subjected to persecution. A Christian worldview, church wisdom, and biblical quotations lived on in the people's consciousness, preserved in songs, proverbs, and sayings, even though people forgot completely where they had come from.

I have already given you as an example the excursion to the monastery of St. Cyril of White Lake that resulted in preaching Christianity. Here is another example. Soviet power could not prevent people from reading Dostoyevsky, even though he was not studied at school. This great writer was a profoundly religious man, and his works are imbued with Christian ideas. The instructions of Starets Zosima in *The Brothers Karamazov* were largely borrowed from the writings of early church fathers, in particular from St. Isaac the Syrian, a Christian mystic of the seventh century. So while works by the holy fathers were not published and the writings of St. Isaac the Syrian were impossible to obtain, Dostoyevsky was widely read and appreciated.

Russian culture, transformed by the Christian content with which it was imbued, has thus proved to be more powerful than all the efforts to destroy religion. This is our answer to the theory and practice of inculturation. It is not inculturation of Christianity in the sense that it has to change its content and message according to the standards and expectations of different cultures, but it is rather the affirmation of cultures in the process of their transformation and transfiguration in encountering the one Gospel. Culture cannot be used for tactical purposes; culture should become a bearer of the message of Christ.

However, those forms of culture and art which promote not spiritual growth but passions, instincts, and decay of human personality represent an anti-culture; anti-art cannot be the church's ally. Violent passions of rebellion against peace, harmony, life, and God generate not only anti-culture but also anti-Christianity. Is it not the devil's presence that is felt in some forms of today's culture, plunging people into the dark depths of passion? The mission of the church today is a struggle for humanity "against the rulers, against the authorities, against the cosmic powers of this present darkness, against the spiritual forces of evil in the heavenly places" (Eph. 6:12). To help human persons out of the embrace of anti-culture and anti-Christianity, to bring them back to God—this is the urgent task we face today.

MISSION AND PROSELYTISM

I would like to touch upon yet another problem which has become especially acute owing to the changes that have taken place and continue to take place in East European countries. This is the problem of proselytism, which, in my opinion, belongs to and has to be dealt with in the framework of the conference theme. It is more than a purely theological or church relationships issue. It is primarily an expression of cultural and ideological clashes, as newcomers try both to impose their own culturally conditioned form of Christianity on other Christians and to save them from the communist past. In my reflections I will again proceed from the context which is closest to me, namely, the reality in Russia yesterday and today.

For the last three decades of its existence under Soviet rule, the Russian Orthodox Church, despite the severe restriction on religious freedom, maintained a living link with Christians of other confessions. Ecumenical contacts developed first of all within the USSR itself, where Christians of various confessions lived peacefully side by side. Solidarity in the face of a common adversary united us—Orthodox, Catholics, Protestants. It was the only way to survive under a totalitarian regime. Ecumenical contacts consolidated on the international level as well. The Soviet government between the '60s and '80s was afraid of the church's influence on the people and of extensive ecumenical activity. Nevertheless, they began to allow us to go abroad and participate in ecumenical meetings when they realized that the absence of the Russian church from those meetings would only serve to intensify what was being said in the West about religious oppression in the USSR.

One of the achievements of our church wisdom was that we managed to secure the permission of the authorities to join the World Council of Churches. The atheistic state leaders could not help but realize that the role and influence of the Russian Orthodox Church in the world would only grow if it joined the WCC, but they took the risk. They also permitted the church to hold peace meetings in the USSR with the participation of Christians from other countries. All this helped to make the condition of the Russian church known in the world, even though its representatives were forced to keep silent when asked about the real state of affairs. The religious and ecclesiastical situation in the USSR became an ever more constant item on the agenda of international Christian organizations as the Helsinki process drew world public attention to it. The external activity of the Russian Orthodox Church and its cooperation with the Christian world were among the factors that contributed to the growing authority of the church and, indirectly, to the collapse of the atheistic system.

International Christian solidarity was not the least reason for the failure to destroy the church in the Soviet Union. The support other Christians proffered during our hardest times helped the church in its struggle for survival. We are profoundly grateful to those Christians who showed solidarity with us and did not let the godless powers crush the church. We thank those who took the risk of sending or bringing copies of the Bible and other religious books into our country. These books were then reprinted by *samizdat* (self-publishing), a powerful underground network. We thank Christians of other confessions and the ecumenical movement for the support we felt throughout those long and difficult years.

We expected that with the coming of religious freedom these relations would develop further and that other Christians would support us in a new, no less difficult situation, as the Russian Orthodox Church suddenly found itself before a door wide open to the broadest possible religious freedom and a huge field for missionary work. We sincerely hoped that we would be supported in this task.

Our hopes, however, were not fulfilled. As soon as freedom for missionary work was allowed, a crusade began against the Russian church, even as it began recovering from a prolonged disease, standing on its feet with weakened muscles. Hordes of missionaries dashed in, believing the former Soviet Union to be a vast missionary territory. They behaved as though no local churches existed, no Gospel was being proclaimed. They began preaching without even making an effort to familiarize themselves with the Russian cultural heritage or to learn the Russian language. In most cases the intention was not to preach Christ and the Gospel, but to tear our faithful away from their traditional churches and recruit them into their own communities. Perhaps these missionaries sincerely believed that they were dealing with non-Christian or atheistic communist people, not suspecting that our culture was formed by Christianity and that our Christianity survived through the blood of martyrs and confessors, through the courage of bishops, theologians, and laypeople asserting their faith.

Missionaries from abroad came with dollars, buying people with so-called humanitarian aid and promises to send them abroad for study or rest. We expected that our fellow Christians would support and help us in our own missionary service. In reality, however, they have started fighting with our church, like boxers in a ring with their pumped-up muscles, delivering blows. The annual budget of some of the invading missionary organizations amounts to dozens of millions of dollars. They have bought time on radio and television and have used their financial resources to the utmost in order to buy people.

All this has led to an almost complete rupture of the ecumenical relations developed during the previous decades. An overwhelming majority of the population refused to accept this activity, which offends people's national and religious sentiments by ignoring their spiritual and cultural tradition. Indeed, given the lack of religious education, people tend to make no distinctions between the militant missionaries we are speaking about and ordinary people of other faiths or confessions. For many of Russia today, "non-Orthodox" means those who have come to destroy the spiritual unity of the people and the Orthodox faith—spiritual colonizers who by fair means or foul try to tear the people away from the church.

What is happening in Russia and other counties of the former "Eastern bloc" can be described as an ecumenical disaster of the late twentieth century, as it has canceled out the incredible efforts of the last forty years in the ecumenical field. At the same time, among those who have been involved in proselytism in our territory are not only sects but even our partners in the ecumenical movement, including some WCC member churches.

I would like to state with all clarity: ecumenism and proselytism are incompatible. Incompatible also are mission and spiritual enslavement, the preaching of Christ and violence to people's conscience, the proclamation of the Gospel and bribery.

In general, any competitive or parallel mission is fraught with threats to the unity of the church and fraternal relations among Christian churches. We are grieved to see these zealous missionaries from abroad creating their own church structures at our expense, thus bearing witness to anything but ecumenical solidarity. At the same time, not only is damage being done to the Orthodox Church, but also the tremendous ecumenical efforts toward Christian unity are coming to naught. It can be said that joint ecumenical efforts have now become blocked by the unrestrained "assault from the West." What is even more frightening is that the credibility of Christian witness is declining in the secular world as it watches the competition, enmity, and mutual attacks raging among various Christian communities.

Proselytism is not some narrow religious activity generated by a wrong understanding of missionary tasks. Proselytism is the fact of invasion by another culture, even if Christian, but developing according to its own laws and having its own history and tradition. This invasion is taking place after the old missionary patterns of colonial times. It is not merely a desire to reveal Christ to people—people who have confessed Christianity for over a thousand years at that—but also to refashion their culture in the Western mode.

Clearly, it is impossible to bear common Christian witness in a situation where each other's religious traditions and cultures are not respected. We call upon the WCC to take up the problem of proselytism with all seriousness to help avoid new divisions, so painful and difficult to heal. Such divisions within the Christian community are inadmissible, especially in an age of rapid secularization of the world community and globalization of its culture through global communications, computer networks, telecommunications, and eventually the common market. If the churches do not make special efforts to transform this community by the power of the Gospel, they risk marginalizing themselves and becoming foreigners in their own countries. This is even more probable as the technological society becomes increasingly engaged in searching for ways of meeting its spiritual needs. Unfortunately, it is apt to find them not in faith in our Lord Jesus Christ but in such fields as psychoanalysis, social psychology, and sexology, on the one hand, and in "new religious movements" and sects which consciously want to replace Christianity, on the other. In this situation we as Christians should find strength first to consolidate our own energies and resources and then bring the word of reconciliation to the world.

The missionary situation as it has developed in Russia and the other republics of the former Soviet Union appears to have reached a deadlock. Yet there is a way out of it. It lies in basing mission on the fundamental principle of early Christian ecclesiology: the principle of the local church. This stipulates that the church in a given place shall be fully responsible for its people before God. This principle can be applied not only to the Russian situation, but to Christian mission in the world in general, on the understanding that nobody anywhere shall ignore a local church. To ignore a local church means to break a whole into pieces, to tear the seamless robe of Christ. Missionary efforts from abroad should be made in each place as a support and assistance to the indigenous church or churches. The same principle should be included in the basis of missionary work in the twenty-first century. Indeed, even where a Christian church was founded by foreign missionaries, it has long since become part of that place and culture. Everyone who, armed with the Bible, sets off to enlighten peoples should remember that by the end of the twentieth century there are indigenous Christian churches virtually everywhere. Independent actions taken by missionary groups at the expense of these churches represent an attempt to redraw the map of the world, and wherever they are taken there is always tension, alienation, bitterness.

The holy martyr Cyprian of Carthage wrote about the church schisms of his time: "Who is so impious and perfidious and so infected with the passion for strife that he believes that he can or dare break the unity of God, the robe of the Lord, the church of Christ?" This question can well be addressed in our day to those who act to the detriment of local churches, tearing the faithful away from the church and thus excommunicating themselves from the world Christian community. St. Cyprian made it clear that these people were enemies of the church and Christian faith: "What unity is respected, what love is cherished or what love is contemplated by him who, indulging in strife, cuts the church, ruins faith, disturbs peace, eradicates love, defiles unity? . . . Indeed, he arms himself against the church and impedes divine construction; he is an enemy of the sanctuary, an agitator against the sacrifice of Christ, a betrayer of the faith and devotion; he is an apostate."

These words uttered in the third century are still relevant today. At the end of the twentieth century we can state that the work of sectarians and schismatics to destroy the unity of churches continues. And this work is not Christian mission, it is spiritual colonialism. Our urgent task therefore is to get rid of colonial practices and develop a new attitude to mission—or rather, to return to the apostolic and early church understanding of mission not as enslaving or bribing people but rather as liberating and bringing them into the light of Christ's truth. The twentieth century has been the time of a mass collapse of colonial regimes and the liberation of peoples, nations, and regions from foreign domination, from the yoke of foreign cultures. The colonial ideology should be overcome in the realm of church and mission as well. Indeed, for many peoples in the southern hemisphere, Christianization meant, above all, Europeanization and destruction of their traditional culture, which the Europeans believed to be low and pagan.

Dear brothers and sisters, the reality described above as being relevant to both national and global contexts presents a considerable challenge to individual churches, to the world Christian community, and to the entire human civilization. We can see how sinful and demonic elements acting in the world and in what is called the cultural sphere have led to a personal moral crisis which leads, in turn, to a global crisis of civilization. If we save the person we will save the culture, civilization, and our common future.

We witness today the fulfillment of apocalyptic prophecies, the decay of human personality, and the mass rejection of fundamental norms of morality. A triumph of the forces of evil may lead to the spiritual death of humanity. In the human community, however, there remain elements which hinder and restrain that triumph (2 Thess. 2:7). These are the good elements expressed through a Christianized culture, transformed by the Gospel. We can see fruits of this good everywhere in the world, including Russia, where by God's grace thousands of churches and hundreds of monasteries have been restored and millions of people have recovered their Christianized culture, making it not only the form but also the content of their lives.

Responding to this reality, the entire world Christian community needs to become conscious of its mission in a broader and bolder way. We should discern the apostolic sources of the uncompromising desire to transform the world around us. Some fifteen years ago one of my brother Russian bishops was summoned to a local official in charge of atheistic work who said to him: "Why do you gather children for a Christmas-tree party? It's not your function. You should meet religious needs." (Obviously he meant conducting worship services for pensioners.) This is what the bishop answered: "My religious need is to change the world." We should come to the same understanding of our missionary service, even if humanly we have no chance, just as the apostles of Christ humanly had no chance. But their mission succeeded and transformed the world, because they walked together, uniting—not separating—people. And a miracle occurred, because where people act in unity there is Christ acting together with them.

Our mission, dear brothers and sisters, is a mission of "one hope," a mission for salvation, for a spiritual transformation of humanity and every particular person, for the kingdom of God in people's hearts. If we follow in Christ's steps without turning back, if we join one another in common witness to the world, supporting one another, not competing, then the Lord will support us and give us new strength and breathe a new spirit into the world Christian mission. Only in this way will we be able to restore the spirit of Christ in those who have fallen away from the church, those who are lukewarm and searching. Only in this way will we be able to enter a new millennium as a spiritually strong civilization knowing the meaning of its existence.

4.

INTERRELIGIOUS RELATIONS IN RUSSIA
AFTER 1917

———————◆———————

Aleksandr Shchipkov

This chapter examines the general development of inter-denominational relations in Russia from 1917 to the present day, and outlines briefly sociological and statistical data, the composition of religious groups, their geographical spread and distribution, and the nature of interreligious contacts.

The chapter will further try to identify areas of potential religious conflicts and possible accusations of proselytism. In the sphere of religious inter-relationships there are no simple situations. Problems will always exist and the degree of their complexity or even "danger" can only be defined in comparison with an even more complex problem in a neighboring region or in another period of history.

SOCIOLOGY

Interreligious relationships of the past century cannot be discussed without drawing on sociological research; therefore, we will examine the legacy of our predecessors who studied questions of religion in Soviet Russia. Perhaps with their help we will be able to find some authentic information about the dynamics of religious belief in twentieth-century Russia.

In pre-revolutionary Russia, the degree of religiosity in society was assessed only by the gathering of statistics, which aimed more at determining the respondents' adherence to a particular denomination from a formal legal perspective than ascertaining the real convictions and mutual relationships between them. After 1917, the Communist Party became the prime mover in sociological analysis of religion. The Union of Militant Atheists, founded in 1925, was the first proponent of this. Excluding personal memoirs, the only formal sources of information about religious life in the 1920s and 1930s are reports from the Propaganda Department of the Central Committee of the Russian Communist Party (Bolsheviks)—publications in atheist journals with such evocative names as *Bezbozhnik* (*The Atheist*) and *Antireligioznik*. This overt ideological position effectively made researchers participants in interreligious relations. In 1929, a sociological survey was conducted in one of Moscow's factories: out of twelve thousand questionnaires, eight thousand were not returned; workers did not want to talk about their beliefs. Of those which were returned, about 10 percent called themselves believers. Despite the obvious lack of clarity in the results, sociologists reported that 90 percent of the workers in the city were free from "the opium of religion." This bore no relation to the reality of the situation.

Thus, the particular nature of "red sociology" must be taken into account. It is essential to correct statistics and the analysis of material relating to the number of religious organizations, number of members, number of religious buildings, scope of preaching activity, number of clergy, and confessional literature. In 1937, a general census of the population was conducted.[1] Questions relating to religious convictions were included in the census form (on Stalin's orders), but five million people declined to answer these. Nevertheless, 50 percent of the respondents openly stated in a state survey that they had religious beliefs. This was after the "atheist five-year plan," after a systematic policy of genocide among the clergy, at the height of large-scale repressions. The quality and confessional loyalty of believers in Soviet Russia may be disputed, but those who maintain that the general process of secularization affected Russia more deeply than Europe or the United States are wrong. The Soviet experience "distorted" religious teachings, but did not eradicate religiosity itself.

Soviet sociology of religion is not only characterized by its militancy, but also by the haphazard nature of its research. In the 1940s and 1950s the war with Germany and the liberalization of state policies toward the church led to a decrease in atheist propaganda and related research projects. In 1954, the Central Committee of the CPSU passed its famous resolution, "On the shortcomings in atheist propaganda and measures for its improvement." In 1960, the 22nd Party Congress passed the Khrushchev program for the construction of communism by 1980, after which there would be no room for outmoded religious prejudices. Atheist propaganda and sociological research were revitalized and given official state support. In comparison with the 1920s, the ideological demands of Khrushchev and Brezhnev had shifted: a "scientific" basis for the need to overcome religion in a socialist society was demanded. Although such a requirement interfered with academic objectivity, now at least it became possible to produce authentic statistics, especially in regional studies where the ideological controls were not so stringent.

---

[1] V. B. Zhironovskaya, *Vsesoyuzniy perpis' naseleniya 1937 goda* (Moscow, 1990).

In the 1970s, following the signing of the Helsinki Accords and a short-lived mild ideological thaw, researchers dared to discover new characteristics of mass religiosity, reporting a stabilization and even *growth* in religiosity in certain regions, a significant lowering of the average age of religious believers, and a corresponding growth in their level of education. While in Russia as a whole the degree of religious adherence in the 1980s was said officially to be about 10 percent, sociologists discovered it to be much higher in the provinces: Gorki *oblast* 21 percent; Mari ASSR 24 percent; Tatariya 40 percent; Checheno-Ingushetiya 50 percent.[2] Traditionally, Muslim regions always showed a higher level of religious observance (including, paradoxically, among the local Russian-speaking population).[3] In addition, regional surveys demonstrated the number of convinced atheists stood at around 20 to 30 percent.[4] All told, the number of wavering and indifferent (in other words, potentially religious believers, with a vague, non-dogmatic religious consciousness) remained around 50 percent of the population of Soviet Russia. These figures were not widely known and long gathered dust in dissertations written by provincial researchers. But once they are taken into account, it is not surprising that there was a sharp rise in religious observance after the liberalization following *perestroika*. Consider the statistics denoting the religious adherence of the population of Russia gathered by the All-Russian Centre for the Study of Public Opinion: 1988, 18.6 percent; 1991, 39 percent; 1993, 43 percent; 1995, 64.2 percent.[5]

This steep jump in religious adherence in the post-*perestroika* period suggests that a concealed (or amorphous) religiosity existed in the preceding Soviet period. This should be taken into account when studying current foreign missionary activity. Missionaries mistakenly believe they are coming to an atheist country and consequently fail to understand why their religious activity within the country is perceived as proselytism. A reduction in the Orthodox share of this population does not mean a general decline in religious belief.

Soviet studies on religion fell short because they aimed principally at measuring the general level of religiosity and at explaining the attitudes of differing social and generational groups of the population toward religion. There were scarcely any surveys conducted on actual religious belief. And the only comparative analyses were some ethnological studies conducted by academics researching the appearance of "ethno-confessional communities" and the formation of "sub-ethno-confessional groups" (e.g., Old Believers and the "bap-

---

[2] V. I. Garadzha, *Sotsiologiya religiya* (Moscow, 1996), 224.

[3] This phenomenon is confirmed by as yet unpublished research by the Centre of Sociology of the Russian Scientific Fund led by S. B. Filatov, which was undertaken in Tatariya in 1996.

[4] V. A. Sudenko, *Kharakter religioznosti gorodskogo naseleniya i tendentsiya yeye izmeneniya* (Ph.D. diss., Moscow, 1972).

[5] Garadzha, *Sotsiologiya religiya*, 226.

tized" Tatars).[6] These studies focused, however, on ethnic and inter-ethnic problems, and religion was of secondary interest.

Although the sociology of religion is now acquiring a civilized face, it would be wrong to say that the phenomenon of "ideological directives" in Russia has completely died out. Sociologists still, at times, seek out an ideological imperative and appease the orientation of the ruling class. For example, a group of researchers at St. Petersburg State University in 1995 announced that according to the results of their research, 94.8 percent of religious believers in St. Petersburg were Orthodox.[7] If one takes into account the general secularization of society, the growth of the new-age religions, and the large number of national minorities living in St. Petersburg (Finns, Germans, Tatars, etc.) who traditionally adhere to "national" faiths (such as Lutheranism, Islam, and so on), then this figure of 94.8 percent must be disproportionately high, exaggerated to suit the prevailing politics of the time.

Contemporary sociology of religion tends to study the reasons for the sharp increase in religiosity in Russia—whether it was a result of the publicity given to the Millennium celebrations in Russia, of current trends and fashions, or of other secondary factors. It has claimed (1) that religion became the symbol of spiritual opposition to the collapsing Marxist ideology (claiming that those surveyed would often declare their religiosity to underline their rejection of the former values and their new moral choice, while essentially remaining nonbelievers); and (2) that the restructuring of social relationships and the economic crisis evoked a general feeling of uncertainty and defenselessness (claiming that religion became a refuge and was in increased demand).

Both these interpretations are influenced by the old atheist school of the study of religion, and do not correspond to reality. Religion did not suddenly emerge during the years of *perestroika*, but had always been the sole spiritual antidote to Marxism during the Soviet era. Neither does the second thesis withstand examination. The statement that the general crisis in society has created a demand for religion (Marxists continue to explain everything in terms of economic relationships) is reminiscent of the primitive explanation that religious faith in God is like a person's displaying fear before a storm.

In conclusion, it is clear that a significant number of people (no fewer than 50 percent) living in Soviet Russia, despite atheist education programs, *preserved* various forms of religiosity and, more important, *imparted them to the next generation*. Thus, the academic problem for contemporary sociology of religion is not to explain the phenomenon of the religious "boom," but to

---

[6] V. I. Puchkov, "Integriruyushchaya i dezintegriruyushchaya rol' religii v etnicheskom protsessye," *Rasy I Narody* (Moscow, 1991), 22-29. L. I. Sherstova, "Etnokonfessional'naya obshchnost'" *K probleme evolyutsii subetnosov*, in ibid., 29-44; A. N. Inatov, *Etnokonfessional'naya obshchnost' kak sotsial'noye yavleniye* (Ph.D. diss., Moscow, 1980).

[7] "Rossiya snova stanovitsa pravoslavnoi'," *Derzhava* 6/7 (1995): 10.

clarify the religious beliefs of the population along confessional lines, to understand what the beliefs of the citizens of Russia are, and to determine the areas where the interests of various religious movements intersect.

GEOGRAPHICAL DISTRIBUTION

Religious beliefs are now less and less linked with national identity, so it is difficult to define the geographical borders of a particular faith. A literal association of religion and ethnicity can lead to errors. Thus, the vast majority of reference books and encyclopedias show that, in addition to Russians, large groups of Finno-Ugric and Turkish peoples profess Orthodoxy—Karelians, Vepsy, Komi, Udmurts, Mari, Mordovians, Chuvash, Khakass, Shory, Evenks, Yakut, Chukchi, Alsuti, Yukagirs, Mansi, Khants, Western Buryats in the Irkutsk *oblast*, a proportion of Kalmyks, and some Tatars *(kryasheny)*. Moreover, Ukrainians, Belorussians, Moldavians, Bulgarians, Gagauz, and Greeks living on Russian territory also profess Orthodoxy. And the nationalities listed comprise only one-fifth of the nationalities in Russia. These and other peoples profess Orthodoxy, but not all do. Thus some Mari today worship their own ancient pagan gods, others hold dual pagan/Orthodox beliefs, while still others, about equal in number, are committed to Orthodoxy or to the Lutheran faith (as introduced by Finnish missionaries).

In Yakutiya, for example, there are two main groups: Orthodoxy and shamanism. Karelians have almost all adopted Lutheranism, but their closest neighbors, the ethnically related Vepsy, are Orthodox. The overwhelming majority of Orthodox believers are Russians. But in the True Orthodox Church, more than 50 percent belong to other national minorities. The choice of an "anti-state" faith is perhaps linked with the traditionally anti-state feelings of national minorities which have been present since Tsarist times. During the Soviet era the Catacomb Church existed in Chuvashiya, Mordovia, Nizhigorodchina, the Baikal region, and the Altai district. True Orthodox Church parishes are now concentrated in Kashira, Moscow, St. Petersburg, and Kursk. Before the introduction of the restrictive 1997 law, there was a tendency within this movement toward legalization and to extending its influence to major urban centers.

The majority of Catholics in Central Russia are Germans and Poles, though ethnic Russians comprise up to 40 percent. In some Siberian regions like Irkutsk, though, Catholic parishes are almost entirely made up of Russians. Currently, former Polish Catholic churches are being restored and parishes are being established around them. If this trend continues, every major city of the Russian Federation will have at least one restored or new Catholic church by the beginning of the next century. The main concentration of Catholics today is in the Volga region (Saratov region), an area of compact ethnic German settlement. In Western Russia (Kaliningrad, Smolensk, and Bryansk regions) and in Western Siberia (Novosibirsk, Omsk, and Krasnoyarsk regions), there are areas of compact Polish settlement.

While Catholicism has obviously become russified, Lutheranism is more prominent among the Finno-Ugric peoples of the Komi, Mordovian Udmurts, and the people of the Mari El Republic. They had no previous contact with Lutheranism, but were receptive to it, for it is the faith of Western Finno-Ugric peoples. Lutherans are concentrated in northwest Russia in the Leningrad *oblast* in Karelia, and in Moscow and Nizhni Novgorod. Lutheranism is also developing where the Volga Germans are settled: Povolzhe, Omsk, Tomsk, and Krasnoyarsk, where Germans were exiled during the Second World War.

It is easier to define areas where Islam or Buddhism are practiced. Bashkiria, Chelyabinsk and Orenburg *oblasts*, Tatariya, Nizhegorodchina, the Lower Volga, and the Caucasus republics are all areas of compact settlement of groups professing Islam. These include Tatars, Bashkirs, Kabardins, Cherkess, Adygei, Abazars, Balkars, Karachai, Avars, Ingush, and Chechens.

Buryatiya, Kalmykia, and Tuva are traditionally Buddhist areas, but the influence of Buddhism has spread far beyond the boundaries of these republics and is gaining much ground in Russia. The largest centers of "Russian" Buddhism are St. Petersburg and Ulyanovsk.

The arbitrary redrawing of national borders and the forced migration of ethnic, social, and confessional groups has had a direct impact on the current religious landscape of Russia. The Stalinist resettlement of peoples began at the end of the 1920s with the liquidation of the *kulaks*. In the Tomsk *oblast* alone, 100,000 *kulaks* were sent into exile from 1929 to 1931, and they were the most loyal adherents of Orthodoxy.[8] Thus the proportion of Orthodox believers in Central Russia fell accordingly. Stalinist deportations rose sharply at the time of the Second World War. Siberian settlements received Lutherans (Latvians, Estonians, Finns, Karelians, Volga Germans), Catholics (Lithuanians, Western Belorussians, Volga Germans, Poles), and Muslims (Balkars, Crimean Tatars, Chechens, Meskhetian Turks). The huge resettlement of Buddhists was linked with the exile of Koreans at the end of the Second World War and the mass deportations of Kalmyks to Siberia in 1943. Tens of millions of people were deported during the Soviet era, which affected the "confessional geography" of the country.

By extending its borders in the middle of the twentieth century, Russia also "acquired" Ukrainian Eastern-rite Catholics, Orthodox Moldavians, Catholics of Western Belorussia, and Jehovah's Witnesses communities, whose numbers had begun to grow in these territories by 1939. Deportations were conducted along religious lines as well as national lines. Jehovah's Witnesses, Baptists, Adventists, and Pentecostals were all deported. Once in Siberia, these communities continued to exist and grow. The Chernogorsk Pentecostals, who lived in Khakassiya and campaigned in the 1970s for exit visas from the USSR, were the descendants of exiled settlers from Ukraine. Other factors influenced the shape of regional confessional profiles, including migration due to industrialization, wartime evacuation of heavy industries east of the Urals, compul-

---

[8] V. N. Uimanov, *Massoviye repressii v Zapadnoi Sibirii* (Ph.D. diss., Tomsk, 1992).

sory selection at the end of the 1940s for the development of the Far East, settlement programs in the 1950s and beginning of the 1960s, the building of KamAz, the Baikal-Amur railway, and other accelerated work projects.

An overview of the current religious movements in Russia reveals many religious variations. The European part of Russia from Pskov to Samara and from Arkhangelsk to Krasnodar can be considered the bastion of Orthodoxy. Finno-Ugric Lutheranism borders the Orthodox to the north (Karelia, the Komi republic, Leningrad *oblast*) and is spreading along the Kama and the Volga through Udmurtia, Mari El, and Mordovia, where it joins the German Lutheranism of the Lower Volga (Saratov, Volgograd). To the south of the Orthodox lands are the Caspian lowlands, dominated by Kalmyk Buddhists and Islam in the Northern Caucasus region. Two "meridians"—with sharply defined regional characteristics—separate this heartland from Asia. These are the republics of the Lower Volga—Udmurtia, Mari El, Chuvashia, and Mordovia, where Christianity is being superseded by an active revival of national paganism. To the east of these republics are the predominantly Muslim Tataria and Bashkiria. The Ural mountains with their huge industrial complexes, such as Perm, Yekaterinburg, Kurgass, Chelyabinsk, and Orenburg, extend along a north-south axis following the 60th meridian. Recent sociological surveys have shown that the Urals region has been more susceptible to secularization than the rest of Russia, and has engendered its own particular spiritual traditions which adapt easily to new-age cults and are less amenable to traditional formal religion.[9] The Urals region has an abundance of local home-grown sects. Thus the Christian heartland and Christian Siberia are divided by two belts: an Islamic-pagan one and a "secularized" one.

The Khants, Mansi, Nenets, Evenks, and other peoples who inhabit the northern regions of Western and Central Siberia have preserved a firmly rooted dual belief, worshiping both the Christian God and their own ancestral deities. Given the very low density of the population, they have practically no influence on the religious life of Siberia. To the east, in the more developed Yakutia, there are complex religious processes underway. The competition for influence between Orthodox and shamanist Yakuts is gathering strength. The most intense religious life beyond the Urals can be found along the southern borders of Western, Central, and Eastern Siberia, the Far East, and the Primorye (Pacific Coast). The shamanism of the mountain Altai and the Khakass, as well as Tuvin and Buryat Buddhism, represent non-Christian religious movements. A complex set of national problems caused by Russian pogroms at the beginning of the 1990s caused a mass emigration of Russians from Tuva. In the whole of Tuva, there were only three Orthodox parishes in 1996. Ethnic and religious relationships are more harmonious in Buryatia.

---

[9] Sociological Center of the Russian Academic Fund (director S. B. Filatov). Partial results of research conducted in the Urals are described in the article by S. B. Filatov and A. V. Shchipkov, "Ural, Prel'sheniye monitarizmom," *Druzhba narodov* 12 (1996): 132-46.

Present-day Christian life in Siberia has evolved under two main influences: the migration mentioned above, and active missionary work. Muscovite Orthodoxy is noticeably weaker in its influence here than in European Russia. Old Believers present a significant challenge to the Moscow Patriarchate, with parishes all over Siberia. There is also the Russian Orthodox Church Abroad, which has more appeal among Siberians than among the inhabitants of Central Russia. And mission activity has brought Catholic parishes to practically every major town. There are major Catholic centers in Krasnoyarsk, Irkutsk, and Khabarovsk, which attract mainly educated people.

Protestant churches are enjoying even greater popularity in Siberia. Lutheranism, introduced by Germans exiled to Siberia, is developing around Omsk and Kemerova. Because of its long isolation, this branch of Lutheranism has preserved a Pietist tradition, and its services are close to those of the Baptist church in terms of rituals and traditions of worship. Among the traditional Protestant denominations, the Baptists, Seventh-day Adventists, and Pentecostals are strong. The new charismatic churches are also enjoying success, with missionaries in training not only for Siberia, but Mongolia and China as well.

STATISTICS

Statistical information was not only kept secret during the Soviet era, but was frequently distorted in order to "demonstrate" the dying out of religious prejudices. Figures now available to us, despite their incompleteness and deficiencies, can help to form a general impression of the religious dynamic from 1917 to 1997.

Before the revolution in the Russian Empire there were 65 percent Orthodox, 10 percent Old Believers of all groups, 8 percent Catholics, 4.5 percent Protestants of all denominations, 6 percent Muslims, and 4 percent Jews. In autumn 1990, a liberal law on freedom of conscience was passed. According to figures published in January 1991, the religious affiliations of citizens of the USSR in total were as follows: 22 percent Orthodox, 0.8 percent Old Believers, 5.5 percent Catholics, 3 percent Protestants, 18.5 percent Muslims, and 0.2 percent Jews.[10] The sharp decline in the percentages of Jews and Old Believers during the Soviet period is striking; it is the result of the closed nature of these groups, which do not missionize. The above figures are for the whole of the USSR; if the figures were based on the Russian Republic alone, the percentage of Muslims would fall accordingly. Various other beliefs not present in Russia before 1917 (such as charismatic Protestantism, Hare Krishna, new-age religions, and occultism) also came onto the scene.

The Orthodox Church was the first to suffer from repression. In 1917 there were seventy-seven thousand churches; by 1926 this had fallen to twenty-seven

---

[10] *Religiozniye obiedineniya Rossiiskoi Federatsii* (Moscow, 1996), 242.

thousand and in 1938 there were only a few hundred churches still open. According to NKVD figures for 1926-28, the number of Catholic parishes also diminished by 13 percent. This same period witnessed a significant increase in the number of Old Believers (by 13 percent), Muslims (33 percent), and Protestants (22 percent).[11] This growth can be explained by at least two circumstances. First, "religious liberty" declared by the Bolsheviks was accorded to those faiths whose rights had been restricted before the revolution. Thus Baptists, Evangelicals, Lutherans, and other confessions had a short-lived opportunity to preach and expand their activity, provided they expressed loyalty to the Soviet authorities. Second, as noted by the All-Union Congress of Anti-Religious Departments of Academic Institutes of the USSR in 1930, a process of "rejection of formal Orthodoxy and a return to the faith of our forefathers" was taking place. Old Believers, Protestants, and other denominations no longer needed to conceal their religious orientation. However, by the middle of the 1930s all religious activity was reduced to a bare minimum, and by 1939 there were only fourteen thousand functioning religious communities of all confessions in the entire Soviet Union.[12]

During the Second World War a reversal took place. Germany (in the occupied territories) and Stalin (in the free territories) started to open churches, particularly Orthodox ones. Muslims, Baptists, and Evangelicals also experienced a relaxation of controls. An improbable event took place in 1945: the Mari were allowed to conduct a universal pagan prayer ritual "in honor of victory over Germany." It was attended by tens of thousands of believers and lasted for more than a week. This underscores the fact that contemporary Volga paganism is based on a religious inheritance.[13]

From 1943 to 1949 the general number of registered communities increased from 16,000 to 20,459. The number of Orthodox parishes increased from 10,243 to 14,329. Then, parishes gradually began to be closed. By 1953 Stalin had closed 1,183 religious communities, including 820 Orthodox parishes. By 1964, Khrushchev had closed 6,479 communities, including 5,550 Orthodox. Brezhnev at first continued this policy of closing religious communities, but in 1970 changed direction. The reduction in the number of Orthodox parishes continued, but the number of registered communities of other faiths began to increase. This policy was maintained under Andropov, Chernenko, and Gorbachev up until 1987: from 1970 to 1987, 525 Orthodox parishes were closed and 809 religious communities of other faiths were registered.[14] This unexpected phenomenon testifies to the particularly negative attitudes of the Communist Party toward Orthodoxy. The ideological department of the Central Committee of the CPSU was preparing a huge antireligious campaign to

---

[11] *Gosudarstvennotserkovniye otnosheniya v Rossii* (Moscow, 1996), 240.

[12] Ibid., 241.

[13] S. Filatov and A. Shchipkov, *Povolzhskiye narody v poiskakh natsional'noi very* (Moscow, 1996), 279.

[14] Uimanov, *Massoviye repressii v Zapadnoi Sibrrii*, 242-43.

Table 4-1
State Registration of Religious Communities in the Russian Federation
January 10, 1993, to January 1, 1996

Denomination	1993	1996	Growth Factor*
Baha'i	8	20	2.50
Buddhism	52	124	2.38
Charismatic Churches	52	136	2.62
Council of Churches of Evangelical Christian-Baptists, *Initsiativniki*	11	32	2.91
Evangelical Apostolic Churches (separate branch of Pentecostalism)	12	22	1.83
Islam	2534	2494	0.98
Jehovah's Witnesses	44	129	2.93
Judaism	40	80	2.00
Krishna Consciousness Movement	58	112	1.93
Lutherans (total)	75	141	1.88
Methodists	14	48	3.43
Mormons	1	9	9.00
New Apostolic Church	24	61	2.54
Non-Denominational Protestant Ministry Organization	86	213	2.48
Old Believers (total)	108	164	1.52
Pagan Communities	2	7	3.50
Pentecostals	114	351	3.08
Presbyterian Churches	30	129	4.30
Roman Catholic Church	73	183	2.51
Russian Free Orthodox Church	57	98	1.72
Russian Orthodox Church (Moscow Patriarchate)	4566	7195	1.58
Seventh-day Adventists	114	222	1.95
True Orthodox Church	11	26	2.36
Unification Church (Moonies)	1	7	7.00
Union of Evangelical Christian Churches	37	248	6.70
Union of Evangelical Christians-Baptists of the Russian Federation	433	677	1.56

*The growth factor is calculated by dividing the 1996 number by the 1993 number.

coincide with the Millennium celebrations in 1988. There was also increased activity among Protestants and Muslims. The uncompromising movement of the *Initsiativniki* (reformers) within the Baptist Church forced the authorities to make concessions such as registering new churches and transferring buildings to them. Thus in Leningrad, even before *perestroika*, Baptists were given derelict Orthodox churches to restore and use as their places of worship.[15] Conversely, the conformism of the Russian Orthodox Church and its willingness to support the policies of the Communist Party did not reap any benefits: Orthodox parishes continued to be closed. In 1990, the recognition of the right to freedom of conscience and its incorporation into the Law on Religious Associations made all religions equal before the law and even acted as a stimulus to active missionary work.

Let us examine the growth of some religious organizations from 1993 to 1996 (see Table 4-1 on page 86). Of fifty-four registered religious organizations, twenty-six of the most active and significant, from a cultural and political point of view, have been selected. The figures in the Table illustrate the development of religious communities during a period of liberalization, and we can interpret them without having to allow for ideological manipulation of the statistics. The high level of activity of the Unification Church and the Mormons is immediately striking. Mormons began their missionary activity on the periphery in Orenburg, where they founded a huge church. Local inhabitants, both Orthodox and Catholic, are extremely suspicious of the Mormons and see them as dangerous rivals. The Jehovah's Witnesses have seen a significant growth in numbers, with their largest community in St. Petersburg. At present the mass media are waging a concerted campaign against them, reflecting subconscious public opinion. Perhaps it is the "Americanness" of these faiths that attracts Russians, given the current fashion—which may be waning—for all things American in Russia today.

The growth among the Protestant denominations yields an informative perspective. Korean Presbyterians have increased the number of their churches fourfold, while the Charismatics increased by a factor of 2.62. The traditional Russian Protestant groups, such as the Baptists, Evangelicals, and Pentecostals, are witnessing steady growth. Stalin forced all Evangelicals to join the centralized All-Union Council of Evangelical Christians-Baptists, but some broke away both during the 1960s and under *perestroika*; these, too, are now experiencing growth. Today there are particular contradictions and tensions between the two branches, further complicated by the fact that each has its own "initiative" movement which does not recognize the state. The table above does not include all Baptist and Evangelical groups, whose number is a dozen or more.

---

[15] This state of affairs led to an acute conflict between the Orthodox and the Baptists (All-Union Council of Evangelical Christians-Baptists) in St. Petersburg in the 1990s.

Although the growth rates of the Seventh-day Adventists and Lutherans are high, their growth has slowed from the beginning of the 1990s. Catholic parishes increased by a factor of 2.5.

The Orthodox Church—mainstream and sectarian—is growing more slowly than the Catholic and Protestant churches. The True Orthodox Church (2.36) is growing faster than the others, but groups bearing this name are registered with the state; they do not necessarily have direct links with the genuinely Catacomb parishes, which are still opposed to entering into any legal agreement with the "anti-Christ" (the state).

The growth of Judaism, despite the effects of emigration, is significant, as well as that of Buddhism. The decline in the number of Islamic communities is explained by the fact that during the war in Chechnya no information on the number of communities was gathered.

AREAS OF COMMON INTEREST

The situation in Russia is extremely complex with respect to proselytism: A generation is still living which continues to carry the burden of the effects of atheist propaganda. The numerous ethnic passions and divisions have not abated. And a bitter battle for political power is taking place in Russia. Against this background new religions are emerging, and old religions are developing. In one sense, the desire to proselytize is natural for every believer and church, for the passionate desire to demonstrate the truth of one's own god is entirely natural. Current conflicts between religious organizations are brought about not so much through direct attempts to proselytize, but by disorientation and a lack of comprehension in the face of new and unaccustomed development of religious movements. The very fact that the religious landscape of Russia is changing engenders discomfort within churches and sparks disputes, sometimes even conflicts, between religious groups.

For example, the division of Russian Orthodoxy into three branches has provoked a whole series of internal conflicts within a single denomination. The ninety-eight parishes of the Russian Church Abroad and the twenty-six (registered only) parishes of the True Orthodox Church attract potential members not so much from the Catholic or Protestant churches, as from the Russian Orthodox Church of the Moscow Patriarchate. Whole parishes (including parishioners, church buildings, and ceremonial objects) often transfer their allegiance, as happened in Suzdal.

The emergence of previously unknown sects—including the Unification Church, the Baha'i faith, Scientology, the Hare Krishna movement, the Mormon faith, the Cult of Vissarion, tantrism, Jehovah's Witnesses, Zoroastrianism, and neo-paganism—has inspired a range of emotions in the Russian people—from astonishment to xenophobia. Other movements which first appeared in Russia shortly before 1917—including the New Apostolic Movement, the Salvation Army, the Quakers, and others—are also perceived, not entirely correctly, as new phenomena.

The Russian Protestant movement possesses a host of contradictions and conflicts, many of which can be traced back to the structural and ideological reordering of forces during the Soviet era. The split of the *Initsiativniki* from the All-Union Council of Evangelical Christians-Baptists, which took place at the beginning of the 1960s, precipitated by the activity of the Council for Religious Affairs, is still having repercussions. In the USA the transfer of membership from one Protestant denomination to another is a common occurrence; so is the adoption by old churches of more modern forms of worship. Western missionaries carry some of this over into Russia, and traditional Russian Baptists and Evangelicals often perceive this as proselytism. In turn, the whole of the Russian Protestant movement faces accusations of proselytism from the Russian Orthodox Church, and occasionally from the Muslims, who are concerned by the growing number of conversions to Protestantism among the Tatars and Bashkirs. Let us examine the following table of statistics:

Table 4-2
Number of Orthodox and Protestant Communities in 1995

Region	Number of Orthodox Communities	Number of Protestant Communities
Amurskaya	15	23
Buryatiya	17	21
Irkutskaya *oblast*	34	42
Jewish Autonomous Region	6	7
Kaliningradskaya *oblast*	44	55
Kareliya	37	41
Khabarovsk *krai*	24	43
Khakassiya	3	11
Komi	17	27
Primorsky *krai*	30	50
Sakhalin	26	42
Tuva	3	4
Yakutiya	9	22
Yamalo-Nenets Autonomous District	8	10

Out of the eighty-eight regions of the Russian Federation, this table shows fourteen in which the number of Protestant churches exceeds the Orthodox. It is in these locales that one may expect possible escalation in the conflict between these two Christian groups in the near future. European Russia is represented only by Kaliningrad, the old Prussian city of Königsberg, which was incorporated into Russia after the Second World War. The religious life of Siberia, however, is becoming more Protestant by the day. It is perhaps in Siberia then, that the vector of religious development of Russia as a whole will evolve. In Buryatiya the number of Protestant churches (twenty-one) also exceeds the number of Buddhist communities (eleven), which may indicate another area of potential conflict.

When considering tensions in Orthodox-Protestant relations we should also note the recent tensions in the southern regions of Western Siberia and Khakassiya, where the charismatic movement, led by the Church of the Glorification, is extremely active. In Khakassiya, the authority of this charismatic movement has spread not only among the people, but also within state structures. The Moscow Patriarchate responded by establishing a separate diocese in Khakassiya in 1995.

In Central Russia the most acute conflict seems to be between the Moscow Patriarchate and the Seventh-day Adventists. The worst conflict is not in Tula, the center of Russian Adventism, but in Nizhni Novgorod—where the sister of the provincial governor, Boris Nemtsov, has become an influential Adventist television preacher.

There are also instances when Protestants have waged war against Orthodoxy. Thus, in St. Petersburg at the beginning of the 1990s, a group of young Baptist believers belonging to the All-Union Council of Evangelical Christians-Baptists was excommunicated by the elders; the elders claimed they had had too much contact with Orthodox believers. As a result, there has been a flow of St. Petersburg Baptists to the Orthodox Church over the last few years.

A description of the more "Catholic" regions in 1995 also reveals a high concentration in Siberia (see Table 4-3).[16]

Table 4-3
Catholic Communities in 1995

Region	Number of Catholic Communities
Altai *krai*	12
Irkutsk *oblast*	5
Kalininigrad *oblast*	18
Kemerovo *oblast*	6
Krasnoyarsk *krai*	13
Moscow	5
Novosibirsk *oblast*	3
Omsk *oblast*	16
Rostov *oblast*	5
St. Petersburg and districts	10
Volgograd *oblast*	5

The growth of Catholics in both capitals and in the traditional Catholic/German areas of settlement (Kaliningrad, Volgograd) has been influenced by historical factors and is therefore unlikely to cause serious conflict. The same is true for the Armenian Catholics (Rostov). However, the same growth in Siberia, despite the huge growth in Protestantism, may give rise to Orthodox-

---

[16] Uimanov, *Massoviye repressii v Zapadnoi Sibrrii*, 242-43.

Catholic tensions. This is especially true in Altai, where four of the twelve religious communities belong to the former Greek-Catholic exiles in Ukrainian settlements.

The historical disagreements between Catholics and Protestants were never reflected in Russia, since both denominations faced identical problems "in the face of Orthodoxy." But discord sometimes exists between the two, most recently over the issue of church property. In Pyatigorsk, for example, an American Protestant mission of the New Apostolic Church took out a long-term lease on the Catholic Church of the Transfiguration, which, by presidential decree, should have been transferred to the Catholic community.[17]

A complex situation is developing in Kaliningrad, where some of the Orthodox churches have become Catholic and Protestant places of worship. The population is 78 percent Russian, but prospects for the development of Catholicism are significant, because of (1) the developing cultural and religious ties with Germany; (2) its proximity to Catholic Poland and Lithuania; and (3) the migration of Russian Germans into the region.[18]

Just as not all Russians are Orthodox, Catholicism in Russia has tended to become russified, and not just as a result of proselytism. The russification of Catholicism both delights and appalls the leadership of the Apostolic Administration, which is striving to preserve a good relationship with the Moscow Patriarchate. But the conduct of some Catholic print and electronic media in Russia is perhaps provocative. These Catholic media actively support the reforming wing of the Russian Orthodox Church, bordering on the "Lutheranization" of Orthodoxy, against the traditionalists and preach a mixture of Orthodox-Catholic ecumenism. They behave as if dogmatic, historical, and cultural problems resulting from the Great Schism of the tenth century do not exist. Such ill-advised conduct, which many Orthodox interpret as interference in its internal affairs, inspires anti-Catholic sentiment in Orthodox Church circles. Thus, at the January 1997 diocesan meeting in Moscow, the conservative section of the Orthodox clergy demanded that the Patriarch defrock any Orthodox priests who had been cooperating with the Catholic media on Russian soil.

In considering the ethnic profile of Russian Catholicism, we should note the declining observance of the traditionally Catholic Poles. Unlike the Volga Germans, there was no mass emigration of ethnic Poles from Russia. Instead, this huge diaspora became absorbed into either Orthodoxy or atheism. According to the parish priest in the small Yakut town of Aldan, of eight hundred Polish families not one attends mass, while 12 percent of the parishes consisted of Yakuts by 1997.

In concluding this brief survey, we should say a few words about Russian Islam. Public opinion considers Islam a huge, politicized religious organiza-

[17] *Katolitsizm, protestantizm, armianskaia apolstol'skaia tserkov' v Rossii* (Moscow, 1995), 32.

[18] Ibid., 34.

tion, a structured ideological monolith that fears no external competition in the light of its national exclusivity. The reality is different. Russian Islam is plagued by unending conflicts and contradictions, and is divided into several muftiates (Tatariya, Bashkiriya, the Lower Volga, and the Caucasus). Although practicing Muslims rarely convert to Christianity, Islamic spiritual leaders have often spoken out against the proselytizing activity of various Protestant missions. This may be because, in Tatariya and Bashkiriya, a significant number of Tatars and Bashkirs have joined the New Apostolic Church or one of the many charismatic movements. And in 1994, the central press stated that fourteen thousand Kazan Tatars had been converted to Christianity.[19] While these figures are likely to be exaggerated, it is important to note their significance for the future, as relations between Russian Islam and Russian Orthodoxy have never been entirely problem-free.

The *kryasheny* (baptized) in Tatariya have also caused tensions. These are Tatars who became Christian during the time of Ivan the Terrible and have preserved their Christian beliefs to the present. In Kazan today there are five Orthodox *kryasheny* parishes with the liturgy in the Tatar language. In the five centuries of their existence the *kryasheny* have become a distinct ethno-confessional community. While the existence of these parishes does not indicate a large-scale conversion of Tatars to Orthodoxy, their very existence annoys the Muslim Tatars. When Tatars (mainly women) *convert* to Orthodoxy, they attend Russian rather than *kryasheny* parishes. However, the majority of nominal Muslims who abandon their traditional beliefs tend to join new religious movements of the Eastern and Hindu persuasions, especially the Baha'i faith.

While on the topic of proselytism, we must also note the public declarations of the Krishna Consciousness Movement and the Church of Scientology, made almost simultaneously in 1996. On their own initiative they declared their complete renunciation of proselytism, in order to soften the effect of anti-sectarian declarations by mainstream Christian and Muslim religions.

From these observations, two conclusions may be drawn: First, in post-Soviet Russia, a great transformation of religious ideas and a consequent shift in relationships among various religious movements, confessions, and churches is taking place. Second, current and possible future interreligious conflicts are caused primarily by the massive breakdown in the religious and ideological assumptions of an entire people, and not by the individual "proselytizing" interests of particular religious groups.

---

[19] *NG Religiya* 1 (1997): 4 (supplement to *Niezavisimaia gazeta*).

5.

RUSSIAN CATHOLICISM: RELIC OR REALITY?

———————◆———————

Sergei Filatov and Lyudmila Vorontsova

After almost fifty years of nonexistence, Catholicism once more exists on Russian soil. Despite the religious diversity of our society and the religious eclecticism of the majority of our contemporaries, no other religious confession arouses such passionate emotions and often outright hostility. This tendency finds its most vivid and grotesque expression in the so-called patriotic press, which regularly detects signs of a Catholic conspiracy that threatens the very existence of Orthodoxy, and indeed of Russia itself. Russians can, of course, choose not to pay attention to these myths, typically perpetuated by the radical nationalist camp, if only on the grounds that they represent an insignificant proportion of the population. But this is not merely a question of nationalism. The senior clergy of the Moscow Patriarchate in their public pronouncements often speak of "the dangers of Catholic expansionism" and of Catholic "proselytism," expressing indignation at the presence of a Catholic bishop in Moscow. It is well known that since 1990 Patriarch Aleksii II has refused to meet the pope. The Russian Orthodox bishops and a large proportion of the clergy share an anti-Catholic phobia, barely even willing to acknowledge the existence of Catholicism in Russia. However critical we may be of this attitude, the very intransigence of the modern episcopate demands careful examination and explanation.

Moreover, this anti-Catholicism is easily mirrored by the state authorities, especially on a regional level (predominantly in Central Russia). Attempts to infringe the rights of Catholics are frequent and varied. For example, Catholic priests who are foreign citizens, in particular Ptolomeusz Kuczmik in Smolensk and Krzysztof Niemejski in Astrakhan, encounter constant difficulties over the extension of their visas. The result is that, for years, they have felt that they are on the brink of expulsion from the country. Under the current administration of Aleksandr Rutskoi, the local priest in Kursk, Iosif Gunchag, has been told that he is an undesirable element who should no longer be seen in the town. The Kursk administration is further refusing even to consider the question of returning the local Catholic Church to the community.[1] In 1997, the head of the local administration in Altai province overruled a 1993 decision to return a pre-revolutionary church building to the Catholic community, basing this decision on the fact that "the Catholic community is small and has few prospects."[2] Catholics everywhere are facing problems over the return of church buildings: they have been campaigning for years over the return of pre-revolutionary churches in Moscow (SS Peter and Paul), Smolensk, Kazan, Saratov, Nizhni Novgorod, Krasnoyarsk, Kursk, Belgorod, and many other towns. The church buildings are a separate issue from the impudent and completely unjustifiable practice of extorting money from Catholic communities. This practice perhaps hearkens back to certain traditions and primitive instincts of the Russian authorities, which in recent times have been revived in their oldest forms.

ORTHODOX-CATHOLIC RELATIONS IN RUSSIAN HISTORY

Anti-Catholic intolerance cannot simply be explained by reference to a general intolerance of believers of other faiths. Russia now has Muslims, Buddhists, and even Protestants, who have encountered difficulties—mainly due to their missionary activity. Catholic missionary activity, if it even exists in Russia, has very limited influence. Moreover, the official position of the Vatican, shared by the majority of influential Catholic organizations, is a genuine renunciation of proselytism. Contemporary intolerance of Russian Catholicism must be examined in the general context of the Russian spiritual and political culture with an understanding of the historical significance for Russians of conversion to Catholicism.

In the early years, Russia was open to both Greek and Roman missionaries. The adoption of one particular faith, at the end of the tenth century, was not made on the basis of its dogma, for the theological differences between Western and Eastern Christianity were beyond the understanding of the unsophisticated population of Ancient Rus. The new faith was received on the basis of its cultural traditions and the attractiveness of its ceremonies. It was not so much the teaching of this faith which attracted, but the appeal and "beauty" of the ritual; indeed the cultural component was often the determining factor in the attitude of the Russian people toward Catholicism.

But over the centuries, Russian national consciousness has been built on an opposition to the "West"—with this multilayered concept frequently inter-

---

[1] Lawrence Uzzell, "Authorities Block Catholic Worship in Russian Heartland South of Moscow," *Keston News Service*, 21 March 1997.
[2] *Svet Evangeliya* [Moscow] 17 (1997).

preted as Catholicism itself. Russian "spirituality," statehood, and culture were all seen as antithetical to "papism." While certain European innovations in the fields of technological advancement, fashion, and the arts were welcomed, theological innovations did not readily cross this religious divide, thus preserving the Russian sense of spiritual superiority. *Pravoslaviye* (literally, "right belief") stood against *ne-pravoslaviye* ("wrong belief")—in other words, Catholicism.

Anti-Catholic feeling was not only inextricably bound up with religiosity, but national consciousness, patriotism, and belief in a particular system of government. From the thirteenth century, when Prince Alexander Nevsky heroically defeated the Catholics at Chudskoye Lake and wisely submitted to the Tatar-Mongols, an anti-Catholic state ideology began to evolve; this ideology stated that a true patriot knew no more constant or perilous an enemy than the West. The ideological link between Orthodoxy and autocracy quickly became reciprocal: not only was the supreme ruler the defender of the one true faith, but Orthodoxy itself sanctified and strengthened the God-given authority of the autocrat, who was equally at risk from the corrupting Latin influences of the West. Ivan the Terrible revealed the essence of the Russian anti-Catholic phobia in a letter to Andrei Kurbsky. Explaining his hatred of Catholics, the Russian autocrat wrote: "Their rulers do not rule, they follow the directions of their subjects. Russian rulers, by contrast, do not follow the whim of their nobles and aristocrats, they are sovereign." A state system where "rulers do not rule" can only exist, according to Ivan the Terrible, where the people are "godless."[3] Thus, the well-known trinity of "Orthodoxy, Autocracy, and Nationality" has ancient roots. It reflects a formulation of national identity that has been created through the centuries, an identity which is not just anti-Western, but anti-Catholic in its origins. In the minds of the devoted Russian people, any perceived threat from the Vatican represented a danger not only to the purity of their faith, but to autocracy itself.

The indissoluble link between anti-Catholic feeling and loyalty to the state system is underlined by an interesting counter-example from the modern era. At the beginning of the 1920s, Patriarch Tikhon and a number of other prominent Orthodox bishops, not previously known for their love of the Vatican, displayed an interested and sympathetic attitude toward Catholics and were open to ecumenical contacts. The Russian Orthodox Church was under total religious repression at the time and no longer knew the form of autocratic government it had known in the past.[4]

Similar pro-Catholic attitudes first began to make themselves felt at the beginning of the modern era, and always directly coincided with periods of

[3] "Perepiska Ivana Groznogo s Andreyem Kurbskim," *Nauka* (Leningrad, 1979), 123-26.

[4] Prince P. M. Volkonsky, "Russkiye katoliki na priyome u Patriarkha Tikhona," in *Logos* 48 (Brussels/Moscow, 1993), 123-29.

accelerated modernization and abatement of autocracy. Such was the case at the end of the seventeenth and beginning of the eighteenth centuries, when Peter the Great instituted the administrative and cultural reforms, marking a significant break with religious isolationism; the first Catholic churches soon appeared in Moscow, St. Petersburg, and Astrakhan. Thereafter, Catholic communities, made up of Poles, Germans, and other Western Europeans, began to form over the years, until there were Catholic parishes in all the major towns of the Russian Empire. Parishioners included civil servants, military officers, merchants, and artisans. The Russians treated these Catholics as if no religious difference existed between them. This was the situation at the beginning of the nineteenth century, when the reforms of the young emperor Alexander I and his desire for Russia to become more open to Western Europe led to an unprecedented, albeit short-lived, period of religious liberalization—including a new growth of pro-Catholic tendencies. The first Russian conversions to Catholicism, involving almost exclusively members of the upper classes, occurred during this period. Almost all of the converts were later forced to emigrate because of the repressive policies of the authorities.

The next stage of Russian modernization took place at the beginning of the twentieth century, and marked a definitive transformation in the fortunes of Catholicism in Russia. Ethnic Russian Catholic parishes began to appear for the first time. And by 1907, the official structures of the Russian Catholic Church of the Eastern Rite were being formed. This short-lived period of the legal existence of the Russian Catholic Church was characterized by the hostile reactions of the Russian Orthodox Church and Russian nationalists. But even more prevalent were the negative, neurotic reactions of the Polish clergy, who had become used to seeing Catholicism in Russia as their national church; for them, the appearance of ethnic Russian parishioners was nothing short of scandalous.[5]

The current era of reforms, which began with Gorbachev's *perestroika*, has brought new challenges to Russia. The transition from years of official atheism to "religious renaissance" has given unique opportunities to the Catholic Church in Russia. Official atheism took its toll more on the Catholic Church than on the centuries-old and firmly rooted traditions. The Russian Catholic Church and its parishioners were subjected to systematic and brutal repression during the Soviet era. Not a single new Catholic parish was registered with the authorities between 1917 and 1991. The Catholic hierarchy was annihilated in the purges of 1937. Indeed, it seemed that Russian Catholicism had disappeared forever. For decades, the very survival of the Russian Catholic Church rested upon a mere two parishes, which were strictly controlled by the Soviet authorities; at the time, Polish, German, and Lithuanian Catholics were traveling to Poland or Lithuania to attend services.

---

[5] A. Yudin, "Religiya i Vselenskaya Tserkov: sudby rossiiskogo katolichestva," in *Religiya I demokratiya: Na puti k svobode sovesti*, 2d ed., "Progress" (Moscow, 1993), 478.

Even before *perestroika*, however, Russian Catholicism made an unexpected reappearance. In the 1970s, a pro-Catholic mood penetrated the Russian Orthodox clergy, up to the highest levels. Orthodox Metropolitan Nikodim (Rotov), as head of the Leningrad diocese, was responsible for a rekindling of interest in Catholicism in Leningrad. His influence spurred the emergence of pro-Catholic sentiments in Orthodox Church circles and instituted a movement for Christian unity. Fathers Mark Smirnov and Amvrosi Gribkov played a particular role in this movement, which led ultimately to the first Catholic conversions in Leningrad. In Moscow, students and followers of Father Aleksandr Men founded the Catholic community of Vladimir Nikiforov, which was destroyed by the KGB in 1983.

During this time, a new generation of underground Catholic communities sprang up, led by "independent" priests. Many spontaneous individual conversions furthered the Catholic revival. These individuals were baptized and received into the church by priests who had entered the country illegally from Poland, Czechoslovakia, and France.[6] Many such spontaneous personal conversions to Catholicism occurred, even in the post-Soviet period.

The stories of Nataliya Komdurova and Alexsei Kikshaev provide salient examples. Nataliya Komdurova, a young Russian intellectual in the town Naberezhniye Chelny, came to a conviction of the truth of Catholicism as part of a personal spiritual quest. Following her conversion, she attracted a large group of both Russians and Tatars, who had no previous Catholic roots, to her newfound faith. She has now established a large and viable Catholic community in her town. Aleksei Kikshaev, a Kalmyk from Elista, was an amateur theologian. Through his studies of religious literature and reflections about God, he became convicted of the truth of the Catholic faith. At the beginning of *perestroika* he moved from Kalmykia to L'vov, went to a Latin-rite church, and approached the priest and requested baptism. After questioning Kikshaev, the parish priest concluded that he was not quite ready for baptism and gave him some literature, suggesting that he study some more and give the matter further reflection. A year later the young Kalmyk passed the test and was baptized. The new convert started a vigorous campaign in Elista, calling upon his compatriots to receive the true faith. Many of the Kalmyk intelligentsia joined Catholicism as a result of his impassioned sermons. Kikshaev gathered together the few remaining elderly Catholic Poles and Germans to form a community. He also met several times with Archbishop Tadeusz Kondrusiewicz, who agreed to send a priest to Elista, and with the president of Kalmykia, K. Ilyumzhinovi, who pledged his support for the community. Kikshaev eventually became a monk and emigrated to join a French monastery, but he left behind three thriving Catholic communities in Kalmykia.

These individual conversions to Catholicism, characteristic of the intelligentsia in contemporary Russian society, find their ideological roots in the

---

[6] Almost all Russian Catholic priests and activists are Dominicans (Frs. Aleksandr Khmel'nitskiy and Yevgeniy Genrikhs; laymen Ivan Lyupandin and Yuli Schreider).

experiences of members of the Russian nobility who converted to Catholicism in the nineteenth century, such as P. Chaadayev, Z. Volkonskaya, M. Lyurin, and V. Pechorin. These nineteenth-century converts came to the conviction that it was essential to overcome Russia's religious isolationism from Western countries. In the eyes of Russian Catholics, unity with the Roman Church was equally an incorporation into European Christian culture. Many considered the West to be the ideal model of civilization which incorporated "a three-fold unity of culture, religion and mores."[7] These intellectual elite of the nineteenth century also turned to Catholicism based upon their negative assessment of the state of Russia. Chaadayev expressed this most vividly when he wrote that the Russian Empire was characterized by "a constant, all-pervading absence of the concepts of duty, justice, law and order."[8] He attributed this problem of Russian backwardness (when compared to the more developed Western European nations) to the fact that Russia adopted Christianity from a Byzantium "despised by all peoples," which he believed would lead nowhere when seeking to establish the ideals of the Kingdom of God on earth. Contemporary Russian Catholics, in essence, follow the same paths and attempt to resolve the same philosophical dilemmas as their aristocratic forebears from the nineteenth century.

CATHOLICISM IN RUSSIA TODAY

In 1991, following the Gorbachev reforms, the Catholic hierarchy was reestablished in Russia. The country was divided into two dioceses: a European one, with its center in Moscow, headed by a Pole from Belarus, Tadeusz Kondrusiewicz; and an Eastern one, with its center in Novosibirsk, headed by a German, Josef Werth. This marked the beginning of a gradual revival of all the Catholic parishes which had existed before the revolution.

The current official Vatican position is that Catholicism in Russia is being revived along strictly ethnic lines: among Poles, Germans, Lithuanians, and Latvians, all "ethnic" Catholics. However, many cultural barriers between Russians and non-Russians have disappeared; the majority of Poles, Germans, Lithuanians, and Latvians have intermarried and become russified to such an extent that many have forgotten their mother tongue. As a rule, services held in the languages of these "ethnic" Catholics are simply incomprehensible to them. Thus, in many parishes, the dividing line between Russians and Poles or Germans is increasingly hard to determine.

Today, the pre-revolutionary antagonisms between Poles and Russians are often absent. In some towns (including Yekaterinburg, Irkutsk, Orenburg, and Astrakhan), Polish priests command great authority and deep respect through-

---

[7] P. Chaadayev, *Stat'i i pisma* (Moscow, 1989).
[8] Ibid.

out the communities, attracting hundreds of new Russian converts. The parish priest of the Catholic Church in Irkutsk, the Salvatorian Ignacy Pawlus, is a brilliant and somewhat atypical representative of the Catholic clergy. A deep love for Russia and Russian culture brought him from Krakow to Irkutsk in 1990. According to him, "Russia can still become the heart of the world, just as Germany is now the nerve center of the world." Father Ignacy adopted Russian citizenship in Irkutsk and conducts regular masses to pray for the revival of Russia. When the town authorities asked him to facilitate the receipt of Western humanitarian aid, he categorically refused, saying, "It is shameful for a great country such as Russia to beg for handouts." And so the Irkutsk parish finances its own charitable work. Father Ignacy described the basic sociological precept governing his ministry: "Communism denied people a conscience. This happened in Russia and in Poland. If during my lifetime I am able to awaken the voice of conscience, if only in a few hundred people, it will be my gift to Russia and the Russian state." Through his ministry, Father Ignacy has come to command unbelievable authority—so much so that we have heard one diehard Russian nationalist, who hates the West and Roman Catholicism, state, "I am not going to talk about Father Ignacy; he is a good priest."

However, ethnic conflicts are not altogether a thing of the past. There remains some discontent among Russian priests and laypeople at perceived Polish and Polish-Belorussian "nationalism." Even Archbishop Kondrusiewicz has sometimes become a target for criticism. The most frequent causes of these conflicts are both the attitude of Russian Poles and the perceived desire of newly arrived Polish priests to turn new parishes into exclusive Polish religious and cultural centers. In Polish Catholic circles in Moscow and St. Petersburg, there are people who express openly nationalist and anti-Russian views. The prior of the Dominican community in Moscow, Andrzej Belyat, has become notorious for such views. He has said, "From childhood I have wanted to kill communists and Russians. But after I settled among them I came to the conclusion that they were even worse than I thought."

Nationalist tensions do not present the only problems for the Catholic Church in Russia. Difficulties have also begun to surface between the church hierarchy and the laity, due to sociocultural differences. Kondrusiewicz and his immediate colleagues—mainly Poles—came originally from peasant and working-class families in Belarus. They moved to Russia shortly before the collapse of the Soviet Union and gained Russian citizenship. These people bravely proclaimed their faith during the Soviet period and all suffered persecution to some extent. But to find a common language with the Moscow and St. Petersburg intelligentsia may be more difficult than standing up to the KGB. Of the numerous priests and monks who have come from Poland into Russia, Kondrusiewicz tends to prefer those who have a similar level of education and background; it is easier for him to relate to them. It is much harder, however, for the educated Russian laity to relate to them. For example, in the central Russian town of Tula, young Russian Catholic activists have effectively broken away from the parish. They claim, "We received the Catholic faith, not Polish citizenship. Perhaps it would be a good thing if Polish priests were denied visas, then Russian Catholicism could quietly gather strength without their domineering attitudes and for the next ten or so years we could simply travel abroad to receive the spiritual nourishment we need in the meantime." Fortunately, this position is an extreme, atypical demonstration of a tendency within the church.

Another issue surrounding the renewal of Catholicism in Russian is the question of the Eastern Rite. This issue, thought to belong only to history, was suddenly revived in the mid-1990s. This has an immediate relevance for Catholics brought up in the Russian Orthodox tradition who do not wish to be under the jurisdiction of the Moscow Patriarchate. The desire to restore a separate Russian Catholic Church sometimes stems from a reaction to Polish nationals, but usually the discussion centers on the revival of the Russian Catholic Church of the Eastern Rite, a church effectively liquidated from the territory of the USSR in 1946. The de facto leader and apologist for this Greek Catholic movement is Ivan Lupandin.[9]

At present there are semi-legal unregulated Russian Eastern Rite Catholic groups in Moscow, Tula, Kaluga, Vologda, and other towns, mainly in European Russia. The religious supplement of *Nezavisimaya gazeta* published a letter in June 1997, unexpectedly launching this movement. The letter from Aleksandr Beryozkin, a member of the Greek Catholic movement, announced the formation of the "Brotherhood for the Reunification of Orthodoxy." It further assured its readers that Russian Catholics would overcome all obstacles and eventually reestablish their "local church."

It is no secret that many people, mainly from the believing intelligentsia who have access to objective information about Catholicism, are not only convinced that the unity of the Church is more important than human considerations since it is the will of Christ. They act in accordance with their conscience, that is they become Catholics. There are not many Catholic churches in the provinces, and it is not possible for everyone to travel one hundred kilometres to get to church. An absurd situation from the ecclesiastical point of view arises: a local church exists (the Russian Catholic Church is recognized as such by the Acts of the Florentine Council, which have not been annulled) which is denied the right to any existence. It may be possible to say, that after a period of confusion, laypeople themselves have realized that they are part of a genuine, quite numerous church in unity with Rome. People unite almost spontaneously, sometimes informally, sometimes through offering hospitality to one another, sometimes as genuine "parishes without a

---

[9] I. Lupandin, "Dekret II Vatikanskogo Sobora o Vostochnykh katolicheskikh Tserkvakh i sud'ba Katolicheskoi Tserkvi vostochnogo obriada v Rossii (1917-1995)," in *Teologiya* [Moscow] 5 (July-December 1994), 100-108.

priest." The "Brotherhood for the Reunification with Orthodoxy" was recently created, the aims of which are: to gain recognition of the right for the reunited church to have its own pastors; and to collect signatures to a petition asking that Rome re-establishes the episcopate. We hope that such initiatives are not interpreted as "aggression from the Vatican," since the question is of the reunification of the church "from below."[10]

These Russian Eastern Rite Catholic groups maintain close ties to Western Ukrainian and Belorussian Greek Catholics, with whom they have an affinity in terms of religious practice and mentality. The Catholic Eastern Rite priest in Grodno, Viktor Danilov, is gradually being recognized as a leading exponent of the Greek Catholic cause, in Russia as well as Belarus.

The Moscow Patriarchate is categorically opposed to the establishment of Eastern Rite churches in Russia, a view shared by the Vatican. But Eastern Rite parishes already exist, and they continue to grow in number and strength. Moreover, the movement for the reestablishment of Eastern Rite Catholicism has a long and firmly rooted tradition in Russian philosophical and religious thought.

Attempts to find a rapprochement of these two church-cultural traditions, of Russian Orthodoxy and Roman Catholicism, were being made as early as the beginning of the nineteenth century. These ideas gained wider currency only at the beginning of the twentieth century, when the great Russian philosopher Vladimir Soloviev promoted Greek Catholic ideas. Soloviev's work helped to dispel the cultural and religious isolationism of the time; it facilitated a wider knowledge of the spiritual values of the Western Church without doing violence to Orthodox thinking. The pro-Catholic and ecumenical ideas expressed by Soloviev and his contemporary Russian philosophers paved the way for the establishment of the Russian Eastern Rite Catholic Church in 1907. Priests Aleksei Zerchaninov and Leonid Fyodorov were the de facto founders of the Greek Catholic Church, as it became known. Aleksei Zerchaninov was a simple village priest before becoming convinced of the truth of Catholicism. Leonid Fyodorov, who was also drawn to Catholicism, left the St. Petersburg Theological Academy during his third year and set off for Rome, dedicating his whole life to the Greek Catholic cause from that day forward. He became head of the Exarchate of the Russian Catholic Church in May 1917.

Thus, two rites have coexisted in Russian Catholicism since before the revolution,[11] and so have two spiritual and intellectual traditions. At the beginning

---

[10] *NG -Religiya* 7 (July 1997).

[11] Vladimir and Anna (Ekaterina) Abrikosov, members of a famous merchant family, founded a community that played a significant role in the preservation of Eastern Rite Catholicism after the revolution. This community miraculously survived policies of the communist authorities aimed at eradicating Russian Catholicism, and its members continued to observe the Eastern Rite in secret.

of the twentieth century, the Latin Rite was generally followed in Polish and German Catholic communities, and the majority of Russian Catholics turned to the Eastern Rite. Leonid Fyodorov described the need for the Eastern Rite in the following terms:

> It is always necessary to make a distinction between the universal idea of the church and its forms. The spirit of Christ, the spirit of pure Catholicism, not only does not necessarily demand one particular form, but may develop in different directions. Our tendency to mimic everything Latin and to value the Latin Rite more than the Eastern I see only as a demonstration of Eastern slavishness and our typical Russian self-abnegation for the sake of humility which is contrary to pride.[12]

The Greek Catholic tradition thus exemplifies contradictions inherent to Russia itself: on the one hand, there is a desire for unity with the church universal; on the other hand, there are the unpleasant realities of Russian life and a desire to preserve Russia's own religious and national traditions.

The cultural component is very important for all Russian Catholics, whether they are observers of the Eastern or the Latin Rite. When foreign priests come from the West, they bring not only a universal Catholic faith, but also their own national traditions of religious life, and Catholic folklore, which they (sometimes without realizing it) try to instill on Russian soil. Many Polish priests do this consciously, believing that they are, in fact, reviving Polish parishes. But Polish culture is not the only culture imported through the church. The parishes in Nizhni Novgorod and Vladimir are influenced by Italian culture; in Chelyabinsk, Ufa, and Marx one may find a German cultural influence; in Samara, Vladikavkaz, and Nal'chik, Irish culture resides; in Voronezh and Yakutsk, Slovak culture is evident; in Kazan, Argentinian cultural influences hold sway. In Vladivostok, the American priest, Miron Effing, has even incorporated the American festival of Thanksgiving into the church calendar, and it is now enthusiastically celebrated by Catholics in the Far East.

Russian Catholics of the Latin Rite have, understandably, reacted against all of this "foreignness." The need to russify Catholicism, to root it in Russian spiritual and cultural traditions, began to be discussed both in the Catholic press and at various meetings of Catholic lay activists during 1996-97. Various proposals have arisen, including the honoring of Orthodox saints canonized after the division of the church in 1054; the introduction of elements of the Orthodox liturgy into the Latin Rite; and the rejection of those liturgical practices which clearly emanate from a Polish cultural tradition.[13] The need to russify Catholicism originated among the Russian Catholic intelligentsia, and has now found an ardent supporter in the person of Stanislaw Opiela, the head of the Jesuit order in Russia. For example, Opiela asserted that foreign

---

[12] Quoted by Yudin, "Religiya i Vselenskaya Tserkov," 472.
[13] S. Mikhailov, "Yeshcho raz o russkikh katolikakh," *Svet Evangeliya* 20 (1997).

priests arriving in Russia should have to study Russian Orthodox spirituality and Russian culture as part of their "inculturalization" into Russia.[14]

Russian Catholicism has achieved much in the last eight years of reforms, after having been almost totally destroyed in the communist era. According to official Catholic statistics, there are around 500,000 Catholics in Russia.[15] This number, together with the Vatican's projection regarding future growth of the church, points to an additional three million people for whom a conversion to Catholicism would represent a return to the faith of their forefathers.[16] Of course, no one can say with certainty how many will actually return to the Catholic faith, or how many Russians (and Tatars, Yakuts, and others) will find God in the Catholic Church. Just seven years ago, no one foresaw that the Armenians would play such a significant role in Russian Catholicism. But in recent years hundreds of Armenian families belonging to the Catholic tradition have moved to Russia from the Caucasus region. By the end of 1997, Armenians comprised the majority of parishioners in the Catholic communities in Krasnodar, Sochi, Rostov-on-Don, and some other southern towns.

In 1997 there were around 250 registered Catholic parishes in Russia. Of these, only 25 are operating in churches which belonged to them before the Revolution; five have built new buildings. The majority holds services in apartments or in rented accommodations. Regional differences play a key role in the development of Catholic parishes. In Central Russia, where Orthodoxy is most firmly rooted, Catholics experience great difficulty in establishing their church, and they encounter powerful opposition from both state authorities and public opinion. In the Eastern regions, such as the Lower Volga, the Urals, and Siberia, Catholicism is developing naturally and easily. Public opinion in some towns—Irkutsk, Krasnoyarsk, and Orenburg—readily accepts Catholicism as a valid alternative to Russian Orthodoxy.

Today, all the clergy (with the exception of four Russians who were secretly ordained during the Soviet period) are foreigners, mainly Poles. The two operational Catholic seminaries, in St. Petersburg and Novosibirsk, will ordain the first Russian priests in 1999. But in May 1997, Vadim Shaikevich, a native Muscovite and a Russian of Polish extraction, was publicly ordained. Shaikevich is a graduate of the philology faculty of Moscow State University and the Wroclaw seminary.[17]

This sparsity of native Russians among the Catholic clergy obviously limits the activity of the church. Even so, the impact of some Catholic initiatives, such as the magazine *Istina i Zhizn* ("Truth and Life"), published with funding from the Dominicans, and the *Blagovest* ("Good News") radio station,

---

[14] *Svet Evangeliya* 14 (1997).

[15] The authors estimate the figure to be closer to 150,000, but that is still a significant number for a church just recovering from oppression.

[16] A. Barmin, "Katolicheskoye prisutstviye v sovremennoi Rossii," in *Religiya I prava cheloveka: Na puti k svobode sovesti*, 3d ed. (Moscow, Nauka, 1996), 124.

[17] *Svet Evangeliya* 19 (1997).

can be felt far beyond the confines of the immediate Catholic community. The cultural, educational, and charitable programs of the Catholic Church in several provincial towns have played a significant role in drawing public attention to the activity of the church on the regional level.

The increased participation in contemporary Russian Catholicism cannot be explained in terms of the missionary activity of the church, for it is negligible. Rather, the increase exists because there is a natural, spontaneous attraction to Catholicism among certain sections of Russian society. This can be seen by looking at the sociological profile of Catholic parishes: the majority of parishioners are young, mainly students and members of the intelligentsia. That is, the parishioners are from the most active and sensitive sections of society, which feel more acutely the exigencies of the times. The generally high level of education among the parishioners (mainly artists, teachers, and academics) gives Catholicism greater influence and appeal than, for example, the Baptist Church. Catholics are, as a rule, well-educated with a Western outlook; for many of them the concepts of culture and freedom are linked primarily with the Catholic Church.

This natural development and growth of Russian Catholicism is affected by the hostile activity of the Moscow Patriarchate, and by the tension between the Vatican and the Moscow Patriarchate. Although some Russian Orthodox clergy, including some bishops, are tolerant or favorably disposed toward the Catholic Church, they are in a clear minority and have no influence over policy. Influential clergy, including the Patriarch and the Chairman of the Department for External Church Relations, Metropolitan Kirill, constantly accuse Catholics of proselytism, expansionism, and spiritual aggression. Any gains made by Russian Catholics are seen as losses for Orthodoxy. The Patriarch, reacting to Catholic protests about the discriminatory nature of the 1997 Law on Freedom of Conscience, virtually denied the validity of the Catholics' right to existence: "Where have you seen the historical presence of Catholics in today's Russia? Before the Revolution in the Russian Empire, Catholics mainly lived in Poland, but you cannot claim that there is a Catholic tradition in modern Russia. Even if there are Catholics here, in Moscow they tend to belong to the foreign diplomatic community."[18] Catholics are being pressured to move the diocesan center from Moscow to St. Petersburg, and they are being asked to refrain from creating new dioceses in the future. Representatives of the episcopate of the Russian Orthodox Church indicate, through their speeches, that they see any normalization of the life of the Roman Catholic Church in Russia as unacceptable. Their desire, thinly veiled, is nothing less than the disappearance of Russian Catholicism.

Some church publications which are more nationalist than conservative in tone express a persistent hatred of Catholicism. For example, the paper *Pravoslavnaya Moskva* ("Orthodox Moscow") has consistently campaigned against the charitable work of Pro Deo et Fratribus, a Catholic organization,

---

[18] *Izvestiya*, 5 August 1997.

directed from Pereyaslavl Zalessky. This organization built a drug rehabilitation center in the village of Gagarinka. This center, employing the best doctors and organized according to the very latest medical research, helps to cure young people from Moscow and St. Petersburg of their drug dependency by distancing them from an "at risk" environment for a long period of time, teaching them work skills, and helping them regain their health. Pro Deo et Fratribus also began an initiative in Gagrinka to work with children who are mentally or physically handicapped. The authors have personally seen ten- to thirteen-year-old children, helped by Catholic monks, learn to hold a spoon for the first time. Nevertheless, *Pravoslavnaya Moskva* expressed that such "corruption of minors" in the sacred motherland of the holy Prince Aleksandr Nevsky insulted the religious sentiments of the Russian people. The paper further claimed that the Catholic charity workers were vampires, and that those local inhabitants who defended their friends in Pro Deo et Fratribus were betraying their country.

Currently, almost all revivals of Catholic parishes have been in places where they existed before 1917 (there are a few exceptions, mainly in Siberia, where many Poles and Germans were sent into exile by the Bolsheviks). The Vatican is seeking to preserve and improve its relationship with the Moscow Patriarchate through pursuing such a policy aimed exclusively at reviving pre-revolutionary, so-called ethnic parishes. Unfortunately, this policy is impracticable. It is impossible to differentiate between Russians, Poles, and Germans, and no Catholic priest can prevent a Russian, even one baptized into the Orthodox Church, from becoming a Catholic.[19] Moreover, the Vatican's attempts to preserve good relations with the Moscow Patriarchate by the voluntary restriction of its activity to the revival of "ethnic parishes" are justifiably seen as lacking in sincerity, for Catholic churches everywhere are full of Russians. A standard pattern encapsulates the creation of Catholic parishes: a group of elderly Russian Poles or Germans asks the diocese to send a priest, and then, four to six years later, the majority of parishioners in this so-called ethnic parish are young Russian intellectuals. Additionally, the current situation of prompting "ethnic parishes" is causing a neurotic reaction among Russian Catholics and evoking schismatic tendencies within the Catholic Church itself. For example, some groups have established links with the Lefebvre movement in the West, and there have even been attempts to create underground Orthodox "Latin Rite" parishes.

Any efforts made by Catholic parishes to establish close ecumenical links with Orthodox churches usually lead to friendly relations with only two or three more liberal priests in a given diocese. The conservative Orthodox majority usually responds by accusing these liberal-minded clerics of heretical and schismatic tendencies, and by accusing the Catholics of seeking to under-

---

[19] When such attempts have been made, they have only inspired hatred toward both Russian Orthodoxy and toward "the Polish mafia" for refusing entrance to the Catholic Church.

mine their church. Conversely, a policy aimed at building bridges between the two traditions may lessen the conflict "at the top" but would lead to increased tensions and conflicts at lower levels. But there is still a long way to go before the relationship at the highest level can be described as fraternal. The Moscow Patriarchate would seemingly be most pleased if Catholicism in Russia simply disappeared—but this is not a realistic possibility. Even if the Vatican recalled all its priests, some form of non-conformist Russian Catholicism, perhaps operating independent of any authority, would continue to exist.

Despite the position of the hierarchy, there is a growing tendency among Orthodox not to see any difference between Orthodoxy and Catholicism. Of course, this is not completely new, as even Gogol said that he could not see any difference between the two churches; for him they were still one church, which made conversion from Orthodoxy to Catholicism pointless.[20] Similar opinions are fairly common among both lay people and among the clergy. Two recent cases gained enormous publicity because those involved were punished by the Patriarchate. The famous icon painter, priest-monk Zinon, was suspended because he had taken communion at a Catholic service[21]; and in Obninsk, the local dean, Abbot Rostislav, was removed from his post and sent to the Tikhonov monastery to mend his ways for a similar misdemeanor.[22] However, not only liberals have a fraternal feeling toward the "sister church." Regular reading of the newspaper *Tat'ianin' den,* the unofficial mouthpiece of conservative Orthodox intellectuals, reveals not only constant criticisms of contemporary Catholicism for its "modernism" and "renovationism" but also belies an emphasis upon a common spiritual heritage and an alliance with pre–Vatican II Catholicism.

The issue is further muddied because of the difficulty in assessing whether Russian Catholicism or Russian Orthodoxy is more liberal. One provincial Catholic priest gave this rather unexpected evaluation in an interview with the authors:

> Catholics, even liberal Catholics, in their daily lives are usually far more traditional than the Orthodox. They go more regularly to church, pray more often, take communion more often, take the teachings of the church on sexual morality and family life more seriously, and so on. The conservatism of the Orthodox is proclaimed mainly for effect; in their conduct and way of life the Orthodox are far more modern and "renovationist."

In the final assessment, the majority of contemporary Russian Catholics view the adoption of the Catholic faith neither as a break with, nor a return to,

---

[20] N. V. Gogol, *Polnoye sobraniye sochinenii v 14-ti tomakh* (1937-1952), 9:118: "I will not alter my religion. . . . For our faith, like the Catholic faith, is one and the same and for these reasons there is absolutely no need to change one for the other."

[21] *Radonezh* 33 (December 1996), 15.

[22] *Metafrazis* (1997), 8.

the faith of their forebears. Becoming a Catholic is, rather, a discovery of Christ and Christianity, a participation in the creation of a new cultural and religious way of life. The agonizing doubts and spiritual quests of Chaadayev and Pechorin are incomprehensible to these new converts to Catholicism from Soviet atheism. In this era of post-Soviet confusion, when national ideologies have crumbled, these converts see their future and the future of their country not just in being with Christ, but in the wider context of Christianity and Western civilization. While they recognize that Russia will never become a Catholic country, they nevertheless, by their very existence, issue a spiritual and intellectual challenge to Russian Orthodoxy. This challenge might, in the future, force the "dominant church" to reject its general opposition to the West.

Contemporary Russian Catholics choose the Catholic faith for many of the same reasons as their nineteenth-century predecessors: the unpleasantness of contemporary Russian life, economic chaos, political excesses, and a cultural void. Converts to Russian Catholicism also reject Russian Orthodoxy—discredited by its links with communism, and characterized by authoritarianism, moral bankruptcy, nationalism, and anti-intellectualism.

New Russian Catholics do not, though, typically see a sharp, direct opposition between Russia and the West. They have not inherited Chaadayev's vision of Russia as a negative Non-entity which may or may not become Something. Becoming a Catholic entails a rejection of the old dilemmas and contradictions of the Russian soul. For today's new Russian Catholic converts the age-old dichotomies of "Russia or the world," "Democracy or the Church," "West or East," "Christ or the Grand Inquisitor," and "red or white" are simply irrelevant. These Catholics generally share the same basic philosophical outlook as the majority of "anonymous" unchurched Russian believers who are "just Christian." From this point of view, contemporary Russian Catholicism has a past, a present, and a future.

6.

PROSELYTIZING AND THE MUSLIM *UMMA* OF RUSSIA

Historical Heritage or Ethno-national Threat?

◆

Donna E. Arzt

Any study of religions and religious conflict in Russia must treat Islam as a special case. For one, Islamic concepts of community, of proselytizing, and of interfaith relations are unique and cannot easily be assimilated to Christian, Judaic, or European human rights models. For another, most Muslims of the Soviet empire were non-Slavic peoples living in their own eponymous republics or autonomous regions, which had been originally demarcated in order to insulate them from Turkish and Iranian influences. Therefore, their relations with non-Muslims in the post-Soviet era are as much a question of ethnicity, geopolitics, and nationalism as of religious doctrine.

The concept and practice of proselytizing within Islamic thought and history is closely connected with the survival and identity of the *umma*, the Muslim community of believers, which is traditionally a political unit as well as a spiritual one. Today, the various Muslim communities of post-Soviet Russia are confronted both with the legacy of Communism's secularistic leveling and with a type of interreligious tension that often takes on political and even racist manifestations. This constitutes another reason why the problem of proselytizing must, for the Muslim *umma* of Russia, be addressed as an aspect of the nationalism question as much as a question of religious freedom.

Russia's Muslims have not, for the most part, been the recent target of Western-supported evangelical movements—nor, for that matter, have they

---

This chapter is excerpted from the author's article in *Emory International Law Review* 12 (1998): 413-75.

historically made great efforts to convert the Slavic population away from Christianity. Nevertheless, they have always been the subject of "Russification" campaigns and currently play an important role in Russia's geopolitical strategy within the Commonwealth of Independent States, vis-à-vis the West and in the greater Islamic world. The conflict in Chechnya, for instance, represents a potential shattering of the ever fragile post-Soviet federalism as much as it does the possible advent of politicized Islamism in Eurasia. Hence, Russia's Muslim communities cannot be studied endogenously or autonomously from Russian political, economic, and security interests.

This study will first introduce some of the relevant legal, historical, and demographic background. This contextual section will be followed by a series of cross-sectional views of the growing politicization of relations between Islam and Orthodoxy within Russian society and polity, focusing on the period after 1979, and particularly after 1991.

PROSELYTIZING IN ISLAMIC LAW

Although Islam accepts both the Jewish and Christian Testaments as books of revelation, albeit inferior to the Qur'an, it does not adopt their use of the term *proselyte* as either "a resident alien in the land" or one who has left her religious community and converted to another religion.[1] The more positively connoted term *evangelical* is, similarly, of Christian origin, while *missionary* is associated by Muslims with Western colonialism and "Orientalist" thinking. *Conversion,* too, evokes images of the Crusades.[2]

The Arabic word *tabligh* roughly translates as "proselytization," while *al-Da'wa* is "the Call to Preaching." But these are used much less often than *jihad,* which itself is frequently misunderstood by non-Muslims when translated into English as "Holy War." In fact, it is more accurately translated as the duty to "struggle" or "sacrifice." The struggle can be personal and internal, as against cravings and temptations that prevent one from behaving virtuously, or it can be communal and external, which requires combating evil and spreading the cause of Allah among the unbelievers. Most scholars of Islam consider the forms of *jihad* which involve armed fighting to be defensive, limited to resisting external aggression, and thus only transitory.[3] Because Islam

---

[1] See Eugene P. Heideman, "Proselytism, Mission and the Bible," *International Bulletin of Missionary Research* 20 (1996): 10-12.

[2] See Betty Beard, "Antioch Conversion Tactics Rile Muslims," *Arizona Republic* (August 19, 1995). See generally Edward W. Said, *Culture and Imperialism* (New York, 1993); id., *Covering Islam: How the Media and the Experts Determine How We See the Rest of the World* (New York, 1981); id., *Orientalism* (New York, 1978).

[3] See Donna E. Arzt, "The Treatment of Religious Dissidents under Classical and Contemporary Islamic Law," in John Witte Jr. and Johan D. Van Der Vyver, *Religious Human Rights in Global Perspective: Religious Perspectives* (The Hague, 1996): 387, 411-12; Ibrahim Malik, *"Jihad*—Its Development and Relevance," *Palestine-*

does not separate the temporal and spiritual spheres of life, *jihad* can have the quality of political organizing: "The mission facing the Muslim is first to reform individual hearts and minds, and on the basis of that to reform society, and ultimately, the good society will install the virtuous state," in the words of Hassan al-Banna, the Egyptian founder of the Muslim Brotherhood.[4]

Yet *jihad*, along with its corollary, *hijirat*, meaning "migration," has historically served as a rallying cry for territorial expansion of Islamic rule. "[M]igration has been a persistent and recurring feature in the Islamic faith, and its successful evolution and propagation. Migration was intended to protect the faithful from further persecution, weaken the society of 'non-believers,' and enable them to take part in the creation of a new Islamic community."[5] Some Islamic jurists argue that the only legitimate reason for Muslims to remain outside the *dar al-Islam*, that is, outside their own states, is *da'wa*, proselytization.[6] Moreover, dying in battle has been considered the highest form of witness to Allah, for which one will attain paradise in the hereafter.[7]

While Muslims have a duty to propagate Islam among non-Muslims ("infidels"), Islamic law prohibits non-Muslims living under Muslim rule from propagating their faith among Muslims and from preventing one of their own from converting to Islam. This further intensifies the potential antagonism. Conversely, for Muslims, submission to foreign domination is a religious crime; actual conversion to another religion was traditionally a capital offense.[8] However, "recognition of the right of non-Muslims to live according to their convictions and at the same time in peaceful harmony and close cooperation with

---

Israel Journal 1 (1994): 26-34; Abdulaziz A. Sachedina, "The Development of *Jihad* in Islamic Revelation and History," in *Cross, Crescent and Sword: The Justification and Limitation of War in Western and Islamic Tradition*, ed. James Turner Johnson and John Kelsay (New York, 1990), 35-50.

[4] Sami Zubaida, "Trajectories of Political Islam," *Index on Censorship* 4 (1996): 151 (quoting Hassan al-Banna, *The Reform of Self and Society*).

[5] "Human Rights, Migration and Asylum: The 'Three Traditions' in Middle Eastern-Islamic Civilizations" 4 (paper prepared by a group of unnamed Islamic scholars for the United Nations High Commissioner on Refugees) [hereafter "Three Traditions"]. See also Sami A. Aldeeb Abu-Sahlieh, "The Islamic Conception of Migration," *International Migration Review* 30 (1996): 37.

[6] Dale F. Eickelman and James Piscatori, eds., *Muslim Travellers: Pilgrimage, Migration and Religious Imagination* (London, 1990), 37, 259, citing Ismail R. Faruqi, *The* Hijirah: *The Necessity of Its* Iqamat or Vergegenw' Artigung (1985).

[7] See John Esposito, *The Islamic Threat: Myth or Reality* (New York, 1992), 33; Majid Khadduri, *The Islamic Conception of Justice* (Balitmore, 1984), 164-70; Abdulaziz A. Sachedina, "Freedom of Conscience and Religion in the Qur'an," in *Human Rights and the Conflict of Cultures: Western and Islamic Perspectives on Religious Liberty*, ed. David Little, et al. (Columbia, S.C., 1988), 84.

[8] See Abdullahi A. An-Na'im, *Toward an Islamic Reformation: Civil Liberties, Human Rights and International Law* (Syracuse, 1990), 88-91, 140-49; id., "Civil Rights in the Islamic Constitutional Tradition: Shared Ideals and Divergent Regimes," *John Marshall Law Review* 25 (1992): 289.

Muslims was one of the Prophet's prominent achievements."[9] Islamic law grants the protected status of *dhimma* to communities of the other monotheisms—Christianity, Judaism, and Zoroastrianism. Freedom to practice their religion, including freedom from pressure to convert, was one of the traditional privileges of *dhimmis*.[10]

For most of the twentieth century, only a portion of the Muslim population of the Soviet Union could be classified as adhering to traditional Islamic beliefs. Therefore, the duty of *jihad* was not a persistent factor in relations with the rest of the country's population, at least not in the republics, such as Russia, where Muslims were not a majority. This began to change in the late 1970s, when a growing sense of Soviet Muslim identity became galvanized by Islamist movements in Iran, Afghanistan, and elsewhere outside the country. Nevertheless, proselytizing is a traditional function of Sufi brotherhoods, the mystical societies which in Daghestan and Central Asia survived into the Communist era and which earlier had played an important role in converting African, Balkan, Turkish, and Caucasian peoples of the Russian Empire to Islam.[11]

MUSLIMS IN SOVIET AND POST-SOVIET RUSSIA

GEOGRAPHICAL DISTRIBUTION

Although Muslims can be found throughout the former USSR, major groupings within the Russian Federation are easily identifiable geographically. In the early 1940s, Stalin's authorities divided the USSR's Muslim communities into four "spiritual directorates" which, though intended to serve as control mechanisms for Moscow, also reflected the four major geographical and political groupings of the Muslim population in this century. The first two regions—corresponding to the Spiritual Directorate of Central Asia and Kazakhstan and the Spiritual Directorate of the Transcaucasian Muslims, which covers the Georgian, Armenian, and Azerbaijan Republics—are beyond the scope of this study, as they are outside the present boundaries of the post-Soviet Russian Federation.[12] The third was the Spiritual Directorate of the

---

[9] See "Three Traditions," 5.

[10] See Bernard Lewis, *The Jews of Islam* (Princeton, N.J., 1984); Donna E. Arzt, "Heroes or Heretics: Religious Dissidents under Islamic Law," *Wisconsin International Law Journal* 14 (1996): 349, 381-83.

[11] See Uwe Halbach, "'Holy War' Against Czarism: The Links Between Sufis and Jihad in the Nineteenth-Century Anti-colonial Resistance Against Russia," in *Muslim Communities Reemerge: Historical Perspectives on Nationality, Politics and Opposition in the Former Soviet Union and Yugoslavia*, ed. Andreas Kappeler, et al. (Durham, N.C., 1994), 251-76 [hereafter *Muslim Communities Reemerge*].

[12] This is not to say they are insignificant concentrations of Muslim believers. Indeed, about 65 percent of the USSR's Muslim population during the Stalin era lived in Central Asia and Kazakhstan.

Muslims of European Russia and Siberia, most of whom resided in the former Tatar, Bashkir, and Chuvash ASSRs in the forest-steppe zone along the middle of the Volga River. The fourth was the Spiritual Directorate of the Northern Caucasus and Daghestan, located between the Black Sea and the Caspian Sea, covering the old Chechen-Ingush, Daghestani and Kabardo-Balkar ASSRs, as well as Adygeia and the autonomous provinces of Karachai-Cherkess and North Ossetia.[13]

While the Volga Muslims reside in an isolated enclave in the middle of Russia, the North Caucasus "mountain peoples," particularly the Daghestanians, live contiguous to the now-independent Shi'ite Muslim state of Azerbaijan. This state is itself contiguous to Iran, thus making the North Caucasus a latent frontier between Russia and the Middle East. Naturally, the North Caucasus communities historically maintained closer ties to the Muslim centers of Baghdad, Cairo, and Damascus, while the Volga Muslims have traditionally had closer contact with Christians. Unlike the rest of the Muslim communities of the former USSR, which predominantly follow the Hanafi rite of Sunni jurisprudence, the Muslims of Daghestan are Sunnis of the Shafe'i rite, their communities still heavily permeated by Sufi mystical movements.[14]

THE SOVIET ERA

Islam at first suffered less under the Soviets than did Orthodoxy or Judaism. However, Communist protection of Islam was short-lived. In Lenin's December 1917 "Message to Working Muslims in Russia and the Orient," the first Soviet leader declared "free and unassailable . . . your creed and customs, your national and cultural institutions," from that time onward.[15] Yet, as it did with other religions, official Soviet policy split Soviet Islam into official and unofficial sectors. The former served artifically to give the appearance of Muslim support for the Communist regime under the aegis of the Party-controlled Council of Religious Affairs. This official sector, however, constituted perhaps no more than 1 percent of all Islamic activity in the country.[16] In this respect, the Bolsheviks misunderstood their Muslim subjects, because Islam as a religion lacks the clerical hierarchy and extensive institutions of other forms of

---

[13] See Shirin Akiner, *Islamic Peoples of the Soviet Union* (London, 1986), 33-36; Alexandre Bennigsen, "Religion and Atheism among Soviet Muslims," in *Islam in the Contemporary World*, ed. Cyriac K. Pullapilly (Notre Dame, 1980), 228-29.

[14] Bennigsen, "Religion and Atheism," 229. The Hanafi school was the official school of the Ottoman Empire, which indicates the lineage of the majority of the former USSR's Muslims.

[15] Hans Bräker, "Soviet Policy Toward Islam," in *Muslim Communities Reemerge*, 163.

[16] G. M. Yemelianova, "Russia and Islam: The History and Prospects of a Relationship," *Asian Affairs* 26 (1995): 278, 285.

monotheism. It thrives, instead, in its informal sector, which was able to out-live the Communist yoke.

The Russian Revolution was particularly bloody and long-lasting in the Caucasus. Not until 1936 did the Bolsheviks fully subdue the Daghestan-Chechnya revolt, a widespread movement of guerilla-fighting mountaineers of the Naqshbandi brotherhood, begun in 1920. Sharia courts were then abol-ished, *waqf* (religious society) property was nationalized, and Sufi leaders were executed or otherwise purged, even though Sufi doctrine resembled Commu-nism in some egalitarian respects.[17] The USSR, along with the Central Asian and Transcaucasian republics, penalized certain Islamic practices such as bride purchase, deeming them "Crimes Involving Vestiges of Local Customs."[18] However, in Tatarstan, which was made into an autonomous republic in 1920, fewer mosques were destroyed than in the Caucasus, though *medressehs* (reli-gious schools) there were permanently closed after the revolution.

One of Stalin's first purge victims was Mirsaid Sultan Galiev, the most promi-nent Muslim Communist Party member, who opposed the Party's nationality policy for conserving the non-Russian peoples in a "colonial state." After his show trial, thousands of high-ranking Muslim clerics and intellectuals disap-peared under indictments for crimes such as "being Sultan-Galievists," "bour-geois-nationalists," "pan-Turkists," "pan-Islamicists," and the usual "anti-Communists, spies and traitors."[19]

By 1937, after twenty years of Communist atheistic propaganda,[20] approxi-mately 15 percent of adult Muslims of the Soviet Union described themselves

---

[17] In both Islam and Communism, "collective values are more important than individual ones . . . and both define the individual in terms of his or her service to society as a whole. In both systems power is personified by a strong political figure who is also an ideological or spiritual leader" with charisma. Alexei V. Malashenko, "Islam Versus Communism: The Experience of Coexistence," in *Russia's Muslim Frontiers: New Directions in Cross-Cultural Analysis,* ed. Dale F. Eickelman (Bloomington, Ind., 1993), 63. On the other hand, the Sufis advocate private owner-ship of land and free enterprise. Marie Broxup, "Political Trends in Soviet Islam after the Afghanistan War," in *Muslim Communities Reemerge,* 304, 311.

[18] Georg Brunner, "The Status of Muslims in the Federative Systems of the Soviet Union and Yugoslavia," in *Muslim Communities Reemerge,* 183, 197.

[19] Arthur Sagadeev, "Great Power Ideology and the Muslim Nations of the CIS," in *Central Asia and the Caucasus after the Soviet Union,* ed. Mohiaddin Mesbahi (Gainesville, Fla., 1994), 235.

[20] A 1954 article by Lutsyan Klimovich gave the official Communist view of Islam as "an anti-scientific reactionary world concept, alien and inimical to the scientific Marxist-Leninist world concept. Islam is in opposition to the optimistic and life-affirming materialistic teaching; it is incompatible with the fundamental interests of the Soviet peoples: it prevents believers [in Communism] from being active and con-scientious constructors of the communist society." See Walter Kolarz, *Religion in the Soviet Union* (New York, 1962), 405 (quoting Lutsyan Klimovich in *Zorya Vostoka*).

as non-believers, while Islamic illiteracy was growing among those who re-mained in the faith.[21] During the Stalinist period, "'[h]igh' Islam suffered seri-ous damage: the development of traditional religious-philosophical thought was undermined after losing its audience; the modernist branches were up-rooted; Muslim education and Koranic knowledge were strictly localized; and the circle of those who were officially allowed to conduct religious services was greatly narrowed."[22] By contrast, the "Islam of the masses" was able to consolidate. As a result, "while the sense of confessional fraternity and knowl-edge of basic Islamic teachings declined, the rituals and local cults not only survived but became the main distinctive signs of ethnicity."[23]

Despite the compulsory teaching of the Russian language and the termina-tion of schools in which native Turkish, Iranian, and Caucasian languages were taught, the penetration of Russian into Muslim communities was rela-tively slow and shallow. (Conversely, Russians living in Muslim republics were not required to learn the indigenous tongues; only a very few ever did.) How-ever, in the late 1920s, languages written in Arabic were forcibly converted to the Latin alphabet; Stalin soon thereafter ordered that they be written in Cyrillic. Thus, while Soviet Muslims often refused to learn Russian, they became more and more cut off from their own cultural heritage and from the rest of the Islamic world outside the USSR.[24]

In 1944, after a new revolt broke out in Chechnya, virtually the entire Chechen and Ingush populations along with the area's smaller communities of Karachays, Balkars, Avars, Muslim Ossetians and Cherkess—a total of be-tween 425,000 and 800,000 people—were forcibly deported to Siberia and Kazakhstan, for ostensible "treason and collaboration with the enemy."[25] While

---

[21] Sergei A. Panarin, "The Ethnohistorical Dynamics of Muslim Societies within Russia and the CIS," in Mesbahi, *Central Asia and the Caucacus*, 23.

[22] Ibid.

[23] Ibid.

[24] Ibid., 24-26; Sagadeev, "Great Power Ideology," 236-37. Currently, for example, less than 1 percent of Russians living in Kazakhstan claim to have fluency in the Kazakh language. Ibid., 237. By contrast, in 1979, over 97 percent of Chechens and Ingush claimed their native language as their mother tongue. Alexandre Bennigsen and Marie Broxup, *The Islamic Threat to the Soviet State* (New York, 1983), 33. See M. N. Guboglo, "The General and Particular in the Development of the Linguistic Life of Soviet Society," in *The Soviet Multi-National State*, ed. Martha B. Olcott (Armonk, N.Y., 1990), 246; M. N. Guboglo, "Factors and Tendencies of the Devel-opment of Bilingualism among the Russian Population Living in the Union Repub-lics," in ibid., 258.

[25] The low estimate is from "Edge of Empire," *Index on Censorship* (July-August 1997), 58, 60. The high estimate is from Bennigsen and Broxup, *The Islamic Threat*, 32. The latter authors label these deportations a case of "unsuccessful genocide," as opposed to the "successful genocide" through deportation of the Crimean Tatars and the Meskhetians, both also Muslim peoples. Ibid., 28-31.

World War II provided the pretext of military necessity, the deportations served a more punitive function. Simultaneously, tens of thousands of Russians and Ukrainians were implanted, in order to make the future restoration of the Chechen-Ingush ASSR impossible and to create a more "loyal" and "reliable" border with Turkey.[26]

Systematic persecution of Sufi brotherhoods in the Caucasus continued through the Khrushchev era, with members being criminally accused of economic sabotage, terrorism, and armed rebellion. The deported Chechens and Ingush began an unauthorized return home, despite arrest orders and the prohibited sale of rail tickets to them. "Alarmed by Khrushchev's failure to refer to [their deportation] in his speech at the Twentieth [Communist Party] Congress, the Chechens and Ingush sent a delegation to Moscow."[27] When they began to restore their ancestors' cemeteries and rebury the dead they had carried back from Central Asia, it became clear to the authorities that they were back in the Caucasus for good. They were therefore officially allowed to return in 1957, with a Kremlin decree that cleared them of the charge of collective treason.[28]

Until 1979, official Soviet propaganda trumpeted the idea that any kind of link between Islam and ethno-nationalism among the Turkish peoples of the USSR was fanciful, a mere mirage. Two world events in 1979—the militant Islamic revolution in Iran and the Soviet invasion of Afghanistan—acted as a catalyst within the USSR's Muslim *umma*, precipitating a heightened apprehension by Soviet officials of "the potentially subversive effects of dynamic Islam on their own rigidly controlled Muslim peoples."[29] Home-grown fundamentalist movements, mostly in Central Asia, were influenced by the Afghan *mujaheddin*, who were successfully battling the increasingly dejected Red Army, as well as by the growing disenchantment with socialism throughout the Middle East. Sufis stepped up their underground activities in the Caucasus, distributing Islamic books, organizing religious ceremonies, even operating clandestine Sharia courts. The number of North Caucasians reportedly belonging to *murid* groups in the 1980s, about sixty thousand, was virtually the same as in 1917.[30]

---

[26] Alexander Moiseevich Nekrich, *The Punished Peoples: The Deportation and Fate of Soviet Minorities at the End of the Second World War* (New York, 1978), 58-60, 104-5. See also Alexandre Bennigsen and S. Enders Wimbush, *Mystics and Commissars: Sufism in the Soviet Union* (Berkeley, Calif., 1985), at 25-29. Even after the deportations, small groups of guerilla fighters were active in the higher mountains of Chechnya, Ingushetia, and eastern Ossetia. Ibid., 29.

[27] Nekrich, *The Punished Peoples*, 135.

[28] The rehabilitation decree represented not so much a change in official policy as a recognition of the fait accompli on the ground. See Bennigsen and Broxup, *The Islamic Threat*, 32.

[29] Alexandre Bennigsen and S. Enders Wimbush, *Muslims of the Soviet Empire* (Bloomington, Ind., 1986), 37.

[30] Broxup, "Political Trends in Soviet Islam," 310.

In sum, despite the overall Soviet destruction of over thirty thousand mosques, the closing of over fourteen thousand Islamic religious schools, and the loss over the decades of approximately forty-five thousand Muslim clerics,[31] traditional Muslim culture was substantially able to survive Soviet rule. Due to Islam's inherent flexibility and adaptability, and because, unlike Christianity, the practice of Islam does not require an official clergy and formal religious premises, it continued to be "a key institution of socialization for the bulk of Soviet Muslims. Failing to understand the dual ethno-religious nature of the Muslim identity, the Soviet atheistic advance, though devastating for the Muslim elite, mosques, *medressehs*, and *mazars*, failed to eradicate Islam itself."[32] With the coming of *perestroika*, Soviet Islam could easily undergo a renaissance, having never really been extinguished.

THE GORBACHEV ERA

When Mikhail Gorbachev stepped into the Communist Party's leadership in 1985, he inherited a country in which the Ayatollah Khomeni's Iranian messianism and Afghan *mujaheddin* agitation and propaganda, as well as other external Muslim influences, were aggravating domestic Muslim political ferment, which had begun even before 1979.[33] His predecessors, Brezhnev and Andropov, the latter in particular, had assumed that Soviet nationality problems had been resolved "successfully, permanently and irrevocably."[34] With not a single Muslim advisor in his Politburo, and no personal experience working in a Muslim region, Gorbachev continued his forebears' policy of limiting Islamic activity to a small group of officially licensed institutions and using the party press to attack vehemently all manifestations of Islamic religious revival.

---

[31] Sagadeev, "Great Power Ideology," 235. See also "The President of the Islamic Center: There Should Be No Privileged Religion," *Pravda* (December 3, 1992), 3, translated in *Current Digest of the Soviet Press* 43/48 (1992): 13. On the Soviet destruction of mosques, see also Broxup, "Political Trends in Soviet Islam," 306-7.

[32] Yemelianova, "Russia and Islam," 285. "The potentially explosive power of Islam in the Soviet Union derives from the ethnic identity of the Turkic and Iranian peoples in the Caucasus-Transcaucasus and Central Asia as well as from their religious convictions. Islam's 'revival' after World War II can be traced in large degree to Moscow's ignorance of the strength of these identities." Bräker, "Soviet Policy toward Islam," 175. See also Malashenko, "Islam versus Communism," 66-67.

[33] Allen Hetmanek, "The Mullahs vs. Moscow: Armenia May Be Just the Beginning for Gorbachev," *Washington Post* (September 25, 1988). In 1988, the Russian newspaper *Literaturnaia Gazeta* speculated on "Khomeini's dream." "It is that the Islamic revolution be victorious throughout the whole Muslim world, from Morocco in the West to Indonesia in the East." Sabrina Petra Ramet, "Religious Policy in the Era of Gorbachev," in *Religious Policy in the Soviet Union*, ed. Sabrina Petra Ramet (Cambridge, 1993), 40.

[34] Bräker, "Soviet Policy toward Islam," 70.

In November 1986, Gorbachev gave a hard-line speech to Communist Party functionaries, calling for "a decisive and unconditional struggle against religious manifestations" and a strengthening of atheist propaganda. He also criticized local Party members who had personally participated in religious rituals for "pandering to obsolete views." Significantly, the speech was delivered in Tashkent, so it was naturally interpreted as an attack on Islam.[35]

A secret Politburo resolution that same year reportedly declared that Islam was a hindrance to Soviet social and economic development, while Vladimir Kryuchkov, the head of the KGB, stated openly in the Supreme Soviet that Islam "is a very dangerous thing, in view of its fanaticism and unscrupulousness in choosing ways and means."[36] Even as recently as 1988, Muslims who preached Islam were expelled from the Communist Party and the Communist Youth League, while *mullahs* who were not approved by the government were subject to official pressure. Gorbachev's "*glasnost* press" continued to condemn Islamic radio broadcasts from Iran and elsewhere in the Middle East, while official propaganda still promoted atheism and secular Soviet ceremonies instead of Islamic ones. More than thirty Muslim dissidents were reported to be held in custody on religion charges in 1988, while armed force was used in 1991 against fundamentalist Muslim demonstrators in Daghestan.[37] The most violent use of force during the entire Gorbachev regime occurred in "Black January" 1990, when Soviet troops crushed a popular rebellion along the Azerbaijan border with Iran. This was a pointedly different response than that which he gave to rebellions within the Eastern European orbit. The head of the Muslim clergy of the Caucasus accordingly condemned Gorbachev for using fear of Islam as an excuse for authorizing brute force there.[38]

Kremlin demographers were also becoming uneasy about rapid population growth in Central Asia, especially given increasing nationalistic rumblings in the region. When Gorbachev's administration ordered "surplus labor" from Central Asia to migrate to parts of the USSR where there was a shortage of workers, the Kremlin's rationale may have embraced their assimilation and

---

[35] Ibid., 175; Bryan Brumley, "Behind the Ethnic Rioting in Moslem Soviet Central Asia," *Associated Press* (December 20, 1986).

[36] Brumley, "Behind the Ethnic Rioting"; T. Saidbayev, "Russia Is Not Threatened by an Islamic Revolution," *Izvestia* (November 28, 1992), translated in *Current Digest of the Post-Soviet Press* 43/48 (1992): 12.

[37] "Union of Soviet Socialist Republics," *United States Department of State Country Reports, 1988* (1989): 1224; Malashenko, "Islam versus Communism," 75. In 1989, a group of Muslims seized a closed mosque in the village of Nizhny Dzhengutai, Daghestan, while several hundred in the North Caucasus town of Makhachkala stormed the headquarters of the Spiritual Board of Muslims, demanding a new mosque and the removal of the locale's official mufti. Ramet, "Religious Policy in the Era of Gorbachev," 40-41.

[38] Robert V. Barylski, "The Russian Federation and Eurasia's Islamic Crescent," *Europe-Asia Studies* 46 (1994): 396.

not economic productivity alone.[39] Moreover, Kremlin recognition that nearly 90 percent of the country's energy and mineral resources were located in the Transcaucasus, Kazakhstan, and the trans-Ural territories may have inspired Gorbachev's geopolitical campaign to promote Russia as belonging to the "Common European Home," and simultaneously as a kind of "bridge" to the Asia-Pacific region, Russia's supposed "natural sphere of influence."[40]

It was not until 1989, on the 1,100th anniversary of the adoption of Islam in the Volga and Urals, that the Gorbachev regime began to see the expediency of permitting new editions of the Qur'an and prayer books to be published, along with the ceremonial laying of cornerstones for new mosques and the reopening of those long closed; the latter was sometimes in reaction to Muslim threats to seize and reopen them by force.[41] Religious groups were sometimes permitted to import Qur'ans—even while individuals might find them confiscated at the border—so long as the organizations agreed to register under the 1990 law on freedom of religion.[42]

Contemporary Socio-demographic Status

In the Russian Federation today, an estimated twelve to twenty million Muslims constitute approximately 8 to 12 percent of the overall population of 160 million.[43] That ranks Russia on a par with Saudi Arabia, Syria, Malaysia, and

---

[39] See Bohdan Nahaylo, "Gorbachev Faces Resurgence of Nationalism," *Wall Street Journal* (December 24, 1986). In 1986 it was predicted that by the turn of the century, between one in four and one in five Soviet citizens (even more among those of draft age) would be Muslim. Ibid.

[40] Milan L. Hauner, "The Disintegration of the Soviet Eurasian Empire: An Ongoing Debate," in Mesbahi, *Central Asia and the Caucasus*, 222-23.

[41] See "Declaration of 6 June 1989 to the Council for Religious Affairs of the R.S.F.S.R.," in Felix Corley, ed., *Religion in the Soviet Union: An Archival Reader* (Houndmills, 1996), 332-33. Compared to over 26,000 functioning mosques in the Tsarist empire of 1912, and 200 at the end of the Brezhnev era (including 69 built between 1977 and 1983), more than 600 mosques functioned with official permission in the USSR in 1987. Gorbachev permitted a preparatory school for imams and muezzins to open in Ufa, in the Bashkir A.S.S.R. in 1989, and an Islamic college opened in Tajikistan in 1990. Ramet, "Religious Policy in the Era of Gorbachev," 40.

[42] For information on the expanded freedom of groups to import the Qur'an, see "Union of Soviet Socialist Republics," *United States Department of State Country Reports, 1990* (1991).

[43] This percentage is similar to the 10 percent of Muslims living in France, which gives closer attention to their integration than any other European country, including Russia. See Milton Viorst, "The Muslims of France," *Foreign Affairs* 75 (1996): 78-96. Based on a high population estimate of 20 million, the regional distribution of Muslims has recently been reported as: Daghestan, 2.2 million; Bashkortostan (Bashkiria), 2.5 million; Tatarstan, 2 million; Chechnya, 1 million; Kabardino-Balkaria, 0.7 million; Karachaevo-Cherkessia, 0.4 million; Ingushetia, 0.3 million; North Ossetia, 0.2 million; Adygeya, 0.1 million; Central Russia, 3.2 million; the Volga region, 1 million; and Siberia and the Far East, 0.5 million. "Muslim Leader Elected to Russian *Duma*," *Jamestown Foundation Monitor* 2 (1996).

Iraq as among the largest Muslim states in the world, behind only Egypt and Indonesia. In contrast to Russian Orthodox Christians, who tend not to self-identify as such unless they are firmly committed believers, or to Soviet Jews, who until recent decades were a predominantly assimilated population, a Muslim in Russia will usually profess to being Muslim, regardless of how loosely he or she adheres to Islamic precepts and practices.[44] Today, Muslim religious identification and practice in Russia appear to be growing rapidly, especially in comparison to Russian Orthodox practice. This surge is evidenced in statistics—the geometric increase in registered Muslim associations from 382 to 2,600 between 1990 and 1993; the establishment of forty spiritual directorates of Muslims since 1990; and the tripling of Muslim congregations, from 870 to 2,349, between 1991 and early 1996, during which time Russian Orthodox congregations merely doubled in number.[45] According to a recent Moscow-based study, "Muslims go to mosques twice as often as Orthodox believers go to church, they pray more, and they are more diligent about observing religious rituals and prescriptions." (However, as many as 90 percent of Russian Muslims may not know the Qur'an and break basic Islamic norms such as refraining from alcohol.[46]) As with other religious groups in Russia, Muslim youth tend to be more observant than their parents' generation. Enough of them desired to fill the acute need for Muslim clergy that new training institutions could open in the early 1990s in Moscow and Khazan.

The Muslims living in the Russian Federation today are made up of more than twenty different ethnic groups, composed of Turkish or Caucasian and, to a lesser extent, Iranian peoples,[47] in addition to ethnic Russians and Ukrainians who converted to Islam. The largest groups are the Tatars, Bashkirs, and Kazakhs (all Turkish), and the Chechens, Avars, and Kabardinians (all Caucasian). Not more than 30 percent of the Ossetians (an Iranian people) identify today as Muslims, although as many as half were Muslims before 1914.[48] For most of Soviet history through the present, these groups have tended to have higher rates of natural increase, and generally larger families,

---

[44] Akiner, *Islamic Peoples of the Soviet Union*, 2. See also Bennigsen, "Religion and Atheism," 222-37.

[45] Alexander Kudryavtsev, "The State Cannot Be Neutral," *Nezavisimaya gazeta* (July 30, 1993), translated in *Current Digest of the Post-Soviet Press* 45/30 (1993): 19; Edith Coron, "Russia's Religious Revival," *Christian Science Monitor* (November 25, 1996); "The Most Believers Are Found among Young People: Religious Life in the Mirror of Statistics and Sociology," *Moskovskiye novosti* 11 (1996), translated in *Current Digest of the Post-Soviet Press* 48/13 (1996): 20.

[46] "The Most Believers Are Found among Young People." See also Sergei Filatov, "Religion, Power and Nationhood in Sovereign Bashkortostan" (unpublished manuscript on file with Keston Institute, May 1997), 16.

[47] See Table 6-1 below.

[48] See Akiner, *Islamic Peoples of the Soviet Union*, 41; Ronald Wixman, *The Peoples of the USSR: An Ethnographic Handbook* (Armonk, N.Y., 1984), 151-52. While a small portion of the country's Muslims are converted Slavs, information on the size of this group is difficult to acquire.

Table 6-1
Muslims of the Russian Federation
(By Ethnic Group over 100,000)
From 1989 USSR All-Union Census

Muslim Ethnic Group	Population
Tatars	5,543,000
Bashkirs	1,345,000
Chechens	899,000
Kazakhs	636,000
Avars	544,000
Kabardinians (Circassians)	386,000
Dargins	353,000
Azerbaijanis	336,000
Kumyks	277,000
Lezghins	257,000
Ingushes	215,000
Karachays	150,000
Digor Ossetians*	130,000
Uzbeks	127,000
Adgeys (Circassians)	125,000
Laks	106,000
TOTAL**	11,699,000

*Estimate of 130,000 based on population of 402,000 for all Ossetians, most of whom are Eastern Orthodox.
**Additional Muslim ethnic groups with populations each under 100,000 are Nogay Tatars, Tabassarans, Aguly, Rutuls, and Tsakhurs, all in Daghestan.

than other Soviet nationalities. A rapid process of urbanization is underway in the oil-rich Tatarstan-Bashkiria enclave, which has traditionally been more heavily influenced by Russian culture and more heavily settled by ethnic Russians than has the North Caucasus. The latter region is in fact more rural now than it was in earlier decades.[49]

FEDERATION-WIDE MOVEMENTS

Perhaps the most striking and potentially most significant development within Muslim Russia today is the recent establishment of a number of independent, country-wide political organizations, the first since the Russian Muslims' Union, which had a faction in all four pre-revolutionary Dumas before it was banned by the Bolsheviks. During the Soviet era, official organizations of Muslim clergy were infiltrated by the Secret Services, which monitored and steered them, as it did associations of other religions[50]; until *glasnost*, independent organizations were prohibited.

Before the USSR's dissolution, the Islamic Revival (or Renaissance) Party claimed to have between ten thousand and thirty thousand members in Central Asia, in the Caucasus, along the Volga, and in the Urals. Created in 1990, its activities were banned in Tajikistan and Uzbekistan, even though its leadership claimed it was not a secessionist group and rejected terrorist and extremist methods. "We are not thinking about creating a state of our own," its

---

[49] Panarin, "The Ethnohistorical Dynamics of Muslim Societies," 29-31.

[50] See "Report from Iakov Peters, Director of the Eastern Division of the GPU, to Iaroslavskii, September 22, 1923, on the Muslim Clergy," in *Revelations from the Russian Archives: Documents in English Translation,* ed. Diane P. Koenker and Ronald D. Bachman (Washington, 1997), 454.

leadership stated. "We want only to protect the interests of the Soviet Union's Moslem minority, which the state-appointed official imams and mullahs are unable to protect."[51] More particularly as to the question of proselytizing, Valiakhmed Sadur, a member of the Party's council of theologians, stated in an interview in *Izvestia*:

> We want Islam to undergo a revival in areas from which it has been driven out and to spread to regions where it is unknown altogether or where people have a distorted notion of it. From this aim, another goal of ours follows—to protect true believers from persecution, from deliberate lies with respect to our faith, and from distortions arising from a poor knowledge of Islam.[52]

More recently, in 1995, the Union of Russia's Muslims, taking its name from the pre-revolutionary Duma party, held its first Congress in Moscow with over one hundred delegates from sixty-three member-states of the Russian Federation. Although it claims that it is a social movement and not a political party, its objective is to have a full list of candidates for seats in every parliamentary constitutency. Currently, the twenty-six Muslim deputies, most of whom belong to the "Russia Is Our Home" Party, constitute only 3 percent of the Duma, out of a nation-wide Muslim population of four or more times that percentage.[53] Like the Islamic Revival Party, the Union must also fight the oft-repeated but unproven rumor that it is "backed by petrodollars" from Middle Eastern states.[54]

---

[51] "Is There a Threat of Islamic Fundamentalism?" *Izvestia* (January 8, 1991), translated in *Current Digest of the Soviet Press* 43/1 (1991): 17.

[52] Ibid. See also Alexei Uspensky, "They Are Trying to Represent Us as Extremists," *Soviet Press Digest* (June 6, 1991); Malashenko, "Islam versus Communism," 71-74.

[53] James Meek, "Islamic Russia Forms Own Party," *The Guardian* (September 2, 1995). The twenty-six Muslim deputies do not operate as a caucus, although the chair of the Union of Muslims of Russia, Nadirshakh Khachilaev, a Daghestani who was elected to the Duma in December 1996, intends to establish a Muslim faction. "Muslim Union Plans to Set Up Faction in Russian Parliament," *Jamestown Foundation Monitor* 2/233 (1996).

[54] For instance, a news article about the Union of Muslims of Russia states: "The new movement is unlikely to have financial problems in the upcoming elections. Independent observers believe it is backed by petrodollars from Middle Eastern countries that would like to establish influence [among] groups in Russia." Sergei Kudryashov, "With Thoughts of Allah and a Faction in the Duma," *Kommersant-Daily* (August 15, 1995), translated in *Current Digest of the Post-Soviet Press* 47/33 (1995): 14. See also Natalya Menshikova and Boris Petrovich, "Qaddafi Has Reached Out for the State Duma," *Moskovsky Komsomolets*, translated in *Russian Press Digest* (September 5, 1995) (stating that, "[a]ccording to information which Moskovsky Komsomolets cannot confirm, Colonel Qaddafi and King Fahd are behind some of the sponsors"). The Union denies that it is receiving funds from abroad. See "Press Conference on the Results of the First Congress of the Union of Muslims of Russia," *Official Kremlin International News Broadcast* (September 6, 1995).

It also insists that it is a purely secular organization. The Union's mission statement declares:

> We want to emphasize the secular character of our organization. We consider the Muslim community in its historically shaped form of civilization as multi-ethnic but at the same time a single confessional, historical and cultural community on the territory of Russia. . . . Muslims are looking with hope to the future of Russia, and are expecting that a reborn strong Russia will reliably protect the interests of all its citizens and peoples.[55]

Yet given the inherent consolidation of the political and the spiritual in Islam, it is not so apparent how such an organization can be considered secular. Indeed, the leading Muslim clergy of Moscow and Kazan have distanced themselves from the Union, on the basis that the Federation's law on freedom of religion prohibits religious organizations from taking part in elections.[56] The same interpretation was made by the Central Electoral Committee, which twice refused to register the Union as a political party, even after the latter had won a court ruling.[57]

Perhaps more significant was the objection of the Russian Orthodox hierarchy. Despite the prior participation of Christian Democratic parties in post-Soviet Russian electoral politics, some of which allegedly have the Church's support,[58] Patriarch Aleksii II formally called upon the Muslim clergy to refrain from participating in the Union. His statement inaccurately noted:

> For the first time in Russia, where the overwhelming majority of the population professes Orthodoxy or is linked to that faith by historical and cultural roots, a large organization making Islam its symbol has entered the political struggle. This inclusion of the religious factor in the political struggle could inevitably prompt the Orthodox community to

---

[55] Ibid.

[56] Richard Boudreaux, "Russian Muslims Form Electoral Bloc," *Los Angeles Times* (September 4, 1995).

[57] "Press Conference with the Islamic Press Center of Russia regarding the Upcoming Elections to the State Duma," *Official Kremlin International News Broadcast* (November 16, 1995).

[58] According to Abdul Vakhed Niyazov, co-chair of the executive committee of the Union: "[T]he Russian Orthodox Church is quite seriously taking part in lobbying for various movements. I know, for instance, that the third line in the list of the Derzhava movement is taken up by a representative of the Church." "Press Conference on the Results of the First Congress of the Union of Muslims of Russia." On the Christian Democratic parties, see also Mikhail Sivertsev, "Civil Society and Religion in Traditional Political Culture: The Case of Russia," in *The Politics of Religion in Russia and the New States of Eurasia*, ed. Michael Bourdeaux (Armonk, N.Y., 1995), 75, 97-98.

take steps in response, which could inject confrontation into Orthodox-Muslim relations and lead to a new schism in society.[59]

The Union subsequently met with the patriarch to convince him that it is a purely secular organization and "there is no need to worry that the religious factor will be used for political purposes or to fear potential 'confrontations in Orthodox-Muslim relations.'"[60] The Union has called for greater government investment in the Muslim regions of Russia, Arab language studies in all Russian high schools, scholarships for young Muslims to study abroad, and public funds to assist pilgrims traveling to Mecca for the *Haj*.[61] It also advocates a peaceful solution to the Chechen conflict, one that promotes the continuation of a strong federal state of Russia. According to its co-chairman, Abdul-Vakhed Niyazov: "This is our Motherland. Our organization stands for constructive cooperation with the government. We strongly object to the allegedly destructive role of which the Islamic community is often accused."[62] He also expressed hope that Russia would recognize itself as "a state where Christianity and Islam have co-existed for centuries," and thereby, in its foreign policy, direct more attention to the international Muslim community and take a more balanced approach to mediating crises such as Bosnia, where Russia has clearly backed the Serbs. Niyazov believes that the Chechen conflict has at least had the positive effect of shaking up the Muslim community of Russia and making it more politically aware.[63]

Perhaps the clearest indication of the current vibrancy of Russia's Muslim population is the formation of yet a third political organization, the similarly named Muslims of Russia. It too takes a statist stance. According to its chairman, Mukaddas Bibarsov, Imam of the Volga region:

Without question, we advocate a united Russia. The breakup of the Soviet Union was an enormous tragedy for Russian Muslims. . . . A great many foreign Muslim leaders are now asking us not to do anything to promote the [further] breakup of Russia. Russia must remain a cultural

---

[59] "Don't Divide Voters into Muslims and Christians," *Rossiiskaya Gazeta* (September 1, 1995), translated in *Current Digest of the Post-Soviet Press* 47/35 (1995): 17.

[60] Valery Musin, "Contenders: Union of Muslims Intends to Be Sure the Faithful Are 'Adequately' Represented in Government," *Sevodnya* (September 2, 1995), translated in *Current Digest of the Post-Soviet Press* 47/35 (1995): 17. The Union seems in fact to have encouraged another new political party, the Christians of Russia electoral association. See Viktor Khamrayev, "Alternative: 'Christians of Russia' Intends to Combat Nationalism 'Arrayed in Orthodox Garments,'" *Sevodnya* (September 8, 1995), translated in *Current Digest of the Post-Soviet Press* 47/38 (1995): 8.

[61] Boudreaux, "Russian Muslims Form Electoral Bloc."

[62] "Russian Moslems Resolve to Reject Separatism," *Passport* (January/February 1996): 34-35.

[63] Ibid.

counterweight to the West. If Chechnya secedes from Russia, a chain reaction could begin.[64]

Other new organizations include the Union of Muftis of the Russian Federation and regional groups such as Muslims of Tatarstan. According to Duma Deputy Ramazan Abdulatipov, the purpose of these groups—and the inevitable umbrella organizations needed to coordinate all of them—is not to oppose any other religious communities but "to conduct an inter-confessional dialogue," to counter the perception that Islam poses an extremist threat to Russian stability, and to educate the Russian public about "the tremendous moral, spiritual and legal potential of Islam" and Muslim culture.[65] Proselytizing among non-Muslims is not an apparent objective of these groups.

MUSLIMS IN THE CAPITAL CITY

Since 1989, the number of Muslims in Moscow has grown, from a quarter million to about one million, including 800,000 in Moscow proper and the rest in Moscow Province. Most of them are Tatars, the second largest nationality in the city after ethnic Russians. Tatars began settling in Moscow as early as the fifteenth century, at the invitation of Catherine the Great.[66] Despite this relatively long history, anti-Muslim feeling runs high among Muscovites. In the fall of 1993, for instance, the All-Russia Center for the Study of Public Opinion recorded a 60 percent rate of "anti-black" sentiment, the same percentage that in a 1995 poll "completely approved" of official city policies designed to evict non-Russians from the capital. Other studies give rates of 30 to 34 percent who "distrust blacks." Russians consistently rate peoples of the Caucasus as those they dislike the most. Approximately one fourth of all advertisements for Moscow rental apartments stipulate that Caucasians should not apply.[67]

---

[64] Igor Rotar, "Muslims of Russia Hold Congress But Haven't Yet Decided Whom to Vote for," *Izvestia* (April 16, 1996), translated in *Current Digest of the Post-Soviet Press* 48/15 (1996): 13.

[65] "Press Conference with State Duma Deputy Ramazan Abdulatipov regarding the Position of Muslims in Russia," *Official Kremlin International News Broadcast* (December 16, 1996).

[66] James Walsh, "An Islamic Renaissance in Russia Acquires a Keener Edge, and Urgency, under Moscow's Hammering," *Time International* 147/8 (1996); Yelena Lebedeva, "A Black Stone with Red Paint: Muscovites Oppose the Construction of a Muslim Center in Russia's Capital," *Moskovskiye novosti* no. 32 (August 7-14, 1994), translated in *Current Digest of the Post-Soviet Press* 46/32 (1994): 1. The number of ethnic Ukrainians in Moscow may approach that of Tatars.

[67] Lebedeva, "A Black Stone with Red Paint"; "Russia: Crime or Simply Punishment? Racist Attacks by Moscow Law Enforcement," *A Human Rights Watch/Helsinki Report* 7/12 (September 1995): 4, 7, 9. The latter-reported study registered levels of "distrust." Azerbaijanis, Armenians, and Chechens (the first and last of which are Muslim) as a group were trusted less than any group other than Gypsies. Ibid. See

The designation "anti-black" is no misprint. Although peoples from the Caucasus and other parts of southern Russia—very often, Muslims—are just that, Caucasians, they are perceived by ethnic Russians as "different" on racial grounds. The prejudice is not limited to members of the public. Human Rights Watch has reported that the most frequent victims of ethnically motivated attacks committed by police, Interior Ministry special forces (known and feared as "OMON"), and road patrol officers are people from the Caucasus Mountains (including Christian Georgians and Armenians as well as Muslim Chechens, Azerbaijanis, and Kurds), the Middle East, Central Asia, the Far East, and Africa. "There also appears to be a rough correlation between skin color and abuse: the darker the skins or less Slavic the features a person has, the worse the treatment is by law enforcement officials."[68]

Chechens are especially prone to being rounded up and often deported under a series of 1993 city and federal ordinances on "regulating the residences of refugees," fighting crime, and implementing the *propiska* (residence requirement) system. Significantly, this *propiska* system had been ruled a violation of the international and constitutional rights to freedom of movement by the USSR Constitutional Supervision Committee two years *prior* to 1993.[69] Moscow Mayor Yuri Luzhkov, a close ally of Boris Yeltsin, stated that he would consider repealing his decrees requiring the registration of Chechens as "foreigners" and recognize them as "Russians" only when Chechen officials signed a peace accord with Russia to end the war there. In July of 1996, after the third bomb in a month exploded in Moscow, but before any perpetrators or suspects were identified, Luzhkov declared that "the entire Chechen diaspora must be evicted from Moscow!"[70]

The Chechen war is not the only justification cited for these policies. During the state of emergency declared by Yeltsin during the hard-liners' parliamentary rebellion in early October 1993, Moscow authorities stepped up the purge of Chechens and other dark-skinned peoples. They deported a reported four thousand to nine thousand, detained sixty-seven thousand others, and inspired ten thousand more to flee the city.[71] Since there was no obvious con-

---

also "Russians Lately Polled by Their Country's Centre for the Study of Public Opinion," *Financial Times* (June 1, 1992).

[68] "Russia: Crime or Simply Punishment?," 3-7.

[69] Ibid. See Article 34 of the Russian Constitution and Article 12 of the International Covenant on Civil and Political Rights. Moreover, the CIS treaty guarantees freedom of movement between former Soviet republics. Ibid.

[70] *ITAR-TASS* (Moscow) (August 2, 1995), available in *OMRI Daily Digest* No. 151, Part I (August 4, 1995); "Russia," *United States Department of State Country Reports* (1996).

[71] See Celestine Bohlen, "Russia's Ethnic Tapestry Is Threaded through with Bigotry," *New York Times* (January 9, 1994); Margaret Shapiro, "Yeltsin Lifts State of Emergency; Police Retain Tough Anti-Crime Measures," *Washington Post* (October 19, 1993); Howard Witt, "Rights Activists Say Moscow Crime Purge Propelled by Racism," *Los Angeles Daily News* (October 15, 1993).

nection between the coup attempt and the Chechen war or the alleged "Chechen crime wave," the former was used to rationalize the need to campaign against the latter. Similar "clean-ups" of predominantly Muslim persons displaced from CIS countries occurred in anticipation of Moscow's 850th birthday festivities in September 1997.[72]

RUSSIA AND ISLAM

THE RUSSIAN POLITICAL LEADERSHIP ON ISLAM

The relationship of Boris Yeltsin's administration to the Islam question is both more sophisticated and more complex than was Gorbachev's, given the former's decision to wage all-out war in Chechnya. In a televised speech in December 1994, while Russian troops were deployed in Grozny, Yeltsin attempted to portray the Chechen rebellion, with its ethno-religious trappings, as camouflage for organized drug and weapons traffickers, counterfeiting, and other illegal activity. "Through deception, through playing on patriotic [nationalistic] and religious feelings, and through money and threats," he explained, "these [Chechen] forces have been able to get part of the local population involved in the armed struggle."[73] Yet coupled with the popular equation made by many ethnic Russians that "mafiosi–Caucasian–Muslim" are "all links in a single chain,"[74] the television audience could have heard its president justifying the war as a crusade—or Crusade with a capital C—to reclaim Russian territory from corrupt Islam.

Appealing to the North Caucasus mountain peoples, Yeltsin insisted that "Russia is not the enemy of the Muslims." He continued, "Any people living on Russia's territory has the right to preserve its natural distinctiveness and its own traditions."[75] This sentiment, that "Russia does not oppose Islam as a religion," would be echoed by then Foreign Affairs Minister Yevgeny Primakov, himself a scholar of the Middle East, in September 1996. However, Primakov drew a distinction between Islamic fundamentalism—a "natural response to historical developments, such as the former persecution of Islam," a phenomenon which "we must learn to respect and reckon with"—and Islamic extremism, which he associated with ethnic discord and civil strife, and from which Russia may rightfully erect a barrier.[76]

---

[72] See "Moscow: Open Season, Closed City," *A Human Rights Watch/Helsinki Report* 9/10(D) (September 1997).

[73] "Address by Boris Yeltsin in Connection with the Situation in the Chechen Republic," *Rossiiskaya gazeta* (December 29, 1994), translated in *Current Digest of the Post-Soviet Press* 46/52 (1995): 7.

[74] See Lebedeva, "A Black Stone with Red Paint."

[75] "Address by Boris Yeltsin in Connection with the Situation in the Chechen Republic."

[76] Yevgeny Primakov, "Russia Doesn't Oppose Islam: We Do Not Equate Islamic Fundamentalism with Islamic Extremism," *Nezavisimaya gazeta* (September 18, 1996), translated in *Current Digest of the Post-Soviet Press* 48/40 (1996): 32.

It is noteworthy, however, that Yeltsin, who like Gorbachev has not a single Muslim in his administration, characterized the Chechens as "a people living on Russia's territory," not as members of the Russian Federation or even as citizens. Though not as overtly exclusionist as Alexander Lebed's outrageous remarks about "foul foreign sects" during the June 1996 Russian presidential campaign,[77] Yeltsin's more subtle comments, coupled with the Russian military's documented targeting of Chechen civilians,[78] are not likely to elude the grasp of the rest of Russia's Muslim communities and the neighboring states of Central Asia.

Vasily Likhachev, the deputy speaker of the upper house of the Russian Parliament and chair of Tatarstan's State Council, denounced "attempts by certain political forces to play 'the Islamic card' and drive a wedge between members of the Orthodox and Muslim religions" during recent Duma hearings on Chechnya.[79] At least one Western analyst has warned that if Yeltsin continues to foster the impression that the war is a Russian struggle against Islam, "he will find the leaders in Kazan, Ufa and other Muslim centers within the Russian Federation less interested in talking with him and more willing to listen to those who argue that these autonomous republics need real independence."[80]

Despite Yeltsin's Chechnya policy and his ambivalent attitude toward Russia's Muslim population, both the Islamic Cultural Center, which was founded in 1991, and the Union of Muslims of Russia, founded in 1995, backed him in the 1996 presidential election, rather than the self-styled "Muslim Communist," Aman Tuleyev. (Another Muslim group, Nur, supported the reformer Yavlinsky.) The two groups sent Yeltsin a joint message, stating in part,

----

[77] Alexander Lebed included Islam, as well as Russian Orthodoxy and Buddhism, in his list of Russia's "established, traditional religions." Richard Boudreaux, "Yeltsin Aide Denounces Foreigners, Urges Curbs," *Los Angeles Times* (June 28, 1996). See also Meek, "Islamic Russia Forms Own Party." He also excluded Judaism, Catholicism, and Protestantism when he attacked "mould and scum" such as Mormons and the Japanese sect Aum Supreme Truth as a direct threat to Russia's security and its "established, traditional religions"—Orthodoxy, Islam, and Buddhism. See Phil Reeves, "Yeltsin's New Ally Reveals His Darker Side," *The Independent* (June 28, 1996). Perhaps significantly, Lebed's remarks were made at a meeting of Cossacks. Ibid. A few weeks later, Lebed added Judaism and Catholicism, but not Protestantism, to his list. Larry Witham, "Lebed's Perspective on Religion Upsets Many," *Washington Times* (July 20, 1996).

[78] See Sarah Brown, "Modern Tales of the Russian Army," *World Policy Journal* (Spring 1997): 61; "Russia/Chechnya: A Legacy of Abuse," *A Human Rights Watch/ Helsinki Report* 9/2(D) (January 1997); "Russia: Partisan War in Chechnya on the Eve of the WWII Commemoration," *A Human Rights Watch/Helsinki Report* 7/8 (May 1995).

[79] "Parliamentary Official Warns Politicians Not to Play the 'Islamic Card,'" *BBC Summary of World Broadcasts* (October 18, 1996).

[80] Paul Goble, "Russia: Analysis from Washington: Moscow's Latest Muslim Problem," *Radio Free Europe/Radio Liberty Broadcast* (October 3, 1996).

At a time when power is being energetically sought by forces of *revanche* that are not concealing their threats to reverse reforms at any price and establish a hard-line Communist dictatorship, Russia's Muslims are becoming more and more convinced that you are the one, in alliance with the democratic forces, who can protect the country from impending totalitarianism.[81]

It is not clear to what extent these organizations reflect Muslim popular opinion, or whether their attitude toward Yeltsin remains firm now that he has signed the 1997 law on religious freedom.

THE RUSSIAN ORTHODOX CHURCH AND ISLAM

Although the 1993 Russian Constitution provides that "the Russian Federation shall be a secular state; no religion may be instituted as state-sponsored or mandatory religion,"[82] much evidence exists that the Russian Orthodox Church is replacing the Communist Party as a monopolistic force within Russian society and state. This Orthodox resurgence has not been lost on the country's Muslims, and Sheikh Ravil Gainutdin of the Islamic Cultural Center of Moscow has criticized the country's policy of treating the Orthodox faith alone as a "privileged religion, that is, the state religion," which he labels a persistent "ideology of the tsarist empire."[83] Other Russian Muslims complain that the country's armed forces now provide religious services for Christian but not for Muslim soldiers, that naval ships are now being officially christened, and that government support for the restoration of cathedrals and the observance of Christmas as a national holiday have turned Orthodoxy into the state religion, with no comparable sponsorship of Muslim commemorations.[84]

Keeping in mind that the Church does not itself speak as a single voice, recent Russian Orthodox attitudes and statements regarding Islam can be said to fall into three broad categories: those that ignore the role of Islam within Russian history and culture; those that posit an inherent antagonism between Islam and Orthodoxy; and those that reach out to the Muslim communities as

---

[81] Serafim Shakhov, "Union of Muslims Doesn't Believe Zyuganovites Are Sincere," *Rossiiskiy Vesti* (May 6, 1996), translated in *Current Digest of the Post-Soviet Press* 48/18 (1996): 12. See also Malashenko, "Islam versus Communism."

[82] Konstitutsiia RF (Constitution of the Russian Federation), art. 14(1) (1993), translated in Vladimir V. Belyakov and Walter J. Raymond, eds., *Constitution of the Russian Federation* (Lawrenceville, Va., 1994) [hereafter Konst. RF].

[83] "The President of the Islamic Center."

[84] "Press Conference with State Duma Deputy Ramazan Abdulatipov regarding the Position of Muslims in Russia," *Official Kremlin International News Broadcast* (December 16, 1996); Boudreaux, "Russian Muslims Form Electoral Bloc." See generally Gennady Vdovin, "Plus the Clericalization of the Entire Country," *Nezavisimaya Gazeta* (September 12, 1992), translated in *Current Digest of the Post-Soviet Press* (October 7, 1992): 20.

allies in the struggle against infiltrating Western influences. While the latter type seems to be on the ascent, it is still, according to observers, "extremely hard for the Orthodox Church to come to terms with the fact that Russia is now a pluralistic society," or indeed, that it always was. Given "the prerevolutionary role of the Orthodox Church, there was not even a dormant tradition of sensitivity to other denominations to resurrect" after the fall of Communism.[85]

Commonplace are Metropolitan Kirill's views that Russia has always been a Russian Orthodox country, that the Church has made the greatest contribution over time to the formation of Russian culture and statehood, and that nothing could remove the Christian core from Russian culture.[86] While such comments can vex the country's twelve to twenty million Muslims, whose history within Eurasia predates Orthodoxy, they undoubtedly sting when made in the particular context of Orthodox-Islam relations. For instance, during a recent controversy over construction of an Islamic cultural center in Moscow, Father Georgy, the priest at the nearby Church of the Archangel Michael, explained his opposition to the center:

> Moscow has always been and will continue to be a holy city for the Orthodox. It has always been known as the oldest capital, as a golden-domed city built of white stag. But they want to make us into "nobodies with no heritage." We pray to God that everything turns out all right. But all the same, Moscow is the third Rome, not the second Mecca.[87]

While Church officials have not been lumping Muslims into the same threatening class of foreign proselytizers who are allegedly using techniques of "poisonous seduction" to snatch believers away from Orthodoxy,[88] others have broadcast ominous warnings about the coming global religious conflagration in which Islam and Orthodoxy (the former sometimes reputed to be "aligned with the Vatican," as evidenced, ostensibly, by the confederation of Croats and Muslims within Bosnia-Herzegovina) "will either distance themselves from

---

[85] Michael Bourdeaux, "Glasnost and Gospel: The Emergence of Religious Pluralism," in Bourdeaux, *The Politics of Religion in Russia*, 125. "The USSR did not permit the establishment of a council of churches. Individual denominations and religions were sometimes brought together in conferences or to sign documents in support of Soviet policies, but this was an entirely artificial and mainly propagandistic exercise that basically had nothing to do with ecumenical initiative." Ibid.

[86] See Kirill's chapter herein.

[87] Lebedeva, "A Black Stone with Red Paint." It is unclear whether by "they" he meant Muslims or the city's secular authorities, but the effect is the same.

[88] Indeed, Metropolitan Kirill's speech does not mention Islam in this context. See Kirill's chapter herein. See also the interview with Patriarch Aleksii II in Mikhail Morgulis, "Russia's 'Pope,'" *Christianity Today* 39/7 (June 19, 1995) (using the "seductive poison" metaphor).

each other or blend in a turmoil of mutual destruction."[89] That the Russian Orthodox patriarch himself has seen fit to condemn Bosnian Muslims and Catholic Croats, but pointedly not Orthodox Serbs, for escalating armed combat in the demilitarized zones of the former Yugoslavia, may indicate that this apocalyptic vision has more than just grass-roots appeal.[90] Other ominous sentiments include the observation that recent conflicts between the Russian Orthodox Church and the Vatican will "play into the hands of the Islamic fundamentalists, building up their influence in the Muslim world."[91]

Yet consciousness about common linkages between the two faiths currently seems to prevail over antagonistic views. Because Russia's Muslims are for the most part ethnically distinct from the Slavic population, Islam does not present a competitive threat to the Church. Thus, it was willing to support the 1997 Law on the Freedom of Conscience, which recognized Islam, as well as Buddhism and Judaism, as one of the historic faiths of Russia.[92] Perhaps this endorsement caused no risk to the Church's view that an Orthodox believer is anyone who was baptized as an infant,[93] because a Russian Muslim too is a Muslim from birth; hence, there is no real overlap. Patriarch Aleksii and Sheik-ul Islam Talgat Taju Din could therefore jointly state their concern about seven Russians forcibly held in Afghanistan by the paramilitary Taliban movement, which was reportedly trying to convert them to Islam. "We call on the leaders of Taliban not to interfere with our compatriots' freedom of conscience and their choice of world-view," said the two leaders in their joint statement.[94]

The Russian Orthodox Church is also reaching out to the wider Muslim world. In one of a series of contacts between the Moscow Patriarchate and the head of Iran's Islamic Council, it was mutually noted that Orthodoxy and Islam are each "the basis of morality, patriotism and the revival of the spiritual bases in the peoples of the two countries . . . [both of whose young people]

---

[89] Eduard Volodin, "Catholicism with Its 'Protestant Makeweight' Steps up Expansion against Orthodoxy; Islam Poses Another Threat," *Soviet Press Digest* (August 23, 1992).

[90] "Russian Patriarch Condemns Bosnian Muslims and Croatia Over Latest Fighting," *BBC Summary of World Broadcasts* (August 11, 1995).

[91] Grigory Borin, "Koran Is All Right, While the Bible Is Being Torn to Pieces," *Megapolis-Express*, 19, translated in *Russian Press Digest* (March 12, 1992).

[92] Church spokesmen have explicitly said that Muslim social-service workers pose no conflict, and spiritual representatives of Islam can serve Muslim prisoners, so long as they do not proselytize to non-Muslim convicts. Leonid Shinkaryov, "Orthodox Church Rivals Vie for Role in Prisons," *Izvestia* (June 8, 1994), translated in *Current Digest of the Post-Soviet Press* (June 29, 1994).

[93] See the chapter by Mark Elliott and Anita Deyneka herein.

[94] The joint statement continued, "The reported attempts at forcible conversion of the Russian nationals to Islam 'evoke not only protest on the part of Christian and Moslem believers but also concern about the fate of inter-religious peace in Russia and the Commonwealth of Independent States.'" "ITAR-TASS Domestic News Digest of August," *TASS* (August 25, 1995).

need protection from the propaganda of cruelty, violence and immorality, which is rampant in modern society."[95] Both Orthodoxy and Islam view themselves as guardians against the onslaught of negative Western influences, secular as well as spiritual. And while the theological similarities between the two religions are beyond the scope of this study, the Islamic attitude toward apostasy, traditionally a capital offense, seems to be captured in the reaction to the delivery of bibles and humanitarian aid by an American Protestant ministry: "Changing your faith is treachery," according to Father Vladimir, a priest in the village of Semkhoz, eighty kilometers (fifty miles) north of Moscow.[96]

Perhaps it was his successful trip to Central Asia in late 1996 that convinced Patriarch Aleksii of the compatibility of the two religions. "All of us, both Orthodox Christians and Moslems, have come out from seventy years of spiritual captivity, [with] one fate in common and the same problems relating to the revival of spiritual principles."[97] While the nascent "Eurasian Orthodox-Muslim" movement, which was endorsed by the Moscow Patriarchate in 1993, may never achieve its true aim of resurrecting the Soviet Union,[98] its anti-Western message may serve a subsidiary, but more transcendent, objective of launching a lasting alliance between these two major faiths on the continent.

RUSSIA, EURASIA, AND TRANSNATIONAL ISLAM

Russia's policy toward its domestic Muslim population and its geopolitical strategies within Southern Europe and the Middle East have been interdependent for centuries, long before, as well as during and after, the Soviet era.[99] This was inevitable given that most of the country's Muslim communities have historically been located along its southern flank, thereby serving as a bulwark against what had been the Ottoman and Persian Empires. Control of the

---

[95] "Russian Patriarch and Iranian Parliament Speaker Praise Religious Revival," *BBC Summary of World Broadcasts* (April 12, 1997). Meetings between the ROC leadership and high Iranian clergy took place in Iran in September 1996 and in Moscow in February 1997. Konstantin Kozeyev, "Iranian Clergymen to Visit Russia, Meet the Patriarch," *TASS* (February 11, 1997); "Newspaper Commentary Notes Western Angst at Growing Irano-Russian Ties," *BBC Summary of World Broadcasts* (April 21, 1997).

[96] Alan Philips, "Bible-Burning Cloud over Russian Freedom," *Electronic Telegraph* 647 (March 3, 1997).

[97] Olga Kostromina, "Russian Patriarch Pleased With Respect for Orthodoxy in Asia," *TASS* (November 20, 1996).

[98] John B. Dunlop, "The Russian Orthodox Church as an 'Empire-Saving' Institution," in Bourdeaux, *The Politics of Religion in Russia*, 17-19.

[99] "Most notable in this regard were relations with the Ottoman Empire, which had stood forth as the defender of the Muslims of the Russian Empire since the sixteenth century." Andreas Kappeler, "Czarist Policy toward the Muslims of the Russian Empire," in *Muslim Communities Reemerge*, 141, 150.

Transcaucasus, particularly the region contiguous to Chechnya and Daghestan, would "give Moscow a foothold in the Middle East with which to exert influence and pressure on Turkey, Iran and points south."[100] While Russia's comprehensive foreign policy toward Islamic and majority-Muslim countries is beyond the scope of this study, a few observations relevant to the concepts of proselytizing and *jihad* are in order. These concern both the region that Moscow refers to as "the near abroad," meaning the former constituent republics of the Soviet Union that are now independent states, and "the far abroad," that is, the rest of the world.

With the dissolution of the Soviet Union, the "near abroad" has suddenly become part of the geopolitical framework of the greater Islamic world. Boris Yeltsin and his advisors—particularly Prime Minister Yevgeny Primakov, the Middle East specialist—cannot help but take note of the efforts made by Pakistan, Iran, and the newly neo-Islamic government in Turkey to provide economic assistance, trade, and investment in the Transcaucasus, particularly in Shi'ite Azerbaijan and the Central Asian states. Iran in particular has actively assisted in opening new mosques in the region.[101] Azerbaijan was the scene of the first outbreak of ethno-national tension in the Gorbachev era, and while downplaying the intention to secede, the spokesman for the Azeri People's Front commented at that time,

> Yes, our struggle contains elements of a *jihad*: gathering as an entire community and swearing that we will stand until the end. . . . [W]e, in accordance with our religion, are relying only on ourselves. Although we know that the entire Moslem world, Iran and Turkey stand behind us.[102]

The Middle East may be creeping even closer than "the near abroad," as evidenced by the support—or at least alleged support—for the Chechen rebels coming from Iran, Pakistan, Saudi Arabia, and even the United Arab Emirates. Moscow has complained about weapons smuggled in from the first two sources, while hundreds of Qur'ans and prayer books were discovered in stacks at the airport in Daghestan, awaiting delivery to Grozny.[103] At the height of the bloodshed, the Saudi Arabian Council of Ministers expressed "regret in

---

[100] Richard Pipes, "The Caucasus: A New Middle Eastern Tinderbox?," <www.IntellectualCapital.com/issues/97/0410/icworld.html>.

[101] Ted Robert Gurr, *Minorities at Risk: A Global View of the Ethnopolitical Conflicts* (Washington, 1993), 200-201; Sergei Strokan, "Geopolitics: Teheran '94," *Moskovskiye novosti* (December 4-11, 1994): 12, translated in *Current Digest of the Post-Soviet Press* 46/48 (December 28, 1994): 19; Vyacheslav Yelogin, "The Islamic Factor Card," *Rossiiskaya gazeta*, translated in *Soviet Press Digest* (May 10, 1992).

[102] "The Caucasus in Flames," *Kommunist* (December 16, 1989): 4, translated in *Current Digest of the Soviet Press* 41/52 (January 24, 1990): 13.

[103] Boris Bachorz, "Arabs Send Korans to War-Weary Chechnya," *Agence France-Presse* (March 21, 1996).

connection with the Russian armed intervention in the Chechen Republic and urge[d] the states of the Islamic world and all friendly, peace-loving states to help bring about an end to Russian armed actions against Chechnya."[104] While this statement does not in itself accuse Russia of conducting an anti-Islamic crusade, its issuance caused much consternation in Moscow, coming as it did from the guardian of the Muslim holy places of Mecca and Medina.

By aligning itself with the Orthodox Serbs within the ongoing conflict in the former Yugoslavia, Russia has continued the tradition established by Catherine the Great, who, in 1768, had forced the Turkish Sultan to recognize Russia as the protector of all Orthodox Christians in the Ottoman Empire. Her act has been said to have initiated "an ongoing anti-Muslim role [for Russia] of natural ally and protector of the oppressed (that is, Orthodox Christian) peoples in the Balkans in their search for the right to self-determination."[105] The continuation of this policy does not sit well with Muslims, who have criticized Moscow for not reining in the genocidal exploits of the Bosnian Serbs. Moreover, Russia continues to maintain that it has an obligation to protect the interests of its former nationals living in the newly independent Transcaucas and Central Asian states. Better that they should be identified as ethnic Russians, perhaps, than as Orthodox Christians.

The Chechen and Bosnian conflicts are not the only Russian-associated enterprises to look suspiciously anti-Muslim in Islamic eyes. Beyond Chechnya, Moscow's major military commitment is in Tajikistan, where 100,000 troops have, since 1992, been bolstering the Communist government in a civil war against radical Islamic opposition forces. Add to that Russia's support for Christian Armenia against Shi'ite Muslim Azerbaijan and its siding with Christian Georgia against its separatist Muslim enclave of Abkhazia, as well as Moscow's renewal of diplomatic ties with Israel (whose population has swelled in recent years with the emigration of Russian Jews), and it becomes understandable why "Russia is being seen more and more negatively in Islamic eyes." In the view of Russian political analyst Andrei Piontkowsky, "If it continues, it is not impossible to imagine Russia taking over from America as enemy number one" to Muslims worldwide.[106]

Russia and the United States share a common perspective on the Islamic world: both have an inordinate fear of "Islamic fundamentalism," or more accurately,

---

[104] Konstantin Eggert, "Islamic World Reacts to Events in Chechnya from Riyadh," *Izvestia* (December 15, 1994), translated in *Current Digest of the Post-Soviet Press* 46/51 (January 18, 1995): 16.

[105] Francine Friedman, *The Bosnian Muslims: Denial of a Nation* (Boulder, 1996), 39.

[106] Mike Trickey, "Rise of Islam Sets Off Alarms in the Kremlin," *The Ottawa Citizen* (October 4, 1996). Russia's support for Iraq and Iran is seen not as a sign of friendship but as Russian anti-Americanism, according to Piontkowsky. Ibid. But since Abkhazia is, in fact, only 20 percent Muslim, Russia's position in that conflict may be more opportunistic than religious. See Barylski, "The Russian Federation," 402; Pipes, "The Caucasus."

militant Islamic revivalism. In the Russian media, these terms, particularly the former, are used with the same phobic connotations as in the Western press.[107] Moreover, Moscow is still suffering the post-traumatic stress of "Afghanistan syndrome," in which *mujahadin* backed by Pakistan, Iran, Saudi Arabia, and Egypt liberated the country from Soviet occupation, leaving the message that "the new *jihad* need not stop at the [former Soviet Union's] border." Reports from the field warned the Kremlin that some [Afghan] rebel leaders intended to carry the struggle into Soviet Central Asia.[108] Even though the United States backed the Islamic militants in that conflict, the West can be seen to have implicitly delegated to Russia the role of "container" of the "Islamic threat" on behalf of "Euro-Atlantic civilization." After all, Russia's closer proximity heightens its fear of being "encircled" by the Islamic world.[109]

Ultimately, Russia shares a more significant strategic interest with Turkey, Iran, Tajikistan, and the other Central Asian and Middle Eastern states than it does with the West. These interests include the prevention of domestic and regional conflicts that could threaten their joint or several territorial integrity, political stability, and control over oil resources. Whether it ultimately defines itself as European, Asia, or Eurasian, Russia must be careful to promote "transcivilizational cooperation" even as it condemns religious and national extremism.[110]

ISLAM AND PROSELYTISM UNDER RUSSIAN LAW

Prior to the dissolution of the Soviet Union, religious proselytizing by any group in the USSR was prohibited and criminalized, while "anti-religious proselytizing" was encouraged and, in fact, part of state policy. Thus, both Stalin's 1936 Constitution and Brezhnev's 1977 updated Charter distinguished between "freedom of religious worship," which was limited to professing beliefs and performing rites, and the actual freedom "to conduct atheistic propaganda."[111] Soviet criminal codes penalized "active participation . . . under the guise of preaching religious doctrines" in "the organizing or directing of a group" whose activity is "connected with . . . inducing citizens to refuse social activity or performance of civic duties," including "mass dissemination" of documents that urge nonobservance of legislation on religious cults.[112]

---

[107] See Sagadeev, "Great Power Ideology," 241-43.

[108] Barylski, "The Russian Federation," 394-95. Some fifteen to twenty thousand Arabs reportedly fought in Afghanistan against the USSR. Ibid., 395.

[109] Sagadeev, "Great Power Ideology," 273, 279.

[110] Barylski, "The Russian Federation," 413.

[111] Konstitutsiia U.S.S.R. [Constitution], art. 124 (fundamental law of the Union of Soviet Socialist Republics) (1936); Konstitutsia U.S.S.R. [Constitution], art. 52 124 (fundamental law of the Union of Soviet Socialist Republics) (1977) [hereafter "1977 Constitution"].

[112] Criminal Code arts. 142, 227 (RSFSR), translated in Harold J. Berman and James W. Spindler, *Soviet Criminal Law and Procedure: The RSFSR Codes* (Cambridge, 1972), 73, n.73.

Organizers of "atheistic upbringing" were trained to counter religiosity, which was thought to be particularly prevalent among housewives, though it was noted in 1984 that "Islam presents special problems for atheistic propagandists because of the extent to which religion permeates daily life."[113]

Formally, this situation changed in October 1990 with the adoption of the USSR Law on Freedom of Conscience and Religious Organizations[114] (the "1990 law"), which replaced anti-religious legislation from 1929, and which in Article 3 permitted every citizen "to express and disseminate convictions associated with his attitude toward religion."[115] The same article also prohibited "compulsion of any kind" regarding a citizen's "determination of his attitude toward religion."[116] A similar Russian Law on Freedom of Conscience and Religious Belief was adopted the same month,[117] later becoming effective in the post-Soviet Russian Federation and bolstered by the guarantees of religious freedom promulgated in the 1993 Russian Constitution.[118] Nevertheless, the new Russian Constitution and legislation continued, as in the Soviet era, to prohibit the incitement of discord and hatred on religious grounds, to require separation of church and state,[119] and to prohibit religious parties.[120]

---

[113] M. Vagabov, "Beyond the Bounds of Family Traditions," *Nauka i religia* (1984): 3, translated in "How Atheists Work with Traditionally Religious Moslem Women in Daghestan," *Current Digest of the Soviet Press* 36 (1984): 14. See generally John Anderson, "Out of the Kitchen, Out of the Temple: Religion, Atheism and Women in the Soviet Union," in Ramet, *Religious Policy in the Soviet Union*, 206-28.

[114] Law of the Union of Soviet Socialist Republics on Freedom of Conscience and Religious Organizations (October 1, 1990), translated in *Religion in the Soviet Republics*, ed. Igor Troyanovsky (San Francisco, 1991), 23.

[115] Ibid., art. 3.

[116] Ibid.

[117] Law of the Russian Soviet Federative Socialist Republic on Freedom of Worship (October 25, 1990), translated in Troyanovsky, *Religion in the Soviet Republics*, 31 [hereafter "1990 Russian Law"].

[118] Article 28 of the 1993 Russian Constitution states: "Everyone shall be guaranteed the right to freedom of conscience, to freedom of religious worship, including the right to profess, individually or jointly with others, any religion, or to profess no religion, to freely choose, possess and disseminate religious or other beliefs, and to act in conformity with them." Konst. RF, art. 28 (1993).

[119] Article 52 of the 1977 USSR Constitution prohibited "incitement of hostility or hatred on religious grounds." 1977 Constitution, art. 52. Article 6 of the 1990 Russian Law on religious freedom continues this prohibition. Article 8 of the same law, which provides for separation of religion and state, allows religious organizations to participate in political elections and campaigns but not to support financially or otherwise participate in the activities of political parties. See also Konst. RF, arts. 14, 29.2.

[120] Muslims were represented by their own faction in all four pre-revolutionary Dumas. "Russian Moslems Resolve to Reject Separatism," *Passport* (January/February, 1996): 34. In 1991, the Islamic Renaissance Party handed the former Supreme Soviet a demand that it be legalized. See A. Karpov, "The Islamic Party Is Still Outlawed," *Soviet Press Digest* (September 11, 1991): 1. A similar demand has recently been made by the new Union of Muslims of Russia.

The 1990 Law's provisions on the activity of religious organizations, particularly Article 14 concerning "professional religious work," led to an early 1990s renaissance of religious activity by indigenous and foreign-based religious groups, including Muslims. However, there followed soon thereafter a backlash of proposed legislation that, inter alia, would have amended Article 14 to prohibit religious activity on Russian territory by noncitizens, foreign organizations, and their representatives, and would have required registration of all indigenous religious groups. An initial version of these changes, strongly supported by the Russian Orthodox Church, officially appointed Muslim spiritual leaders, a plurality of popular opinion, right-wing nationalists, and even the Communist Party, was passed by the Duma. The legislation, however, was vetoed by Boris Yeltsin, who subsequently dissolved the legislature after the aborted coup of 1993.[121]

Yeltsin vetoed a later permutation of the amended legislation in July 1997 on the grounds that numerous provisions would still "curb constitutional human and civil rights and freedoms, make confessions unequal and are inconsistent with Russia's international commitments." Moreover, he stated, signing it could "trigger religious strife in the country."[122] Nevertheless, further attempts to enact broad restrictions on missionary and other activity by "nontraditional," "foreign," and minority religions persisted on the federal level. These efforts culminated in new legislation, effective October 1, 1997, which Yeltsin finally signed into law, despite the fact that it was substantially similar to the version he vetoed in July.

The 1997 Russian Federation Law on Freedom of Conscience and on Religious Associations (the 1997 Law), places Islam in a "second tier" classification along with Christianity, Islam, Buddhism, and Judaism. Islam stands below the especially venerated Russian Orthodox Church but above other religions and creeds which are not considered "an inseparable part of the historical heritage of Russia's peoples."[123] If the 1997 Law can be said to represent a fear

---

[121] According to the Russian Department of State and Law, Yeltsin rejected the amendments because they contradicted the Russian Constitution. "Yeltsin Rejects Changes to Russia's Religious Freedom Law," *Church and State* (April 1995): 21. See Vadim Sazonov, "Poll: A New Symbiosis," *Nezavisimaya Gazeta* (August 12, 1993): 5, translated in *Current Digest of the Post-Soviet Press* 45/32 (1993): 25. Supreme Mufti Ravil Gaynutdin, head of the Spiritual Board of Muslims of Central European Russia, reportedly agreed with the Russian Orthodox Church that activities of foreign missionaries should be tightly regulated. "Duma Approves Amendments to Law on Freedom of Religion," *BBC Summary of World Broadcasts* (July 12, 1996).

[122] Letter from Boris Nikolaevich Yeltsin, president of the Russian Federation, to G. N. Seleznev, president of the State Duma, and E. S. Stoev, president of the Federation Council (July 23, 1997); Daniel Williams, "Yeltsin Vetoes Bill to Curb Many Religions," *Washington Post* (July 23, 1997): A18.

[123] Russian Federation Law on Freedom of Conscience Law and on Religious Associations, Federal Law No. 125-FZ (September 26, 1997), preamble, translated by Lawrence A. Uzzell in *Emory International Law Review* 12 (1998): 657-80 [1997 Law].

of penetration from "outside," non-indigenous faiths, particularly those that are more modern and/or more zealous in their expansionist activities, Islam has an ambiguous status. It represents *both* an inside *and* an outside faith, and while it is not more modern than Orthodoxy, it is certainly more zealous.

As Jeremy Gunn details in his chapter herein, the 1997 Law establishes a complex series of registration requirements and statuses, contingent on a religious association's geographic distribution, length of proven existence in Russia, and type of activities. It also contains vague provisions which might be interpreted to "restrict the freedom of a religious association to disseminate its faith to non-members, especially minors, or to set up new congregations where it is not already registered," making them "vulnerable to the caprice and graft of central and local Russian bureaucrats."[124] Its most notorious provision is Article 9.1, which discriminates between religious organizations which have confirmation from the organs of government that they have existed on the territory of Russia for at least fifteen years, and those that do not. The latter will not be able to publish newspapers or distribute religious literature; invite foreign preachers; hold worship services in hospitals, senior citizens' homes, schools, orphanages, or prisons; form educational establishments; or obtain tax relief. Nor will their clergy be exempt from military service.[125]

The fifteen-year period was not selected arbitrarily. The year 1982 predates Gorbachev's *perestroika*; before then, most religions operated underground to avoid harassment and arrest by Communist authorities. Although Islam's roots in Russia are much more ancient, many of its newer manifestations developed after 1982. For instance, of the more than fifteen hundred mosques functioning in Russia today, approximately thirteen hundred were opened after 1983.[126] Not all of these fall under the jurisdiction of the Central Council of the Ecclesiastical Board of Muslims of Russia, which means they may not be "grandfathered" in under its preexisting registration. Other independent Muslim organizations may also be affected; it was not until 1989, for example, that Muslim groups first became involved in charitable work.[127]

Although the official leadership of Russian Muslims is reported to have approved of the 1997 Law, it is far from popular among the majority of Muslims and the more independent voices in the *umma*. Calling the new law "a great evil," the president of the Supreme Coordination Center of the Ecclesiastical Board of Muslims of Russia, Nafigulla Ashirov, has vehemently protested that it "tramples on the rights of religious organizations of long standing . . .

---

[124] Jim Nichol, "Russia's Religion Law: Assessments and Implications," *Memorandum from the Department of State* (September 26, 1997): 4 (quoting Keston Institute).

[125] Dave Carpenter, "Russia's Parliament Passes Religion Bill," *Associated Press* (September 24, 1997).

[126] Tatiana Varzanova, "Muslims Are Opening Mosques, Although Some Are Obstructed," available at <www.stetson.edu/~psteeves/relnews>. On the number of mosques in 1983, see above note 41.

[127] Ramet, "Religious Policy in the Era of Gorbachev," 40.

[and] does not conform with the democratic principles of Russia and the Islamic religion." According to Ashirov, the law is a "direct insult to the principles of the Muslim religion" because, unlike Orthodoxy, Islam is not hierarchical. "When a Muslim society simply receives the blessing of Almighty Allah, it has the right to exist and it does not need the blessing of any Islamic patriarchs," let alone the bureaucrats of an ostensibly secular, democratic state.[128]

This insight illustrates how the legislation attempts to force other religions such as Islam into an Orthodox-centric frame. For instance, Article 8 divides religious organizations into local and centralized forms, allowing centralized ones (those with three or more local organizations) which have been registered in Russia for fifty or more years to use the words *Russia* or *Russian* in their titles. Even though the country's Muslims have been so organized since Stalin created the centralized "spiritual Directorates" in the early 1940s, this structure has never been organic to Islam, which is inherently decentralized.

Among the law's particular proscriptions which might be invoked against Muslim congregations is its prohibition on "actions entailing coercion of an individual." This prohibition addresses, in particular, actions "forcing members and followers of the religious association or other persons to alienate property which belongs to them for the use of the religious association."[129] One of the five "pillars" of Islam is to give *zakat* (alms) for the support of the faith and the poor, while *"submission* to the One God in all things is the central theme of Islam."[130] The law also provides for liquidation of religious organizations, banning of their activities, or refusal of re-registration for, inter alia, "propaganda of war, the igniting of social, racial, national or religious dissension or hatred between people, [or for] hindering a citizen from leaving a religious association by threatening harm to life, health, or property if there is a danger of this threat's actually being carried out, or by using force or other illegal actions."[131] Islam's traditional prohibition on apostasy, defined to include conversion to another religion, and its more extreme expressions of *jihad*, could very easily run afoul of these provisions of the new law.[132]

One need look no further than the recent past to realize that speculation concerning possible restrictive applications of the law against Muslims is not farfetched. In the city of Balashikh, near Moscow, the local administrator has refused since late 1996 to allocate land for construction of a mosque, on the grounds that "Islam is not traditional for this region of Russia."[133] Similar

---

[128] Ashirov's view was expressed at a hearing of the Duma Committee on Human Rights on August 28, 1997. *Tserkovno-obshchestvennyi Vestnik* (September 4, 1997), translated at <www.stetson.edu/~psteeves/relnews/council2808.html>.

[129] 1997 Law, ch. I, art. 3.6, ch. II, art. 14.2.

[130] See C. G. Weeramantry, *Islamic Jurisprudence: An International Perspective* (New York, 1988), 8.

[131] 1997 Law, ch. II, art. 14.2; ch. IV art. 27.3. See also ibid., ch. I, art. 3.6.

[132] See Arzt, "The Treatment of Religious Dissidents."

[133] Varzanova, "Muslims Are Opening Mosques."

interpretations could be applied in any region other than those where Muslims form a majority. Other religious groups—"traditional" to Russia generally, if not a particular locale—have already experienced this kind of official obstruction after the adoption of the religion law. Given the harassment that Chechens and other Muslim Caucasians have previously experienced at the hands of private thugs as well as the official militia in Moscow, the new law can be expected to incite further ethnic tension, both in the capital and without.

CONCLUSION

Only in 1990, on the verge of the collapse of the Soviet empire, would a Russian academic at a conference on Muslim societies be able to summarize the Soviet Union's situation this way: "Twenty years ago we considered religious beliefs to be dying. Now we are reaping the harvest of this neglect."[134] Surely Leonid Brezhnev would have been awakened from his customary torpor had he been aware in the 1970s of the imminent renaissance in the cultural, political, and religious identity of Russia's Muslims.

Islam has the potential of being linked with political and ideological resistance, and has been so linked in Russian history, particularly during periods of intensive Russification campaigns against cultural minorities. Therefore, while Muslim-Christian ideological conflict is not currently a flashpoint, in pointed contrast to the struggle of Orthodoxy vis-à-vis the rest of Christianity, the former risks being kindled in a backlash against excessive Russian governmental coercion in Chechnya and other parts of the Caucasus, for instance, or even in Moscow. But such a development is not predetermined, unless the majority persists in refusing to recognize that one can be "Russian" without being either a Slav or an Orthodox believer, just as one can be "English" without being a white Anglo-Saxon Anglican.

This is not a prescription for the adoption of an Anglo-American or Western model. Islam and Russian Orthodoxy, in fact, have more in common with each other than either does with the individualistic Western forms of Christianity. Russia is a Eurasian state, situated between East and West, with Islam an integral, indigenous part of its social fabric. Or, as explained by Sheikh Nafibulla Ashirov, chair of the executive committee of the Supreme Information Center of the Muslim Directorates of Russia:

> Allah created us as different tribes and has bestowed on us different cultures, different faces, different shaped eyes, different clothes. This forms the beauty of the world. If forests consisted only of birch trees or spruce trees, it would not be so interesting to walk in such forests. . . . Nature

---

[134] Dale F. Eickelman and Kamran Pasha, "Muslim Societies and Politics: Soviet and U.S. Approaches—A Conference Report," *Middle East Journal* 45/4 (Autumn 1991): 632.

created by Allah cannot be made uniform. It will resist such attempts. The same is true of people. . . . Our history proves it. An attempt was made to turn it all into Russians with a family name, first name and given name. But this attempt failed. Because this is unnatural.[135]

---

[135] "Press Conference with the Islamic Press Center of Russia regarding the Up-coming Elections to the State Duma." A similar parable is told by First Deputy Secretary Tatarkhan Kubanov in describing the goal of the Union of Muslims of Russia to work "in the name of Russia's prosperity": "A wise man said that 'til now Russia was like a bird with only one wing. When it tried to fly using just this one wing, it circled and fell. Now after the unification with Muslims, Russia has acquired a second wing that will lift this bird higher and further." "Press Conference on the Results of the First Congress of the Union of Muslims of Russia." The Russian politician Vasily Likhachev has similarly noted, "Russia has existed and will always exist in its historical niche between East and West, combining both in its national character and having the legacy of two great religions—Christianity and Islam." "Parliamentary Official Warns Politicians."

7.

RELATIONS BETWEEN RUSSIAN ORTHODOXY AND JUDAISM

———————◆———————

Yuriy Tabak

Any discussion of the relationship between Russian Orthodoxy and Judaism requires a careful definition of terms. For centuries, the terms *evrei* (Hebrew) and *iudei* (Jew) have been used interchangeably, even though *iudei* has a distinct meaning. Thus, secularized Jews have broken away from the religious community but have not lost their cultural and ethnic identity. Secularized Jews who no longer observe the faith nonetheless recognize the significance of traditional Jewish religious values. In this sense, the term *iudei* as conventionally applied in Russia to those who practice the Jewish faith is too narrow a term to denote the wider concept of *evreistvo* (Jewry) understood by today's Russian Orthodox Christian. Moreover, the very meaning of the word *iudei* in its historical and religious context is complex and contradictory. For this reason the wider term *evrei* is more apt, and it is that term which I have in mind in this chapter.

THE PLACE OF JUDAISM IN THE HOLY TRADITION

Contemporary attitudes of the Russian Orthodox Church toward Jews and Judaism can be properly understood only against a historical backdrop.[1] The Jewish-Orthodox relationship dates to the founding of the Russian state, when Jews from Western Europe and Khazars settled on the territory of Kievan Rus in the ninth and tenth centuries. It appears that the Jewish community was

---

[1] For a bibliography (in Russian) of historical relations between Orthodoxy and the Jewish community, see Zh. P. Likhtenburg, *Ot pervovo do poslednievo iz pravednikov. K istorii evreisko-khristianskikh otnoshenii* (Moscow, 1996), 107-8.

strong both socially and economically: Kievan Jews studied in the famous Jewish educational institutions of Europe, and Kiev was a leading trading center between East and West, with trade being conducted mainly by Jews and Italians.[2] Jewish religious influence was also significant from early times. It is no accident that in the *History of the Baptism of Rus* there is an account of how Prince Vladimir chose the future monotheistic state religion to replace old pagan beliefs, with Judaism as one of the pagan alternatives. Although the provenance and historical reliability of the *History* is unknown,[3] Kievan Rus clearly witnessed sharp polemic between Christians and Jews as evidenced by the strong anti-Jewish passages in the "Speeches of a Philosopher" contained in the *History*.

The Russian Orthodox Church, in the beginning, may well have employed anti-Jewish rhetoric mainly in the service of apologetics. But after the establishment of Christianity the polemic continued, as seen in the manuscripts of the time, such as *Sermon on Law and Grace* by the first Russian Metropolitan (Illarion), the thirteenth-century *Tolkovaya Paleia: Arkhivskiy khronograf*, and other works.[4] Alongside the polemical writings, there were practical attempts to convert Jews to Orthodoxy. The well-known episode in the *Life of St. Feodosiy*, when "the saint scolded the Jews and argued with them about Christ, calling them apostates and transgressors," provides a salient example.[5] The economic prosperity of the Jews, at times, led to increased hostility and hatred toward them. Thus was established the problematic situation of the Jews in ancient Russia, mirroring the situation of Jews in Western Europe—where periods of comparative calm and economic prosperity alternated with periods of religious repression, "bloody slander," and pogroms. The first pogrom in Ancient Rus took place in 1113, when the Jewish quarter in Kiev was destroyed.

As the Russian state developed further, the Jewish community remained effectively a persecuted ethnic and religious minority. The social and religious persecution of the Russian Jewish population assumed forms common to the West: exclusion from the professions, forced baptism, and bloody pogroms. The numerous Jewish ghettos in Western European towns could be compared to the Pale of Settlement in Imperial Russia. In Europe, the authorities blamed Jewish influences for the Albigensian and other heretical movements in the Catholic world, and subjected Jews to cruel persecution. Likewise in Russia,

[2] *Evreiskaya entsiklopediya* (St. Petersburg, 1906-12), 9:516-17.

[3] See, for example, M. Yu Braichevskiy, *Utverzhdeniye khristianstva na Rusi* (Kiev, 1989), 217-23.

[4] S. Dudakov, *Istoriya odnovo mira* (Moscow, 1993), 9-14.

[5] It is not inconceivable that some Jews were baptized against their will, along with a significant proportion of the pagan Slav population, and that this was designed to test the loyalty of the Jews and expose any secret heresy. See G. M. Barats, *Povesti i skazaniya drevnerusskoi pis'mennosti, imeiushchiye otnosheniye k evreiam i evreistvu* (Kiev, 1906).

the fifteenth-century "Judaizing" movement brought a number of misfortunes to the Jewish community.[6]

In both Europe and Russia, state policy and official practice were governed by a series of shifting ideological, economic, and social factors. The inevitable result was variation in the degree of repression of Jews. The Christian community, linked by numerous trading and economic ties to the Jewish community, maintained a relatively neutral attitude toward the Jews during the calm periods; even individual personal friendships were not uncommon.[7] But the mixture of fear and hatred of Jews, characteristic of medieval Christian consciousness, never completely disappeared: these latent emotions smoldered beneath the socio-economic necessity of maintaining the status quo. With the emergence of any new circumstances in society, whether in the social, economic, religious, or governmental spheres, or in the internal dynamics of the Jewish-Christian debate, these latent emotions quickly reached the boiling point. The defenseless Jewish community would then become the target of harsh economic measures, a pawn in political games, or a convenient focus for the lower classes to vent their own discontent.[8]

The fundamental difference between anti-Jewish measures in Europe and anti-Jewish measures in Russia lies in the roles of the churches.[9] Western church policy in relation to the Jews was unsettled. The history of the Roman Catholic Church contains many examples—including Popes Innocent IV and Gregory X—of a tolerant and humane attitude toward Jews, protecting them from tyranny and the worst anti-Semitic attacks. However, many negative examples may also be adduced, where church authorities initiated or readily participated in anti-Semitic legislation and policy. At times, the Western Church even adopted a more actively anti-Semitic position than the state, which periodically defended the Jewish community.[10]

---

[6] *Evreiskaya entsyklopedia*, 2:115-16; *Kratkaya evreiskaya entsyklopedia* (Jerusalem, 1976), 7:289.

[7] See further J. Katz, *Jews in Medieval Europe* (Jerusalem, 1997) (now available in Russian).

[8] For works analyzing the roots of anti-Semitism and its manifestations in the Christian world, see Gavin I. Langmuir, *History, Religion and Anti-Semitism* (New York, 1990), and Yves Chevalier, *L'antisemitisme* (Paris, 1988).

[9] In pointing out the differences between the Western Church and Russian Orthodox Church regarding their attitudes toward the Jews, it does not follow that this is an example of the usual opposition of West versus East or Catholicism versus Orthodoxy. The policies of local Eastern Orthodox churches toward the Jews varied widely—from the relatively tolerant attitude (primarily in the new era) of the Serbian and Bulgarian churches to the clearly anti-Semitic views of the Greek Orthodox and particularly the Romanian Orthodox churches. See *Kratkaya evreiskaya entsyklopedia*, 6:729-33.

[10] See generally Malcolm Hay, *The Blood of Your Brother* (Jerusalem, 1991) (now available in Russian).

Conversely, the complicity of the Russian Orthodox Church in active anti-Semitism is much harder to show. All anti-Jewish decisions were made by state administrative organs, acting on the authority of emperors, state committees, and ministries. Even if the Ecclesiastical Collegium under Peter (and, later, the Holy Synod) agreed with and approved anti-Jewish measures, these institutions were essentially government departments. Before Peter the Great, when the Church preserved some degree of independence, it is hard to find any definite statements of an official anti-Jewish policy in the decisions of local and diocesan councils, decrees of the Patriarch, or elsewhere. Although one might assume that the church authorities had an influence on the state in implementing anti-Jewish measures, there is no conclusive evidence to support such an assumption.[11] Undoubtedly, the Russian Church can be criticized for its total submission to the state in the synodical period (after the abolition of the Patriarchate in the early eighteenth century), for its inability to express an independent opinion, and for its failure to demonstrate love for the neighbor through defending those who were persecuted—as the basic teaching of the Gospel would dictate. Unlike the Western Church, the Russian Orthodox Church took no steps to protect the Jews. But also unlike the Western churches, it developed no anti-Semitic policies.

While the Church's official statements were largely silent about the Jews, individual clerics and priests of the Russian Orthodox Church did betray anti-Semitic attitudes. The cruelest attacks on Jews can be found in Orthodox polemics, in the sermons and speeches of the most illustrious clerics and hierarchs of the Russian Orthodox Church—from Iosif of Volokolamsk to St. John of Kronstadt. At the end of the nineteenth century, the anti-Semitic views of Archbishop Nikon of Vologda, Hieromonk Iliodor (Trufanov), and Archpriest Ioann Vostorgov were widely known. Because an official church position had not been formulated, these individuals were merely reflecting the general population's widely held negative attitudes toward the Jews.

By contrast, though, many Russian Orthodox clerics, including senior hierarchs, openly defended persecuted Jews—at least from the second half of the nineteenth century. In Russia, perhaps more than in the West, church hierarchs and theology professors advocated the social rights of Jews, refuting accusations that Jews *conducted* pogroms and ritual sacrifices and were organizing a "world-

---

[11] The entry on "Orthodoxy" in the *Kratkaya evreiskaya entsiklopedia*, devoted to the Russian Orthodox Church (7:733-43), gives numerous examples of persecution of the Jews in Russia, including religious persecution, but gives no evidence of the direct participation of the Church, either in legislative terms or in the conduct of policy. Although the authors of the article state that the active role of the Church in inciting the government to conduct anti-Jewish acts (for example, in the case of Ivan the Terrible's policy in the defeated territories) is "obvious," no facts are given to support this.

wide conspiracy."[12] Soloviev, Bulgakov, Ilyin, and other prominent Russian religious philosophers played an active role in this Jewish-rights movement. But neither numerous speeches by the Christian community nor impassioned appeals on behalf of the Jews could alter the Russian population's general hatred of Jews, which had existed since medieval times. State and religious laws accompanied and reinforced these prevailing attitudes about Jews.

While Jews in Europe began gradually to gain broader religious and social rights, in Russia the conditions of Jews deteriorated. In contrast to the West, Russia's liberal and democratic tendencies were too weak to stand against the reactionary authoritarian views that permeated all levels of public life.[13]

Moreover, Russian Orthodox beliefs about Jews rest on changeless religious teachings—formulated through ecumenical councils and set down in Holy Tradition, which is deemed to be "from God." This "Holy Tradition" embraces the whole historical experience of the Church—the Bible, service books, and prayer books; the decrees of the ecumenical councils; the writings of the Holy Fathers; the lives of the saints; the canon law, iconography, music, and architecture.[14] Holy Tradition, by its very definition, is "sacred"; its religious and cultural values and relevance are beyond question. And the Holy Tradition dating from the period of the fathers is overtly anti-Semitic. Both in the decisions of the ecumenical councils and in the works of the holy fathers, Jews are called "murderers of God" and "a despised people." St. John Chrysostom called the Jews "unclean and foul" and the synagogue "a refuge of demons." Nearly all of the most respected church fathers echo similar sentiments toward the Jews, including the most respected church activists from Bishop Ignatiy Bryanchannikov to St. John of Kronstadt.[15] Not one church father of Russian Orthodoxy has professed a genuine love for the Jews, in accordance with the biblical commandments. Generations of Christians were educated in this "teaching of contempt" in relation to Jews. Whereas Western churches have developed a new position regarding Judaism, Russian Orthodox teaching still rests on medieval conceptions. Thus the most extreme Russian Orthodox anti-Semites can logically claim that their monstrous anti-Jewish invective is based upon "church teaching." Given this history, it seems rather inappropriate for modern authors angrily to denounce anti-Semites as

---

[12] See *Pravoslavnaya tserkov I sevreii: XIX-XX vv.* The most important extracts from the speeches of Russian church hierarchs in defense of the Jews can be found in the important article by V. N. Toporov, "Spor ili druzhba?" *ABQUINOX. Sbornik pamyati o. Aleksandra Mena* (Moscow, 1991), 91-162.

[13] See Richard Pipes, *Rossiya pri starom rezhime* (Moscow, 1993).

[14] Archpriest Foma Khonko, *Osnovy pravoslaviya* (New York, 1987), 9.

[15] See T. Reinach, *Textes d'auteurs grecs et romains relatifs au judaisme* (Paris, 1895) (and subsequent editions); and *Israiil v proshlom, nastoyashchem I budushchem* (Sergiev Posad, 1915); Protoierei Ioann Sergiev (Kronstadtskiy), *Nachalo I konets nashevo zemnovo mira* (St. Petersburg, 1904).

less than "true Christians,"[16] for such pronouncements must implicitly include the most respected pillars of the Orthodox Church on the list of "pseudo-Christians," given the unfortunate two-thousand-year history of Judeo-Christian relations.

Some observers have sought to define "true Christianity" by identifying those positive tendencies in Christian history which opposed anti-Semitism, looking in particular to the Orthodox traditions of the late-nineteenth and early-twentieth centuries.[17] These attempts have been only partly successful, for in condemning anti-Semitism and advocating religious tolerance, most Orthodox priests saw the resolution of the Jewish question only in terms of conversion to Christianity (in the "last days"). They attributed the Jewish reluctance to accept Christianity not only to the unworthiness of Christians, but to the spiritual "blindness" of the Jews. The Jews were often not perceived as brothers and sisters, but as enemies who had to be "loved." This infelicitous position has been proved by a large body of Western academic research to be unsuccessful in rooting out Christian anti-Semitism,[18] despite the opinions of contemporary liberal Orthodox thinkers and Russian religious philosophers.

JUDAISM AND RUSSIAN ORTHODOXY TODAY

With these historical tensions from Russian Orthodoxy as a whole in mind, it is useful to divide current Russian Orthodox Christians into four main groups for further assessment of their attitudes toward Jews and Judaism.

First, a relatively small but active part of the lower clergy, in which monks play an important role together with lay activists, belong to a number of social and political movements operating mainly under the banner of Orthodoxy. These movements combine anti-Jewish and anti-Western (including Western Christian) ideologies, often with anti-democratic tendencies as well. The Russian National Council, the Russian National Union, the Union of Orthodox Brothers, and others are among such organizations whose membership includes many prominent cultural figures, writers, artists, and cinematographers. The journals *Moskva* and *Molodaya gvardiya;* the newspapers *Zavtra, Russkiy vestnik*, and *Russkaya gazeta;* and dozens of books from ideologues express the views of these groups.[19] They promote various ideas regarding the salva-

---

[16] See articles by M. Chaikovskiy and Z.A. Krakhmal'nikova in *Russkaya ideia I evrei* (Moscow, 1994).

[17] See *Pravoslavnaya tserkov I evreii: XIX-XX vv.*

[18] See A. Roy Eckhardt, *Elder and Younger Brothers* (New York, 1967), and sources cited therein.

[19] Some of these papers which say they are "Orthodox" (e.g., *Zemshchina, Tushino, Russkoye Voskreseniye,* and others) concentrate almost entirely on the Jewish question, and advocate the most virulent anti-Semitism. They are periodically tried in court on grounds of incitement to racial hatred, but receive no substantial punishment.

tion of Russia from the "Jewish conspiracy"—from the screening of the ethnic and religious background of prospective governmental officials to mass expulsion of the Jewish community.[20]

Second, the overwhelming majority of rural and urban parish priests and laypeople who regularly attend church is characterized by a relatively low level of religious education and church life centered on conscientious observance of Orthodox rituals and fasts. The Jewish-Christian debate has no bearing on their everyday lives, although some harbor a degree of underlying suspicion and fear of the Jews, arising from their sketchy knowledge of Holy Tradition regarding the Jews "who crucified Christ."[21] While this negative attitude toward Jews is generally passive, a changing social and political climate or incitement from the first group might stimulate a growth in religious aggression toward the Jews, as has occurred more than once in Russian history. Both education and democratization as a means to reduce religious intolerance are particularly important to discourage the anti-Semitic tendencies of this group.

Third, there is the church leadership and the main authors and exponents of the official church position. The senior hierarchs of the church ascended to their positions during the Communist era, and this has undoubtedly left its mark on their psychological outlook and the way they conduct church policy. Because of the financial and economic dependency of the Church on the state, the hierarchy necessarily gauges the strength of competing ideologies in the state organs of power before developing general positions. The church leadership wavers between adherence to the conservative tradition and the demands of the political establishment. At the same time, any important socio-political movement in modern Russia, resting on "national patriotic," democratic reformist, or other principles, must struggle to define the role and position of Orthodoxy in modern society, as has been demonstrated by the conflict concerning the 1997 Law on Freedom of Conscience.[22] The church hierarchy must

---

[20] "Poetomu my dolzhny gnat' IKH v sheiu" *Russkoye Voskreseniye* 4/12 (1997): 4.

[21] See *Pravoslavnaya tserkov i evrei: XIX-XX vv*, containing the first and, to my knowledge, the only sociological study which compares the attitudes of Orthodox and atheists to Jews (V. Bozenko, "Antisemitizm I pravoslaviye v sovremennoi Rossii," 99-106), published in 1992. Both Orthodox and atheists were categorized according to age and education. The author concluded that there is a lower level of anti-Semitism among Orthodox believers than among atheists. However, Bozenko did not take into account a very important factor—that the majority of those surveyed were nominally Orthodox, in the context of the traditional identification "Russian = Orthodox." The more systematic approach of L. Byzov and S. Filatov yields different results. According to their research, practicing Orthodox Christians are more prejudiced in their attitude toward Jews and Judaism than non-believers. "Religiya i obschestvo sevodnya," in *Religiya i Demokratiya*, 9-42.

[22] See "Materially parliamentskikh slushanii: Svoboda sovesti I prava cheloveka v Rossiiskoi Federatsii," *Analiticheskiy vypusk* (Moscow, 1995), No. 13.

navigate among a host of other factors, too, when deciding official church positions, including competing socio-religious interests, internal power struggles, and the need to preserve face in Western church circles.

The current ideological positions of the Russian Orthodox Church mirror the same tendencies of Russian politics: uncertainty and instability. These two features characterize every area of church life, including liturgical reform, social policy, the ecumenical movement—and the issue of anti-Semitism. On the one hand, it appeared that the Patriarch of Moscow and All Russia, Aleksii II, had defined the position of the Russian Orthodox Church in a 1991 speech to the rabbis of New York.[23] The Patriarch addressed the Jews as "brothers" and strenuously rejected all forms of anti-Semitism. However, the speech aroused strong criticism both from the Russian Orthodox Church Abroad and from the Moscow Patriarchate, especially the monastic community, and it seems to have had little lasting impact on the church's attitudes toward Jews. On the other hand, the anti-Semitic sermons, articles, and speeches of the now deceased Metropolitan of St. Petersburg and Ladoga, Ioann (Snychev), have been widely circulated in the past few years.[24] The Moscow Patriarchate's response has been limited to the inadequate statement that these are merely the personal views of the Metropolitan. Neither has the Moscow Patriarchate reacted to the dozens of openly anti-Semitic books published by Orthodox authors, nor to the articles published in the fascist and neo-fascist press, which call themselves "Orthodox." In cathedrals and Orthodox bookstalls, it is possible to buy a copy of the viciously anti-Semitic *Protocols of the Elders of Zion* printed under the title of a book by S. Nielus, *Velikoye v malom*. At times, even the Church itself has published openly anti-Semitic books.[25]

The hierarchy has not responded to the few clergy and laypeople who are troubled by the problem of anti-Semitism, nor to the appeals of Western theologians on the same question.[26] Instead, with the exception of Metropolitan Ioann and his followers, the Russian Orthodox hierarchy prefers not to touch the Jewish question at all, but instead to make general appeals for tolerance as

---

[23] See "Speech by Patriarch Aleksii to the Rabbis of New York, 13 November 1991." Issued in Russian by TOO Pallada publishers, 1992. "Molim vas–prislushaityes," *Russkaya pravoslavnaya tserkov v sovetskoye vremya* 2 (Moscow, 1995): 335-38. Rumor has it that some sections of the monastic community have even stopped using the Patriarch's name at the celebration of the liturgy.

[24] The basic ideas of Metropolitan Ioann can be found in his book *Samoderzhaviye dukha* (St. Petersburg, 1994). See also a detailed review in I. Levinskaya, "Rannyy Gitler, Pozdniy Stalin, niezlobniy Ivan Grozniy I drugiye," *Bar'ier* (St. Petersburg, 1994): 11-13.

[25] See, e.g., the "memoirs" of Prince Zhevakhov, prepared for publication by the publishing department of the Spasso Preobrazhenskiy Staropigal'ny Monastery.

[26] See *Pravoslavnaya tserkov I evrei: XIX-XX vv*, 81, 82, 92; Yu. Tabak, "Ochen aktual'no, no sovremenno secretno," *Megapolis-Express* 18/30 (August 1990): 13.

they hope to avoid criticism from both the conservative and democratic factions in the Church.

Fourth, there are priests campaigning for a renewal in church life who advocate ecumenical dialogue with members of other Christian denominations and strongly condemn Orthodox anti-Semitism. The views of this group are reflected in the journals *Logos* and *Strannitsy*, in the newspapers *Russkaya mysl, Sevodnya,* and *Nezavisimaya gazeta,* and in the broadcasts of the Moscow-based radio station *Sofia.* Some laypeople, the majority of whom are parishioners of Moscow churches, share these views. However, this group of priests and laypeople is very small, and adherents of this position are constantly attacked by conservative factions in the Muscovite clergy.[27] Moreover, the contradictions inherent in the Russian Orthodox position do not allow this group of Orthodox believers to present a potent theological argument in support of its position.[28]

What concrete outcomes may emerge from these attitudes of the Russian Orthodox Church and its members toward the Jews? Overt religious persecution of the Jews in its medieval forms seems unlikely—in part because Russia will hopefully continue to follow a civilized and democratic path,[29] and in part because, sadly, the Russian Jewish community is slowly diminishing. The Russian Jewish population at the end of 1993, based on the official census, was estimated at less than 400,000.[30] Most practicing religious Jews have emigrated, and the overwhelming majority of those who remain are almost entirely assimilated and secularized. The continuation of democratization and the removal of the notorious "fifth paragraph" from passports (designating Jews as a separate nationality) will probably speed up this process of assimilation. Furthermore, a number of the Jewish intelligentsia have converted to Christianity over the last few decades,[31] and a series of complex sociological

---

[27] See *Russkaya mysl* (October 24-30, 1994): 8-9.

[28] Only archpriest Vitali Borovoy has tried to find the reasons for the sin of anti-Semitism in the Orthodox Church tradition. See V. Borovoy "Christian Orthodoxy in the Modern World," in "Orthodox Christians and Jews on Continuity and Renewal," *Immanuel* 26/27 (Jerusalem, 1994).

[29] There are admittedly single tragic events, such as the recent desecration of Jewish graves and the arson attack on the Moscow synagogue, which unfortunately may recur in the future, indicating that anti-Semitism has not died out. But this type of vandalism at present is more a product of racism or general hooliganism than a conscious demonstration of religious (Christian) anti-Semitism.

[30] *Kratkaya Yevreiskaya Entsiklopediya* (Jerusalem, 1994), vol. 7, col. 402. Admittedly, the statistical data for the Jewish population of Russia given in foreign sources are usually higher than the data of Russian statistics, sometimes almost twice as high (I am grateful to Professor Donna Arzt for this information).

[31] See T. Ptushkina G. Yeremeyev, "U Kosmy I Damiana," in *Pravoslavnaya tserkov I evereii: XIX-XX vv,* 118-23; L. Vorontsova and S. Filatov, "Rossiiskiye evreii I Tserkov v zerkale sotsiologii," in ibid., 130, 133.

factors still divides the Christian and Jewish communities, rendering attempts at dialogue and mutual understanding much more difficult.[32]

However, neither the low probability of pogroms nor the objective difficulties in Judeo-Christian relations should become an excuse for stagnation in Christian religious thought. For it is only through reevaluation of the central issues for the Christian—of the fate of Israel, of the Jewish roots of Christianity, and of anti-Semitism as the worst sin in the history of Christianity—that "the crisis of the medieval world view" (to use Soloviev's expression) can be overcome. And only then can Orthodox-Jewish relations take a decisive step forward, following in the footsteps of Western Christians.

---

[32] See Yu. Tabak: "The Difficulties and Perspectives of Jewish Christian Interreligious Dialogue," in *Dia-Logos. Religia i obshchestvo 1997* (Moscow, 1997), 43-60.

8.

SEVENTH-DAY ADVENTISTS

——————◆——————

Mikhail M. Kulakov

The Seventh-day Adventist movement, the beginnings of which in Russia go back to 1886,[1] has one system of beliefs and practices which is more or less common to all Adventists in 172 countries. All of its major missionary endeavors are coordinated and directed from the movement's headquarters in Silver Spring, Maryland, USA. One of many Christian groups of Western origin in the former Soviet Union, the Adventist movement in Russia has experienced a dramatic recent increase in members: membership tripled from 34,146 in 1990 to 98,963 by the end of 1994.[2] This growth stems from a series of joint evangelistic efforts by both foreign and local evangelists. This chapter examines some important recent developments within the Adventist church in Russia, paying special attention to the relationships between foreign and indigenous Adventists in Russia and to Adventist attitudes toward other Christian churches and the ecumenical movement.

RELATIONSHIPS WITH OTHER CHRISTIAN CHURCHES AND RELIGIOUS ORGANIZATIONS[3]

Few Adventists are aware of the important official statement on relationships with other religious bodies adopted by the Adventist General Conference ex-

---

[1] For the history of Adventists in Russia, *S dobroi vest'yu k svoim sootechestvennikam: Istoriya Tserkvi khristian adventistov sed'mogo dnya v Rossii* (Zaoksky, 1996).

[2] See the report by Ted N. Wilson, the former president of the Adventist EuroAsia Division, "Bozhii chudesa . . . ," *Adventistski Vestnik* 3 (1995): 11.

[3] For a review of early Adventist attitudes to cooperation in evangelism and foreign missions, see Keith A. Francis, "Adventist Attitudes to the World Missionary Conference," *Studies in Church History* 32.

ecutive committee in 1926. This statement now forms a part of the "General Conference Working Policy O 75,"[4] but is strangely absent from the Russian edition of this document. Here are some excerpts from the statement:

1. We recognize those agencies that lift up Christ before men as a part of the divine plan for evangelization of the world, and we hold in high esteem Christian men and women in other communions who are engaged in winning souls to Christ.
2. When interdivision work brings us in contact with other Christian societies and religious bodies, the spirit of Christian courtesy, frankness, and fairness shall prevail at all times.
3. If a change of conviction leads a member of our church to feel no longer in harmony with Seventh-day Adventist faith and practice, we recognize not only the right but also the responsibility of that member to change, without opprobrium, religious affiliation in accord with belief. We expect other religious bodies to respond in the same spirit of religious liberty. . . .
6. The Seventh-day Adventist Church is unable to confine its mission to restricted geographical areas because of its understanding of the gospel commission's mandate. . . . Any restriction which limits witness to specified geographical areas . . . becomes an abridgement of the gospel commission. The Seventh-day Adventist Church also acknowledges the rights of other religious persuasions to operate without geographic restrictions.[5]

A typical Adventist attitude toward other Christian churches is largely determined by the understanding that the Adventist Church is the only true "remnant" (spoken of in Rev. 12:17), which all faithful children of God from other churches are invited to join. The attitude to other church structures (but not individuals within those institutions) as "fallen" ecclesial bodies is partly based on the interpretation of the "threefold union" of Revelation 16:13-14 found in the writings of Adventist pioneer Ellen G. White.[6] In "Testimonies for the Church" she wrote:

When Protestantism shall stretch her hand across the gulf to grasp the hand of the Roman power, when she shall reach over the abyss to clasp hands with spiritualism, when, under the influence of this threefold union, our country [USA] shall repudiate every principle of its Constitution as a Protes-

---

[4] For the complete text of the statement, see policy O 75, "Relationships with Other Christian Churches and Religious Organizations," in *Working Policy of the General Conference of Seventh-day Adventists* (Washington, D.C., 1996), 401-3.

[5] Ibid.

[6] Adventists believe that the gift of prophesy was manifested in the church through the writings of Ellen G. White. They also hold that her writings do not in any way take the place of the Bible.

tant and republican government . . . then we may know that the time has come for the marvelous working of Satan and that the end is near.[7]

The Adventist community is not monolithic in its thinking on this matter, however. There are a considerable number of Adventist pastors who subscribe to a more inclusive and complex understanding of the "remnant." They emphasize that E. G. White also suggested that our ministers should seek to come near to the ministers of other denominations and involve themselves in various evangelistic and academic projects with them.

One positive practical development in the area of interdenominational relations was the recent decision taken by the leaders of the Euro-Asia Division of the Adventist Church to establish public relations and religious liberty departments at all levels of the Russian Adventist organization. In July 1996 a special educational seminar was held in Moscow for the newly elected local leaders of this department and for religious liberty specialists from other denominations.[8] Two quite different opinions were expressed and debated during the seminar: (1) that within the Russian Orthodox tradition there are writers and Bible commentators whose works Adventists can safely use for their edification— for example, the commentaries of Russian Orthodox theologians such as Professor A. P. Lopukhin; and (2) that the Russian Orthodox Church is a "fallen" ecclesial body which consists of a mixture of paganism and superstition, and that nothing wholesome can be found in its teachings. These two divergent views roughly reflect the wide spectrum of attitudes toward the Russian Orthodox Church found among Russian Adventists at large. The leaders of the Euro-Asian Division are currently taking a number of concrete steps to raise the level of education and competence of the pastors in the area of interdenominational relations. However, the urgency of the complex modern religious and sociopolitical situation demands immediate action. Virtually none of the significant Adventist books and monographs dealing with interchurch relations and religious liberty issues have been translated into Russian yet.

ADVENTISTS AND THE ECUMENICAL MOVEMENT[9]

Representatives of the Adventist Church participate in the various councils of churches (whether national, regional, or international) only as observers or

---

[7] Ellen G. White, *Testimonies for the Church,* 9 vols. (Mountain View, Calif., 1948), 5:451.

[8] See the special report issued by the Adventist Department of Public Relations in Moscow, "Otdel obschestvennykh svyazei i religioznoi svobody EvroAsiatskogo divisiona Tserkvi ASD soobshchaet," *Adventistski Vestnik* 3 (1996): 20-21.

[9] For a thorough treatment of the history of the ecumenical movement from the Adventist perspective, see Bert B. Beach, *Ecumenism: Boon or Bane?* (Washington, D.C., 1974). A brief summary of the Adventist position on ecumenical cooperation by Bert B. Beach can be found in the report "Otversta velikaya i shirokaya dver' . . . ," *Adventistski Vestnik* 4 (1995): 12-13.

consultants. The Adventist attitude to the World Council of Churches is in many ways similar to the position of a number of conservative evangelical groups. The study document officially released by the General Conference of Seventh-day Adventists in connection with their world session in New Orleans, Louisiana, in June 1985, remarks:

> While the Seventh-day Adventist Church does not completely condemn the ecumenical movement and its main organizational manifestation, the World Council of Churches, she has been critical of various aspects and activities. Few would wish to deny that ecumenism has had laudable aims and some positive influences. Its great goal is visible Christian unity. No Adventist can be opposed to the unity Christ Himself prayed for. The ecumenical movement has promoted kinder interchurch relations with more dialogue and less diatribe and helped remove unfounded prejudices. Through its various organizations and activities, the ecumenical movement has provided more accurate and updated information on churches, spoken for religious liberty and human rights, combated against the evils of racism, and drawn attention to socioeconomic implications of the gospel. In all this the intentions have been good and some of the fruit palatable. However, in the total picture, the banes tend to outweigh the boons.[10]

Among the "banes" the document mentions: the WCC's disregard of the issues of heresy and apostasy; "little emphasis on personal sanctification and revival"; "the danger that ecumenical quicksands of doctrinal softness will suck churches into denominational death"; unacceptable understanding of biblical authority and apocalyptic prophecy; shifting of the emphasis in evangelism from personal conversion to changing unjust structures in society; unacceptable understanding of sociopolitical responsibility; and the "somewhat ambiguous" WCC stance on religious liberty in more recent years.[11] With regard to ecumenical cooperation the document states:

> Should Adventists cooperate ecumenically? Adventists should cooperate insofar as the authentic gospel is proclaimed and crying human needs are being met. The Seventh-day Adventist Church wants no entangling memberships and refuses any compromising relationships that might tend to water down her distinct witness. However, Adventists wish to be "conscientious cooperators." The ecumenical movement as an agency of co-

---

[10] For the complete text of the statement see "Seventh-day Adventists and the Ecumenical Movement" in *Statements, Guidelines & Other Documents. A Compilation.* (Communication Department, General Conference, Seventh-day Adventist Church, 1996), 99-108.

[11] Ibid., 100-104.

operation has acceptable aspects; as an agency for organic unity of churches, it is much more suspect.[12]

COOPERATION IN THE AREA OF RELIGIOUS LIBERTY

The sphere of religious liberty represents one area where Adventists on the whole show a high degree of interdenominational cooperation. The International Religious Liberty Association (IRLA) was formed in Moscow in 1992 on the initiative and with the financial support of the Adventist Church.[13] It has played a significant and positive role in the consolidation of efforts of many of those concerned about the freedom of conscience in Russia and the principle of the separation of church and state. Leading Russian human rights activists, such as Gleb Yakunin and V. V. Borshchev, and specialists in the legal aspects of religious freedom, such as Dr. Yuri Rozenbaum and Anatoli Pchelintsev, have joined the association. However, the present leadership of the Russian Adventist Church believes that it is becoming increasingly difficult to ensure that the Russian section of IRLA continues to remain a representative and influential body faithful to its original goals and moderate methods, and that, due to recent changes in leadership, it may turn into a forum for radical human rights activists and religious minorities. The Moscow Patriarchate has already indicated that it is not prepared to share membership of the association on a par with representatives of new religious movements and those Russian Orthodox groups which do not recognize its authority. The present leaders of the Adventist Church are not unanimous in their understanding of the significance of IRLA's activities for the overall Christian mission in Russia. Those who react cautiously to pleas for greater denominational openness, social involvement, and dialogue believe that recognition and influence in society will rise naturally in proportion to the increase in membership and hence insist that all available funds and human resources should be channeled exclusively to direct "soul winning" activities understood in traditional terms.

SPECIFIC PROBLEMS OF MISSION IN RUSSIA

PUBLISHING

One of the first fruits of *perestroika* and the new state law on the freedom of the press, the Adventist publishing house "The Source of Life" in Zaoksky, Tula *oblast,* was established in 1992. In its first four years of operation it has

---

[12] Ibid., 105.

[13] For more information on IRLA, see its publication *Svoboda i Sovest': Zhurnal mezhdunarodnoi assotsiatsii relgioznoi svobody* (Zaoksky, 1992).

produced fourteen million copies of about seventy titles of books and brochures. However, most of these publications are translations from English, with only a few exceptions. The director of the publishing house, Roy Terretta, has a clear understanding of the general anti-Western backlash prevailing across the country today and of the need for books written by Russian authors in which Christian ideas and principles are illustrated by stories or tales familiar to Russians from their youth—something that would always be missing in translated literature, no matter how well it was done.[14] He is concerned about the need to nurture and develop local authors, but this is not an easy task.

Russian Adventists and other Protestant denominations have already missed a unique opportunity to give their able young people professional training in creative writing and Christian journalism. In the wake of *perestroika,* the department of journalism of Moscow State University extended such an offer to national religious organizations, and only the Russian Orthodox Church took advantage of the opportunity.

THEOLOGICAL EDUCATION

Only established in 1988, Zaoksky Theological Seminary is steadily developing its programs of intensive pastoral training at both undergraduate and graduate levels.[15] Of all the Protestant educational institutions recently opened in Russia, it is probably the largest and the best equipped. One of the most difficult challenges which the administration currently faces is the challenge of contextualizing educational programs which have been largely imported from the West. Should there be any contextualization, any reference to and any dialogue with the Eastern Orthodox tradition at all? Has God's Spirit been active in Russia before the arrival of Protestant Evangelicals, and if so, to what extent? While a handful of Zaoksky seminary teachers have embarked on a serious study of the Eastern Orthodox tradition, the question is far from being resolved. The textbooks written for Western Protestant educational institutions usually make no reference to the Eastern Orthodox tradition and the history of Christianity in Eastern Europe.

CHRISTIAN BROADCASTING AND INTERCHURCH OPENNESS

Established in 1991, the "Voice of Hope" Christian radio station was among the first to broadcast on such national state channels as "Radio Russia" and "Radio-1," whose transmitters cover almost the whole territory of the Russian Federation. "Voice of Hope" is one of the few denominational radio stations which concentrate not on narrow confessional doctrinal instruction but

---

[14] On the current state of denominational journalism, see O. Zhigankov, "Sila pechatnogo slova," *Adventistski Vestnik* 4 (1994): 23-24.

[15] For more information on Zaoksky Seminary, see Mikhail M. Kulakov, *God's Soviet Miracles* (Boise, Idaho, 1993).

on drawing the attention of listeners to basic Christian values and providing a Christian perspective on current events.[16] The station's producers quite often invite prominent figures of other Christian denominations (including the Russian Orthodox Church) to take part in the programs. Such openness is not always well received by those within Adventist circles who would prefer to hear the direct preaching of some of the distinctively Adventist doctrinal teachings. Yet the positive results and the authority which this station enjoys on a national level do not give these critics enough grounds for enforcing ideological censorship from within. The station's mail shows that many Orthodox people regularly listen to this program. The station's producers say that the philosophy behind their programming is not to promote a particular church, but to stimulate and nourish in their listeners a drive for genuine spiritual life, and as further contact with listeners reveals, many find spiritual fulfillment not in the Adventist Church but in various Protestant and Orthodox churches.

According to a 1996 study conducted by the department of journalism of Moscow State University, the largest listening audience of the "Voice of Hope" consists of those who have "no specific religious orientation." The study thus concludes that this station "can be regarded as the leader in modern Christian radio broadcasting in Russia."[17] The work of this station is clearly one of the successful Russian experiments in interchurch openness, bridge-building, and cultural sensitivity in media evangelism.

A MODEL OF NATURAL INTEGRATION

The Russian Christian Grammar School in Tula is a good example of how it is possible to have a high commitment to evangelism alongside an equally high degree of confessional openness and toleration. Established in 1991 through the enthusiasm and vision of its present director, Maria Grishutkina,[18] the school has grown into an accredited institution of some 30 teachers and 150 students, and offers a complete program of secondary education.

Mrs. Grishutkina says that although the members of the teaching staff do not belong to one denomination, they all share the common Bible-based philosophy of Christian education adopted by the school. Only 40 percent of the teaching staff are members of the local Seventh-day Adventist church, which is rather atypical for Adventist church schools both in Russia and abroad.[19] Several of the other teachers consider themselves Russian Orthodox by birth. The

---

[16] See Valeri Demidov, "Golos Nadezhdy: Pyat' let v efire," *Adventistski Vestnik* 3 (1996): 5-8.

[17] M. M. Lukina, *Khristianskiye programmy na kanalakh natsional'nogo radioveshchyaniya Rossii (Opyt kachestvennogo issledovaniya)* (Moscow, 1996), 41.

[18] See Olga Filatova, "K Tebe vedut stopy moi," *Adventistski Vestnik* 1 (1995): 21-23.

[19] For the official Adventist position on this issue, see "Seventh-day Adventist Philosophy of Education," policy FE 05 40, "Achievement of Objectives," in *Working Policy*, 207.

school is successfully exploring a number of creative ways to teach central Bible themes without a special emphasis on distinctively Adventist or Russian Orthodox interpretations. The emphasis is rather on creating an atmosphere conducive to the natural development of a Christian world view and the ability to think for oneself. Less than 10 percent of the students are Adventist, which is also unusual for an Adventist school. The students represent almost every sector of Russian society: quite a number are from the affluent families of "new Russians." In Tula the school is well known for its high academic and moral standards and is felt by some to present healthy competition to the Russian Orthodox Grammar School directed by Father Lev Makhno. Some claim that the Orthodox grammar school was opened to counterbalance the Adventist initiative; at that time a number of non-Adventist teachers initially employed by Mrs. Grishutkina quickly changed camps when they were offered a higher salary by Father Makhno.

Despite this and other setbacks (some, unfortunately, from within her own confession), Mrs. Grishutkina is convinced that building an exclusivist denominational fortress (be it Adventist or Russian Orthodox) is counterproductive to the task of scattering the seeds of the Gospel.

THE PROS AND CONS OF FOREIGN MISSIONARIES[20]

For decades before *perestroika*, Adventists in the Soviet Union tried to reestablish official contact with their central leadership (the General Conference) and to be formally incorporated into the world body of their fellow believers. This became possible only in 1990, when the Soviet Division (later renamed the Euro-Asia Division) was established. At that time, only Soviet government officials were alarmed by the prospect of a heavy foreign presence and its possible consequences.

Adventist believers in the Soviet Union were anxious to work with their brothers and sisters from the United States, Europe, and Australia in open evangelism. The funds may have been raised in the West and the plans drawn up in Washington, but the enthusiasm of local Russian believers has been crucial to the overall success of the mission. During the first half of 1994, Adventist pastors in the Commonwealth of Independent States held 120 evangelistic campaigns, baptized about 6,000 members, and founded 40 new churches. In the same year, international evangelists from the Americas, Europe, and Australia held 35 campaigns, baptized about 5,000 members, and set up 18 new churches.

In 1992, some leaders in the General Conference became convinced that it would be easier to take advantage of the new opportunities in the CIS if the local organization were administered by Western leadership; an election took place at the end of the year. The new Western leaders (the president, the treasurer, and several departmental directors) have introduced a number of changes,

---

[20] The text of this section is an updated and slightly changed version of M. Kulakov's article "Foreign Missionaries: Boon or Bane?" *Frontier: Religion East and West* (June-August 1995): 1-2.

including a more effective system of administration and financial accountability, and also modern means of electronic communication. The non-Russian origin of the new leaders tends to be seen by some national Adventists as a stabilizing and unifying factor at a time of ethnic tension and growing nationalism.

A centralized construction department has been set up in Moscow through which donations for the building of new churches in the CIS are channeled and where Western construction specialists and accountants supervise the projects. This centralization has brought outside funds to many congregations, both established and new, which could never otherwise have afforded a new church building. This urgent need for new buildings and trained pastors for some three hundred new congregations is just one of the "joyful dilemmas" created by rapid evangelistic success.

Many local Adventists in Russia realize that they have benefited considerably from Western involvement in administration and evangelism. The Western presence has helped them to feel themselves a part of one large family of believers scattered around the world. Through effective advertising, foreign evangelists have helped the local church to make itself known to large segments of society which would otherwise be beyond its reach. (For example, many educated and professional people have joined the church.) The self-assurance of visiting evangelists from the free world has helped local believers to overcome their inferiority complex, developed as a result of unbridled atheistic propaganda and decades of persecution for their religious beliefs.

During the years 1990-94, local pastors were able to attend meetings between foreign evangelists and high-ranking state officials in central Russia and the outlying districts. At last they feel themselves to be respectable members of society whose needs should be taken into account.

On the negative side, however, some national church leaders now believe that with the advance of Western evangelists, local lay members and pastors have developed a kind of "consumer" attitude and a spirit of dependence. They have quickly become used to expecting funds for advertising, hall rental, and salaries to come from abroad rather than locally. While in the past most aspects of church life, including church-building and public outreach, were carried out through local initiatives, that dimension has now decreased. There is a fear that some local believers have lost faith in solving their problems by directly addressing God and instead rely upon the help of their more affluent Western brothers and sisters.

Any sophisticated Westerner coming to Russia needs humility and perception to be aware of local people's opinions and insights. The lack of international exposure and professional training among local pastors is often mistaken for a lack of wisdom and practical experience. This naturally offends local people and creates unnecessary tensions and barriers between national and foreign workers. Another divisive factor is the standard of living and the remuneration of Western missionaries working in Russia. Some Russian pastors joke that "the life of a Western missionary in Moscow is not a life of sacrifice but life in paradise" compared with the poor living conditions and meager salaries of the local workers.

Regarding public evangelistic meetings, it is generally recognized among Adventists in Russia and abroad that the time for large-scale campaigns, like Mark Finley's 1993 crusade at the Olympic stadium in Moscow, has passed. While public evangelistic meetings still attract considerable numbers of people in some parts of Russia, the initial interest has largely subsided. Adventist leaders are now encouraging small-scale meetings conducted by indigenous evangelists, for one of the weaknesses of short, intensive, and baptism-oriented outreach efforts is that there is no provision for those who are not yet prepared (due to intellectual, emotional, or social reasons) to be baptized and formally enter the Adventist Church at the end of such meetings. Many thoughtful, questioning individuals who have attended meetings but are unable to come to terms with baptism thus experience a spiritual anticlimax. This has prompted some pastors to consider new and more culturally sensitive forms of evangelism with a focus on dialogue, personal friendship, and natural social integration which, they believe, could have a more lasting and far reaching spiritual influence on the community in the long run.

THE NEW EXTERNAL BARRIERS

While Russian society in general was in a state of great flux and the people showed remarkable openness and tolerance toward all types of religious witness from 1989 to 1993, the ensuing years have seen a merger of the movements of national and religious restoration. Many Adventist pastors in various Russian provinces today observe that when government officials deal with religious matters, they often appear unwilling to upset local Orthodox clergy and nationalist activists by granting permission to carry out evangelistic outreach in their area. In many places there is no trace of the openness and favor to foreign evangelists which local officials used to extend three or four years ago. Perhaps it can even be said that the principal forces active within Russian society have accepted de facto the idea of one national religion. The question of whether Russia is to be a secular or a religious state is still debated—but mostly within the narrow circles of specialists and politicians.

On the whole, however, it seems that this direct encounter between Christians from East and West has been healthy and instructive for both sides. Many feel that Providence is teaching the East and the West some important lessons.

DEEPER ISSUES OF THE ADVENTIST MISSION IN RUSSIA[21]

Due to a number of complex historical factors, chief among them the absence of religious freedom in the former USSR, Adventist congregations were forced

---

[21] The text of this section is a somewhat revised version of the article "Razmyshlyaya o nastoyashchem i budushchem Adventisma v Rossii," *TserkovnoObshchestvennyi Vestnik* 4 (November 28, 1996): 11.

to exist in isolation from the rest of society for decades. Constant persecution by the state and an atmosphere of hostility toward all forms of dissent were not at all conducive to forming an attitude of openness toward the larger Russian society and its culture among the majority of the members of Adventist congregations.

During the period 1990-94, thousands of new converts from diverse spheres of society were attracted by the dynamic preaching of foreign and local missionaries and joined Adventist congregations. The majority of local pastors, lacking the necessary experience of communicating with people outside the church, found themselves for the first time immersed in a sea of human needs which required highly delicate treatment and professional pastoral care.

Unfortunately, many new enterprising people who joined Adventist congregations experienced disappointment due to the clash of two almost completely different mindsets. The pastors of Adventist parishes, by and large, have been raised on a few doctrinal brochures and have been introduced neither to Western nor to Russian wider spiritual and cultural heritages. They now find themselves face to face with people from circles which were formerly completely unaccessible to them, such as well-educated intellectuals. It is very difficult for people who have been raised in a narrow confessional subculture, in which members of the community are brought up on the same hymns and books from generation to generation, to understand those who have come to the Christian faith from outside the church. Yet they too have consciously accepted Gospel ideas: some under the influence of the classical Christian writers, others through reading works of the Eastern church fathers and Russian Christian thinkers, still others through the works of music or, most unexpectedly, through a study of the exact sciences. Common to them all is the profession of a so-called non-confessional (or broad) Christianity. Most have not done a thorough study of the complexities and contradictions of the history of Christianity and the development of modern denominations. They are inspired by the idea of the God of love, by the Gospel teaching of redemption, and frequently possess a keen vision of what social significance these ideas could and must have in the life of modern society.

Many of us who are born Adventists are not aware of how such non-confessional Christian consciousness has evolved, and we do not understand these people who have an acute sense of belonging to society as a whole and have very close ties with it. Many Russian Adventists have a real fear that if they begin to interact with the surrounding culture and enter into an open dialogue with it, then, in their own minds and in the minds of those to whom they carry the Gospel message, this would inevitably undermine the authority of the Holy Scriptures and water down the confessional distinctiveness of the teaching which is so precious to them.

Yet only through genuine dialogue with people in this swiftly changing society will we Protestants and Orthodox be able to acquire new language and develop new ways for the expression of our Christian experience in ways which will be understandable to modern men and women. Only in direct interaction will we be able to see the specific problems and needs of each individual and so understand how to fulfill those needs and apply the Gospel message.

We Adventists are primarily concerned with the preservation of our "otherness" in the multi-confessional world and with the preaching of distinctively Adventist doctrines. Yet we do this in a manner which is out of touch with people's everyday lives and thus find ourselves in a position where we do not hear the cry for help from our spiritually starving parishioners. Their foremost need is not a theoretical acquaintance with the peculiarities of our teaching, but an acquisition of the basic Christian understanding of God, the world, and the human person. They need to acquire the elemental experience of relying on God and communicating with God through prayer and corporate worship.

It seems that prominence, public influence, and attractiveness—which the Adventist Church possessed during the period of *perestroika*—had a lot to do with the appropriate style of leadership. National newspapers and magazines and radio and television reported about the first steps of the Adventist Church in developing its prison ministry, the work in orphanages, the construction of Zaoksky Seminary, the publishing house, and the first Russian Christian radio station. These reports were all an outcome of the church presenting a cordial and friendly style of leadership to society—not as another bureaucratic structure with a list of strategic tasks, but as a part of the larger community.

Today some Adventists in Russia are concerned not only about the substantial loss of new members, but also that the church is losing its public image. While internal administration has undoubtedly improved enormously with Western help, it is proving difficult to develop a long-term strategy. New leaders invited from abroad (being honorable in themselves) come to Russia for a short term of office—with no roots in Russian society, lacking a deeper understanding and appreciation of Russian history and culture, and not usually conversant in the local language. They are thus unable to forge strong and natural ties with the society on which the church is expected to exert a lasting spiritual influence.

We can perfect the administrative structure of our organization, equip it with latest technology and modern means of communication, and yet, without honest recognition that besides Adventists, God has here in Russia thousands of those "whose knees have not bowed down to Baal," we are in danger of ending up in a byway of the history of the Russian spiritual revival, embodying that very type of sectarian mentality so aptly described by Nikolay Berdyayev in his work the "Meaning of the Creative Act."

Yet there is a strong hope that under the influence of the Holy Spirit our vision of Christian ministry to society will acquire the necessary breadth and depth. Despite all these inevitable growing pains and the search for a place in the new Russia, the love and faithfulness of our people to God's Word continues to attract thousands of new people to the Adventist Church—who find in it true fulfillment of their spiritual needs.

9.

SECTS AND NEW RELIGIOUS MOVEMENTS IN POST-SOVIET RUSSIA

———————◆———————

Sergei Filatov

The issue of sects and new religious movements has attracted much attention in Russia in the 1990s.[1] Over the last few years, almost all the mass media have devoted significant space to stories of the harmful activities of "totalitarian sects," especially those originating from abroad. During the selection of candidates for the 1996 Russian federal elections, almost half the candidates promised that they would take measures against totalitarian sects and foreign missionaries. The episcopate of the Russian Orthodox Church and many clergy are constantly declaring war against new religious movements and totalitarian sects; such a struggle is seen as one of the main tasks of the church. Why is Russia so concerned about this topic that draws relatively little notice in Western European countries? Why have "totalitarian sects" become one of the most burning issues of the day? A short bit of history provides the necessary context.

During the Soviet era, the authorities strictly controlled all religious activity. There were crackdowns on religious propaganda, and especially on any attempt to create new religious organizations. The communists placed a significant barrier in the way of flowering of any religious activity: the police. Thus, at the beginning of *perestroika*, the religious consciousness of Russian citizens was an amorphous, eclectic mixture of different beliefs, including some fragments of Orthodoxy, Eastern religions, occultism, and others. In retrospect, this is not surprising. For under conditions of censorship, and given the

———————

[1] The author uses the terms *sects* and *new religious movements* interchangeably in this chapter. These are merely descriptive terms, and no negative connotation is intended nor should be assigned to them.—ED.

163

virtual destruction of church traditions and disappearance of a coherent religious world view, simple beliefs—the "fragments" of religious ideologies—spread in a spontaneous and random manner.

In Russia, unlike the West, the label "new religious movements" also attaches to many forms of Christianity (other than Orthodoxy); many sections of society have nevertheless begun to follow such movements after 1988.

But "new religious movements" spread in Russia both before and after *perestroika*. The 1970s saw a growth in the influence of occultism, Eastern religions, witchcraft, and in belief in UFOs, the abominable snowman, and the transmigration of souls. Before *perestroika* these unofficial religions attracted mainly young people and the intelligentsia—sections of society most inclined to soul-searching and questioning their beliefs. However, recent sources have revealed that not only the young, but even representatives of the highest Soviet authorities became interested in new religious movements and employed the services of psychics and astrologers during this time.

Worth noting is that believers in supernatural forces, UFOs, the reincarnation of the soul, Eastern philosophies, and similar beliefs are more often advocates of democratic market transformation than Orthodox Christians or atheists.[2] This eclectic, non-dogmatic religious consciousness has developed parallel to the growth in pro-market forces and spread it further. *Perestroika* undermined the ideological rigor of the system and sparked a general philosophical malaise in society—a society which has now slipped easily into a game without rules in the post-Soviet regime.

FOREIGN MISSIONARY GROUPS

This current ideological vacuum and philosophical malaise has provided a fertile ground for sects and so-called totalitarian sects, a fact not unnoticed by leaders of the most influential and wealthy international sects. In the first years of *perestroika* the most prominent and fastest-growing sects were those from abroad—especially the Unification Church (Moonies), the Aum sect Shri Chinmoy, and Scientology. The social atmosphere in the late 1980s and early 1990s was more receptive to them than at any other time. Religion in general had been rehabilitated, but ignorance regarding religious matters was so great among the Soviet people, from the president of the USSR down to the ordinary citizens, that few could tell the difference between Syoko Asahara and Moon, on the one hand, and the pope, Patriarch Aleksii II, and Billy Graham, on the other. For example, some events could have only occurred during such a situation—during *perestroika*: Gorbachev's meeting with Moon in the Kremlin in April 1990; the participation of the secretary of the State Security Committee, O. Lobov, in the leadership of the Aum Association at the Russo-Japanese

---

[2] L. Vorontsova and S. Filatov, "Vo shto seichas veryat rysskiye ludi?" *Logos* 48 (Brussels/Moscow, 1993): 242-43.

University; and the lavish official opening of the first Scientology laboratory in the most prestigious higher education institution in the land, Moscow State University.

The Unification Church was the first and most zealous of the missionary sects to establish a presence in Russia. Moon had expressed an interest in Russia long before *perestroika*. His missionaries first entered the country illegally—that is, on tourist visas—at the beginning of the 1980s. After 1985, the Unification Church was fully prepared to launch a missionary campaign. The process of the sect's registration began in 1989 when leading Soviet publications published interviews with Moon following a conference organized by the Moonies, to which the Novosti Press sent a dozen journalists. All remaining barriers to legalization quickly disappeared after Gorbachev's meeting with Moon in 1990, and in 1992 the Unification Church was officially registered by the Russian Ministry of Justice. The group established a centralized system in Russia, with its administration in Moscow and six departments throughout the country.

The activity of the sect was basically unrestricted until the end of 1994, and it conducted an impressive range of programs. Its efforts concentrated on the young: on students, schoolteachers, and university lecturers, as well as on the state authorities. All told, tens of thousands of inhabitants of the former Soviet Union (some figures put the number at eighty thousand) participated in numerous conferences, seminars, and study trips to various towns in the CIS and the United States. At the beginning of the 1990s the Moonies gained wide access to schools and higher educational establishments, working closely with the Ministry of Education and regional education authorities. In 1994, two thousand Russian schools used "moral textbooks" provided by the Moonies. For the Moonies, it was a unique and great achievement to have such easy access to children in Russia.

The Moonies sought to establish close relationships with local authorities, and succeeded in some regions of Russia. For example, in Yekaterinburg, the Unification Church had such a close relationship with the administration of Governor A. Strakhov that the Moonies, at the instigation of his staff, actively campaigned for his candidacy in the elections against E. Russell.

Despite such vast effort in Russia, the Moonies' cause seems to have been less than successful. Even at its peak in 1993-94, the number of full members of the cult, according to official statistics, did not exceed five thousand.[3] The state began an antisectarian campaign in late 1994, with the Moonies one of its major targets. Local authorities have gradually ceased contact with them, and by 1997 few educational institutions would still grant them access. The authorities have stopped registering the Moonies, and have subjected them to such pressure in some regions that the Moonies have had to cease their activities. At the same time, Moon stopped underwriting the Russian section of the church in 1995, desiring it to be self-financing.

---

[3] *Pravoslavnaya Moskva* 34 (1996).

As a result of these situations, membership in the sect has fallen dramatically; according to A. Shtern and other experts, there were fewer than three thousand members in 1997. Moreover, the gradual changes in the leadership of the Russian section of the Unification Church, replacing foreigners with Russians, has not had the desired effect. Nikolai Dikin, appointed as leader of the Russian division in 1995, has not been able to bring Russian Moonies out of this crisis, despite his firsthand knowledge of "Russian realities." But it is not only the Moonies' large-scale, well-financed program that failed.

Syoko Asahara first made an appearance in Russia in the spring of 1992, receiving the warmest welcome in the highest echelons of power. He hired the largest and most prestigious concert halls for his rallies, and bought airtime from the leading radio and television companies. The Russian Aum Organization mostly attracted people who practiced yoga and meditation, many of whom had been members of yoga groups in the 1970s and 1980s. The primitivism and accessibility of Syoko Asahara's interpretation of Buddhist theology and practice were popular draws. But despite the large numbers who attended Aum gatherings, which attracted many with an interest in Eastern mysticism, the actual membership of the Aum organization never exceeded two thousand—even at the height of its popularity in early 1995.

After the cult was routed in Japan in mid-1995, Russian security broke up the leadership of the Russian Aum cult. After a short-lived resistance, the Russian organization quickly faded, though there are still a few small groups of followers of the "Enlightened Teacher" in some Russian towns who continue to idolize him.

The well-organized Scientology cult, with its network of "colleges," "management courses," and bookshops, has succeeded only in confusing the whole country.[4] Those who have been drawn deeper into the cult have faced bitter disappointment.

INDIGENOUS NEW RELIGIOUS MOVEMENTS

The reason foreign missionaries, despite their great efforts, have experienced such limited success in Russia is likely because they are unable to adapt to the realities of Russia and to the Russian mentality. Filling the "spiritual vacuum" in Russia, which appears to be so easy, has proven difficult for foreign sects. Those sects which have developed on Russian soil have generally fared better than the foreign sects. This is due, at least in part, to the fact that these indigenous Russian sects build their teachings, brick by brick, on those religious ideologies which are currently most widespread in Russian society. These beliefs are many and varied.

---

[4] D. Dokuchayev, C. Mirzeyeva, and E. Yakovleva, "Prodavtsi Neva," *Izvestiya* (September 12, 1996).

ECLECTIC RUSSIAN BELIEFS

Perhaps the most obvious and ubiquitous beliefs are the pseudo-religious teachings linked with health issues and alternative medicine. Psychics and magicians, inventors of diets and "lifestyles" almost always base their lucrative practices on some kind of general religious principles; in the post-Soviet era the spiritual aspect of alternative medicine is expanding. Healing is the basis for the appearance of many new sects. But, more than that, it is also an almost indispensable element of sects founded on completely different ideological grounds.

Simplified Eastern beliefs and their remnants have also become more widespread in Russia since the 1970s. These include many adaptations of Buddhism, Hinduism, and yoga. The Rerikh movement, inspired by an early-twentieth-century Russian family which dabbled in various forms of Far Eastern and occult spirituality, plays a particular role in the adaptation of all kinds of Eastern beliefs to the conditions of modern Russia. Although the Rerikh movement is loosely organized into various clubs and associations which conduct lectures and seminars, it has so far not formed itself into a strict and disciplined organization. However, many of its ideas inspire other sectarian organizations, such as the Bogema religion in the Saratov province and the Bazhov movement in the Chelyabinsk province. These other sects recruit from among members of the Rerikh movement, and sometimes from among their leaders.

The most important philosophical element of Russians' contemporary religious outlook consists of pseudo-scientific ideologies. These beliefs include belief in UFOs (held by 70 percent of Russian citizens), the abominable snowman, and contact with extraterrestrial civilizations. There are also many theories (or superstitions) about so-called great scientists who are able to alter the whole universe either for good or evil. Pseudo-psychological religious ideas promise a transformation of the soul or the means to achieve unlimited power over one's fellow beings. Nearly two-thirds of society is seduced by a belief in astrology. Ideas abound relating to the age of Aquarius and the creation of the higher race of Aquarius; these tie in easily with beliefs about the end of the world and the election of a particular sect.

Because of the low level of religious education and the chaotic nature of today's religious renaissance, even the Orthodox intellectual environment has become fertile soil for the emergence of religious teachings which are not only far from Orthodox beliefs, but far from Christianity itself. A clear example of this kind of "para-Orthodox" sectarianism can be seen in the "underground community" of the so-called "bishop of Kashirsk, archbishop of Moscow, metropolitan of Siberia, patriarch of All Russia, the bailiff of the Revelation of John the Word of God, the Lamb of the Testament Lazarus (Vasil'ev) and the *Bogorodichny Tsentr*" (the Center of the Mother of God).

In the mid-1990s, comparatively late, paganism joined the list of ideologies of modern Russian sectarianism.[5] Paganism is not, of course, entirely new to

---

[5] See further Sergei Filatov, "The Revival of National Paganism in Russia" (unpublished manuscript, June 1998).

Russia; tiny groups of worshipers of the Slav god Perun existed before *perestroika.* However, the restoration of ancient Russian paganism is quite difficult, for the pantheon of Slav gods inspires no recognition in the Russian soul. The tradition has long been severed and the remaining elements in folklore are very few. Therefore, Russians often create pagan communities where they worship ancient German gods, adopt the beliefs of Native American Indians, and find truth in the shamanism of Chukotka, the Caucasus, or abroad—all at the same time! The ultimate demonstration of the weakness of paganism in the Russian religious tradition lies in the appearance of sects which invent their own form of paganism.

Almost all of the major sects which have emerged in the 1990s possess an eclectic combination of all these primitive beliefs. There are three main sects: *Velikoye Beloye Bratstvo* (Great White Brotherhood); *Tserkov poslednevo zaveta* (the Church of the Last Testament) also known as the Sect of Vissarion; and the *Bogorodichny Tsentr* (the Center of the Mother of God). The first of these is the most extreme and well organized.

THE GREAT WHITE BROTHERHOOD

The Great White Brotherhood emerged out of the spiritual quest of a Ukrainian with a doctorate in engineering, Yuri Krivonogov. At the end of the 1970s, Krivonogov became interested in psychology, occultism, and various religious teachings—including theosophy, yoga, and the teachings of Rerikh and Aivankhov.

He traveled all over the USSR to spread his beliefs, and met a journalist, Marina Tsvigun, on one of these trips; Tsvigun left her husband and son for him. Krivonogov and Tsvigun founded a medical center called *Atma* (Institute of the Soul), which used alternative methods of healing and cooperated with the Center of Self Awareness and Higher Yoga (which was affiliated with the Kiev Charity and Health Fund). *Atma* was affiliated with the esoteric Moscow firm Academy of Health, which now exists under the title Yoga Academy. The Ukrainian Ministry of Internal Affairs began a criminal investigation of the activity of Krivonogov and Tsvigun following accusations of misappropriation of funds. They then moved to Russia, where they began their main activity, declaring themselves to be religious teachers (gurus) and forming a community of followers. As the sect grew in numbers, its teachings evolved—the Krivonogovs declared themselves to be divine (the "divine duo," calling themselves Ioann Svami and Maria Devi) and developed their own eclectic religious teaching, *Yusmalos* (a Russian contraction of their two first names and the word *logos*).

The divine duo established a special program of activity based on a three-and-a-half year time scale (1260 days). During this period, the duo and their devoted followers were to preach the message of *Yusmalos*, calling all to repentance and to the recognition of the "Virgin Mary" (Maria Devi) as a "living god." They believed the end of the world was to occur in Autumn 1993, when Marina Tsvigun reached the age of thirty-three. According to the expectations of their followers, Ioann Svami and the Virgin Mary would be killed, and would then be resurrected after the third day. The last judgment would take place following their resurrection. Transfiguration and "eternal life" awaited believers in *Yusmalos*, while the unbeliever would face "eternal torture." In October 1993, nearly all the members of the sect traveled to Kiev, where they occupied the Cathedral of St. Sophia to await the end of the world.

But the Kiev militia arrested Krivonogov, Tsvigun, and the most active members of the sect, because it had been banned in Ukraine. The members of the sect stood firm, even in prison, holding on to their beliefs and going on a hunger strike. The majority of the sect members were eventually released, but the authorities continued to detain Krivonogov, Tsvigun, and their closest associate, apostle Piotr Kovalchuk (the main steward and administrator). In February 1996, the courts sentenced Maria Devi to four years' imprisonment, Ioann Svami to seven years, and apostle Piotr Kovalchuk to six years.

During the detention and investigation, Krivonogov and Tsvigun had a falling out and all the unpleasant details of their private life—fights, domestic violence, and so on—came to light. Tsvigun declared that Krivonogov was a traitor, cursing him as "Cain." In prison she married Kovalchuk, declaring him to be the apostle John-Peter. The "white brothers" subsequently received letters only from the "Virgin Mary" and not from the "fallen Cain." In her letters, Tsvigun claimed that Ioann Svami had consistently distorted her divine thoughts and prophecies. She had, apparently, never predicted that the end of the world would happen at a specific time.

In an interview with *Izvestiya,* Tsvigun stated that she would resume leadership of her church upon release from prison. She even predicted a glittering future:

> We are no more dangerous than the Krishna movement and no one persecutes them. Of course, my teaching is more complete—I have been able to bring together Christian and Eastern teachings and preach the program of "Yusmalos," which aims to save and revive Slavic culture.[6]

Tsvigun has recently begun preparing her eighteen-year-old son from her first marriage to join in the leadership of the cult. And in August 1997 Marina Tsvigun and Piotr Kovalchuk were released under amnesty from prison.

After the arrest of its leaders, the sect was disorganized for a time. Its membership fell noticeably, even though it had not been large to begin with. But repression did not lead to the disappearance of the sect. It simply forced it to follow a more secretive existence.

The current organizational structure of the sect is reminiscent of a regiment, in which every officer is responsible for two or three soldiers—but at the beginning of the battle it turns into a ramshackle group of rank-and-file mem-

---

[6] *Izvestiya* (January 9, 1997).

bers and fellow-travelers at the expense of mobilization. While the goddess was serving her time in prison, the "apostles" Sergei Solov'ev (Ierofan), Gennadii Polishchuk (Gibar), Aleksandr Zhuravel' (Israil'), and someone called "Vulan" were leaders of the sect.

The teaching of *Yusmalos* combines elements of Christianity, the Rerikh movement, and the Buddhist and Krishna meditation techniques which Krivonogov practiced for a number of years. *Yusmalos* is thus rooted in four main sources: yoga (diet), Hare Krishna (meditation techniques), the Rerikh movement, and Christianity. The adopted names of the two leaders, the idea of the Trinity (which they interpret differently), the resurrection on the third day, and the idea of the Last Judgment all come from Christian traditions.

At first, Krivonogov called himself Adam, while Tsvigun was Elena Rerikh. This combination of Christianity with the Rerikh movement developed further as the divine duo, Iosif and Maria Devi, appeared. It is possible to infer from the writings of the Great White Brotherhood that the role of Christ in the family of Iosif and Maria Devi was reserved for Marina Tsvigun's son, who lived with them for a time before returning to his father. Soon after that, Maria received a new name—Maria Devi Khristos—and she announced that a unification of the spirit of Jesus Christ and the Virgin Mary had taken place on April 11, 1990, in "Bethlehem" (Donetsk). She said that since the date of this unification, her body was the receptacle of the one god. Tsvigun then adopted the name Mother of the World—Virgin Mary—Christ. Unlike Tsvigun, the "divine spark" was not as apparent in the person of Krivonogov. Krivonogov has been an endless array of figures: Adam, Joseph, John the Baptist, Elijah, David, Prince Vladimir, and Archangel Michael. In the end he became Ioann Svami.

The Great White Brotherhood hates any external authority, whether the Communist Party, the KGB, Yeltsin, Kravchuk, or Kuchma. *Yusmalos* teaches that the "Center of the One Universal Religion" is on Slavic soil: "God is Russian." Of the 144,000 saints and elect all are said to be Slavs. "Everything has already been sold out to the Jewish-Masonic conspiracy of the antiChrist (USA, Israel)." They defend "Slav interests," displaying a blatant nationalism devoid of any true cultural and religious tradition. The Brotherhood favors the establishment of a strong state, which should defend the "one true teaching." It supports the principle of private property, opposes a centralized economy, and sympathizes with the interests of the small traders and kiosk owners. The Great White Brotherhood is one of the most extreme, fanatical, ascetic, and disciplined of the post-Soviet sects. In order to free themselves from "state indoctrination," members of the Brotherhood have to isolate themselves as much as possible from all external influences; television, films, radio, tapes, any printed matter, and electronic media are all banned. In justification of this, the leadership argues that "Satanic energies are everywhere and people are being turned into bio-robots." But even more stringent methods are required. Members are not allowed to sleep for more than four hours a day. Their diet is restricted to one vegetarian meal a day. Sexual intercourse is banned.

Followers are not allowed any contact, even accidental, with people (or even with animals). And they are advised to douse themselves with cold water and go barefoot.[7]

However, according to the statements of Tsvigun, the ideology of the Great White Brotherhood gradually became more "liberal" after the expulsion of Krivonogov. For example, the goddess now refuses to name the date for the end of the world, and she has called on her followers to stop fasting and otherwise generally relax the ascetic regime adopted within the Brotherhood.

Interestingly, as was the case with the foreign missionary sects, the disparity between the extreme reactions of society and the insignificance of the Great White Brotherhood movement itself is striking. Despite loud public outcries against the sect, it never had a large following. Before the arrest of the duo, membership numbered less than four thousand; after 1993, membership declined to only three or four hundred, despite no serious repression in Russia similar to the repression of Ukraine.[8]

THE CHURCH OF THE LAST TESTAMENT
SECT OF VISSARION

The Sect of Vissarion is an even better example of the type of beliefs currently being espoused in Russia. The history of the sect arises from the biography of its "living god," Sergei Torop. He was born into a family of builders on January 14, 1961, in Krasnodar. His parents were nonbelievers. Until the age of six he was brought up by his grandmother, who had links with the Old Believers. She influenced his spiritual development, and Torop still keeps her picture among his icons. In 1968, his family moved to work in Minusinsk, Krasnodar province. After he finished school, Sergei Torop did his military service, and after demobilization, he entered the lower ranks of the militia. After the military, he worked in various occupations, studied occultism and Christianity, and took up painting. Torop's religious interests stem from his involvement in the martial arts, yoga, and the Rerikh cult. He is clearly a skilled orator, capable of speaking for five hours at a stretch. (This serves his preaching activity well.)

In May 1990, at the age of twenty-nine, Torop announced that his "memory had been opened," "the scales fell from his eyes," and he learned that he was the "son of God," who was to be called Vissarion. According to Torop, the Heavenly Father himself baptized him on January 14, 1991 (prior to this he had not been baptized into any religion), and the Heavenly Father commis-

---

[7] L. I. Grigoryeva, "Istoriya vozniknoveniya, osobennosti veroucheniya i kul'tovoi praktiki i sposobi vozdeistviya na psikhiku v religioznom dvizhenii Beloye Bratstvo," *Religiya, tserkov'v Rossii i za rubezhem*, Informatsionnii byulleten, no. 2 (Moscow, 1994), 27-30.

[8] Despite frequent allegations of heinous and scandalous activity, including murders, ritual self-mutilation, orgies, and the like, no such activities ever occurred.

sioned him to preach the One True Religion. Torop first preached near Minusinsk on August 18, 1991. For Vissarionites this day is marked almost as a founder's festival, and it is also linked with the Moscow coup against Gorbachev. After this, Torop traveled all over Russia, preaching his religion. He was particularly successful in St. Petersburg, but also attracted followers in other republics of the former USSR, especially in Latvia.

In 1994, Torop announced that people must settle in the Sayansk hills to obtain salvation. There, on the Sukhoi mountain (Kurgansk region, Krasnoyar province), his followers would survive the coming end of the world. The One Faith Community obtained official registration in 1994, and in 1995 the closed joint-stock company *Tabrat*, formed by the settlers, began to create an "experimental ecological settlement" (as it was described in official documentation). Vissarionites from various towns all over the country have begun to sell their flats and move to villages around the Sukhoi mountain. The village of Cheremshanka, not far from the regional center Kurganino, has become the sect's central location. Vissarionites constructed a tower for Vissarion not far from the village. Though Vissarion spends much of his time traveling around the country, his wife and three children make their permanent home in Cheremshanka. The sect has begun to build the Asun city on a large tract of land on the Sukhoi mountain (250 hectares); as of early 1997 it had just finished building a road to the site. The Vissarionites built their first church in Cheremshanka in 1996, and they live in a disciplined community life. The two thousand Vissarionites in the surrounding villages all remain in the immediate vicinity, as they are forbidden to leave the community.[9]

A formal organization and priesthood is developing relatively slowly in the sect of Vissarion. There were only two recognized assistants in the community during the early years. Sergei Chevalkov, a former missile specialist, retired colonel, and now an "elder of the One Faith," heads administrative and financial matters. Vadim Red'kin is the main theologian, responsible for setting down the teachings of the cult and editing divine texts. Vissarion finally consecrated two "high priests" in 1995: Vladimir Kupunkin, a former musician who is developing a range of services, matins, vespers, and liturgies; and Aleksandr Beloshapkin.

Vitali Savitsky, a deputy of the State Duma and leader of the Christian Democratic Union, campaigned against totalitarian sects, and set his sights on the Vissarionites in 1995. Savitsky denounced the Vissarionites in the mass media and traveled to Kurganino, calling upon the authorities to act against the followers of Vissarion. The local authorities enacted a few measures, but these only insulted the members of the sect and did not really threaten its survival. After Savitsky's death in a car crash in late 1995, the Vissarionites have been largely left alone. Consequently, their settlement has continued to develop. Despite the negative attitudes of the authorities and public opinion,

---

[9] S. Kobish, "Cerdtse mira na Tiber-Kule," *Ogonyok* 3 (1996): 26–30.

the Church of the Last Testament had eight officially registered communities in 1997, and undoubtedly many more unregistered communities.

Vissarion teaches that he has brought the ultimate religion to the world. Before him, four religions had been revealed to the world: Taoism, Buddhism, Christianity, and Islam. Vissarion draws upon the spiritual riches of these religions to open to humanity the mysteries of the One World Religion. The advent of the One Religion marks the end of the "Kingdom of Force," and the beginning of the "Kingdom of Soul" (which is the Kingdom of God).

Although Vissarion's teaching about the divine nature is vague and vacillating, it does have some discernible features. His view of the divine nature includes the concept of the Trinity (which is similar to the Christian concept) as well as an additional deity—Mother Earth (or Mother Nature).

While he acknowledges the One (the Great Father of the Universe, the Absolute) to be the creator of all that exists, Torop is not a strict monotheist even about the first person of the Godhead. For Vissarion, at times, speaks of an independent Heavenly Father (sometimes called the Son of the One), who is the great father of human souls; and at other times there is a kind of Extraterrestrial Reason, which is independent of the One. While it is possible that this threefold division of the first person of the Trinity will disappear as Vissarion's teaching develops, it is also possible that it will lead to the transformation of the Trinity into the Four, the Five, or even more. The third person of the Trinity, the Holy Spirit, is a "beneficial energy, which enters the chosen in order that with its help they can create godly works among people." This third person of the Trinity also has a colleague, the Spirit of Life, which gives physical strength and is represented as "material energy." The second person of the Trinity is "the one and only son," the incarnation of Christ," the "radiant being of the Heavenly Father," and "the Son-God born of the union of the Spirit of Life and the energy of the Heart of Mother Earth." This second person is Vissarion himself.

In addition to these variations on the Christian Trinity, Vissarion's teaching represents the earth as virtually another divine being, which he calls Mother Earth. "The pagans worshiped her, understanding that she embodied some kind of being, the energy of the heart." The earth, he continues, treats this harmful, fallen human race as if it were a sickness to be dealt with, as something to be overcome. Thus, the earth is preparing to take radical action, and we can already see signs of this as humans have started to degenerate and cells have started to mutate. These are the beginnings of the Last Judgment, in which most people will perish. Vissarion teaches that the counterpart of the biblical flood will soon occur—a fifteen-year drought that will annihilate the human race. Followers of Vissarion, however, will be transformed to a "new state of being"; they will transmute. Russia has a special role to play in the transformation of the earth to a new quality of existence, for it is in Russia that the Son of God will "create a new union between God and man" and will conclude a third and final testament. Those people who have "converted to a new state" (that is, the followers of Vissarion), will be received into the Kingdom of God, which will exist in material form on a transformed earth.

Vissarion acknowledges the existence of the Anti-Christ on the earth, who manifests himself in two persons—both of whom exist in Russia. Vissarion knows one of them, but he will not reveal the person's name. He offers only that the person was born in 1962, is charming and intelligent, worked with "psychological weapons," and will be elected to the Duma.

God has not called Vissarion to work miracles, because people should receive Vissarion's teachings freely rather than through fear. These teachings include that a person can appear on the earth up to ten times. Each appearance is an opportunity for spiritual growth, after which the soul will go either to heaven or hell. Vissarion also teaches that the universe is developing according to the Law of Expediency. This law proclaims that everything that exists operates on the principle of self-interest, and aims to interfere with others as little as possible, but will cooperate with others on the basis of mutual benefit. The Law of Expediency also advances the notion of "karma," or the "boomerang effect," which states that everything you give out into the world will return to you multiplied. The universe will react to a person's activity, rewarding good works with blessings and cutting short any deeds which cause harm to other members of the community. The Law of Expediency manifests itself most extremely in the truth that "if the minority interferes with or threatens the activity of the majority, then it must be destroyed for the good of the majority."

The theme of sincerity lies at core of Vissarion's teaching; each person should live according to the dictates of the heart rather than the head. Although there are sixty-one commandments, extramarital sex is not forbidden—as Vissarion says that sexual desire is not sinful. He also claims that any untruth which brings good is wise and appropriate. Strict vegetarianism is one of the few strict rules in Vissarion's teaching; such vegetarianism is even, at times, augmented by additional dietary restrictions, including bans on bread and honey.

Just as few commandments are burdensome, neither are the divine services strictly regulated. Before founding their settlement on Sukhoi mountain, Vissarionites simply worshiped Mother Earth. They would gather in a circle, raise their arms, and praise Mother Earth and the teaching of Vissarion. They would also sew special clothing and make amulets in the Russian style. Since 1996, the sect has instituted a whole series of additional services and practices. The recitation of psalms by the priest now forms the main element of the service. Worship of the Father is the main element of the Vissarionite service. The Eucharist is only of secondary importance, for Christ is incarnate in Vissarion and it is impossible to partake of the bread and wine when the living bread, Vissarion, is present in the flesh. Therefore, Vissarionites make their communion of the Word from the mouth of "god." The "Eucharist," also called the "communion of fire," that is celebrated during the liturgy has a completely different meaning from that of Christianity. The Vissarionite faithful make their communion of "hot water," which is pure spring water. (Only the high priest witnesses the "burning" of the water, which happens outside the earthly realm.) This communion of fire is a means of receiving energy from God the Father.[10]

CENTER OF THE MOTHER OF GOD

The *Bogorodichny Tsentr* is a less eclectic sect which grew out of Orthodoxy, though it is considered a heresy. It originated within Orthodoxy out of the prophesies of the writer Veniamin Bereslavsky. This new prophet "heard the voice of the Mother of God" in 1984, and she dictated more than twenty volumes of "God-breathed" texts to him. The religious organization itself was not formed until sometime in 1988-89.[11]

Bereslavsky's teachings claim that the physical and spiritual world have undergone significant changes since the time when the Lord gave humans the Old Testament and the New Testament. Because of this, a Third Testament needs to be imparted to humans before the Thousand Year Kingdom can begin. This Third Testament would come from the Virgin Mary through the "prophet" Ioann Bereslavsky. Since 1984 (the date of his first vision), God has revealed himself exclusively through the Virgin Mary and her "uncorrupted heart." Previously the only source of grace was the Eucharist. But now Mary has been given a mystical grace, without which the eucharistic grace from Christ is ineffective. The atoning mission of Christ will gradually be fulfilled and replaced by the atoning mission of Mary, whose heart is suffering at the sight of the fallen world. It is Mary who will stand in judgment over this fallen world.

Mary's appearances at Lourdes, Fatima, Medjugorje, Cairo, and other places evidence her desire to help humanity by showing the path to salvation through the transformation of the church, particularly through the Orthodox Church. This path of transformation has five mystical milestones, three of which have already been crossed: (1) the appearance in March 1917 of the icon "Derzhavnaya"; (2) the mighty victory of Mary over the "red communist dragon" in August 1991; (3) the birth of the Church of the Uncorrupted Virgin (another name for the *Bogorodichny Tsentr*). There are two remaining spiritual milestones which have yet to be passed: (4) a huge vision of the image of the Mother of God will appear in the sky; and (5) the outpouring of the so-called Solar Pentecost.

The renewal of the Orthodox Church will be nurtured in the bosom of the Church of the Mother of God, that is, the *Bogorodichny Tsentr*. In this church, a renewal of a priesthood free from the sins of the "red church" (the Russian Orthodox Church), is taking place. However, only those who do not carry the "ancestral ban," and who preserve the "hereditary capability of serving oth-

---

[10] "Noviye religiozniye organizatsii Rossii destruktivnovo i okkul'tnovo kharaktera," *Belgorod* (1997): 163-71.

[11] "Bogosloviye neporochnovo serdsta," Sostaviteli: Sobor ottsov Novoi Svyatoi Rusi-arkhiyep Amvrosii arkiyep. Aleksandr, arkhiyep: Paisii i dr. Moscow, *Izdatel'stvo Novaya Svyataya Rus'*.

ers," can become "priests of the Virgin Mary." These can only be men, or the "fathers of Our Lady."

One of the main features of the sect is the devaluation of human sexuality. Bereslavsky declares that a man can only be free when he has liberated himself from the cult of woman (that is, wives and mothers), a cult which remains "on the genital level" (the original text uses expressions which are unfit for print). Every person bears the sins of the human race, which are transmitted from generation to generation by the sexual acts of women. In order to combat this evil, the sect has a carefully concealed rite of the "negation of mother." In the community, women are treated as second-class citizens. The *Bogorodichny Tsentr* teaches that women crucified Christ (highlighting the collective image of the sinful origins of women on earth) and then blamed it on the Jews. This belief in the sinful origins of woman is based on the secretive nature of the female gender, personified in the theological texts of the *Bogorodichny Tsentr* by the "mother of the AntiChrist" or "the Whore of Babylon."

According to Bereslavsky's teaching, humanity is now entering the ultimate phase of Christian history. The "last times" are coming. But Marian eschatology promises the transformation of the world rather than the end of the world. If repentance and conversion to the "true Marian faith" take place, then the Virgin will substitute the "quiet sleep of transformation" for the Last Judgment. During the coming Thousand Year Kingdom, the world will be organized according to true spiritual principles, and "state Christianity" will be replaced by "the Christian state." The present monasteries and communities of the *Bogorodichny Tsentr* will become the models and centers of such a "Christian state," and "Mary, the first anointed" will head the new state.

The *Bogorodichny Tsentr* honors the last Russian emperor and has even elevated Grigori Rasputin to its calendar of saints. However, this bow to monarchism is merely symbolic and does not have any direct influence on the sociopolitical situation. In practice, these devotees campaign for freedom of conscience and ecumenism, for it is only through the observance of these norms that their survival is possible in Russia. They also maintain that the accession of democrats to power is attributable to the divine influence of the Mother of God. They claim that the Virgin Mary intervened both in August 1991 and in October 1993. They further support the economic free-market system. This also works to their advantage, as their publications and mass undertakings indicate that they are doing extremely well.

Ioann Bereslavsky retains a unique place in the hierarchy of the religion. The movement reveres him as a prophet, and he is called either archbishop, patriarch, or matriarch. He must fulfill the special mission of opening up "the secrets of the last times," which are tied to the special role of Mary. He unites the Old Testament and the Third Testament, in the same way that John the Baptist joined the Old Testament with the New Testament. The literature states that the prophet Ioann, sent by God to Russia, carries "the fullness of truth."[12]

---

[12] "Noviye religiozniye organizatsii," 319-28.

The *Bogorodichny Tsentr* was the first of the indigenous Russian sects to appear. It has found some generous financial sponsors, and has hardly been touched by repressive measures of the authorities; some fifteen of its communities have received official registration. But despite adequate financing, not much repression, and even a mass public relations campaign in 1994 (to counter a broad anti-sectarian campaign in Russia), this organization has never amassed large numbers—maintaining a membership of only two or three thousand.

OTHER INDIGENOUS GROUPS

While the *Bogorodichniki'*, the White Brotherhood, and the Vissarionites are the most widely known of the indigenous Russian sects, there are dozens, if not hundreds, of less well-known, less-organized, and less-widespread indigenous sects. It is impossible to tell which of them may attract significant public attention in the future. Even so, it is the author's opinion that two sects are most likely to attract further attention—the Bogema religion and the Cossack religious movement, *Kruglik*.

THE BOGEMA RELIGION

On March 20, 1991, Nadezhda Kosova, while at her home in Balakovo in Saratov province, saw a vision of the Creator of the Universe—the Central Reason of the Universe. Kosova claims that she, and also her mother and her son, communicated with this Reason until May 15, 1991. It revealed to them the secret knowledge and teaching of the Bogema religion. Kosova shared her "knowledge" with others, who believed this new teaching and formed the Community of Like-Thinkers in June 1991. Its members called themselves *Bogemtsy*. Kosova gradually formulated the teaching of the Bogema religion, creating a unique mythology, cult, forms of worship, symbolism, rituals, alternative methods of healing, and culture (artists' cooperatives, poetry, and music). According to official literature, the establishment of the sect "began with the presentation of the Bogema religion, which took place on 22 June 1993 in the Palace of Builders in the town of Balakovo."[13] The Bogema religion, then, is a religion created by Nadezhda Kosova.

Following registration in Saratov, the sect began to create sister organizations to spread its teachings and alternative therapies. And the *Bogemtsy* tried to organize a community life in Balakovo from 1994 to 1996. They rented a kindergarten and tried to control one of the schools in the town. But the municipal administration reacted negatively toward them and restricted their activity through fiscal and administrative measures. So in early 1996, most of the community (including Kosova) moved to Cheremshany near Khvalinsk,

---

[13] The Report of the Main Teacher of the Bogema Religion to the Open Central Gathering of Bogemtsy (Autumn 1994).

where they began renting part of a sanatorium—paying for it not with money but with their labor. The sanatorium is situated in the buildings of what was formerly an Old Believer monastery, Cheremshansy—one of its main centers before the revolution. The Saratov community of Belokrinitsy Old Believers has recently broached the issue of the return of its monastery, so the *Bogemtsy* are faced with renewed problems.

A fire broke out in the sanatorium in January 1997, destroying many passports and official documents of the community—along with a significant amount of its property. Arson has not been ruled out. But the local authorities are currently well-disposed toward the *Bogemtsy*, and the community plans to build a Bogema Center in Cheremshany. The community lives a closed life and does not allow strangers in.

The teachings of the Bogema religion consist of a synthesis of Rerikh, Christianity, and religious impressions gained through "contacts." The *Bogemtsy* attempt to "Russify" the religion of Rerikh through Christianity. The New Testament and Agni-Yoga serve as the main sources of literature. The mythology of the *Bogemtsy* rests upon the belief that six thousand years ago the earth was called Bogema and its inhabitants were called *Bogemtsy*.[14] This was a highly developed civilization. The *Bogemsty* were godlike beings; the length of their lives was directly dependent on the degree to which higher Reason had an effect on them, and they could live for as long as one thousand years. The *Bogemtsy* who lived according to the laws of the Cosmos had a heightened spirituality and could transform energies at will. Bogema was a "virginal garden" where no one dug or tilled the soil. The *Bogemtsy* fed and clothed themselves through the transformation of energy. Everyone had a "telepathic link with the Creator," and death merely marked the completion of life on the first level of existence, after which they returned to life on the second level on other planets.

Bogema was, and still is, a "female" planet where women possess great power. Six thousand years ago the "godlike woman" allowed Evil to enter her mind, and it produced pride, which spread like an infection. Infected by the force of evil, Bogema stopped performing its main function in the universe— the universal exchange of energy. Bogema gradually deteriorated into a "pirate civilization," which became the center for the production of evil energies in the universe. Fortunately, the Creator had preserved "contacts" on the earth. These "contacts" are people with a heightened spiritual potential, capable of acting as a counterbalance to the disharmony of the earth and preventing it from succumbing to ultimate destruction. Nadezhda Kosova is one of these contacts. Her advent marks the end of the pirate civilization and the beginning of a transition to the revival of Bogema and the *Bogemtsy*. Their first task is to

---

[14] The provenance of the term *Bogema* is unknown. It appears that Kosova created a new word from the contraction of the word *bog* (God) and *zemlya* (earth)— maybe simply for the resonance of the word. She was likely unaware of any connection to gypsies (the French word *bohème* means gypsy woman).

reorient the "true exchange of energy" so that it flows in the proper direction; the orientation of energy exchange had been reversed as a result of transgression. If the inhabitants of the earth fail to heed the appeals of the Bogemtsy, a terrible catastrophe will take place in the year 2000: the earth will leave its orbit.[15]

The female occupies a place of prime significance in the Bogema religion. Woman is the bearer of positive energies. Man carries negative energies, and it is only with the help of woman that he is able to reach a normal spiritual state. The era of the Woman-mother on the earth dates from the moment of Kosova's vision in her flat. The preeminence given to women in the Bogema religion, and the accompanying negativism toward men, possibly stem from the dynamics within Kosova's own family.

The Bogema religion supposedly encompasses all world religions. At the end of the second millennium the earth will be given over to the authority of Jesus Christ, who will return to earth to take the *Bogemtsy* into the "universal Brotherhood" which represents the sum of all rational civilizations. The Trinity—understood by the *Bogemtsy* to be the Triunity of the Creator (God the Father), the Virgin Mary, and Christ—directs the entire process of the revival of Bogema. Two earthly beings, the mother and the son (the Virgin Mary and Christ), became the "symbols of the Humanity of the Universe." Soon, after two or three years, the functions of the "holy beings" (the Virgin Mary and Christ) will be transferred to Kosova herself and her son.

The Bogema religion uses various symbols: a green disk represents the Creator; three disks (orange, red, and yellow) represent the Mother of the World; and an equilateral triangle of three colors (green, blue, and orange) represents Christ. The six-pointed star and the red rose are also symbols of the sect. The Bogema religion has also established rituals of fire worship. Communion consists of bread, wine, or holy water, depending on the communicant's age and situation. Believers are baptized with water, fire, and the holy spirit. There is also a marriage rite. But the most poetic rite is the "committal of the flesh of the departed soul to the holy fire," a funeral to "protect the planet from the spread of all manner of harmful viruses, bacteria, and microbes." The body is to be burned on a funeral pyre of aromatic herbs and red roses. The community is young, and so far Kosova's mother is the only member who has died. But according to one of the members of the sect, it was not possible to cremate her because there is no crematorium in Balakov.[16]

Another major component of the community's teaching relates to healing. True believers often pay a small sum of money in order to be "purified from evil energies and made ready for the transition to the era of Woman-mother." The *Bogemtsy* are also active in missionary work on the territory of Saratov province. By 1997, permanent missionary stations had been established in

---

[15] "Podari sebe zhizn," *Balakovo* 1 (1996): 21-26.
[16] Interview by the author.

Saratov, Yershov, Atkarsk, and Krasnoarmeisk, in addition to the community in Balakov, which continues to function.

KRUGLIK

The religious movement Kruglik, or the teaching about the True Cossack Light, is directly linked with the political separatist movement of the Kuban Cossacks. The leader of the group is Dimitri Podlipentsev, an electrical engineer from Krasnodar. Podlipentsev was drawn into the democratic movement during the *perestroika* years, and the Cossack movement attracted him because of his ancestry. Because he was firmly anti-communist, anti-monarchist, and a separatist who supported establishing an independent Cossack republic in the territory of Krasnodar province (Kuban), Podlipentsev suited neither the red nor the white Cossacks. He thus founded his own Cossack movement and became the ataman of the "Kuban Cossack circle." He called himself general-lance-corporal: *general* because he is an ataman, and *lance-corporal* because he was a lance-corporal in the Soviet special troops in the early 1970s.

Podlipentsev initially ran for election to the town Duma, but was unsuccessful. He campaigned to rename Krasnodar as Nova Sych, and, through his newspaper, *Kruglik,* he was highly critical of the local authorities for serving the interests of Moscow. He railed against the red Cossacks for bowing to the authorities and criticized the white Cossacks for their monarchism and their betrayal of Cossack freedom. And he criticized both for their loyalty to the Moscow Patriarchate, which he characterizes as the ideological bastion of Russian interests in the region. Podlipentsev thus gained a reputation as a political extremist and a Cossack nationalist. As a result, he was excluded from regional politics both by the democrats from the liberal wing and by the patriots from the conservative wing. So Podlipentsev created a Cossack National Party in 1997, but soon realized his political career showed little promise. He then became more involved in religious activity, which had always been of interest to him.

At first, the religious teaching about the True Cossack Light served only as an ideological component of the political activity of Dimitri Podlipentsev's group. But as its political activities came to naught, religion gradually came to the fore, turning Cossack political activists into mystics. This religious movement, Kruglik, describes the cosmology and spiritual system of the universe in two ways: metaphorical and scientific. There are thus two documents effectively describing the same thing but using different language. The "scientific" version consists of five closely typed pages which describe the teaching about the Light in dry academic language. The "metaphorical" version is a lengthy text, emulating the style of the synodal translation of the Bible. This text, an idiosyncratic interpretation of the Christian Bible, is presented as the Holy Book of Kruglik. It imparts both basic information about the Atlantic origins of the Cossack people and revelations about the divine ordering of the world.

Members of Kruglik maintain that the Cossacks have always had their own faith, even during times when they professed Orthodoxy. For the Cossacks, Orthodoxy was merely used as a front to cover their secret knowledge of God and the mysteries of the world. This knowledge was contained in special books in the library of the Transfiguration of Christ Monastery in Mezhigorsk (in present-day Ukraine, but closed by the tsarist authorities in 1786). Some of the books disappeared, but others were passed from person to person. Cossacks who chose to attend Orthodox seminaries were supposedly first secretly consecrated in their villages by the Ordained. For example, claims Podlipentsev, only Ordained Cossacks, preservers of the secret faith, studied at the Stavropol seminary until 1917. And the Moscow priests did not even suspect this. Kruglik further attributes Cossacks' tolerance of Buddhism and Islam to the presence of this special non-Orthodox faith.[17]

The Cossacks had their own totems and symbols, including the white deer, the white goose, and, most important, the mountain dragon. A special Cossack saint was the "holy Cossack Georgi the Victory-Giver." Orthodox Muscovites cunningly depicted George slaying a dragon, with the resulting image of a Cossack "cutting down a Cossack sign and symbol." The Cossacks have not been united ever since, and the red Cossacks defeated the whites in the Civil War.

The secret knowledge of Kruglik has been partially lost over the years, and it must be fully restored. Some of it remains in the memories of the Ordained, in manuscripts, and in memoirs. The other way of restoring lost knowledge, employed by the priest Yu I. Troschei (the probable author of this anonymous holy text) and the elder D. V. Podlipentsev, is known as the Stanislavsky method. This method, when completely mastered by the individual, is a means of transmigration into historical figures, studying historical documents, and then imparting the knowledge to one's contemporaries. The most important quality in Kruglik is the ability to communicate with God himself, who is called the Absolute. But this is deemed as special knowledge and is not imparted to the unauthorized.

According to the teaching of Kruglik, the Cossacks are the descendants and inheritors of the "fourth generation of Atlantis" (the lost city of Atlantis), which was called Ass Aki. This name has been preserved in the Russian word for Cossack: *k-az-aki*. Historically, the Cossacks were courageous and sincere people, who had received the "Spark of the Crystal of Light" in their hearts. This Spark of the Crystal of Light, one of the fundamental teachings of Kruglik, denotes the sum of secret knowledge, divine revelation, and the sacred Cossack language which has been imparted to the elect; it is "all knowledge of everything, which God created in his love, before the universe even existed." Because the Cossacks were different from all other humans, God chose to spare them from the Flood.

---

[17] Interview by the author with the plenipotentiary, June 25, 1997.

The Kruglik religion teaches that Assaki (Cossacks) settled the ancient lands of Akhiyava on the coast of the Aegean Sea. Three thousand years later, some of them traveled further to the east, toward the shores of the Caspian Sea. They taught their language to the small tribes living between the Caspian Sea and the Itil' River, and they pitched their *yurts* on the steppes between three inland seas. One day a herald brought an arrow from Ass Aki which struck all the Assaki: "The Virgin has brought the Redemption of the Dimension of Truth into the world. And all trembled for they saw and received at that moment the Spark of the Crystal of Light."

The Holy Book of Kruglik reveals that the genealogy of Mary and of Christ was falsified. In truth, Mary never met Joseph, and Christ never belonged to the house of David. But this fallacy is not surprising, states the Holy Book of Kruglik, for "God will take reason away from anyone who detracts from the teaching of the Light and their name will be removed from the Book of Life."[18] Therefore, the story as told in the four gospels remained distorted, as did the teaching about the Light. The Cossacks, however, preserved the true teaching and served as the primary bearers of the Spark of the Crystal of Light. It is the goal and mission of the Cossacks to revive the true teaching about the Light. They do this at the direction of Christ. For Jesus said, as quoted in the Holy Book of Kruglik,

"While you have the Light with you, believe in the Light, be sons of the Light, the children of the noble white deer. To you, who see and receive the Light, I give the banner of the white flower, symbol of truth and sanctity, for I am convinced that you will be worthy of it. The way the truth and the life will shine in this symbol of the Assaki and you will come to the Father through Me. Do you believe this?" And they answered, "Yes, Lord." The Assaki believed in Jesus and worshiped Him. . . . They did not know that the Jews had vowed to put anyone who believed in the Light to death.[19]

The Kruglik religion asserts that a higher rational cosmic being exists, called the Absolute. He is equal in importance to the Creator God, and counterbalances the Creator God. There is also Chaos, which is universal evil and darkness and acts as a chaotic influence. The Absolute influences the spiritual growth of each individual, increasing its influence at specific times that resonate with the individual's internal spiritual processes. Every person has a "receiver" of sorts in his or her brain; this receiver is a Spark of the Crystal of Light, which, under certain circumstances, tunes in to the "bank of statistics and energies of

---

[18] This quotation is an interpretation and variation of the Book of Revelation, chapter 19.

[19] This quotation is an interpretation and variation of John 12:35.

the Absolute." Anyone insufficiently prepared, or with a low level of spirituality, is incapable of receiving information from the Absolute. Moreover, the force of Chaos tries to distort the receiver and dull the Spark of the Crystal of Light. The Absolute is constantly in a creative state, and is supported by the Knowledge within in the Spark of the Crystal of Light. Only those who master this secret knowledge can receive the Baptism of Truth. And only Kruglik possesses the expertise needed to master this knowledge. This expertise is a secret liturgical religious system called the Teaching of the Light— Early Christianity (that is, it is "pure" Christianity, unblemished by Orthodoxy, Protestantism, or Catholicism).[20] Kruglik teaches that only the individual capable of "knowing the Free Reason of the contemplative Observer" will achieve salvation by attaining the strength which will put him or her beyond the power of death. Such an individual dialogues directly with the Absolute, without the mediation of priests, who "have turned the church into a feeding trough."

This Cossack teaching about the Light is that it is not a repository of dogma, but an experimental laboratory which awaits its great prophet and teacher. The Holy Book of Kruglik foretells the appearance of a prophet. "The one who is able to leave the cares of the world in order to know the Truth of the Reality of the Dimension according to the Virgin, who has brought Light to mankind, will cleanse the Old and New Testaments of their mistakes, made by another hand, he will break the chains." This prophet will probably arise from the current membership of Kruglik, and is likely the anonymous author of the holy text.

The community is currently planning to build a Temple of Light on the Kruglik mountain between the villages of Ispravnaya and Peredovaya. The initial plans call for the planting of an oak tree and placement of a sacrificial altar at the base of the mountain. Additionally, the priestly class in the Kruglik community seems likely to grow. For example, one of the members has been an acolyte for several years in a Krasnodar church, and he plans to be consecrated by the priest Troshchei. Then he will seek ordination in the "church of Isidor" serving under Archbishop Isidor, of the Krasnodar diocese of the Moscow Patriarchate in one of the diocesan churches; he plans simultaneously to remain a secret priest of the True Cossack Faith.[21]

Kruglik has a staunch supporter in the Cossack National Party, which will defend the interests of Kruglik and all Cossacks. The party's goals include reviving the Cossack people through reestablishing the national mythology; promoting the return of the Father of the Nation and the Prophets to the Cossacks; reviving the rite of the ennoblement of Cossack warriors; and reviving the ancient sacral Cossack language for the Cossack elite.

---

[20] This liturgical system is apparently built upon the Stanislavsky method, mentioned above.

[21] Interview by the author.

CONCLUSION

Russian society and foreign observers, as well as the Russian Orthodox Church, Western missionaries, and leaders of indigenous Russian sects, all make the same mistake. They all believe that there is a "spiritual vacuum" in Russia, just waiting to be exploited by some talented prophet of a new religion. But instead of a vacuum, there are rather a host of beliefs in contemporary Russian society, including occultism, paganism, and pseudo-Christianity. And Russians' beliefs and superstitions are complex, eclectic, and changeable. They are also weak; scarcely anyone would be willing to join a formal organization for belief alone.

In the current Russian context, battling "totalitarian sects" is much like fighting a specter. The sects are quickly driven away by the slightest repression, leaving only former adherents to pick up the pieces of their lives. But the beliefs remain even when the sect is gone. To struggle with the beliefs themselves—a struggle waged by the government, by society in general, and even by the Russian Orthodox Church—is much harder. For it is much like fighting one's own shadow, because all aspects of Russian society are wholly infected by this nontraditional religiosity that sparks interest in sects.

10.

THE QUALITY OF MERCY

A Once-only Opportunity

———◆———

Michael Bourdeaux

On February 11, 1986, a diminutive figure, his face wreathed in smiles, strode across the Glienicke Bridge joining one sector of East Berlin to the West. There was a spring in his step, but he was not walking naturally: one of his hands was permanently engaged in holding up his trousers. The KGB had supplied this man with clothing far too large, and its own rules did not permit the possession of a belt, as this could have been used for suicide.

Anatoli Shcharansky had, for most of the eleven years of his imprisonment, been the focus of a worldwide Jewish lobby in favor of the emigration of Soviet Jews to Israel. Many Christian groups and human rights activists had joined in the campaign, impressively led by Shcharansky's wife, Avital. She had been allowed to emigrate immediately after their marriage, with the promise that Anatoli would follow a day later. Instead, he was arrested and sentenced for no specific crime, except "anti-Soviet activity." He had been untiringly energetic in fighting for human rights for everyone under the Soviet system, including the right to emigrate. The petty vengeance of the couple's treatment added force and poignancy to the campaign. "I'm sorry I'm a little late" were reported to be Anatoli's first words to his wife, when he saw her for the first time in over a decade. Ten years after this event, now having changed his name to Natan Sharansky, Anatoli would become minister of trade for the State of Israel.

For millions who saw this episode on television, it was obvious that something basic had changed. Shcharansky's somewhat undignified first steps to freedom were a signal, just under a year into Mikhail Sergeyevich Gorbachev's time as chairman of the Central Committee of the Communist Party, that the Kremlin really did have a new human rights agenda. The words *glasnost* ("openness," literally "giving a voice to") and *perestroika* ("rebuilding, remodeling") entered the currency of world speech.

Two months later, the explosion at Chernobyl reduced to silence those very men in the Kremlin who were proclaiming *glasnost* to the world. Not even Gorbachev in his writings and lectures has publicly reflected on the tremendous effect this tragedy had on his own thinking, but the outcome was clear: a decision to make the USSR a more humane place in which to live. Gorbachev summoned the other great and repressed leader of the human rights campaign, academician Andrei Sakharov, out of enforced exile in Gorky to return to Moscow and participate in the *perestroika* process. Within a year most of the two hundred or so Christian prisoners, representing almost all active denominations, Orthodox, Catholic, and Protestant, had been released to invigorate the campaign for religious liberty, which the government was prepared not only to tolerate but to encourage. The Lithuanian Catholic activists, almost alone, did not benefit from the amnesty, an illustration of just how fearful the communists still were of the potent mixture of religion and nationalism.

The year 1988 put the seal of permanence on the changes. By the end of the year even the Lithuanians had been released, but before this, on April 29, an unprecedented meeting took place in the Kremlin. Gorbachev summoned the leaders of the Orthodox Church and offered them a new deal based on the "common cause" between Christianity and communism.[1]

In other ways, too, 1988 was a key year in the opening up of Christianity in the Soviet Union to Western eyes and concerns. By coincidence or an act of Divine Providence, Gorbachev's *glasnost* coincided precisely with the Orthodox millennium, the celebration in 1988 of the thousand years since the baptism of Prince Vladimir in Kiev. Long uncertain how they could celebrate this anniversary in an atheist society, Patriarch Pimen and the bishops received the green light from Gorbachev to expand the international event they were already organizing. President Reagan visited Moscow in May 1988 and was shown the Danilov Monastery, which, with its restoration well underway, was designated as the focus of the celebration, an event the world witnessed on its television screens. The next month, high-profile delegations from all over the world, including such figures as the archbishop of Canterbury, Billy Graham, and Cardinal Willebrands, representing Pope John Paul II, began to pour into Moscow, later dispersing to Leningrad and Kiev. Never before had the Russian Orthodox Church commanded the attention of the world to such an extent, and reporting in the Soviet media represented a psychological breakthrough of major proportions for those who had until recently been oppressed.

CHARITY AND THE CHURCHES

The fulfillment of Gorbachev's promise that there would be a new law on religion to replace Stalin's blueprint for its suppression passed in 1929 did not

---

[1] For a full account of the events of 1988, see Michael Bourdeaux, *Gorbachev, Glasnost, and the Gospel* (London, 1990).

occur until late in 1990, but in the two and a half years between the Kremlin meeting and the passing of the new law, the churches simply ignored the still-existing legal prohibition against Christian involvement in social activities. For nearly seventy years after the 1917 Revolution the Russian Orthodox Church—indeed all believers—had been banned from participation not only in media and education, but also in charitable work. Meanwhile Christianity in the free world had undergone immense changes in the sphere of social responsibility, which had passed the Russian Church by. For a few happy years following the heyday of *glasnost* the experience of the church in the world outside was seized upon with gratitude and enthusiasm, as the Soviet Union began to open its doors to the world at large.

For a while, *miloserdiye* became one of the resonant words describing the type of society the leadership would like to build. Literally meaning "dear-heartedness," the word is loaded with Christian associations. It is the biblical word for "mercy," *caritas* in Latin, which lies at the basis of the English word "charity." But to say that the church in the Soviet Union could now engage in "charitable activities" does not begin to convey the richness present in the Russian word—particularly striking when not only had the practice of charity been banned for seventy years, but even the word itself had been almost excised from the Soviet dictionary, having the label "obsolete" beside it.

It was only to be expected that there would be considerable opposition to the church's involvement in charity from within the Communist Party. Konstantin Kharchev, chairman of the Council for Religious Affairs, who was to become an apostle of *perestroika*, at first expressed his discontent in a typically forthright image. Addressing the ranks of one of Moscow's most elevated ideological institutions, he asked whether it was right, in this great socialist society, to allow a man's dying vision to be of a believer bringing him a bedpan. Should he go to his grave in the realization that the Soviet State was incapable of organizing someone to bring him this small relief? The debate, in March 1988, was on whether it was correct to allow believers to help out in these most elementary aspects of social care where the Soviet State had so abysmally failed. Kharchev went on: "Another reason why we cannot allow the church to engage in charitable activities is that the Catholics would seize upon it: that well-known Mother Teresa has already offered, also Protestants, Baptists, Adventists. Only the Orthodox Church is too beleaguered to have financial resources available at present for anything like that."[2] Kharchev's speech was virtually the last bastion of resistance to the summoning of Christian resources to supply relief in the huge and growing areas of need which were now being publicly admitted in the social services. Some secrets of a state which had proclaimed itself around the world as the most humane yet known to humankind were now open to public scrutiny in the era of *glasnost*.

By the end of 1989 there was open debate. A priest put forward the argument that the virtue of compassion was so developed in pre-revolutionary

---

[2] *Russkaya mysl*, Paris (May 20, 1988).

society that it was not uncommon for the aristocracy to found hospitals with the best available medical equipment, and titled women sometimes even gave up the comforts their inheritance guaranteed in order to devote their life to nursing the sick, exercising just those virtues so lacking today.[3]

A Succession of Disasters

With the Chernobyl disaster of 1986, the state showed itself from the first to be virtually bereft of the means to offer help on the scale needed, leaving a huge gap to be filled by the charitable work of the church, both at home and internationally. During the period of initial reaction, one could see the Russian Church preparing for a defensive propaganda exercise; for example, Metropolitan Filaret of Minsk stated on May 21, 1986, that some foreigners were trying to "gain political advantage from someone else's grief," a deeply unfair remark, especially in what was now a new context: for the first time in history Western Christian aid could be mediated directly to a Soviet disaster area.[4]

Russia opened up as a recipient of aid long before it became host to the invasion of missionaries and proselytizers. There was a considerable Western response to Chernobyl, which continues in modified form even today. Some Western reactions, however, still seemed tuned to the old propaganda on East-West issues. The Soviet press quoted a visiting pastor from West Germany as saying that the real danger to the world was not nuclear reactors, which will inevitably have accidents from time to time, but the deployment of American nuclear weapons.[5] Archbishop Makari of Ivano-Frankivsk, instead of thanking a major Western agency (Aid to the Church in Need) for its offer of help, criticized it for championing the cause of the Ukrainian Catholic Church.[6]

However, there was also a new note in the pronouncements of one or two of the most forward-looking of the Soviet Church leaders. The head of the Armenian Apostolic Church, Catholicos Vazgen I, who two and a half years later would see his people engulfed by the tragedy of an earthquake in his own homeland, announced the opening of a disaster fund to raise 150,000 rubles to help refugees from Chernobyl. The strong Baptist churches in Kiev did the same and provided temporary accommodation, even sending personnel into the heart of the disaster area. Konstantin Kharchev had already spoken with a different voice, stating in an interview with the atheist monthly *Nauka i religiya* ("Science and Religion") in November 1987 that the churches had donated more than three million rubles for the relief of Chernobyl victims.[7]

Three years after the accident, an estimated twenty thousand people gathered outside the Cathedral of the Assumption in Lviv, Western Ukraine, to

---

[3] *Literaturnaya gazeta*, Moscow (October 4, 1989).
[4] *Keston News Service* (June 12, 1987), 252.
[5] Ibid.
[6] Ibid.
[7] "Guarantees of Freedom," *Nauka i religiya*, Moscow (November 1987), 11.

pray for those who had died, for the health of children, and for those who had been held responsible. Priests from the then-still-outlawed Ukrainian Catholic Church led the service.[8] In all of these enterprises there was a Western presence, either explicitly visible or behind the scenes.

This was a new departure for the churches. They had regularly contributed to the Soviet Peace Fund, but this was purely a government agency over which ordinary people had no control and about the workings of which they had little knowledge. Therefore in no real sense could supporting it be considered an act of "charity." Now it would be possible, even logical, for the churches in the Soviet Union to become recipients of Western aid, first to alleviate disaster, but soon to benefit their own development. The shock of this disaster was undoubtedly a factor which made people question: Why was the Party unprepared to cope with social and humanitarian need? Christians in the Soviet Union had shown by their deeds that they cared more than communists did, and their concern was shared by believers (and nonbelievers) in other countries.

After Chernobyl there followed floods in Georgia and various rail and air crashes. The bishops of the Russian Orthodox Church organized a collection for a serious rail disaster during the *sobor* (council) of June 1988. Most horrific of all in its immediate effect was the massive earthquake which devastated Spitak and Leninakan in Armenia in December 1988. Now not only Catholicos Vazgen, but all other church leaders, struck a new note in their public statements.

A CHANGE OF HEART

Miloserdiye now became a buzz-word in the Soviet press. Earlier the resurrection of old religious terminology would have been unthinkable. In 1988 it became a reality. Soviet citizens had to begin to accustom themselves to headlines such as "Charity for all"[9] and "Hurry to do good."[10] Groups of people began to form charitable societies in response to this call, and they were, in the main, open to support from the West.

Although there was still entrenched opposition to this initiative, some headway was made. The Leningrad *Miloserdiye* Society was the first to register, and it did so on April 5, 1988, just before Gorbachev's meeting with the leaders of the Russian Orthodox Church. Within two months the movement had spread to twenty cities, and on September 16 the first All-Union Conference of the Soviet Mercy and Health Fund, an organization apparently running parallel to the *Miloserdiye* Society, took place. In December the All-Union *Miloserdiye* Society was established. On June 14, 1989, *Literaturnaya gazeta* listed the cities in which the main opposition was to be found. At the same time, some

---

[8] *Keston News Service* (April 27, 1989), 325.
[9] *Sovetskaya Moldavia*, (March 7, 1988).
[10] *Pravda* (September 17, 1988).

city councils were much more enthusiastic and took the initiative, such as that in Rostov, which held a *miloserdiye* week in May 1989, involving all local schools in holding fund-raising fairs. Then the Russian Republic inaugurated an "Action-*Miloserdiye*" six months (August 1989 to February 1990) with a series of charity gala concerts involving many leading performers from at home and abroad. For the first anniversary of the Armenian earthquake, and therefore in good time for Christmas and the New Year, the state issued charity stamps to help continue raising funds for the homeless and the families whose lives had been shattered. All this was a world of new experience, not only for Soviet believers, but for citizens in general, and the Christian world beyond was ready, at least in a few places, to respond.

A charitable activity of an especially sensitive nature was the February 1989 establishment of an Association of Afghan War Veterans, who put relief for mutilated victims and for bereaved families at the top of its agenda. The agency established a foreign bank account, not only to collect donations from abroad, but also to be able to order such essentials as artificial limbs, the manufacture of which remains at a primitive level in the Soviet Union and (to this day) relies primarily on the West to supply the essential requirements. Those continuing to need injections would also be able to secure foreign needles for the purpose and thus avoid the very real extra danger of contracting AIDS—for revelations by the Soviet medical profession itself would soon show that here was another crucial gap in the supply system, which put the whole population in peril.

SISTERS OF MERCY

For decades, all offers of charitable assistance from abroad had been rejected out of hand by the authorities, who often confiscated goods from foreign Christians at entry points and harassed the would-be recipients to an extent intended to deter the donors. For a few years there was a legal method, later abolished, of sending in parcels, but this was always accompanied by punitive taxation.

Among foreign enterprises deserving special mention was the persuasiveness of the redoubtable Mother Teresa of Calcutta in obtaining permission to establish a bridgehead for her Missionaries of Charity. Before the illness which disrupted her life in the second half of 1989, Mother Teresa visited the Soviet Union no fewer than three times in seven months and saw her work firmly established there over that period. It is understandable that some Soviet believers have expressed cynicism at the welcome, little short of ecstatic, which officialdom finally extended to her and which was reflected in the media. "Why can't our own nuns receive premises to do similar work in central city locations? We have hundreds of nuns who can't even follow their vocation openly and our own Catholic Church doesn't have a single convent," was one reaction from a dedicated priest. Nevertheless, taking the longer view, this development was significant, not only for the intrinsic goodness of the act itself, but because it opened an important channel for Western Christian aid, an example to be followed some five years later by the Catholic visionary Father Werenfried van Straaten and his charity, Aid to the Church in Need. This also helped persuade the authorities that they should no longer ban the work of indigenous religious orders.

Mother Teresa had requested permission to establish her work long before 1988; as early as autumn 1987 she had been refused permission to do so. However, in the words of Father Mark (Valeri) Smirnov, one of the foremost figures in the *miloserdiye* movement: "Sorrow has made us wiser."[11] Mother Teresa's first visit in December 1988 was an emergency one in the immediate aftermath of the Armenian earthquake. The second was the following February, by which time she was able to agree to a coordinated program for help in Moscow's Burdenko Hospital, which had a section under Professor Arkadi Lifshits for treating spinal disorders and where several victims of the earthquake were undergoing treatment. All in this group were trained nurses and would be there initially for six months, but with the hope, the professor said, that the arrangement would then be ongoing. A further four nuns, according to Mother Teresa, would go directly to Armenia to participate in the continuing relief work there. She went on to express the hope that some Soviet women would be able to join the order and continue this work. There were already thirty-five nationalities represented among the three thousand sisters of the order, and the group in the Soviet Union represented Italy, India, Poland, and Yugoslavia.

On her third visit, at the end of June 1989, Mother Teresa received a telegram of welcome from Raisa Gorbachev and announced that by now no fewer than thirteen of her sisters were at work in Moscow. Professor Lifshits reported: "All the patients who have been lucky enough to meet sisters of the Order of Mercy speak of the unprecedented warmth of soul coming from these people. Mother Teresa visited the new centers recently opened in Tbilisi and Spitak and said that people had come to her literally day and night to receive a blessing and ask for help."[12] The Moscow civic authorities promised all the necessary provisions for her to develop her work, which was so urgently needed.

These indeed were golden days, giving promise, which would not be fulfilled, of openhanded cooperation between the serious needs of the Soviet Union and spontaneous Christian generosity in the West and beyond. There was no suggestion that Mother Teresa's activity—or any other comparable activity—was a covert means of converting Russia to the Catholic faith. On October 8, 1989, *Moscow News* was able to give the addresses of two permanent premises in the capital, little two- or three-story buildings with gardens, where the seriously ill, including people suffering from AIDS, or the homeless would be able to find shelter. Work would be done by Soviet volunteers supervised by

---

[11] "I Believe in Goodness," Molodyozh Estonii, Tallinn (February 18, 1989), interview with Father Mark Smirnov.

[12] *Keston News Service* (July 20, 1989), 330.

a priest. It is remarkable that an ethnic Albanian, whose people at this time were still denied even the basic right to worship God, was able, in her sunset years, to supervise personally the breaking down of a bastion of Soviet atheism and establish the right of Christian sisters to nurse and to love.

PRISON VISITING, HOSPITALS, PSYCHIATRIC CLINICS, OLD PEOPLE'S HOMES

For believers to establish a precedent, even with visible opposition, of visiting criminals in prison and of bringing them a message of Christian salvation illustrates another breakthrough—one which was momentous for generations of Christian prisoners of conscience who had sought to preach the Gospel while themselves sharing the fate of their fellow-prisoners. This was an area in which Soviet Christians, perhaps for obvious reasons, were ready to take the lead without the need for input or training from the West. In Riga the main Protestant denominations came together to form a Latvian Christian Mission, the principal aims of which were social initiatives and evangelism. They listed prison work as one of the objectives: "Corrective labor colonies are an area for our special attention. Initial practical experience suggests the most positive results."[13] One of the new evangelical Christian publications printed a remarkable article three months later entitled "Within Prison Gates," continuing the story of the Latvian Christian Mission. The "boldness" of the officials of the Ministry of the Interior in Latvia had given Christians the opportunity to preach the Gospel in prisons and to distribute Christian literature. The author noted the diversity of nationalities among the 250 or so people participating in this, while regretting that there were not more Latvians involved. The first visit to a women's prison had been very emotional, thanks especially to the singing of a Baptist choir and a remarkable gesture from a Roman Catholic gardener: "He gave each of the female inmates a daffodil. Afterwards the women told me that this flower, even more than the words accompanying the gesture, had moved them. Many of them had never in their lives received such a gift. And, they went on, though they did not yet understand many of the words which passed over them, yet the feeling of warmth and love remained. This light in the soul could not be confused with anything else."[14]

The second visit, in April 1989, concentrated on a service of worship, prayers, and a question-and-answer session, where everyone observed a great openness to the Word of God. Not all were total strangers to the faith: some had been brought up in it, but had subsequently abandoned it. There were those who requested prayer for them in their own local churches. The prison officials later testified to such an improvement in the outlook and behavior of the inmates that they wanted to establish these services as a regular event. But the

---

[13] *Informatsionny byulleten* (new Baptist newspaper), Moscow (May 1989).
[14] *Khristianskoye slovo* (*Informatsionny byulleten* renamed) (August 1989).

writer pointed out with sadness that so very little Christian follow-up literature was available in Latvian that a unique opportunity was not being taken to
the full. Here was an open door of opportunity for Western believers to help
supply the relevant literature. In post-Soviet times, Russian citizens would request Western advice in setting up more long-term plans for establishing a
systematic prison chaplain service.

The development of Christian work in hospitals, psychiatric clinics, and
old people's homes was less dramatic than in the prisons, but nonetheless was
substantial. One effect of *glasnost* was the general recognition and acknowl-
edgment of the appalling conditions prevalent in every institution set up to
care for people. With no possibility of travel, the populace had accepted the
status quo as standard and inevitable. The main problems fell into two categories: lack of personnel and poor physical conditions. Some sources, including
Kharchev in the speech cited at the beginning of this chapter, claimed that in
the Moscow region alone there was a shortfall of twenty thousand medical
personnel, which in itself could only prejudice the relationship between the
hospital staff and the individual. Add to this a prevalence of filth, overcrowd-
ing, and sometimes the lack of even the most elementary needs of clinical
medicine and the picture which emerged, to the surprise of millions in the
West, was of conditions inferior to some parts of the Third World.

An article in *Literaturnaya gazeta* charting the growth of the *miloserdiye*
movement opened with a horrifying description of corruption and negligence
in an old people's home in Voronezh, a city of approximately one million,
three hundred miles south of Moscow. Nurses expected extra private payment
before they would give even the most elementary nursing care, and sanitary
conditions were such that there was only one shower room to two hundred
people. Clearly, someone made a high-level decision early in 1988 that it might
be possible to alleviate the effects of the enormous shortfall in personnel and
to improve staff-patient relationships if it were possible to summon help from
the only available source which could cost the state nothing: the local churches,
with possible supplementary help from abroad. Mr. Gorbachev virtually suggested such initiatives at his meeting with the leaders of the Russian Orthodox
Church in April 1988.

The response was immediate, though uneven. Leaders of the Russian Orthodox Church correctly claimed that such "charitable" activity had been an
essential part of Christian concern since time immemorial. Nevertheless, they
were clearly caught unprepared, as Soviet law had specifically banned any
such work since 1929. As Father Matvei Stadnyuk, dean of the Moscow Patriarchal Cathedral, stated in an interview with the reformist newspaper
Ogonyok—an article, incidentally, accompanied by a photo of priests in cas-
socks and other believers going about their task of hospital visiting—people
had become passive, had lost the prompting to take initiatives: "Everywhere
they are waiting for some directive . . . a decision, an order, a telephone call.
You can compel someone to go out on a *subbotnik* [so-called voluntary Satur-

day labor, such as tree-planting]—we go, we're used to it. But can you force someone to go and exercise charity? Hardly."[15]

Far fewer people volunteered for charitable work than needed or expected, but the stage was therefore set all the more readily for Western initiative. For example, according to Metropolitan (later Patriarch) Aleksii, there were only eighty-four volunteers in a huge city like Leningrad.[16] Some volunteers dropped it just as quickly as they had taken it up:

> Many parishioners who had taken up charitable work on the spur of the moment abandoned it within a month or two. Some of them, especially young people, proved to be unprepared psychologically for the sight of the suffering of the gravely sick and the dying. The dispersion of believers in the parishes and lack of contact with the local clergy also have a negative effect. The inertia of the stagnation period is still there. The church's estrangement from public life, the blame for which was not hers, resulted in believers adopting a guarded attitude towards society. Today, when the conditions for public activity by Christians are favorable, many of us are not ready for it morally.[17]

This article was important because it was printed in the *Journal of the Moscow Patriarchate,* which has always been among the most timid of publications, and this exercise in self-examination was a new departure not without relevance to the subsequent criticism of Western initiatives by the Russian Orthodox Church. The article went on to state that in one place "about half of the forty people who volunteered for hospital work have dropped out," and the only answer is to bridge the estrangement between the clergy and their flock. If there was no history or practical experience, then there must be parochial libraries, where activists can learn secondhand from the knowledge of others, but that resource is nonexistent, too. Here was a wide-open door to cooperation with the West, but one which the Orthodox Church itself would soon close. At the same time, the article made it clear that even these modest beginnings were achieving positive results:

> For instance, there is a very active group of young men and women. Interestingly, after the hospital was visited by young believers many patients expressed the desire to receive Holy Communion, wear a pectoral cross, have small icons, and memorize prayers. Some of the nurses too wished to receive Holy Communion. . . . A woman of about sixty enters the ward. She holds a book. She tells me she is a parishioner of St. Nicholas Church. She proceeds to read the Lives of Saints to the patients. . . .

---

[15] *Ogonyok,* Moscow (September 1988), 38.

[16] *Moscow News,* Moscow (April 9, 1989).

[17] *Journal of the Moscow Patriarchate* (JMP), Moscow, 3 (March 1989) (English language version, verbatim; reprinted in Russian version June 1989).

Professor Anatolia Fedin, Chief Neuro-Pathologist of Moscow . . . says:
"Since volunteers first appeared in our wards, the nurses and other personnel have shown more consideration for the patients. It is no secret
that we do have cases of rudeness and negligence in hospitals. When
nurses see people come here in their free time to look after the patients,
they begin working better themselves. The volunteers' work is having an
especially strong educative effect on the young nurses."[18]

It is clear that, even had optimum help been sought from abroad, it would
have taken the Orthodox Church years, probably decades, to be in a position
to take advantage of all the new opportunities.

CHILDREN

It was in the sphere of child care that the church made the most significant
breakthrough in its social program. Often the Soviet State, in its attempt universally to impose communist morality, removed children from parents as a
result of a judicial decision and placed them in boarding schools. Into what
conditions? There are dozens of heartbreaking stories from the 1960s continuing right into the 1980s which recount the horror and the shock of the child
victims and their attempts, sometimes successful, to run away. In the Gorbachev
period the appalling conditions in those homes became open for inspection
under *glasnost,* and it was not a pretty sight. One of the extreme ironies in the
volte-face of *perestroika* was the open invitation to Christians in many places
to come in and clean up the mess. In some instances, Westerners received invitations to observe, and this often led to personal involvement as well, though
never to the extent as happened in Romania.

The daily *Sovetskaya Rossiya* published an article about the plight of Soviet
orphans on December 16, 1989. It revealed that no less than 1,100,000 children were currently living in Soviet orphanages. The article went on to focus
on several families which had adopted children, an entirely new practice for
the Soviet Union. There was some interest in the West in receiving Soviet children for adoption, but this never happened to any significant extent. It was the
establishing of regular visits by a group of Orthodox believers which led to an
initiative—requested by the staff of the home itself—to have the children in a
psychiatric hospital baptized. A priest, Father Vladimir Chuvikin, recounted:

We decided that each child should have a baptismal outfit. We bought
48 white shirts, candles, small crosses, and presents, and with a group of
parishioners we went to the children's home. Everyone was in a holiday
mood and looked forward to that Saturday in anticipation as a great
celebration. Two weeks later, 15 April, the children received communion
[there is no confirmation in the Orthodox tradition]. In the future we

---

[18] Ibid., 52-54.

shall support them spiritually and give help to these sick children who so much need human contact and warmth.[19]

AN OPPORTUNITY MISSED

In 1990, the present author wrote these words:

> Organized encouragement and help is now needed from the outside to render good the inevitable deficiencies resulting from atrophy. Much of the good will is there already, but where it is not it should be possible to cultivate it in the present climate. From Brest on the Polish frontier to Vladivostok on the Pacific, training programmes for local organizers are needed on a massive scale. Visual aids, especially video tapes, to illustrate what is being done elsewhere, could encourage believers nationwide. The prospects are limitless, but the lack of preparation for them in the West is frightening.[20]

These words heralded a false dawn, and the fears expressed in the last sentence proved to be only too real. Previously, propagandist spokesmen for the Russian Orthodox Church had claimed all social welfare was safely in the hands of the caring state. Therefore there could at that time have been no question of the Orthodox Church turning to foreign agencies for help. This attitude, expressed by the Russians in public Christian forums in the West over decades, produced its own consequences. Reiterating the message that everything was going well for the Soviet Union led to an atrophy in the West in those very areas where aid agencies might have become active. No tradition arose, so there were precious few ready and able to respond to the humanitarian opportunity which opened up in the Soviet Union in the Gorbachev years. Instead, the immediate collapse of communism would herald the influx of (often untrained) evangelists. Only here and there in the West did the will exist to establish training or exchange programs, and even when there was the desire, the linguistic skills to back this up were insufficiently developed.

One wonders whether, if Western Christians had been better prepared to walk through an open door to an unprecedented welcome, this might have increased understanding and lessened the tensions between East and West over proselytism which bedevil the scene today. Looking at the example of Mother Teresa of Calcutta, one can say with confidence that the involvement of Christians of the Third World would have been practically helpful as well.

---

[19] *Moskovsky tserkovny vestnik* (new Orthodox monthly publication), Moscow (May 1989), 3.

[20] Bourdeaux, *Gorbachev*, 208.

11.

PROTESTANT MISSIONARIES
IN THE FORMER SOVIET UNION
— ◆ —

Mark Elliott and Anita Deyneka

A MODERN MISSION CRUSADE

Because Russian Orthodoxy was the established faith of tsarist Russia, it was for centuries a violation of law for a person baptized into the Orthodox faith to convert to Protestantism. This changed after the Edict of Toleration of 1905; still, for all but the last few years of imperial Russia, traditional Protestant evangelistic outreach and foreign missionaries were almost always legally proscribed. Nevertheless, Evangelicals grew to number several hundred thousand by 1917. This was primarily because of the translation of the Bible into the Russian vernacular, pietistic movements in Russia's German colonies which spread among neighboring Slavic peasants, and the emergence of an Evangelical community among St. Petersburg aristocrats that quickly spread to other classes and other regions of the country.

Although the efforts of a few Evangelical missionaries, such as Dr. F. W. Baedeker and Granville Waldegrave Lord Radstock, promoted the growth of Protestantism in the nineteenth century, comparatively few foreign Evangelical missionaries engaged in ministries to Russia until the late 1980s. In 1917, the Bolshevik Revolution set Russia on a course of official atheism that quickly led to a ban on foreign missionaries and, by the late 1930s, so repressed Soviet citizens of all religious convictions that all faiths were on the verge of institutional extinction.

However, even during the most severe periods of religious persecution, foreign Protestants attempted to support their co-believers behind the Iron Cur-

This article is an excerpt of the authors' earlier article that appeared in *Emory International Law Review* 12 (1998): 361-412.

tain, entering the USSR clandestinely with Christian literature and providing other assistance from the outside, such as shortwave Christian broadcasting. These foreign missionaries were revered by Soviet believers for this assistance. At the same time they were reviled by the Soviet government.

By 1989, with the presidency of Mikhail Gorbachev and his policies of *perestroika* (restructuring) and *glasnost* (openness), Protestant missionaries began to enter the Soviet Union openly. In October 1990, a new law on religion not only provided unprecedented freedom for Soviet religious believers but also opened the doors of the USSR to foreign missionaries. The dissolution of the Soviet Union in December 1991 swung open the doors to Russia even wider.

The change was startling. Some Western Protestants, unable to obtain visas under communism, now found themselves invited to meet with political leaders. For example, in November 1991, nineteen American Evangelical leaders met with Mikhail Gorbachev, then president of the USSR, and also with General Nikolai Stolyarov, an air force general and KGB vice chairman, who told them that "[p]olitical questions cannot be decided until there is sincere *repentance*, a return to faith by the people. . . . I have been a member of the Party for twenty years. In our study of scientific atheism, we were taught that religion divides people. Now we see the opposite: love for God can only unite."[1]

Warmly welcomed by Soviet citizens from all strata of society, the trickle of Protestant missionaries that had entered the USSR before the late 1980s soon swelled to a stream, with evangelists arriving from the United States, Canada, Korea, Germany, Sweden, Finland, and other countries. By 1993, anti-Westernism was on the rise in Russia, and the tide of national sentiment had started to turn against Western missionaries. In September 1997, the Russian Duma passed national legislation restricting religious liberty and foreign missionaries. Increased provincial legislation and administrative practice already had been curbing "nontraditional" faiths for several years and contributed to the air of urgency to both foreign and indigenous Evangelical efforts.

The political upheaval that spelled an end to communist rule in East Central Europe, and which led to the dismantling of the Soviet Union itself, has also transformed the region's churches and East European ministry. Regarding Protestant missionary activity in post-Soviet lands, the seismic changes of this past decade have contributed to a number of major developments, including mission restructuring, mission expansion, unprecedented cooperative efforts alongside an unprecedented proliferation of mission mavericks, and mission specialization.

RESTRUCTURING

Gorbachev's stress in the late 1980s upon *glasnost* and *perestroika* triggered a major restructuring in East European ministry as well. Proceeding as usual

---

[1] Philip Yancey, *Praying with the KGB: A Startling Report from a Shattered Empire* (Portland, Ore., 1992), 32-33.

made less and less sense for Evangelical agencies as the Soviet Union relaxed religious discrimination and restrictions on foreign contacts. Debates became intense in a number of ministries regarding the extent of operations and the number of personnel which should remain abroad and the extent to which personnel should relocate within the country. Also, with the demise of communist governments, missions that stressed *anti*communism had difficulty adjusting to the new politics and suffered financial downturns.[2]

EXPANSION

The unanticipated removal of political barriers in East Central Europe and the Soviet Union in the latter half of the 1980s led to a sharp increase in the number of foreign ministries working in the region: from 150 in 1982, to 311 in 1989, to 691 in 1993, to nearly 1,000 in 1997. Some 561 groups were active in the former Soviet Union in 1997.[3] Quickest to take advantage of new opportunities were parachurch ministries, which are more flexible than church bureaucracies; ministries headed by Slavic immigrants from the region, whose leaders understood the region's languages and cultures firsthand; and ministries with worldwide programs, which could rapidly redeploy substantial resources and personnel to former Soviet Bloc states.

While no precise statistics exist for the current size of the foreign missionary force in post-Soviet territories in 1997, informed estimates are available. In 1993, British author Patrick Johnstone published an admittedly conservative estimate of 1,113 foreign missionaries in the former Soviet Union and 864 in East Central Europe, for a total of 1,977.[4] In 1995, survey work conducted by the *East-West Church and Ministry Report* determined that the twenty-five largest sending agencies, by themselves, had 3,190 nonindigenous missionar-

---

[2] Mark Elliott, "Eastern Europe: Responding to Crisis in the Household of Faith," *Eternity* (July-August 1986): 26-27.

[3] Mark Elliott, ed., *The East European Missions Directory* (Wheaton, Ill., 1989), includes 267 groups—402 if branches are included—and excludes 44 low-profile organizations. Sharon Linzey, et al., eds., *The East-West Christian Organizations Directory*, (1993), includes 691 groups. Paul Hansen, European Secretary of the Lutheran World Federation, estimated 80 groups in 1979. *Religious News Service*, February 27, 1979.

Since 1993, the Institute for East-West Christian Studies has identified some 296 Western agencies not included among the 691 groups listed in Linzey's *Directory*, thus giving a total of 987 for 1997. The figure of 561 ministries from abroad working in the former Soviet Union is based on the following: 377 of the 691 groups in the 1993 *Directory* work there, plus 148 (approximately half of the 296 groups identified since 1993), plus 36 South Korean groups (9 church and 27 parachurch).

[4] Patrick Johnstone, *Operation World* (Carlisle, 1993), 646-47. For a statistical table by country based on *Operation World*, see "Non-Indigenous Protestant Missionaries in Former Communist States of Eurasia," *East-West Church and Ministry Report* (Winter 1994): 5.

ies in the former Soviet Union.[5] Among the numerous smaller ministries, several hundred, who are engaged in such support services as publishing, broadcasting, and relief work, have either no missionaries or no career missionaries stationed in the country. At the same time, hundreds of other smaller agencies appeared to be sponsoring an average of four missionaries each in the mid-1990s. Given these considerations, a total Western missionary community in the former Soviet Union of approximately 4,390 would appear plausible for 1995.[6] In late 1996, an *East-West Church and Ministry Report* survey indicated a one-year increase of 31 percent in the number of Western denominational missionaries in the former Soviet Union, as opposed to parachurch groups.[7] Since it appears that denominational momentum was just reaching a crescendo in 1996-97, in comparison with parachurch groups which mobilized more quickly and may have peaked earlier, a more likely overall estimate for a 1995-96 increase in the Western missionary force in the former Soviet Union might be 15 percent, which would yield a total of 5,049.[8] Adding 557 South Korean missionaries gives a total foreign missionary force of 5,606 in the former Soviet Union in 1997.[9] Finally, if the career-to-short-term ratio of 35/65, which was the case for the twenty-five largest sending agencies, can be applied to all groups, then approximately 1,962 career missionaries from abroad served in the former Soviet Union in 1997. On one hand, this represents a striking increase over the handful of undeclared missionaries in the Soviet Union in 1986. On the other hand, given its population of approximately 287 million people, the former Soviet Union does not command a disproportionate share of the worldwide Protestant missionary effort.[10]

---

[5] "Missionaries to the Former Soviet Union and East Central Europe," *East-West Church and Ministry Report* (Spring 1995): 10; *East-West Church and Ministry Report* (Fall 1995): 3. See Appendix A below.

[6] The total of 4,390 Western missionaries in the former Soviet Union in 1995 is based on 3,190 (from the twenty-five largest agencies) plus 1,200 (from three hundred agencies with an average of four each). The authors wish to thank Peter Deyneka of Russian Ministries for his help in arriving at this estimate.

[7] See Appendix B below.

[8] A total of 5,049 is based on 4,390 in 1995 plus a one-year increase of 15 percent (659).

[9] The authors wish to thank graduate assistant Sharyl Corrado for her extensive survey work in the fall of 1996 on Protestant missionaries in the former Soviet Union. The source for the number of Korean missionaries is an e-mail from David Lee of the GM Torch Center sent to Sharyl Corrado on December 3, 1996.

[10] If the fifteen republics of the former Soviet Union still constituted one nation, the 5,606 Protestant missionaries working there in 1997 would constitute the largest Protestant mission contingent in a single nation worldwide. (No up-to-date breakdown by republic is available.) On the other hand, given a population of approximately 287 million, the Protestant missionary presence in the former Soviet Union in 1997, per capita, was less than that in the five countries with the largest Protestant missionary contingents: Brazil (3,397 in a population of 146,200,000); Japan (3,015 in a population of 124,760,000); Philippines (2,958 in a population of 65,650,000);

In addition to a pronounced increase in foreign missionary activity, *glasnost* also gave new opportunities to indigenous Protestants in the former Soviet Union. One response has been a proliferation of denominations. In part, new church structures were a reaction against the Soviet-imposed unity that had seen Mennonites and even Pentecostals constrained under an Evangelical Christian-Baptist (ECB) umbrella. Also, new freedom allowed Western and Korean denominations to enter, or reenter, the region unimpeded. Whereas in 1986 the Kremlin permitted only one all-union Protestant denomination (Evangelical Christians-Baptists) and a handful of others in particular locales (Lutherans in the Baltics, Methodists in Estonia, Hungarian Reformed in Western Ukraine), by 1997 the former Soviet Union counted thirty-five Protestant denominations.[11]

The past decade has also witnessed an explosion of independent grassroots mission enterprises, distinct from existing church structures. Hundreds of such indigenous initiatives now engage in evangelism; Christian publishing and distribution; compassion ministries in hospitals, orphanages, prisons, and soup kitchens; and professional associations for Christian lawyers, doctors, artists, and entrepreneurs.[12] Three such groups founded in 1988-89, *Svet Evangeliia* (Light of the Gospel) in Rovno, Latvian Christian Mission in Riga, and *Vozmozhnost* (Possibility) Mission in Donetsk, alone support 540 full and part-time workers.[13]

Indigenous ministries and Western agencies such as Campus Crusade, Navigators, InterVarsity, and CoMission are spawning Bible studies and new autonomous congregations that frequently have no affiliation with the formerly all-encompassing Union of Evangelical Christians-Baptists. These newly forming churches appeal especially to new converts who, on one hand, distrust many Orthodox hierarchs and priests who collaborated with the old regime, and yet, on the other hand, find it difficult to conform to Baptist and Pentecostal legalism and cultural isolation. Ultimately, distinct new Protestant denominations are likely to emerge from these parachurch efforts as has happened in the past with such ministry-sponsored churches as Nigeria's SIM-related Evangelical Church of West Africa and the OMS-related Korean Holiness Church.[14]

Kenya (2,322 in a population of 29,300,000); and Papua New Guinea (2,278 in a population of 3,850,000). Johnstone, *Operation World*, 644-49; Brian Hunter, ed., *Statesman's Yearbook*, (London, 1996). (Both the *East-West Church and Ministry Report* survey and Johnstone's statistics used in the above comparison include short-term missionaries. However, the figures are not completely comparable because the total for the former Soviet Union includes short-termers serving three to twenty-four months, whereas Johnstone includes short-termers serving twelve months or more.)

[11] Mark Elliott and Robert Richardson, "Growing Protestant Diversity in the Former Soviet Union," in *Russian Pluralism: Now Irreversible?*, ed. Uri Ra'anan, et al. (New York, 1992), 189, 204 (citing twenty-one denominations, but additional churches now work there). See Appendix C below.

[12] "Indigenous Christian Missions in the Former Soviet Union," *East-West Church and Ministry Report* (Winter 1994): 6.

[13] Elliott and Richardson, "Growing Protestant Diversity," 198.

[14] Ibid., 198-200.

GREATER SUPPORT FOR COOPERATION
AND GREATER INDEPENDENT ACTIVITY

Paradoxically, in former Soviet Bloc states, unprecedented mission cooperation coexists with an unprecedented number of solo, go-it-alone mission mavericks. On the positive side, 1987 to 1989 alone saw Bible delivery partnerships involving some twenty-eight denominations, missions, and Bible societies.[15] Other ongoing, collaborative efforts include eight new Evangelical alliances and twenty-three new Bible societies in former East bloc states; the CoMission's efforts involving eighty-five agencies in a program of Christian ethics and outreach in post-Soviet public schools; the sixty-five-member Albanian Encouragement Project; and the multi-ministry Alliance for Saturation Church Planting.[16] Peter Deyneka Russian Ministries, founded in 1991 specifically to serve as a consultant and catalyst for Slavic ministry partnerships, has advised and assisted over 270 church and parachurch missions now working in the former Soviet Union.[17]

Other collaborative projects are notable. Wycliffe Bible Translators and five denominations (the Alaska Moravian Church, the Presbytery of Yukon-Presbyterian, the United Methodist Church in Alaska, the Evangelical Covenant Church of Alaska, and the Evangelical Lutheran Church of Alaska) have organized the Chukotka Native Christian Ministries.[18] The American Bible Society is assisting the Russian Bible Society in translating Scriptures for seven of the seventy-five languages and dialect groups in Russia. Since 1987 in the former Soviet Union, these Bible societies have published 4,462,576 Bibles, 1,997,259 New Testaments, 1,226,579 Bible tracts, and 4,073,337 Scripture portions, including children's Bibles.[19] To strengthen the estimated 120 Protestant theological training institutions that now exist in the former Soviet Union, the Overseas Council for Theological Education, the Maclellan Foundation, and Russian Ministries joined together to stock an Evangelical theological research library containing approximately 5,000 different titles in Russian. From titles selected from this library and elsewhere, 300,000 copies of 80 different theological textbooks, used by approximately 3,000 students in resi-

---

[15] Mark Elliott, "New Openness in USSR Prompts Massive Bible Shipments to Soviet Christians in 1987-88: A Statistical Overview," *News Network International* (March 20, 1989): 24-31.
[16] Elliott, "East European Missions," 11-12; letter from Paul Stawasz, American Bible Society, to Amy Staufer, Institute for East-West Christian Studies (February 24, 1997). On February 28, 1997, Dwight Gibson, of the World Evangelical Fellowship, reported eight Evangelical alliances in the region: Albania, Bulgaria, Croatia, Czech Republic, Estonia, Hungary, Romania, and Slovakia.
[17] Categories of Networking Relationships, available in Russian Ministries Files, Wheaton, Illinois.
[18] Gary Brumbelow, "The Other Side of Russia: Evangelical Ministries in Siberia," *East-West Church and Ministry Report* (Spring 1995): 1.
[19] Interview with Doris Fisher, American Bible Society (November 26, 1996), available in Russian Ministries Files, Wheaton, Illinois.

dential schools and extension courses and hundreds of churches, have been published or reprinted.[20]

Unfortunately, hundreds of other, more independent-minded new players claim to know what has worked in Christian outreach in the West and boldly step forward with a bewildering array of "proven programs" that they are confident will provide answers in the East. Too often, a free-spirited, "Lone Ranger" approach to ministry ends in what might be called hit-and-run evangelism, producing neglect of discipline for new believers and inattention to respectful partnerships with existing churches. Gross cultural insensitivity on the part of many missionaries stems, in part, from an arrogant attitude which assumes that "the West knows best." Even when Western and Korean ministries are unconscious of their overweening, unbiblical sense of self-importance, Christians in the East readily detect it. The latter have to deal with far too many newcomers more intent on promoting prepackaged strategies than listening to Slavic believers sharing their needs and dreams.

Often, mission miscues result from a lack of appreciation for, and even ignorance of, the culture in question. It may be that the greatest flaw today in missionary orientation for post-Soviet lands is not its brevity, although that frequently is a serious shortcoming. The greatest flaw may be inadequate or nonexistent country-specific and culture-specific preparation (i.e., woefully insufficient study of pertinent languages, literature, and history). Ministry training too often focuses on what might be called generic preparation—the cultivation of skills and outlooks applicable to any cross-cultural experience, be it in Botswana or Belarus—to the neglect of an adequate entree to the specific destination. What are we to make of a mission board, presently preparing missionaries for service in diverse parts of the world, that is sending them together to southern California for a ten-week internship with an Hispanic cross-cultural ministry? If a pre-field, cross-cultural immersion experience is prescribed, why not, rather, send the candidates bound for Russia to Sacramento, to one of its many Slavic immigrant churches to experience more of Russian culture firsthand? And why not send those bound for Nigeria to a ministry internship among African immigrants in Chicago, New York, or London? Greater attention to culture-specific orientation and training would require more staff work and greater decentralization, but it would reap ample dividends in terms of less traumatic culture shock and greater longevity for personnel in the field. Missionaries to Russia, for example, who arrive ignorant of icons and Orthodoxy, Dostoyevsky and Tolstoy, Stanislavsky and Chekhov, and Tchaikovsky and Rachmaninov are not taken seriously.

SPECIALIZATION

Recognizing the miscues of post-communist missions and recalling the region's longstanding tradition of state churches identified with particular nationali-

---

[20] Jack Graves, "Russian Protestant Theological Textbook Project," *East-West Church and Ministry Report* (Fall 1996): 1-2.

ties, one can more readily explain the genesis of various legislative measures to curb Western missionary activity. But ill-advised and ill-informed Christian witness represents only part of the explanation for the hostile reception. Communists, nationalists, and the hierarchs of former state churches also oppose Evangelical missionaries because they are just as often warm, winsome, and loving as they are brash, brazen, and culturally clueless. Opposition, then, is as much a function of what Evangelicals are doing right as it is of what they are doing wrong. It may be argued that so many ministries are having such a beneficial effect in so many places and in so many ways that Evangelical detractors cannot tolerate it. As a result, they seek to restrict freedom of conscience by erecting political barriers which discriminate against arbitrarily defined "nontraditional" faiths.

In the meantime, large numbers of Western ministries are making perhaps their greatest impact for good in former Soviet Bloc states through all manner of specialized assistance, including the following: (1) facilitating in-country radio broadcasting, publishing, and film and video production; (2) partnering with indigenous churches to help provide Sunday school-to-seminary-level training; (3) sharing expertise in marriage, family, youth, prison, alcohol, and drug counseling; and (4) introducing sports, camping, and drama ministries, to name just a sampling of the burgeoning kaleidoscope of Western Evangelical endeavors.

Concrete examples of Evangelical efforts requiring uncommon expertise and unique resources abound. The Children of Russia Project is providing Christian literature to more than 200,000 orphans by delivering mini-libraries of Christian literature to the 1,000 orphanages under the direction of the Russia Ministry of Education.[21] CoCreation is a Moscow-based "cultural society aimed at reaching creative Russians involved in media and the performing arts."[22] Transport for Christ International is ministering to truck drivers within a 3,500 kilometer radius of Moscow.[23] Deaf Opportunity OutReach has organized Bible studies for deaf people and has facilitated the use of Christian ethics and morals curriculum in schools for the deaf.[24] The Salvation Army has proclaimed the gospel on the streets, in theaters, and in prisons; is involved in the rehabilitation of alcoholics; and has distributed tons of food and clothing in Russia and other republics of the former Soviet Union.[25]

---

[21] Brochure of Children of Russia Project, available in Institute for East-West Christian Studies Files, Wheaton, Illinois.

[22] Newsletter of Beverly Nickles of Jesus Name Ministries International (September 18, 1996), available in Institute for East-West Christian Studies Files, Wheaton, Illinois.

[23] Newsletter of Transport for Christ (November 1996), available in Russian Ministries Files, Wheaton, Illinois.

[24] Mission Bulletin of Deaf Opportunity OutReach (1994), available in Institute for East-West Christian Studies Files, Wheaton, Illinois.

[25] Reprint from *Salvation Army Year Book* (London), 183-84, available in Institute for East-West Christian Studies Files, Wheaton, Illinois.

Christian Bridge, Christian Broadcasting Network, the Evangelical Cov-
enant Church, the Evangelical Mennonite Conference Missions Auxiliary, Far
East Broadcasting Company, International Russian Radio/TV, the Missouri
Church Lutheran Synod, Russian Christian Radio, Trans World Radio, World
Radio Missionary Fellowship, and other Western agencies have helped na-
tional churches establish radio studios and stations and produce radio and
television programs.[26] Christian Booksellers Association of America (CBA),
Gospel Light Publications, Russian Ministries (also known as *Assotsiatsiya
Dukhovnoye Vozrozhdeniye*), and other organizations have assisted in establishing distribution networks for Christian literature in the former Soviet
Union.[27] The Christian Medical and Dental Association, Dorcas Aid, Fellowship of Association of Medical Evangelism, Samaritan's Purse, World Vision,
and other organizations have helped to establish Christian medical clinics and
other medically related outreaches.[28] Relating faith, business, and economic
development, the Mennonite Economic Development Association has promoted
a program to provide business training and institutions to help Christians develop micro-enterprises.[29] In addition to training 411 counselors, Kingdom
Ventures organized 114 Christian camps in eight former Soviet republics for
23,000 young people in 1996.[30]

THE NEED TO RETHINK THE RELATIONSHIP
BETWEEN EAST EUROPEAN MISSIONS
AND INDIGENOUS PROTESTANTS AND ORTHODOX

East European ministries have much to learn from both the successes and
failures of two centuries of Western Protestant missions in Africa, Asia, and
Latin America.[31] At the same time, even long-established ministries, highly
respected for their effectiveness elsewhere, need to approach service in post-
Soviet lands with a healthy dose of humility and with many more questions
than answers. The disastrous consequences of seventy-two years of communism in the Soviet Union, not only on the political process and the economy,
but on the psyche of long-suffering citizens, cannot be overestimated. Missions
from abroad must remember that ministry among people long conditioned by

---

[26] See generally Russian Ministries Files, Wheaton, Illinois.

[27] Russian Ministries e-mail (September 12, 1995), available in Russian Ministries Files, Wheaton, Illinois.

[28] See generally Russian Ministries Files, Wheaton, Illinois.

[29] MEDA Bulletin, available in Institute for East-West Christian Studies Files,
Wheaton, Illinois.

[30] Newsletters of Kingdom Ventures, available in Institute for East-West Christian Studies Files, Wheaton, Illinois.

[31] Mark Elliott, "New Opportunities, New Demands in the Old Red Empire,"
Evangelical Missions Quarterly 28 (1992): 36-37.

authoritarian Marxist rule presents circumstances unique in the history of world missions.[32]

It is appropriate for mission agencies to note, of course, that with regard to hardship and deprivation, Botswana and Belarus have suffered alike. At the same time, a discerning Evangelical outreach in post-Soviet Belarus must take into account the wrenching peculiarities of its twentieth-century ordeal: terror, death, and devastation inflicted by Stalin, Hitler, and Chernobyl. Foreign missions to Belarus also need to be aware that, unlike in the case of Botswana, Western missionaries did not constitute the first expression of Christianity in this troubled land. Orthodox and Catholics have been on hand for a millennium, and even indigenous Protestants have had a presence here for more than a century. More than once in public forums has Father Leonid Kishkovsky, ecumenical officer of the Orthodox Church in America, rightly decried a 1991 ministry advertisement in *Christianity Today* that, under a reproduction of an icon, appealed for help in its campaign to take the real Christ to Russia.[33] The implication that without this initiative the real Christ would remain absent from Russia is clearly offensive to Orthodox Christians. But Slavic Evangelicals as well, who managed to survive over one hundred years of tsarist and Soviet attacks on their existence, might take offense. Guidelines for ministry in the East published by the British Evangelical Missionary Alliance agree with Father Kishkovsky: "Mission teams which say 'We are taking Jesus to Russia' show they don't understand the situation at all. Nobody is taking Jesus to Russia. He has been there all the time! His Holy Spirit was moving behind the Iron Curtain before Christians from the West could go there. Remember that many Christians you meet have lived under persecution, whilst you have lived with religious freedom."[34]

East European missions should first recognize the existence of indigenous Evangelical and Orthodox Christians, and, second, should pay them due respect for having outlasted communism.

RETHINKING THE RELATIONSHIP
BETWEEN EAST EUROPEAN MISSIONS
AND INDIGENOUS PROTESTANTS

In order to evaluate the relationship between East European missions and indigenous Protestants, a brief overview of Evangelicals in the Soviet Union as

---

[32] See Juraj Kusneirik, "Post-Modern Culture in Post-Communist Countries," *East-West Church and Ministry Report* (Winter 1994): 1, 2; Annette J. Ford, "Mission Trends in Eastern Europe," *The Christian and Missionary Alliance* (February 1996).

[33] The advertisement appeared in *Christianity Today* 35 (September 16, 1991): 61. See Leonid Kishkovsky, "The Mission of the Russian Orthodox Church after Communism," *East-West Church and Ministry Report* (Summer 1993): 1, 2; Miroslav Volf, "Fishing in the Neighbor's Pond: Mission and Proselytism in Eastern Europe," *International Bulletin of Missionary Research* 20 (1996): 26, 28.

[34] Evangelical Missionary Alliance, *Working in Central and Eastern Europe: Guidelines for Christians* (1994): 3.

of 1990, on the eve of the large influx of Western missionaries, is in order. Protestants included a membership of 1.2 million, with a total community (including children and adherents) of 3 million. Lutherans, at 1.1 million, were mostly non-Slavic (Estonian, Latvian, or German) and outside the Russian heartland (concentrated in the Baltic states or scattered in German enclaves in Central Asia and Siberia). Evangelical Christians-Baptists (746,000 members) could be found in all Soviet republics and included faithful of many nationalities. Geographically, its greatest strength was in European Russia and Ukraine. Pentecostals (700,000 members) in 1990 were just coming into an independent legal existence for the first time. They also drew faithful from various nationalities, but with a predominance of Slavic membership and a stronger than average presence in Ukraine and Siberia. Remaining Protestant groups included Seventh-day Adventists (160,000 members) and two groups confined by law to Western borderlands: Hungarian Reformed in Western Ukraine (200,000 members) and Methodists in Estonia (2,500 members). German Mennonites (7,000 members) by 1990 were already just a shadow of their former presence, thanks to large-scale immigration abroad.[35] In contrast to this short list of recognized denominations as of 1990, some thirty-three Protestant denominations existed by 1997.

Two contrasting perspectives prevail regarding the relationship of ministries from abroad with indigenous Protestants. The first emphasizes that Evangelicals have survived a lengthy and vicious atheist assault on their existence; they have been tested by the refiner's fire firsthand; they are to be commended for their faithfulness. As a result, some perceive that they should receive the lion's share of support from their co-believers abroad. The second ministry perspective stresses the legalism of many former Soviet Bloc Evangelicals, their cultural isolation from the mainstream of society, their authoritarian leadership style, their lack of financial accountability by Western standards, and their frequent inability to absorb new converts who sometimes find the traditional Evangelical subculture cold, constraining, and judgmental. Accordingly, this second perspective argues that the major focus should be on new wineskins; that is, on new churches where those coming to Christ in the wake of communism will find ready acceptance and love. Actually, each conclusion can be debated, but every point in *both* perspectives can be readily documented. That being the case, both partnership with existing denominations and the establishment of new churches would appear to be legitimate strategies for Evangelical ministries. At the same time, it would be more edifying if proponents of the two approaches did not verbally cast those with whom they differ into outer darkness. As a practical matter, foreign ministries, even those committed to new wineskins, should not begin work in any region or city without extending the common courtesy of informing local churches of their plans, asking for advice, and, where possible, offering material assistance.

Although relations between Russian Orthodox and Western Evangelical missionaries have often been antagonistic, Russian Evangelicals initially welcomed their Western counterparts with open arms, rapidly requesting assistance from

---

[35] See Elliott and Richardson, "Growing Protestant Diversity," 205.

foreign Christians and reiterating how grateful they were for such help. Such a reception was not surprising, considering the long and deep relationship between Western and Russian Evangelicals, even during the most repressive years of communism.

Many nationals, including religious leaders such as Grigori Komendant, former president of the Evangelical Christians-Baptists, expressed appreciation and gratitude along the following lines:

> But, praise God, there are those who came to us, sought out our churches and our brothers and sisters, and stayed to labor together with us as partners in the work of spreading the gospel message. To some degree, they cannot become "as one of us" yet their lack of language ability or knowledge of our culture, history, and traditions have been beautifully overcome by their willingness to subject self to the Lord, His work, and to our Russian and Ukrainian fellowships. They labor not to plant American-style churches, but churches in the spirit and tradition of our fellowships and our people. Observing their committed experience and humble dedication, our national workers were challenged and encouraged. As a result, many of our lay preachers were willing to trust the Lord, leave their secular jobs, and commit themselves to full-time Christian service. When they saw that American missionaries were willing to leave a comfortable life to win souls for Christ in Russia, many of our young people were deeply touched and responded to God's call with courage and faith.[36]

Alexander Sorokin, a Christian publisher in St. Petersburg, noted the blessings which the foreign mission movement brought:

> Thousands of missionaries have now come to Russia to help its spiritual revival, and I deeply appreciate their time and deeds. May God bless them! I saw people whose lives were completely changed by the Lord Jesus Christ through those missionaries. Before their conversion, people had anxious looks, but then their faces became clear and smiling. It means that God's peace has come to their hearts. I saw kids' eyes at a summer camp when they received God's love through missionaries. Many children were from broken families and had lack of care. But now they will always link Christian faith with missionary kindness. I saw prisoners who, with the help of missionaries, received hope and strength to endure their terrible circumstances. Praise the Lord for those missionaries who have brought light to Russia.[37]

---

[36] Grigori Komendant, "Certainly," *East-West Church and Ministry Report* (Winter 1996): 2.

[37] Alexander Sorokin, "A Russian Perspective on the Missionary Movement," *East-West Church and Ministry Report* (Winter 1996): 16.

In a letter reflective of thousands of responses received by Western missionaries who provided Christian broadcasts, Bibles, and other materials, one Russian woman described what the broadcasts had meant to her:

> I thank my Lord for you. Thank you for your sermons, thank you for the Good News of salvation. Thank you for showing me the way to God—and for what He means in my life! I wait each week for your programs on Saturday and Sunday. . . . Some of the people I work with have begun to listen to your programs, as well as some of my neighbors with whom I have been able to share the joy of knowing Him. I read the booklets you send me and pass them on to others.[38]

However, even though the contact of Evangelical missionaries with many national Protestants has continued to be close and strong, some Russian Evangelicals have also grown increasingly critical of their co-believers and have become increasingly discerning as they decide with which foreign missionaries they will work. In a 1993 Open Letter of the Missionary Coordinating Council to all Western Missionary Organizations, national Christians from ten former Soviet republics thanked Western missions for their efforts "during decades when Christ's Church in our country had been an object of persecution."[39] Although appreciative, these nationals criticized Westerners who in 1993 were overwhelming the indigenous church:

> In Moscow alone, over one hundred Western organizations were registered. And each one wants to accomplish its program by using the existing church infrastructure, which is still so weak that it cannot resist this pressure, neither organizationally nor spiritually. . . . [I]ndigenous missionary organizations cannot compete with strong western missions and the best people prefer to work for Western organizations and, naturally, for better payment. . . . Finally, instead of assistance and support from Western missionaries, local missions have to defend their own vision of missionary service. Evangelization campaigns, which had been formed under the influence of Western showmanship, produce feelings of protest against Protestantism as a Western way of thinking and culture which is alien to them.[40]

---

[38] Letter from A. P. Kuznetsova of Tula, cited in Newsletter of Russian Christian Radio (August 1996), 1, available in Russian Ministries Files, Wheaton, Illinois.

[39] Otonas Balchunas (Shaulai, Lithuania), Semen Borodin (Krasnodar, Russia), Andrei Bondarenko (Elgava, Latvia), Anatoly Bogatov (Saransk, Mordova), Vassily Davidyuk (Kiev, Ukraine), Piotr Lunichkin (Vladikavkaz, Ossetia), Pavel Pogodin (Nalchik, Kavkaz), Franz Tissen (Saran, Kazakhstan), Henri Fot (Bishkek, Kyrgystan), Victor Shiva (Almaty, Kazakhstan), Open Letter of the Missionary Coordinating Council to All Western Missionary Organizations Interested in Spreading the Gospel in the Former Soviet Union (March 23, 1993), available in Russian Ministries Files, Wheaton, Illinois.

[40] Ibid.

Even national Christian leaders such as Grigori Komendant, who has praised American missionaries, have also criticized them:

> Foreign missionaries, who also have waited for this moment, came rushing to us, it must be said, with many different agendas. It is necessary to report here that there have been negative as well as positive results. Unfortunately, in coming to us, many foreign workers have not considered identifying with us and becoming "one of us." There are those who may look very much like us outwardly, even to the point of learning our language, but they have not been able to "subject" themselves. . . . for Christ's sake. They seem to have more success in "enslaving" others: some they entice with dollars, some they buy with humanitarian aid, and some they seduce with free-wheeling church services or a loose lifestyle.[41]

RETHINKING THE RELATIONSHIP
BETWEEN EAST EUROPEAN MISSIONS
AND EASTERN ORTHODOX

Turning to the relationship of foreign ministries with Eastern Orthodox, some preliminary theological reflections are in order. Orthodox and Evangelical Christians both hold a similar, if not identical, high regard for Scripture. Both also believe in the Trinity, Christ as wholly human and wholly divine, and Christ's death and resurrection as the means of humanity's salvation from sin and death. These and many other historic Christian teachings held in common are enumerated in the Nicene Creed, which both traditions affirm. Given these major, mutually cherished convictions, it would appear that Evangelicals and Orthodox have much more in common theologically than either has in common with modern mainline Protestantism, whether Reformed or Lutheran.[42]

Don Fairbairn, a Cambridge University doctoral student who formerly taught at Donetsk Christian University, notes that the "theological differences separating Eastern Orthodoxy and Evangelicalism are more than cultural."[43] The fundamental distinction for Fairbairn involves contrasting Evangelical and Orthodox understandings of salvation: Evangelical justification by faith *at the outset* of a Christian life, versus Orthodox *theosis* (deification), the "process of becoming acceptable to God—as I practice love, mercy, and justice," *ending* in God's ultimate confirmation of eternal communion with God.[44]

---

[41] Komendant, "Certainly," 2.

[42] See Mark Elliott, "For Christian Understanding, Ignorance Is Not Bliss," *East-West Church and Ministry Report* (Summer 1993): 5. For a discussion of Slavic Evangelical and Orthodox common ground, see Mark Elliott, "Eastern Orthodox and Slavic Evangelicals: What Sets Them Both Apart from Western Evangelicals," *East-West Church and Ministry Report* (Fall 1995): 16.

[43] Don Fairbairn, "Eastern Orthodoxy: Five Protestant Perspectives," *East-West Church and Ministry Report* (Spring 1995): 6-7.

[44] Ibid.

Fairbairn contends that a fundamental distinction between Orthodoxy and Evangelicalism may stem from an Orthodox telescoping or combining of biblical passages concerning salvation and sanctification.[45] It is interesting that a key verse for an Orthodox reading of salvation (2 Pt 1:4; "His divine power has granted to us . . . [to] become partakers of the divine nature") has historically been a key verse for both Wesleyan and Calvinist readings of sanctification. While better relations between the confessions should earnestly be sought, Evangelicals still need to keep in mind that their faith also appears to part company with Orthodoxy over the related question of mediation between God and human. For Evangelicals, Christ alone stands as mediator between human sinfulness and God's holiness. However, it would appear, from a Reformation perspective, that Orthodoxy includes additional mediators between the two: the church, the priest, the divine liturgy, icons, and prayers of supplication to saints. As East European theologian Peter Kuzmic has argued, from an Evangelical perspective, Orthodoxy appears to detract from Christ "by addition."[46]

In Eastern Europe, popularly perceived differences between Orthodox and Evangelical Christians, as opposed to carefully drawn theological distinctions, shed little light but certainly inflame passions. "When we say 'the Church' we always mean the Orthodox Church and no other," reported one respondent in a mid-1980s poll conducted in the Soviet Union.[47] "It has been established by Christ, and has had no deviations, neither left nor right. All the rest are false churches or sects that went astray."[48] In the same survey Russian Evangelicals typically voiced opinions just as intolerant, dismissing Orthodoxy as "a dead Church" with "drunkards" for priests. "They know how to cross themselves, and nothing else. . . . Worshipping those icons, lighting the candles, praying for the dead, it's all idolatry."[49] In the Russian Empire and in the Soviet era, most grassroots Protestants and Orthodox rarely moved beyond such negative stereotypical images of each other. And today it is arguably worse, as more and more Protestant ministries work in East Central Europe and the former Soviet Union. These days, the mutual tolerance and respect among Western Catholics, Protestants, and Orthodox, built up painfully over centuries, frequently evaporate in a flash in the cauldron of ethnic and confessional strife raging from the Balkans to the Baltics.

Soon after communism collapsed, Russian Orthodox Patriarch Aleksii condemned the activities of foreign evangelists:

When the territories of central eastern Europe were opened for the public missionary endeavor and evangelism, the peoples rooted in millennial

---

[45] Don Fairbairn, "Partakers of the Divine Nature," unpublished manuscript, 61.

[46] Mark Elliott, response to Bradley Nassif, "Evangelical Missions in Eastern Orthodox Lands," *Trinity Forum* (Winter 1996): 5.

[47] Eugene Grosman, "A Contribution to Protestant-Orthodox Dialogue in Russia" (Wheaton College Graduate School, 1986), 7, 9 (on file with authors).

[48] Ibid.

[49] Ibid.

Orthodox traditions became objects of proselytism for numerous zeal-
ots calling themselves missionaries and preachers who came from outside to the new markets. . . . Of course our people will also survive this
invasion, as it survived even worse times of persecution and attacks from
the atheist propaganda.[50]

In 1993, Patriarch Aleksii II requested restraint of foreign missionaries entering Russia and also called for restrictions on Western religious broadcasters
on Russian television. In an interview with the Russian newspaper *Nezavisimaya
Gazeta* published just before Easter 1996, the patriarch said that "Russians,
especially the young, continue to be caught in the net of exotic preachers."[51]
    Arguing for increased control of foreign missionaries, Archpriest Viktor
Petluchenko, deputy chairman of the Department for External Church Relations of the Moscow Patriarchate, stated: "I'm not among those who say that
only the Russian Orthodox Church should be in Russia. But missionaries must
be limited. . . . [O]ur people are a very easy target and can be bought easily by
foreign missionaries. They see Americans as coming with a box of food in one
hand and a cross in the other."[52]
    Orthodox opposition to Western missionaries on occasion has been more
overt. On February 3, 1997, two Russian Orthodox priests supervised the
burning of approximately two hundred illustrated children's Bibles that had
been supplied by Josh McDowell Ministries, an American organization which
has provided Christian books and approximately $310 million worth of hu-
manitarian aid since 1991. When volunteers from the organization arrived at
School No. 23 in the village of Semkhoz, about fifty miles north of Moscow,
two priests and approximately twenty-four militant Orthodox blocked their
path. One of the priests, Father Vladimir, stated: "Changing your faith is treachery. If Americans want to help Russia after years of atheism, let them restore
our churches and monasteries or print our own literature. Under the guise of
presents, they are trying to propagate a different faith."[53] Similarly, at a February 26, 1997, board meeting of the All Russian Union of Christian Organizations in Moscow, members asserted that "[t]here are ten Baptist Churches in
Moscow who have been refused by Mayor Yuri Luzhkov rights to land for
church buildings. There is a clear conspiracy between the mayor and the patri-
archy to limit growth of Protestants by denying land rights."[54]
    Although Western missionaries need to apply themselves to a study of his-
tory and culture to understand what prompts Russian Orthodox to such an-

[50] Volf, "Fishing in the Neighbor's Pond," 26.
    [51] Patrick Henry, "Russian Church Seeks Curbs on Other Faiths," *Moscow Times*
(April 30, 1996).
    [52] Frank Brown, "The Next Crusade," *Moscow Times* (November 19, 1994), 3.
    [53] Alan Philips, "Bible-Burning Cloud over Russian Freedom," *Electronic Tele-
graph* (March 3, 1997).
    [54] Russian Ministries e-mail (February 26, 1997), available in Russian Ministries
Files, Wheaton, Illinois.

tagonism toward Evangelicals, they should not feel that they need to apologize for sharing the good news in a Russia without Marx. One major reason for this is demographics. Evangelical ministries are motivated by a desire to support a movement of some three million indigenous Protestants.[55] Also, both Evangelicals from abroad and indigenous Evangelicals are motivated by Russia's huge nonbelieving population. Data from a June 1996 pre-election survey suggest that as many as 67 percent of Russian men and 38 percent of Russian women do not identify themselves as religious believers.[56] While a recent poll indicates a substantive increase in the percentage of Russians claiming affiliation with the Orthodox Church (from 30 percent in 1991 to 50 percent in 1996), the percentage of these respondents who have taken Orthodoxy to heart and who practice their faith is another matter.[57] The June 1996 Russian pre-election survey indicated that believers (50 percent of respondents) were far more often non-observant (37.3 percent) than observant (12.7 percent). And even among self-described observant believers, corporate worship proved to be strikingly erratic. When asked how often they had attended church in the past twelve months, only 10 percent of believers who considered themselves to be observant answered once a week, 13 percent answered once a month, while 55 percent answered that they attend on religious holidays and on family occasions.[58] Just as revealing as the low levels of participation in Orthodox worship is the conclusion of one poll analyst, based on an All-Russia Public Opinion Research Center survey, which suggested "no correlation between religiousness and the expression of a personal moral code."[59]

Evangelicals believe they have an obligation to witness to nominal believers as well as to nonbelievers. But nominalism aside, the current poll figures for Russian nonbelievers are such that indigenous Evangelicals and Evangelical ministries from abroad have ample opportunity to minister to many millions who are spiritually adrift in the former Soviet Union, without ever engaging in

---

[55] Elliott and Richardson, "Growing Protestant Diversity," 205.

[56] Susan Goodrich Lehmann, "Religious Revival in Russia: Significant or Superficial?" presented at the Kennan Institute for Advanced Russian Studies, Washington, D.C. (October 21, 1996), Figure 6. An earlier 1992 survey found a comparable 69 percent of Russian men and 46 percent of Russian women who did not identify themselves as believers. Mark Rhodes, "Religious Believers in Russia," *Radio Free Europe/Radio Liberty Research Report* (April 3, 1992): 60, 61. In contrast, in the post–World War II era, perhaps as few as 10 percent to 15 percent of the population was religious. William C. Fletcher, *Soviet Believers: The Religious Sector of the Population* (Lawrence, Kan., 1981), 67.

[57] "Dramatic Increase in Russians Claiming Religion," *Religion Watch* (January 3, 1997), based on a poll by the All-Russia Public Opinion Research Center.

[58] Lehmann, "Religious Revival" (Figure 1, Table 4). Among the 50% of respondents who identified themselves as believers, 83% considered themselves to be Orthodox. Ibid., Figure 4.

[59] Mark Rhodes, "Russians' Spiritual Values," *East-West Church and Ministry Report* (Fall 1993): 13.

proselytizing; that is, without specifically targeting adherents of one church in an attempt to lure them into another.

However, in Russia, Orthodox and Evangelicals have great difficulty agreeing on a single definition for *proselytism*—stemming from conflicting understandings of what constitutes a believer. Evangelicals assume a personal, conscious commitment to Christ alone as Savior, lived out in worship and life. In contrast, if a Russian has been baptized as an infant, even if faith is dormant or nonexistent, Orthodox consider an Evangelical witness to that person to be proselytizing. Actually, many Orthodox envision an even more expansive prerogative in the East. Since Russia—and Romania, Bulgaria, and Serbia—historically and traditionally have been predominately Orthodox, church leaders in these countries would like to assume a territorial, spiritual protectorate over at least their Slavic populations. Thus, some Orthodox will interpret Evangelical witness even to self-described Russian nonbelievers as proselytism. Oddly enough, such an understanding seems to be underscored by findings which indicate that some respondents who identify themselves as Orthodox, meaning "I am Russian," have little or no acquaintance with Christian teachings and rarely, if ever, attend worship. For example, one poll revealed that "[f]ewer Russian Orthodox than the general population believe that Jesus is the Son of God."[60]

Of course, differentiating proselytism and legitimate proclamation of the gospel can be contentious in the West as well as in the East. Consider a volume of essays edited by Martin Marty and Frederick Greenspahn, entitled *Pushing the Faith: Proselytism and Civility in a Pluralistic World.*[61] In his closing remarks, after a stream of chapters awash with broad condemnations not only of proselytism, but of practically every conception of evangelism, Marty concludes that if the arguments of his contributors were taken to their logical conclusion, it would be a rare occasion when it was ever proper to share any personal spiritual reflection outside church walls.[62] Today, the politically correct Western Christian seems determined to make an idol of tolerance, defined

---

[60] "Disparity between Faith and Practice in Russia," *East-West Church and Ministry Report* (Spring 1996): 14. See also Paul Mojzes, "Ecumenism, Evangelism, and Religious Liberty," *Journal of Ecumenical Studies* 33 (1996): 6. On territorialism and the equation of national and religious identity, see Cecil M. Robeck Jr., "Mission and the Issue of Proselytism," *International Bulletin of Missionary Research* 20 (1996): 3-4. Volf, "Fishing in the Neighbor's Pond," 26; Harold J. Berman, "Religious Rights in Russia at a Time of Tumultuous Transition: A Historical Theory," in *Religious Human Rights in Global Perspective: Legal Perspectives*, ed. Johan van der Vyver and John Witte Jr. (The Hague, 1996), 301-2.

[61] Martin E. Marty, "Conclusion: Proselytism in a Pluralistic World," in *Pushing the Faith: Proselytism and Civility in a Pluralistic World*, ed. Martin E. Marty and Frederick E. Greenspahn (New York, 1988), 155, 158.

[62] Ibid.

today in such a way as to equate almost every profession of conviction as an affront and an offense. If everybody really left everybody else alone, says Marty, "[i]t would be a more comfortable but probably comatose world."[63]

Despite the Soviet Union's concerted, antireligious assault of this century, Orthodoxy is, and probably will remain, the preeminent cultural and religious reality in Russia. Though some will not accept the fact, dissenting Protestants nevertheless have much to offer Russia—even Orthodoxy itself. To begin with, Evangelicalism presently appears to be the only route to faith for some Russians who will never trust an Orthodox hierarchy they see as compromised by its past ties to the Soviet state. Likewise, some better-educated Russians appear to be attracted to Evangelical, rather than Orthodox, Christianity because Reformation churches tend to be more accepting of knowledge and intellectual inquiry as complementary to faith. Finally, Evangelicals can render Orthodoxy a service in the same way that the Reformation stimulated genuine reform within Roman Catholicism. Evangelical activity in a given region can and often does serve as a catalyst, re-energizing Orthodox out of a complacency born of tradition and nominal predominance.[64] As Martin Marty has noted, challengers of the status quo can provide "great stimulus for communities to define themselves" and "to revitalize stagnant cultures."[65] Today the question must be posed: Does the majority faith in Russia—Orthodoxy—have sufficient confidence in itself to tolerate religious dissent? Or will it repeat history and retreat to dependence upon the state to provide it with a legislative advantage, if not a monopoly? Based on Europe's sad experience with state churches, it would appear that nothing could be more deadening to Orthodox spiritual vitality than artificial, secular supports propping up a privileged church.

EVANGELICAL ASSISTANCE TO ORTHODOX

Evangelical ministries working in the East should, of course, require their missionaries to study language, culture, and history.[66] Those bound for Russia should prayerfully determine to their own satisfaction what are the common theological understandings and nonnegotiable differences between Eastern Orthodox and Evangelical Christianity. That settled, the question of practical, day-to-day relationships still looms large. Conclusions will differ. Neverthe-

---

[63] Ibid.

[64] Kent Hill and Mark Elliott, "Are Evangelicals Interlopers?" *East-West Church and Ministry Report* (Summer 1993): 4; W. Cole Durham Jr., "Perspectives on Religious Liberty: A Comparative Framework," in van der Vyver and Witte, *Religious Human Rights,* 16.

[65] Marty, "Conclusion," 158.

[66] See chapter 17 by Anita Deyneka herein.

less, Western ministries should, at the very least, encourage reform-minded elements within the Russian Orthodox Church, many of which receive their inspiration from the example of Father Alexander Men, the winsome and open-hearted Orthodox priest who was murdered by an unknown assailant in 1990. It can be argued that "no single Christian confession alone can reach all of Russia for Christ. . . . Because Russian culture owes an enormous debt to Orthodoxy . . . many Russians likely will remain spiritually lost if a reinvigorated Orthodox Church does not reach them."[67]

Prior to *glasnost*, YMCA work among Russian post–1917 émigrés stood out as perhaps the most strategic and successful instance ever of concerted Protestant assistance to Orthodoxy. Under the able and discerning direction of Episcopalian Paul Anderson, the Russian YMCA Press in Paris played a pivotal role in preserving and undergirding Russian Orthodox cultural life at a time when the Soviet antireligious onslaught and Western indifference might otherwise have extinguished it.[68] This exceptional case history deserves widespread study today as a model for effective, but noninvasive, nonpatronizing interconfessional assistance.

Better understanding among Christian traditions has been a primary concern of a number of initiatives. One is the Society for the Study of Eastern Orthodoxy and Evangelicalism, headed by Dr. Bradley Nassif, an Orthodox scholar with a well-informed understanding of both confessions.[69] Regular meetings have been held at the Billy Graham Center, Wheaton College, Wheaton, Illinois, since 1991. Also, Anglican Jane Ellis, who has written extensively on contemporary Russian Orthodoxy, organized three dialogues (1994-96) in Moscow, directly addressing Orthodox-Evangelical tensions. A third body that hopefully will have success as an agent of improved interconfessional relations, the Christian Inter-Confessional Consultative Committee, emerged from a meeting of 132 representatives of twenty-one church bodies, held in Minsk, Belarus, October 1-3, 1996. Participants from various republics of the former Soviet Union both affirmed "full respect for the spiritual choice of a person" and condemned conversions from one church to another "through ways and means contradicting the spirit of Christian love and violating the freedom of a human person."[70]

Since *glasnost*, direct Protestant assistance to the Russian Orthodox Church has not been overwhelming, but it has been more extensive than is commonly realized. National Council of Churches work teams and mainline Protestant sister-church programs have provided some assistance. In addition, Danish Lutherans, the Episcopal Church, and the United Methodist Committee on

---

[67] Hill and Elliott, "Are Evangelicals Interlopers?" 3.

[68] Matthew L. Miller, "The Russian Ministry of the YMCA: 1899-1939" (M.A. thesis, Wheaton College Graduate School, 1994).

[69] Bradley Nassif, "Evangelical Missions in Eastern Orthodox Lands," *Trinity Forum* (Winter 1996): 2-4.

[70] "Churches Talk in Minsk," *Christian Century* 113 (1996): 1002.

Relief have funneled substantial humanitarian aid through the Moscow Patriarchate. On the whole, however, ecumenical and mainline Protestant ties with Russian Orthodoxy have become more precarious in recent years due to growing grassroots Orthodox distrust of the West, in general, and wariness of mainline Protestant theology, in particular.[71]

Russian Orthodox are of two minds regarding Keston Institute, well known as a champion of Soviet-bloc religious rights for three decades. The hierarchy does not appreciate the work of this interdenominational advocacy group headed by Anglican priest Michael Bourdeaux because Keston, in the past, consistently gave a voice to Orthodox dissidents out of favor with Soviet and church authorities. As a young man, Bourdeaux himself came under the personal influence of Paul Anderson, pioneer analyst of the church in the Soviet Union, and Bourdeaux has always felt himself close to the Orthodox Church, as well as being a strong supporter of practical ecumenism. At present, Keston News Service tenaciously documents and decries the Patriarchate's maneuverings for preferential state treatment. In contrast, those Orthodox who were persecuted for their faith by communists hold Keston in the highest regard for being their voice through the decades of oppression.[72]

Western Evangelicals might be thought to have less substantive relationships with Russian Orthodox than mainline Protestants, since the latter have had longstanding and visible links with the Moscow Patriarchate through the ecumenical movement since 1961. That has become somewhat less the case since *glasnost*. In 1988-89, Open Doors with Brother Andrew provided the Russian Orthodox Church with one million New Testaments; Taizé, with strong French Calvinist support, provided the Patriarchate with another one million New Testaments; and the Swedish Institute for Bible Translation donated seventy-five thousand Russian Orthodox study Bibles.[73]

The American Bible Society (ABS) and the United Bible Societies (UBS), with Evangelical as well as mainline Protestant contributors, have provided major funding and technical support for the revived Russian Bible Society. Effective Orthodox, Baptist, and Pentecostal working relationships in this organization for several years now have made this indigenous Orthodox-Evangelical collaboration perhaps the most significant interconfessional initiative in the former Soviet Union to date. The ABS, the UBS, and the Russian Bible Society were

---

[71] Based on comments at a meeting of Christians Associated for Relationships with Eastern Europe (November 17-18, 1994) Chicago, Illinois, and Mojzes, "Ecumenism, Evangelism, and Religious Liberty," 4-5. For a survey of Orthodox–mainline Protestant contacts see Mark Elliott, "How the Churches Have Seen Their Roles in the USSR," *Pulse* 22 (January 9, 1987): 2.

[72] See generally Jenny Robertson, *Be Our Voice: The Story of Michael Bourdeaux and Keston College* (London, 1984). Aid to the Russian Church, a Christian humanitarian agency formerly headed by Jane Ellis, has focused on assistance to Russian Orthodox since 1973.

[73] Elliott, "New Openness in the USSR," 28-31.

responsible for the publication of 6,459,835 Bibles and New Testaments in the Soviet and post–Soviet Union from 1987 to 1996.[74]

Gospel Light, a California-based Evangelical publisher, is collaborating with the Russian Orthodox Ministry of Education in a potentially unprecedented venture. Gospel Light and the Moscow Patriarchate are jointly producing large quantities of graded Sunday-school literature for use in Orthodox parishes. The intention is to produce materials acceptable to both Orthodox and Evangelicals.[75]

Campus Crusade for Christ has made extensive, if not always successful, efforts to engage the Orthodox in the former Soviet Union. In 1992, Mission Volga, an evangelistic outreach projected as a joint Campus Crusade-Orthodox effort, highlighted the possibilities and the pitfalls of working together. The Moscow Patriarchate considered endorsing the venture, but declined to do so at the last minute. Some Orthodox priests nevertheless participated in the boat ministry, while other Orthodox protested the outreach at several ports of call.[76]

Navigators, International Fellowship of Evangelical Students, and its affiliate, InterVarsity, have made concerted efforts to study Orthodoxy, to develop meaningful relationships with Orthodox believers, and to sponsor interconfessional theological dialogues. Dansk Europamission, Norwegian Mission to the East, and Peter Deyneka Russian Ministries have sponsored rebroadcasts of radio sermons by Father Alexander Men, the Russian Orthodox priest who was martyred in 1990. Russian Ministries also helped underwrite a 1994 Orthodox/Protestant conference on cults in Russia and funded a publication on the cults written by Orthodox writer Andrei Kuraev.[77]

CONCLUSION

Russian society, exhausted by previous exertions and failures, finds itself in some sort of torpid state, apathy, spiritual stupor, despondency. The Russian state has yet to demonstrate signs of rejuvenation and strengthening which are so vital for it. . . . Russian citizenry, blinded by multiple mortal punishments and the extraordinary rise in crime and the general

---

[74] Interview by Anita Deyneka with Doris Fisher, American Bible Society (November 26, 1996), available in Russian Ministries Files, Wheaton, Illinois.

[75] Letter and supporting documents from William T. Greig Jr., chairman, Glint International, to Mark Elliott (February 17, 1997).

[76] R. Vito Nicastro Jr., "Mission Volga: A Case Study in the Tensions between Evangelizing and Proselytizing," *Journal of Ecumenical Studies* (1994): 223-43; "Witnessing on the Volga," *Christianity Today* (October 16, 1992), 77.

[77] Conversations with James Stamoolis, Wheaton College Graduate School (February 25-26, 1997). The book on cults is *Soblazn Neoiazychestva* [*The Temptation of Neopaganism*] (Moscow, 1994).

decline in manners, has steadily regressed. Russian literature has been overwhelmed by a powerful wave of pornography and sensation-mongering.[78]

So wrote the Russian theologian Sergei Bulgakov in 1909. That his words ring as true at the end of the twentieth century as at its beginning not only underscores the long-suffering of the Russian population, but also the urgent need for a fresh approach to the country's multiple crises—political, economic, but above all, moral and spiritual. In Russia, all Christians of good will, Orthodox and non-Orthodox, native and foreign, must focus not on each other but on the true foe—the evil of corrosive, destructive egoism that divides not along any East-West fault line, but as Aleksandr Solzhenitsyn has said, through every human heart.[79] In 1909, in his famous *Vekhi* (*Signposts*) essay, theologian Sergei Bulgakov wrote, "The root of evil lies in the egotism of every individual." Consequently, "[o]nly those renewed from within can implement the required political, economic, cultural and religious renewals in Russia."[80]

Just as in 1909, Russia's gravest troubles today are fundamentally moral and spiritual. No society can endure without the rule of law. But today in Russia few feel any moral compunction to obey the law, which is contradictory and in flux in any case. Nor can a society endure amid pervasive economic crime and a mafia stranglehold on the material lifeblood of the nation. General Nikolai Stolyarov, a former Gorbachev confidant who tried but failed to reform the KGB, declared in 1992 that Russia had rejected the Ten Commandments, and as a result, the entire nation was reaping the dreadful consequences.[81] In 1989, writer Yuri Barabash made the same argument in defending Nikolai Gogol's long-suppressed religious thought:

> It seems that, finally, bit by bit, and with a near fatal time-lag, we are beginning to grasp the point: culture and religion, morality and Christianity, creation and faith are so indissolubly interconnected that the desecration of sacred things, the violation of the Ten Commandments, and the cynical ridicule thereof, once impressed upon us as normal, in fact bear witness to a terrible, yawning emptiness.[82]

Russia's Orthodox and Evangelicals certainly can agree that the cause of the nation's political and economic crises is moral, and in turn, that the solu-

---

[78] Quoted in Peter Sawczak, "Reconstruction, Deconstruction, and the Restoration of Literature in Russia," in *Russia in Search of Its Future*, ed. Amin Saikal and William Maley (Cambridge, 1995), 178, 185.

[79] Aleksandr I. Solzhenitsyn, *The Gulag Archipelago, 1918-1956* (New York, 1973), 168.

[80] William van den Bercken, *Christian Thinking and the End of Communism in Russia* (Utrecht-Leiden, 1993), 24-25 (paraphrasing Bulgakov).

[81] General Nikolai Stolyarov, presentation at Wheaton College (October 2, 1992). See also Yancey, *Praying with the KGB*, 33.

[82] Quoted in Van den Bercken, *Christian Thinking*, 127.

tion to the moral crisis is spiritual. At the same time, what a tragedy it will be if Orthodox and Evangelicals do not make common cause by making amends, as both confessions need to do, for vilifying each other. To this end, both confessions must concentrate on the present moral collapse and its spiritual cure. Orthodox, for their part, should recognize that religious pluralism is unavoidable in a free society and that a renewal of state-enforced Orthodox privilege would only sap its spiritual vitality.[83] Evangelical ministries, for their part, ought to pay a great deal more attention to legitimate Russian sensitivities through substantially improved missionary orientation and through a sober appreciation of their own cultural limitations. There is much constructive work to be done in Russia by all charitably inclined Christians. There should be no time for debilitating "mutual demonization," as Paul Mojzes calls it.[84] The solution is Christian charity, deference, and humility.

---

[83] Elliott and Richardson, "Growing Protestant Diversity," 189-214. Growing religious diversity in Russia would appear to be a function of the collapse of rigid Soviet ideological controls, the resulting dramatic increase in Christian and cult activity from abroad, *and* a resurgence of indigenous pagan, pseudoreligious, and occult influences. In Russia today one finds an inextricable mixture of native and foreign influences in the surge of interest in "the supernatural, the fantastic, the mystical and the esoteric." Valentina G. Brougher, "The Occult in Russian Literature of the 1990s," *Russian Review* 56 (January 1997): 110, 124.

[84] Mojzes, "Ecumenism, Evangelism, and Religious Liberty," 8; see also Berman, "Religious Rights in Russia," 4.

APPENDIX A

Western Missionaries in the Former Soviet Union from the 25 Largest Sending Agencies (1995)*

Organization	Missionaries
Assemblies of God[1]	28
Biblical Education by Extension[2]	12
Calvary Chapel of Costa Mesa[1]	8
Campus Crusade for Christ[2]	23
Child Evangelism Fellowship[1]	25
Christian and Missionary Alliance[1]	39
Church of Christ[**1]	104
Church of the Nazarene[1]	16
Church Resource Ministries	17
Evangelical Free Church Mission[2]	12
Frontiers[2]	118
Greater Europe Mission[2]	18
International Teams	20
Institute in Basic Life Principles[4]	320
InterVarsity Christian Fellowship[3]	32
Lutheran Church—Missouri Synod	32
Navigators	193
OMS International	87
Operation Mobilization	40
Salvation Army[1]	50
Seventh-day Adventists	49
Southern Baptist Convention[2]	80
United World Mission[1]	18
Wesleyan World Mission	38
Youth with a Mission	1,600
Total for 25 Agencies	3,190

[1] all career
[2] majority career
[3] all short term (3 to 24 months)
[4] 20 career, 300 short term
[*] To avoid double counting of many of the 862 one-year CoMission missionaries, this cooperative effort involving 12 sending agencies is not listed separately.
[**] Church of Christ totals do not include 200-300 mission-trip participants (1-6 weeks) because this short term of service falls below the 3- to 24-month designation for short-term missionaries.
SOURCE: *East-West Church and Ministry Report* (Spring 1995), 10; (Fall 1995), 3. Compiled by Pamela Meadows.

APPENDIX B

WESTERN MISSIONARIES IN THE FORMER SOVIET UNION FROM THE 12 LARGEST DENOMINATIONAL SENDING AGENCIES

Denomination	1995	1996
Assemblies of God	28	51
Calvary Chapel of Costa Mesa[1]	8	45
Christian and Missionary Alliance	39[1]	57[2]
Church of Christ[1]	104	ca.104
Church of the Nazarene	16	16
Evangelical Free Church	12	87[3]
Lutheran Church—Missouri Synod	32	35
Salvation Army	50	52
Seventh-day Adventist	49	69[4]
Southern Baptist Convention	80	108[1]
United Methodist Church	ca.15	15[1]
Wesleyan Church	38	41[5]
Total	473	680

[1] all career
[2] 40 career; 17 short term
[3] 25 career; 62 short term
[4] 29 career; 40 short term
[5] 10 career; 31 short term

SOURCE: Compiled by Sharyl Corrado, Mark Elliott, and Pamela Meadows.

APPENDIX C

PROTESTANT DENOMINATIONS IN THE FORMER SOVIET UNION*

Churches Present Since 1917 (Regardless of Official Status)

Evangelical Christian-Baptist
Lutheran
Mennonite
Pentecostal
Seventh-day Adventist

Churches in Lands Annexed in World War II

Hungarian Reformed
   (Transcarpathia)
Methodist
   (now active outside Estonia)

Reemerging Churches

Anglican
Armenian Evangelical and Baptist
Brethren
Church of Christ
Evangelical Christian
Molokane
Salvation Army
United Pentecostal

New Churches

Calvary Chapel
Christian and Missionary Alliance
Christian Life Centers
Christian Reformed
Church of God, Anderson
Church of God, Cleveland
Church of the Nazarene
Estonian Christian Church
Evangelical Covenant
Evangelical Free
Evangelical Presbyterian
Friends
Lutheran Church—Missouri Synod
New Apostolic
Pentecostal Holiness
Presbyterian Church of America
University Bible Fellowship (Korean)
Vineyard Christian Fellowship
Wesleyan
Word of Life

---

* In addition to denominations, the former Soviet Union is witnessing the emergence of unaffiliated Protestant churches founded by Western and indigenous parachurch missions.

SOURCE: Compiled by Mark Elliott, Robert Richardson, and Sharyl Corrado.

Part Two

LEGAL PERSPECTIVES

12.

REFLECTIONS ON CHURCH AND STATE IN RUSSIAN HISTORY

Firuz Kazemzadeh

The law "On Freedom of Conscience and Religious Associations," passed by the Duma in 1997, came as a surprise to many foreign observers as well as to some Russians who had not expected the radical changes the new legislation introduced. The earlier law (1990), adopted in the heady days of drastic reform when old constraints were being swept away and hopes of freedom stood high, had granted equality to all religions and religious associations, decreed that no religion or religious association shall enjoy any advantages or be subjected to any restrictions relative to others, and promised that the state shall be neutral in matters of freedom of worship and belief. The repeal of the liberal law of 1990 and the adoption of the restrictive law of 1997 fit the traditional pattern of relations between the Orthodox Church and the Russian State. Once again, as they had done through the centuries, the Church and the State entered into an alliance that each considered natural and beneficial. Enlightenment notions of religious freedom largely imported from the West could not withstand the pressures generated by ingrained traditions and perceived needs of a nation in crisis.

Relations between Church and State in Russia and their interdependence have had a long and tortuous history. Imported into Kievan Rus in the ninth century from Byzantium, where the emperors reigned supreme, Orthodox Christianity had no tradition of autonomy from the secular power. The Metropolitans of Kiev, Greeks appointed by the Patriarchs of Constantinople, co-existed with their hosts, the grand princes, occupying themselves with spreading the faith, building churches, founding monasteries, bringing enlightenment to a primitive population and, after A.D. 1054, defending Orthodoxy against a schismatic West. The Church diligently served the State, and the State protected the Church. It was, after all, Prince Vladimir who baptized Rus and was in turn canonized by the Church, as was his grandmother Princess Olga, herself an early convert to Christianity. In fact, the Church easily canonized rulers of Kiev and of other principalities of ancient Rus. Of the 180 persons canonized between the introduction of Christianity in the tenth century and the Mongolian conquest in the thirteenth, fully one-third were rulers. "Statistics tell, of course, a very small part of the story; they do reveal a tendency of the Russians and their church to sanctify their princes frequently and, perhaps, rather easily."[1]

When the Kievan state broke up into virtually independent principalities, the Metropolitans of Kiev, appointed by the Patriarch of Constantinople, and directing the spiritual and administrative life of all parishes, managed to preserve both the spiritual and administrative unity of the Church.

The Mongolian invasion, which effectively destroyed the vestiges of the political cohesion of ancient Rus, did not shatter the unity of the Church. Even from devastated Kiev, shrunk to a village after the sack of 1240, the Metropolitans continued to exercise a degree of spiritual and administrative authority over the divided and bleeding land. The tolerant, almost protective, religious policy of the Tatars helped to make the Church the only functioning national institution.

By the year 1300, with Kiev virtually abandoned and uninhabitable, its Metropolitan, Maxim, looked north for support to the principality of Vladimir, whose rulers claimed the title of grand prince of Rus and were eager to use the Church to increase their influence against the various claimants to supremacy among the members of the house of Riurik, the legendary founder of the Kievan Russian state. Maxim transferred his see from Kiev to Vladimir, but ten years later, his successor, Metropolitan Peter, quarreled with Prince Michael, his host, and was induced to move to the then insignificant town of Moscow, whose ruler, Iurii Danilovich, grandson of Alexander Nevskii, hoped to strengthen his own position by assuming the role of the protector of the Church. The transfer of the see of the Metropolitan to Moscow made that city the spiritual capital of Rus and the administrative center of its only national institution. Peter's close relations with Sultan Muhammad Uzbek, Khan of the Golden Horde and its first ruler to embrace Islam, further cemented the ties between Prince Iurii, who had married Uzbek's sister, and his Tatar overlord. Moscow became the Tatars' closest ally in Rus.

Peter sided with Prince Iurii in the latter's struggles with his many Russian enemies and rivals for supremacy, and on Iurii's death loyally supported his brother and successor, Prince Ivan I Kalita (the "Money Bag"), who continued the policies of full cooperation with the Horde and patronage of the Church.[2]

---

[1] Michael Cherniavsky, *Tsar and People* (New Haven, 1961), 4.

[2] See generally E. E. Golubinskii, *Istoriia Kanonizatsii Sviatykh Russkoi Tserkvi*, 2d ed. (Farnborough, England, 1969); George Vernadsky, *The Mongols in Russia* (1969).

Thus, the positions of both Prince Ivan and Metropolitan Peter became virtually impregnable, but Peter secured his status as head of the Russian Church at the cost of serving the interests of the princes of Moscow and of their Tatar overlords. After Peter's death in 1326, Ivan I conducted a successful campaign to have him canonized by the Patriarch of Constantinople, making Moscow a place of pilgrimage and further assuring the spiritual primacy of Moscow among Russian principalities. The symbiosis of Church and State was now firmly established.

It must be noted here that in the fourteenth century no theoretical issues of the relationship between Church and State seem to have been raised. The hierarchs and the secular rulers alike were guided by the needs of the moment and by pragmatic concerns. Moreover, the state of culture in Russia under the Tatars had fallen so low that even the princes tended to be illiterate and most of the clergy knew little of either church history or theology. It was in the late fifteenth century, when Moscow had acquired independence, and its cultural life revived rapidly, that several fundamental theological issues, as well as issues of the relations between Church and State, emerged with dramatic suddenness and force.

The second half of the fifteenth century was, for Russia, a time of stress and turmoil. The fall of Constantinople to the Muslim Turks in 1453 shook Orthodox Christianity to its foundations. The Muscovites could not understand how Tsargrad—the City of Caesar, the second Rome, the abode of the true faith—could have fallen to the godless children of Hagar. Surely, this spiritual disaster presaged a universal catastrophe, some even said the end of the world.

The break that occurred fifteen years earlier, after the Greek Church had bowed to the papacy at Florence in 1438, accepting the primacy of the pope and the hated *filioque*, had further isolated Moscow and thrown its Church on its own resources. Heresies appeared in the independent principality of Novgorod, their poison spreading to Moscow and infecting some members of the ruling family. Some heretics rejected the need for sacraments; others rejected the Trinity itself. Within the Church there arose a movement led by a saintly monk, Nil Maikov, known as Sorskii, from the hermitage he created on the banks of the river Sora. Nil had traveled to the Holy Land and spent time at a monastery on Mount Athos, where he fell under the spell of Hesychasm, the doctrine and practice of quietism and spiritual tranquillity that may have been influenced by Buddhism.

In his teaching, Nil Sorskii stressed, as steps toward ultimate enlightenment, the renunciation of passion, introspection, internal prayer of purification, quietude of spirit (*hesycheia*), yoga-like control of body and breath, contemplation of God, and ecstasy and the experience of the light of God.[3]

Applying his principles to the Church, Nil and his followers declared that monasteries ought not to own land and serfs but rather ought to follow the

---

[3] A. S. Orlov, *Drevniaia Russkaia Literatura* (The Hague, 1970), 206.

examples of Jesus and be free of earthly possessions. Nil and his followers became known as Trans-Volga Elders, "non-covetous" monks or "non-possessors" (*nestiazhateli*). Although few in numbers, they acquired considerable influence because of the purity of their motives, their sincerity, and their skill as propagandists of their views. Grand Prince Ivan III sympathized with the nonpossessors. Monasteries owned about one-third of the land in Muscovy. The grand prince had cast a covetous eye on the enormous monastic wealth and was looking for support within the Church. The nonpossessors could provide such support.

Nil's views ran into fierce opposition from the majority of Church hierarchy led by Joseph Sanin, founder and abbot of a monastery at Volokolamsk.[4] Well-educated for his time and an excellent administrator, Joseph, energetic and tenacious, turned his monastery into a veritable college for the education of clergy and laymen slated for the service of the State.

Joseph first distinguished himself as a prosecutor of heretics. In this he followed the lead of Bishop Gennadii of Novgorod, a relentless heresy hunter and chief antagonist of the Judaizers, a small sect that originated in Gennadii's own city. In 1471, Novgorod welcomed a new prince, Michael, who brought with him a learned Lithuanian Jewish scholar, Skhariia, or Zachary. Skhariia engaged in theological discussions with a few Novgorodian priests who formed a sect that denied the Trinity, the Incarnation, the sacraments, and the Church hierarchy. At about 1481, the sect made its appearance in Moscow, where it soon came to count among its members the monk Zosima, a future Metropolitan, as well as the grand prince's daughter-in-law and several other members of the highest nobility. Ivan III himself was rumored to sympathize with the heretics.

In his campaign against the Judaizers, Joseph Volokolamskii would stop at nothing. He would tolerate no deviation from Orthodoxy, believing that heresy was a crime against both Church and State, that heresy was treason and treason was heresy. In his major work against the heretics, *The Illuminator*, Joseph states that heretics deserve imprisonment and death, that penitent heretics can never be trusted, that civil authorities must put to death those whom the Church identifies as heretics, that people must inform the State on anyone suspected of heresy, and that deceit was permitted to entrap heretics ("divine perfidy").[5]

The issue of heresy was further complicated by the issue of land holding. Ivan III was not only importing Italian architects to raise the new Cathedral of the Dormition of the Virgin, new bell towers, and new walls of the Kremlin, but he was also expanding a new military class that stood outside the old appanage system, was paid by the prince, and was loyal to him alone, thus providing him with an indispensable weapon in the last struggle against the

---

[4] Joseph is known as both Volokolamskii and Volotskii.

[5] Iosif Volotskii, *Prosvetitel* (Moscow, 1903); Michael Karpovich, "Church and State in Russian History," *Russian Review* 3 (1944): 10-14.

traditional appanage order. To pay this new class, the service gentry, the prince needed land, and the largest and most easily available source of land was the Church.

Ivan's desire to secularize monastic properties partly explains his early benevolence toward the heretics and the Trans-Volga Elders. These could weaken the Church's resistance to expropriation of monastic land holdings, thus helping Ivan to increase his independence from the boyars, the old aristocracy jealous of its privileges and unwilling to submit to the autocracy that was gradually reducing that class to the status of mere servants of the Crown.

The boyars also had their eyes on Church lands—some of them for economic reasons—and a few, out of moral conviction, sided with Nil Sorskii's nonpossessors, making it impossible for Ivan III, who feared an alliance between these two groups, to maintain his early tolerant attitude toward religious dissent.

Faced with this threat to Church property, Joseph of Volokolamsk welcomed Ivan's retreat. The three sides in the epic struggle for Russia's body and soul had to be resolved. The resolution was the reaffirmation of the old alliance of Church and State. "Under the terms of the alliance, the Church would support the rising absolutism of the Grand Duke with its own moral prestige, while the Grand Duke would leave the ecclesiastical properties virtually untouched. . . . The alliance between Church and ruler . . . was a very important step toward subjecting the Church entirely to the State, making it a subservient tool of the Grand Duke."[6]

Joseph's compromise with the State had far-reaching consequences. The abbot of Volokolams Monastery was canonized. His religious formalism and ritualism, his glorification of the power of the prince, his hatred of heretics and of all outsiders, and his defense of ecclesiastical wealth became the norms of the official Church. While it continued to harbor spiritually pure individuals, these were marginalized and left without influence on the ecclesiastical institutions. Even the Councils of the Russian Church became subservient to the Crown.

The ideology of the supremacy of Moscow and its ruler was given a universal and metahistorical dimension by the monk Filofei (Philotheus) of Pskov in his famous epistle to Grand Prince Vasilii III. Filofei followed the pattern, already familiar to Russian thinkers, of seeing history as a succession of world empires of three divinely chosen peoples. The first of these was Rome, the pious capital of Orthodox Christianity. But the popes betrayed the faith, embraced error, and led the city to its doom. A second Rome then arose in Constantinople, where the true faith flourished until a Patriarch and an emperor surrendered to the Latin heretics (the Roman Church). Divine retribution was swift and severe. Constantinople fell to the godless Ishmaelites (Muslims), and the true faith was trampled and oppressed.

---

[6] Marc Raeff, "An Early Theorist of Absolutism: Joseph of Volokolamsk," *American Slavic and East European Review* 8 (1949): 7, 81.

But following the fall of the second Rome, the Russian tsardom arose in the north, the only guardian of the divinely revealed faith. Addressing the grand prince with the title of tsar (Caesar), a title that would not be officially assumed by the ruler of Moscow until the coronation of Vasilii's son, Ivan the Terrible, Filofei preached, "Perceive, pious Tsar, how all the Christian realms have converged into yours alone. Two Romes have fallen, and the third stands, and the fourth there shall not be."[7]

The glorification of the princes of Moscow was not confined to Filofei. Spurious genealogies purported to show that the princes of the house of Riurik were related to Roman emperors through a mythic Pruss, the brother or a half-brother of Caesar Augustus. Equally fanciful stories were told of the Byzantine emperor Constantine IX (1042-54), whose realm was purportedly attacked by Prince Vladimir Vsevolodovich of Kiev (1113-25). To secure peace, the emperor sent his crown, his cross, and his neck chain to Vladimir, bidding him to be crowned an independent tsar. That Vladimir would become grand prince of Kiev fifty-nine years after Constantine's death was a minor detail that the mythologizers ignored.[8]

The total power of the ruler over the Church was dramatically demonstrated both in theory and in practice by Ivan IV, or Ivan the Terrible. In his writings, Ivan unequivocally asserted the primacy of secular power and barred any interference by the clergy with the tsar's will. In practice, he treated the Church as the inferior that it was. When Metropolitan Filipp, a monk of exceptional moral character and fortitude, dared to remonstrate with Ivan about the depredations of the *oprichnina*—a system of repression designed by the tsar to exterminate his enemies, most of them imaginary—and publicly to denounce the tsar for the terror he had unleashed in the land, Ivan had the bishops remove Filipp from the metropolitanate. Shortly thereafter the courageous monk, head of the Russian Church, was murdered by Maliuta Skuratov, a brutal companion in crime of the half-demented tsar. The Church meekly submitted, although a century later it canonized Filipp as a martyr.

Ivan the Terrible's reign had dire consequences for the country. The unrestrained and aimless terror, the failed military campaigns in Livonia, the demoralization of the boyar class, the enserfment of peasant masses and the consequent flight of the peasants into the open country to the east and the south left the country shaken and exhausted. Ivan's successor, his sickly and inactive son, Feodor, left the government in the hands of his devious but capable brother-in-law, Boris Godunov.

Boris was keenly aware of the usefulness of the Church as an instrument of the State. To strengthen his own position in Russian society, he cultivated the hierarchy and conducted a veritable campaign for the elevation of the Metro-

[7] George Vernadsky, ed., *A Source Book for Russian History from Early Times to 1917*, 3 vols. (New Haven, 1972), 1:156; V. N. Malinin, *Starets Eleazarova Monastyria Filofei I Ego Poslaniia* (Farnborough, 1901).

[8] See Orlov, *Drevniaia Russkaia Literatura*, 220-21.

politan of Moscow to the rank of a Patriarch. The four ecumenical Patriarchs of the Orthodox Church, those of Constantinople, Jerusalem, Antioch, and Alexandria, were subjects of the Ottoman Muslim Sultan-Caliph. During the preceding decades, they had become dependent on Moscow's support and eager for financial help. In 1586, Moscow was visited by the Patriarch of Antioch, and two years later by Jeremiah, Patriarch of Constantinople, the highest-ranking cleric in the Orthodox Church. Taking advantage of their financial needs, Boris Godunov persuaded them to call a council that would elevate the Metropolitan of Moscow to the rank of Patriarch, making him the fifth Patriarch of the Orthodox Church. Speaking at the installation of Job, the first Patriarch of Moscow, Patriarch Jeremiah of Constantinople made it clear that the Muscovite Church deserved such a high honor because of the power of the monarch. "In all the world [he said] there is [now] but one pious tsar. . . . [It] is here that the ecumenical Patriarch should be, while in old Tsargrad [Constantinople] the Christian faith is being driven out by the infidel Turk's for our sins."[9]

The new rank of its head, useful in Moscow's relations with foreign countries, especially in the East, did not diminish the power of the tsar over the Church at home. At the death of the childless Feodor in 1598, it was Patriarch Job who proposed to the Assembly of the Land to elect Boris Godunov to the vacant throne, thus repaying his debt to Boris. In the subsequent relations between the two there was no question as to who held the upper hand.

The decade of turmoil, known in Russian history as the Time of Troubles, that followed Boris's death came close to destroying the State, and mortally endangered the Church as well. The throne was occupied for a short while by an adventurer pretending to be Dmitrii, the long-deceased youngest son of Ivan the Terrible. This False Dmitrii was sponsored by Polish nobles who were in turn encouraged by the Vatican, which nursed hopes for the conversion of the Russians to Catholicism. There followed several other tsars and pseudo-tsars, none of whom was able to stop the disintegration of the country or defend it against the Catholic Poles, Lutheran Swedes, and the anarchic bands of Cossacks from southern borderlands. At last a broad movement of townspeople, service gentry, and some boyars, with the strong support and blessing of the Church, drove out the invaders and restored a semblance of order. In 1613, the Assembly of the Land elected the sixteen-year-old boy, Michael Romanov, whose father, Feodor, had been forced to become a monk under the name of Filaret. Filaret completely dominated his mild and obedient son, and to the end of his life not only ruled Russia in his son's name, but even used the title of Great Sovereign heretofore reserved exclusively for the tsar. An experienced statesman, intelligent, energetic, and willful, Filaret was elevated to the position of Patriarch, effectively uniting in his person State and Church. Filaret, however, was dedicated more to secular than to ecclesiastical affairs, and used his unique position to promote the

---

[9] See Vernadsky, *A Source Book*, 1:176.

interests of the State. The Time of Troubles was over, and the predominance of the secular authority was fully reestablished.

The solitary and last challenge by the Church, or rather by an individual Patriarch, to the dominant position of the State came in the next generation. Tsar Aleksei Mikhailovich had for his Patriarch an intelligent, well-read, and strong-willed man, Nikon, whose ideas to a great extent reflected the change in the mentality of a segment of Muscovite ruling classes produced by their growing exposure to the West, the influences coming from the newly annexed Ukraine, and the closer relations with the Orthodox churches of the Ottoman Empire. Increased acquaintance with Greek theological literature stimulated the desire to correct sacred texts that had been improperly translated into Russian, while exposure to Catholic thought produced doubts in the legitimacy of the subordination of the Church to the State.

Twenty-five years the tsar's senior, Nikon acquired enormous influence over the mild and impressionable Aleksei Mikhailovich. The Patriarch frequently shared the tsar's meals, engaged him in long conversations, and freely offered advice on affairs of State. Nikon insisted on writing his name next to the tsar's in official documents and began to use the title *Velikii Gosudar* (Great Sovereign), reserved to the tsar alone and previously used by only one uncrowned person, Patriarch Filaret, Tsar Aleksei's grandfather. Such self-aggrandizement aroused much jealousy in governing circles and alarmed the tsar himself.

Aware of the inaccuracies in Russian translations of the Greek sacred texts and of the numerous deviations that had crept into Muscovite liturgical practices over the centuries and had been sanctified by tradition and by official decisions of the Church Council of 1551, Nikon vigorously championed their correction in conformity with Byzantine models. To bitter accusations that he betrayed Holy Rus, the Patriarch replied that while he was a Russian, his faith was Greek.[10] Nikon saw the Muscovite Church as a part of the Church Universal whose standards had been set in Constantinople, not as an autonomous body that possessed all truth. Such a palpable deviation was unacceptable to a large number of priests and monks who perceived Nikon as a heresiarch and opposed his reforms.

The matter was further complicated by Nikon's loud expressions of his conviction that the Church was not subject to secular power but superior to it. In a society steeped in the belief of the tsar's sanctity and the divine provenance of his absolute power, Nikon's assertion of ecclesiastical superiority was seen as yet another deviation from Orthodoxy, an attempt to introduce Catholic papist notions and to pervert ancient truth. When accused of papism, Nikon arrogantly replied: "Why should not one respect the pope for that which is good? There [in Rome] the supreme apostles are Peter and Paul and he serves them."[11]

No Muscovite church hierarch either before or after Nikon put forth the claim of the superiority of spiritual power so clearly and unequivocally. In

---

[10] V. O. Kliuchevskii, *Kurs Russkoi Istorii*, 5 vols. (Moscow, 1987-89), 3:285.
[11] Ibid.

1662, Nikon published a refutation of certain views expressed in the form of questions by the Boyar Simeon Streshnev, a refutation that contained statements worthy of the *Unam Sanctam* of Boniface VIII. Nikon wrote that "episcopal authority is spiritual, while that given to the tsar is of this world; and matters of heavenly, that is, spiritual, authority stand far above those of this world or of temporal [authority]. Hence, it is clear that the tsar must be lower than the prelate and obedient to him, for I also say that the clergy are chosen people and are anointed by the Holy Ghost. And if all Christians owe obedience to the prelates, such obedience is owed still more by him who with his sword forces the insubordinate to obey the prelates."[12]

Nikon then compares episcopal authority to the sun and royal authority to the moon:

> As the moon receives its light from the sun . . . so it is with the tsar. He is consecrated, anointed, and crowned by a prelate, from whom he must therefore receive his perfect light, to wit, his most rightful power and authority. . . . The clergy is the more honored and higher authority than the state itself. . . . The throne of the clergy has been erected in heaven. Who says this? The Heavenly King Himself: "Whatsoever you shall bind on earth shall be bound in heaven. . . . " Thus it is the tsars who are anointed by the priests and not the priests by the tsars. . . . Priestly authority excels civil power as heaven excels earth, yea, and much more so.[13]

Such extreme assertions of ecclesiastical authority were not only unacceptable to the tsar but frightening to the episcopate and even to the ecumenical Patriarchs of the East, who depended on Moscow for protection and financial support. The Muscovite Church, Josephite to the core, hastened to reiterate its loyalty and subordination to the tsar and deposed Nikon. In December 1666, at a Church Council attended not only by the Russian bishops but by the ecumenical Patriarchs of Antioch and Alexandria as well, the hierarchs declared that the deposed Patriarch had offended the tsar, "autocrat of all Great, Little, and White Rus," and plunged the country into turmoil. The Council therefore ratified the Patriarch's deposition and debarred him "from every sacerdotal function."[14]

Nikon had no effective champions. His encounter with the State served only to increase the power of the monarch. The official Church was now facing a major rebellion in its own ranks because of the schism of the Old Believers, as well as from the enemies of all reform and innovation whether inspired by the West or by the East. Thus, the Church needed the autocratic monarchy to save it from the revolt of these xenophobic worshipers of the past. In its zeal to extirpate Old Belief, the Church once again invoked the power of the State and bowed to its supremacy as it had done two centuries earlier.

---

[12] Vernadsky, *A Source Book*, 1:256.
[13] Ibid., 1:256-57.
[14] See ibid., 1:258.

The penetration of Muscovy by Western ideas did not seem to be quite so threatening. Tsar Aleksei, like his predecessors, at least since the days of Ivan III, brought to Moscow foreign military officers, physicians, and technicians of all sorts. The Church was aware that Western ideas were spreading among the Muscovite upper class through foreigners employed by the tsar, Ukrainian clerics and scholars flocking to Moscow, and increased travel by Russians abroad. Tsar Feodor, Aleksei's eldest son, continued to favor foreigners, as did Feodor's two younger brothers and successors, the co-tsars Ivan V and Peter I. The conservative Church called upon the State to save Holy Rus, but it was powerless to prevent Russia's growing contamination by Western beliefs, attitudes, and manners, a contamination that was encouraged and promoted by the monarchy.

In a vain attempt to protect the past and to reassert some semblance of Church authority, Patriarch Joachim in his Testament addressed the co-tsars Ivan and Peter in March 1690, calling upon them to defend the faith, and stating the position of the Church on foreign influences, a position that has not substantially changed to this day. The Patriarch pleaded with the tsars "never to allow any Orthodox Christians in their realm to entertain any close friendly relations with heretics and dissenters—with Latins [Roman Catholics], Lutherans, Calvinists, and godless Tatars (whom our Lord abominates and the Church of God damns for their God-abhorred guiles); but let them be avoided as enemies of God and defamers of the church."[15] The Patriarch, in a strikingly contemporary spirit, wanted the tsars to decree "that men of foreign creeds who come here to this pious realm shall under no circumstances preach their religion, disparage our faith in any conversations, or introduce their alien customs derived from their heresies for the temptation of Christians; they should be forbidden to do all this on pain of severe punishment."[16]

In a postscript to these modern-sounding reflections, Patriarch Joachim added that under no circumstances must the tsars allow "the heretics and dissenters to build Roman [Catholic] temples, Lutheran kirks, or Tatar mosques anywhere in your realm or dominions, nor to bring any new Latin and alien customs, nor to introduce the wearing of foreign dress: for it is not through such practices that piety will spread in a Christian realm or faith in our Lord will grow." Such was the position of the Muscovite Church at the close of the seventeenth century and such, in essence, it has remained.

Joachim did not live to see Peter become the sole tsar and institute reforms that opened not just a window, but gates to the West. Although religious like most of his contemporaries, Peter was anticlerical. Circumstances of his childhood and youth made him fear and hate Old Believers, whose ranks included a number of nobles bent on preventing him from ascending the throne. Throughout Peter's reign Old Believers were persecuted. Their resistance to the tsar, whom many considered Antichrist for his attacks on cherished traditions, his friendship with foreigners, and even his pipe smoking, at times was so fierce as

---

[15] Ibid., 2:362.
[16] Ibid.

to lead to self-immolation. Seemingly the Church was once again being protected against dissidents by the power of the State.

Yet Peter did not trust the church hierarchy, for it too resisted his reforms, albeit passively. When Patriarch Adrian, a timid and ineffectual prelate, died in 1700, Peter left the patriarchal throne vacant, entrusting the administration of the Church to a learned Ukrainian monk, Stefan Iavorskii. Later, the tsar used as his surrogate in running the Church another Ukrainian, Feofan Prokopovich, an opportunist totally dependent on his master for his position in Russian society. Thus the patriarchate lapsed. In its place Peter established a committee, the Holiest Governing Synod, which functioned under a set of rules written by Prokopovich and edited by Peter himself.

The Synod was organized like any other government department under the direct authority of the tsar who appointed one of its officers with the incongruously foreign title of *ober-prokuror* (high procurator), a layman representing the authority of the tsar. The establishment of the Synod signaled the total abolition of ecclesiastical autonomy and the reduction of the Church itself to the status of a government department. The hierarchy did not, and could not, protest this outright takeover of the Church. It had no tradition of independence, no moral strength to withstand the overwhelming might of the autocracy. With the Old Believers it had lost its most determined and its fanatical members.

It is noteworthy that the man who ran the Russian Church during the last years of Peter's reign was also the most outstanding proponent of unlimited royal power. Feofan (Theophanes) Prokopovich was the author of numerous treatises, sermons, exhortations, and government documents that bestowed a divine status on the tsar. Educated in Kiev, the Catholic academies in Cracow and Lvov, and in Rome, Prokopovich was well versed in the classics and Western scholastic literature. However, his political thought was heavily influenced by Lutheran ideas that also appealed to Peter. In stilted, inflated language full not only of biblical citation but also of classical pagan imagery, Prokopovich preached his secularizing sermons in a style that must have offended the sensibilities of many Russian churchmen. Yet they remained silent. Even as the masses boiled with rage at the impious tsar, the official Church faithfully served the State.

For almost two centuries after Peter's rule, the Church acted as an arm of the State, teaching obedience to the government, glorifying absolutism, and serving as a spiritual police. The Holy Synod itself was run by laymen, usually of the most conservative bent. It is enough to mention but one of them, Konstantin Pobedonostsev, confidant of Alexander III and tutor of the future Nicholas II, to illustrate this point.

By and large, the church leadership was satisfied with the arrangement. The tsars never intruded in the domain of doctrine and dogma. They subsidized the golden-domed churches and innumerable monasteries and convents. They let the Church remain undisturbed in its frozen attitudes and ideals, disdaining science, fearing innovation, and mistrusting the West. The Church was grateful to the State for its protection, for discrimination against Old Believers, for limits imposed on the Catholics and Protestants, for severe restrictions placed on foreign and domestic sects, and for occasional help in missionary activity among the Muslims. No wonder conservative statesmen such as Count S. S. Uvarov proposed the tripartite formula of Orthodoxy, Autocracy, and Nationality as a safeguard against the spread of "destructive" ideas that, in his view, had caused great harm in Western Europe. Uvarov's formula was eagerly embraced by the tsars and became a central element of the Russian official ideology until at least 1905. It survives in some minds to this day, although nowadays it is expressed in somewhat different language. Indeed, the contemporary identification of Great Russian ethnicity with Orthodoxy is not only a survival of an aspect of Muscovite exclusiveness and xenophobia, but also the heritage of a carefully cultivated reactionary nineteenth-century philosophy promoted by the tsarist regime. It is significant, however, that the Church was passive in the ideological struggles of the last century, when religious thought in Russia was dominated by laymen from Chaadaev, Gogol, Kireievskii, Khomiakov, Aksakov, Dostoyevskii, and Soloviev to Tolstoy, who was anathematized by the Church for his heterodox views.

After November 1917, the Church, accustomed to existence under the paternalistic control of the State, found itself adrift in the turbulent sea of the revolution. A militantly atheistic regime disestablished the Church, confiscated its properties, desecrated its temples, burned its icons, killed thousands of priests and monks and deprived the rest of citizenship, and reduced that proud institution to the status of a despised semi-legal organization. Trying to cope with this novel and frightening situation, the Church attempted to stand on its own feet. It elected its first Patriarch in more than two hundred years. Its new head, Patriarch Tikhon, was an extreme conservative with old ties to some of the most reactionary organizations in tsarist Russia. Tikhon strongly opposed the Soviet regime and dared to defy it, but the Church had neither the material nor spiritual means of resisting the State, even an atheistic state bent on the destruction of all religion. Tikhon was arrested, tried, convicted, and jailed, whereupon he surrendered and publicly recognized the Soviet government.

For the next seventy years, the Church experienced periods of improved relations with the State, as happened during World War II, when Stalin needed to mobilize the spiritual resources of the Russian people in its mortal struggle with the invading Germans, and periods of severe repression, as was the case under Khrushchev. The Church for its part did not hesitate to address Stalin as the God-given leader of the Soviet people and remained silent about Khrushchev's destruction of thousands of churches and the harassment of monks and priests. Now thoroughly infiltrated by agents of the Soviet secret police, the Church was less than ever able to defend itself. If anything, it continued to hope for a reconciliation, for a return to the symbiotic relationship that had served Church and State so well for hundreds of years. With the dissolution of the Soviet regime, the dream of restoring such a relationship, regaining the protection of the State against religious rivals, and receiving an honored place in the life of the country began to be realized.

13.

THE LAW OF THE RUSSIAN FEDERATION ON THE FREEDOM OF CONSCIENCE AND RELIGIOUS ASSOCIATIONS FROM A HUMAN RIGHTS PERSPECTIVE

◆

T. Jeremy Gunn

THE 1997 LAW ON FREEDOM OF CONSCIENCE AND RELIGIOUS ASSOCIATIONS

On September 26, 1997, Russian President Boris Yeltsin signed into law an act On Freedom of Conscience and Religious Associations (the "1997 Law") that had been vigorously promoted by the Russian Orthodox Church and by Aleksii II, Patriarch of Moscow and All Russia.[1] The 1997 Law grants a broad range of privileges to the Russian Orthodox Church and other "religious or-ganizations" that have operated in the Russian Federation since 1982. But, at the same time, it denies those privileges to other religious associations. The 1997 Law was adopted in the Duma by the overwhelming vote of 358 to 6 (with 4 abstentions), and by a unanimous vote in the Federation Council.

The 1997 Law is now the principal legislation of the Russian Federation regulating the legal status of churches and religious associations. It repealed a

---

This chapter is an excerpt and update of the author's article that appeared in *Emory International Law Review* 12 (1998): 43-99.

[1] On the Freedom of Conscience and on Religious Associations, Federal Law No. 125-FZ (Sept. 26, 1997), translated by Lawrence A. Uzzell in *Emory International Law Review* 12 (1998): 657-80 [hereafter "1997 Law"].

1990 Law on Freedom of Conscience and Religious Belief (the "1990 Law") and became effective on the date it was published.[2] The 1990 Law had guaranteed that all religious associations were to be treated equally by the State. It had provided that:

> All religions and religious associations shall be equal before the laws of the state. No religion or religious association shall enjoy any advantages or be subjected to any restrictions relative to others. In matters of freedom of worship and belief the state shall be neutral, that is, shall not favor any religion or outlook.[3]

Unlike the 1990 Law, which ensured the equality of all religious organizations, the salient feature of the 1997 Law is the sharp distinction it draws between two types of religious associations: favored *religious organizations,* which are granted a series of privileges (including the rights to own property, establish schools, and import religious literature), and less-favored *religious groups,* which are denied virtually all rights except the ability to worship.

Because of the vast disparity between the rights accorded religious organizations and the single right accorded religious groups, the most important provision of the 1997 Law is the clause identifying the criteria for becoming a "religious organization." The relevant clause provides that:

> No fewer than ten citizens of the Russian Federation may be founders of a local religious organization, joining together *as a religious group which must have confirmation from the organs of the local government that it has existed on the given territory for no less than fifteen years,* or confirmation from a centralized religious organization of the same creed that it forms part of its structure.[4]

Therefore, the difference between the rights of religious organizations, as opposed to religious groups, effectively hinges on whether the religious entity is recognized by local governments as having operated in Russia since 1982 or whether it is a branch of a centralized religious organization, such as the Russian Orthodox Church. The Russian Orthodox Church, which actively promoted the 1997 Law, readily qualifies to become a privileged religious organization. Under the 1997 Law, religious associations that have arrived since the downfall of Communism, or that operated underground during Communism but are not recognized by local governments, do not qualify. Thus, if a church

---

[2] Law of the Russian Soviet Socialist Republic on Freedom of Worship (October 25, 1990), translated in *Journal of Church & State* 33 (1991): 191-201, and in Igor Troyanovsky, ed., *Religion in the Soviet Republics* (San Francisco, 1991), 31 [hereafter "1990 Law"].

[3] Ibid., art. 10. See also ibid., art. 5 ("The fundamental guarantees of freedom of worship in the RSFSR shall be . . . equality of religious associations before the law").

[4] 1997 Law, art. 9.1 (emphasis added).

did not operate under the Soviet State—with the profound compromises that such operations necessarily entailed—the church will not be permitted to function if the terms of the 1997 Law are enforced as written.

THE 1997 LAW
AND INTERNATIONAL HUMAN RIGHTS NORMS

The 1997 Law, by repealing the 1990 Law and establishing a two-tier system of religious associations, runs afoul of four major principles of human rights law that are incorporated both in the Constitution of the Russian Federation and in international human rights conventions to which the Russian Federation has pledged itself to adhere.[5] These international human rights conventions include both the International Covenant on Civil and Political Rights ("ICCPR") and the 1950 [European] Convention for the Protection of Human Rights and Fundamental Freedoms ("ECHR" or "European Convention").[6] Russia has ratified both the ICCPR and the European Convention.[7] The first major principle violated is the general right of equality (or "non-discrimination"). The three remaining principles are the substantive rights of (1) freedom of thought, conscience, and religion, (2) freedom of expression, and (3) freedom of association.

THE RUSSIAN CONSTITUTION

Human rights law is controlling law within the Russian Federation under the provisions of the Constitution that guarantee certain enumerated rights as well as the Constitution's provisions that incorporate international human rights law. The supremacy clause requires that all Federal laws comply with the Constitution: "The Constitution of the Russian Federation shall have supreme legal force and direct effect, and shall be applicable throughout the

---

[5] Konstitutsiia RF (Constitution of the Russian Federation)(1993), translated in Vladimir V. Belyakov and Walter J. Raymond, eds., *Constitution of the Russian Federation* (Lawrenceville, Va., 1994) [hereafter "Konst. RF"].

[6] International Covenant on Civil and Political Rights, G.A. Res. 2200A, U.N. GAOR, 21st Sess. Supp. No. 16, U.N. Doc. A/6316 (1966), *United Nations Treaty Series* 999 (1976): 171 [hereafter "ICCPR"]; European Convention for the Protection of Human Rights and Fundamental Freedoms, Nov. 4, 1950, 213 U.N.T.S. 222, as amended by Protocol Nos. 3 & 5 [hereafter "ECHR"]. The High Contracting Parties of the ECHR have ratified a new Protocol 11, which repeals Sections III and IV of the ECHR and establishes a new unified European Court of Human Rights. Protocol 11 became effective as of November 1, 1998.

[7] For the ICCPR, see *Multilateral Treaties Deposited with the Secretary-General* (1997), 120-21. On May 5, 1998, Russia deposited its ratification documents for the ECHR with the Council of Europe Secretariat.

entire territory of the Russian Federation. Laws and other activities of the Russian Federation may not contravene the Constitution of the Russian Federation."[8] Accordingly, to the extent that the 1997 Law contravenes the Constitution, it is either void or voidable.

Moreover, the Constitution guarantees not only that human rights are to be respected in Russia, but that Russian legislation must be consistent with international human rights standards. The Preamble acknowledges that the Constitution was created, in part, for the purpose of declaring that "human rights and liberties" are to be respected in the Russian Federation. The Constitution thereupon requires the state to fill the role of guarantor of those liberties. "State protection for human rights and liberties in the Russian Federation shall be guaranteed."[9] Not only does the Constitution incorporate international law into domestic law, it provides that international law supersedes contravening domestic law:

The commonly recognized principles and norms of the international law and the international treaties of the Russian Federation shall be a component part of its legal system. If an international treaty of the Russian Federation stipulates other rules than those stipulated by the law, *the rules of the international treaty shall apply.*[10]

The Constitution's placement of international law above contravening domestic law applies specifically to international human rights law. Article 17 provides that:

1. The basic rights and liberties in conformity with the commonly recognized principles and norms of the international law shall be recognized and guaranteed in the Russian Federation and under this Constitution.
2. The basic rights and liberties of the human being shall be inalienable and shall belong to everyone from birth.
3. The exercise of rights and liberties of a human being and citizen may not violate the rights and liberties of other persons.[11]

The Russian Constitution guarantees not only rights related to equality, religion, expression, and association, but it also specifically provides that statutory law is superseded by the Russian Constitution and by international human rights norms. To the extent that any law violates rights guaranteed by the Constitution or by international human rights standards, that law should not have effect in the Russian Federation.

---

[8] Konst. RF, art. 15.1.
[9] See ibid., art. 45.1.
[10] Ibid., art. 15.4 (emphasis added).
[11] Ibid., art. 17.

THE 1997 LAW VIOLATES FOUR HUMAN RIGHTS NORMS

The substantive rights guaranteed by the Russian Constitution and by international human rights conventions—including the freedoms of religion, expression, and association—typically are enunciated in two separate clauses. First, a *guarantee clause* identifies the scope of a particular right. Second, a *limitations clause* identifies the circumstances under which a government properly may limit the scope of a guaranteed right. In both the ECHR and the ICCPR, the guarantee clause and the limitations clause are contained in the same article, typically as sections 1 and 2 respectively. For example, the ICCPR's guarantee clause for freedom of association provides that "[e]veryone shall have the right to freedom of association with others."[12] The limitations clause to that guarantee provides, in part, that "[n]o restrictions may be placed on the exercise of this right other than those which are prescribed by law and which are necessary in a democratic society in the interests of national security or public safety, public order, the protection of public health or morals or the protection of the rights and freedoms of others."[13] In the Russian Constitution, the guarantee clauses are contained in separate articles throughout the Constitution, while the single limitations clause, found in Article 55.3, applies to all of the guarantee clauses.

To determine whether a governmental action violates a human rights norm, there are, therefore, two distinct analytical inquiries that must be made. The first inquiry asks whether the legislation (or state action) infringes a right protected by a guarantee clause. If the legislation does not infringe such a right, it is legitimate under human rights law, and there is no need for further analysis. If, however, there is a finding of an infringement, this is only the first step. The second step determines whether the infringement is justifiable under human rights norms. Not all government actions that infringe on rights amount to violations of the law. The European Court has developed a framework for analysis, which I shall follow below.

THE 1997 LAW INFRINGES ON THE RIGHTS OF EQUALITY AND NON-DISCRIMINATION

EQUALITY STANDARDS

The Russian Constitution, the ECHR, and the ICCPR contain generic clauses guaranteeing rights of equality and prohibiting discrimination.

These three articles prohibit discrimination among people on the basis of specified impermissible criteria, including race, sex, nationality, religion, and

---

[12] ICCPR, art. 22.1.
[13] Ibid., art. 22.2.

Equality and Non-Discrimination Clauses

Russian Constitution	ECHR	ICCPR
Article 19 1. All people shall be equal before the law and in the court of law. 2. The state shall guarantee the equality of rights and liberties regardless of sex, race, nationality, language, origin, property or employment status, residence, attitude to religion, convictions, membership of public associations or any other circumstances. Any restrictions of the rights of citizens on social, racial, national, linguistic or religious grounds shall be forbidden.	*Article 14* The enjoyment of the rights and freedoms set forth in this Convention shall be secured without discriminations on any ground such as sex, race, colour, language, religion, political or other opinion, national or social origin, association with a national minority, property, birth or other status.	*Article 26* All persons are equal before the law and are entitled without any discrimination to the equal protection of the law. In this respect, the law shall prohibit any discrimination and guarantee to all persons equal and effective protection against discrimination on any ground such as race, colour, sex, language, religion, political or other opinion, national or social origin, property, birth or other status.

language. All three documents prohibit discrimination among people on the basis of religious belief. The ECHR provides that the "enjoyment of the rights and freedoms set forth in [the ECHR] shall be secured without discrimination on any ground such as . . . religion."[14] The European Court has interpreted Article 14 to mean that "a distinction based essentially on a difference in religion alone is not acceptable."[15] Similarly, the ICCPR similarly provides that "the law shall prohibit any discrimination and guarantee to all persons equal and effective protection against discrimination on any ground such as . . . religion."[16] The Russian Constitution is perhaps the most advanced of the three charters in this regard, because it is not limited to prohibiting discrimination on impermissible grounds, but instead it also affirmatively obligates the "state [to] guarantee the equality of rights and liberties."[17]

---

[14] ECHR, art. 14.

[15] *Hoffmann v. Austria*, 255 Eur. Ct. H.R. (Ser. A), 61 (1993).

[16] ICCPR, art. 26. Even in times of national emergency, when the state is permitted to derogate some rights, the ICCPR prohibits discrimination on the basis of religion. This "non-derogation clause" of the ICCPR provides that even in times

> of a public emergency which threatens the life of the nation[,] the States Parties to the present Covenant may take measures derogating from their obligations under the present Covenant to the extent strictly required by the exigencies of the situation, provided that such measures are not inconsistent with their other obligations under international law and do not involve discrimination solely on the ground of race, colour, sex, language, religion or social origin. Ibid., art. 4.1.

[17] Konst. RF, art. 19.2.

The types of impermissible discrimination explicitly mentioned in the ECHR are not exhaustive. Article 14 prohibits discrimination "on any ground such as" those that are specifically identified, and the European Court itself has affirmed that there are additional grounds that are not specifically enumerated.[18] Neither the Constitution, nor the ICCPR, suggests that the list of prohibited forms of discrimination is complete. Unlike the ECHR, which speaks only of "non-discrimination," the Russian Constitution and the ICCPR identify "equality" as the prevailing norm and specifically charge governments with the role of promoting equality.

The Russian Constitution, the ECHR, and the ICCPR guarantee the rights of equality for both citizens and non-citizens. Article 19 of the Constitution includes one clause that explicitly protects "all people,"[19] one clause that appears to protect all people,[20] and a third clause that refers only to the rights of citizens.[21] The ICCPR also provides, without any reference to citizenship, that "[a]ll persons are equal before the law and are entitled without any discrimination to the equal protection of the law."[22] Although Article 14 of the ECHR does not explicitly state whether its guarantees are for all people or merely for citizens, the European Court has held that the basic rights enumerated in the ECHR, including rights of religion, expression, and association, apply both to citizens and to non-citizens of a state. Moreover, each of the substantive rights clauses of the Constitution, the ECHR, and the ICCPR pertaining to freedom of association, religion, and expression guarantees the rights for "everyone" without regard to citizenship status.

In addition to the non-discrimination and equality clauses described above, the Russian Constitution contains two unique and far-reaching clauses that ensure equality not simply among citizens, but also among associations within the Russian Federation. Article 13.4 provides that "[p]ublic associations shall be equal before the law." Similarly, Article 14.2 provides that "[r]eligious associations shall be separated from the state, and shall be equal before the law." Thus, under its own Constitution, the Russian state is prohibited from discriminating among different types of similarly situated associations.

DISCRIMINATORY PROVISIONS OF THE 1997 LAW

The 1990 Law had guaranteed a wide range of rights to *all* religious associations. Under the 1990 Law, each religious association was entitled to request religious holidays; become a "juridical person" (provided it had a minimum of ten members); found and maintain churches and pilgrimage places; publish and acquire religious literature; engage in charitable activities; maintain con-

---

[18] "The list of prohibited grounds of discrimination as set out in Article 14 is not exhaustive." *James and Others v. United Kingdom*, 98 Eur. Ct. H.R. (Ser. A) at 44 (1986).

[19] Konst. RF, art. 19.1.

[20] See ibid., art. 19.2 (sentence 1).

[21] See ibid., art. 19.2 (sentence 2).

[22] ICCPR, art. 26.

tacts with foreign co-religionists; own buildings and real property; rent real property; engage in commercial business activities; hire laborers; receive tax-exempt status for charitable contributions; and obtain social insurance for the clergy and others.

The 1997 Law, however, guarantees the equality of religious associations with respect to only one issue: "freedom of conscience and creed."[23] Although the 1997 Law guarantees this essential right for all people to hold religious beliefs, this right is so elementary that it essentially states the obvious: no modern, civilized society may infringe on a person's internal beliefs. After recognizing this important, but unremarkable, right, the 1997 Law thereupon draws a sharp discriminatory line between the rights of favored *religious organizations* and disfavored *religious groups*. The 1997 Law provides a litany of benefits and privileges that are available to the favored religious organizations, such as the Russian Orthodox Church, but that are denied to religious groups that did not operate in Russia under the Communist regime. There are at least five separate types of benefits for religious organizations that are denied to religious groups.

First and most important, religious organizations are entitled to become juridical persons, whereas religious groups are not.[24] The rights that follow from becoming juridical persons include the right to own real property, a benefit that is vital to any religious association that wishes to operate churches openly or to provide housing for its clergy.

> Religious organizations [but not religious groups] can own buildings, plots of land, objects for the purpose of production and for social, charitable, educational and other purposes, articles of religious significance, financial means, and other property which is essential for their activity, including that necessary for historical and cultural monuments. Religious organizations [but not religious groups] have the right to own property which has been acquired or created by their own means, by the donations of citizens or of organizations or transferred to them by the State, or acquired by other means in conformity with the laws of the Russian Federation.[25]

Second, the 1997 Law permits favored religious organizations to receive from the state "tax privileges and other privileges."[26] This provision establishes the basis whereby organizations may become tax exempt but disfavored groups may be taxed. By leaving open the possibility of additional, but unspecified, "privileges," religious organizations now have statutory authorization to receive any additional appropriations that the Duma might offer. In addition, the 1997 Law provides that the state may provide "financial . . .

---

[23] 1997 Law, art. 4.3.
[24] See ibid., arts. 8.1, 7.1.
[25] See ibid., arts. 21.1, 21.2.
[26] Ibid., art. 4.3.

material and other aid . . . [for] the restoration, maintenance and protection of buildings and objects which are monuments of history and culture."[27] The state may also provide benefits to schools operated by religious organizations, including "instruction in general educational subjects in educational institutions."[28]

Third, religious organizations are authorized to own and operate educational institutions,[29] own commercial enterprises,[30] found and maintain religious buildings and equipment,[31] and operate theological schools.[32]

Fourth, under the 1997 Law, only religious organizations may conduct charitable activities,[33] and they have sole access to hospitals and prisons for the purpose of ministering.[34]

Fifth, religious organizations are authorized, on their own recognizance, to acquire, import, and distribute religious literature.[35] They are permitted to invite foreign citizens to preach and conduct religious activities.[36] Among religious associations, only organizations are permitted to operate mass media.[37]

The 1997 Law discriminates not only among religious associations but also between citizens and non-citizens. It contains a pro-forma statement acknowledging that foreigners residing in Russia have the right to hold religious beliefs.[38] But the 1997 Law, unlike the 1990 Law that allowed both citizens and non-citizens to found associations for religious activities, imposes significant restrictions on religious activities of non-citizens in several ways.[39]

First, not only does the 1997 Law refuse to recognize foreigners' rights to form religious groups or religious organizations,[40] *it fails even to recognize their right to found religious associations,* unless they permanently reside in the Russian Federation.[41] Foreign religious associations, which may have members residing in Russia, are also prohibited from operating informal associations.[42] Thus, according to the 1997 Law, a group of Hindu engineers working in Moscow would not legally be permitted to form an association to discuss Krishna and Vishnu.

---

[27] Ibid.
[28] Ibid. While religious organizations are entitled to receive assistance in operating their schools, religious groups are not permitted even to operate schools. See ibid., art. 5.3.
[29] See ibid., arts. 5.3, 18.2; see also ibid., art. 19.1.
[30] See ibid., arts. 16.3, 23.
[31] See ibid., art. 16.1.
[32] See ibid., art. 19.1.
[33] See ibid., art. 18.1.
[34] See ibid., art. 16.3.
[35] See ibid., art. 17.1.
[36] See ibid., art. 20.2.
[37] See ibid., art. 18.2.
[38] See ibid., art. 3.1.
[39] 1990 Law, art. 14.
[40] 1997 Law, arts. 7.1, 8.1.
[41] See ibid., art. 6.1.
[42] See ibid., art. 13.2.

Second, the 1997 Law states that "[a] representative body of a foreign religious organization may not engage in liturgical or other religious activities, and does not receive the status of a religious association as established by this federal law."[43] Under this provision, a group of Roman Catholic priests on an official visit to Russia may not legally pray together.

Third, the 1997 Law provides that religious organizations, but not religious groups, "have the right to establish and maintain international links and contacts, including those for the goals of pilgrimages, participation in meetings and other undertakings, for receiving religious education, and also they have the right to invite foreign citizens for these purposes."[44] Moreover, religious organizations, but not groups, "have the exclusive right to invite foreign citizens for professional purposes, including preaching and religious activity in the said organizations in accordance with federal laws."[45]

In conclusion, the 1997 Law clearly discriminates against religious groups in favor of privileged religious organizations. The one-sided benefits to the religious organizations—and derivatively to the members of those organizations—certainly appear to run afoul of the general non-discrimination clauses of the Russian Constitution, the European Convention, and the International Covenant. The one-sided benefits also run afoul of the "equal rights" clauses that protect public associations and religious associations. Finally, the 1997 Law discriminates on the basis of citizenship and imposes discriminatory burdens on aliens.

THE 1997 LAW INFRINGES ON THE SUBSTANTIVE RIGHTS OF FREEDOM OF RELIGION, EXPRESSION, AND ASSOCIATION

FREEDOM OF THOUGHT, CONSCIENCE, AND RELIGION

Article 28 of the Russian Constitution, like Article 9 of the ECHR and Article 18 of the ICCPR, pertains directly to the freedoms of thought, conscience, and religion.

In a recent decision that interpreted the scope of freedom of religion, the European Court considered the question whether Greece, the vast majority of whose citizens are members of the Greek Orthodox Church, might legally impose restrictions on the activities of minority religions.[46] In the *Manoussakis* Case, the Greek government argued that its Constitution, laws, and regulations favoring the Greek Orthodox Church were permissible because of the

---

[43] Ibid., art. 13.2.

[44] Ibid., art. 20.1.

[45] Ibid., art. 20.2.

[46] *Manoussakis and Others v. Greece*, Eur. Ct. H.R. (Ser. A), No. 59/1995/565/651 (Sept. 26, 1996). The European Court recently reaffirmed *Manoussakis* in another case that calls into question Greek laws prohibiting proselytism. See *Larissis v. Greece*, Eur. Ct. H.R. (Ser. A), No. 140/1996/759/958-60, slip op. (Feb. 24, 1998).

Freedom of Thought, Conscience, and Religion Guarantee Clauses

Russian Constitution	ECHR	ICCPR
Article 28 Everyone shall be guaranteed the right to freedom of conscience, to freedom of religious worship, including the right to profess, individually or jointly with others, any religion, or to profess no religion, to freely choose, possess and disseminate religious or other beliefs, and to act in conformity with them.	*Article 9.1* Everyone has the right to freedom of thought, conscience and religion; this right includes freedom to change his religion or belief and freedom, either alone or in community with others and in public or in private, to manifest his religion or belief, in worship, teaching, practice and observance.	*Article 18.1* Everyone shall have the right to freedom of thought, conscience and religion. This right shall include freedom to have or to adopt a religion or belief of his choice, and freedom, either individually or in community with others and in public or private, to manifest his religion or belief in worship, observance, practice and teaching.
Article 14.2 Religious associations shall be separate from the state and shall be equal before the law.		

Freedom of Thought, Conscience, and Religion Limitations Clauses

Russian Constitution	ECHR	ICCPR
Article 55.3 Human and civil rights and liberties may be restricted by the federal law only to the extent required for the protection of the fundamentals of the constitutional system, morality, health, rights, and lawful interests of other persons, for ensuring the defense of the country and the security of the state.	*Article 9.2* Freedom to manifest one's religion or beliefs shall be subject only to such limitations as are prescribed by law and are necessary in a democratic society in the interests of public safety, for the protection of public order, health or morals, or for the protection of the rights and freedoms of others.	*Article 18.3* Freedom to manifest one's religion or beliefs may be subject only to such limitations as are prescribed by law and are necessary to protect public safety, order, health, or morals or the fundamental rights and freedoms of others.

role Orthodoxy plays in Greek life and because of related "historical considerations."[47] The Greek government further argued that its laws restricting the ability of minority religions to open houses of worship were permissible on

---

[47] *Manoussakis*, slip op. 17-18.

"public order grounds" because such churches and houses of worship tended to become centers for illegal proselytizing activities that would undermine the traditional role of the Orthodox Church.[48]

The European Court rejected the arguments of the Greek government and held that "the need to secure true religious pluralism [is] an inherent feature of the notion of a democratic society."[49] This decision of the European Court in support of religious pluralism parallels the United Nations Human Rights Committee's General Comment on Article 18 of the ICCPR. In commenting upon the laws of states that either have established churches or that have a predominant religious faith, the Committee observed that:

> The fact that a religion is recognized as a State religion or that it is established as official or traditional or that its followers comprise the majority of the population, shall not result in any impairment of the enjoyment of any of the rights under the Covenant, including articles 18 and 27, nor in any discrimination against adherents of other religions or nonbelievers. In particular, certain measures discriminating against the latter, such as . . . imposing special restrictions on the practice of other faiths, are not in accordance with the prohibition of discrimination based on religion or belief and the guarantee of equal protection under article 26.[50]

The dominance of one religion in a particular state is not, therefore, a proper rationale for enacting legislation that further favors the dominant religion and discriminates against new or minority religions. Indeed, the Human Rights Committee "views with concern any tendency to discriminate against any religion or belief for any reasons, including the fact that they are newly established, or represent religious minorities that may be the subject of hostility by a predominant religious community."[51] When considering rights related to religion and conscience, the proper touchstone is not the immediate interests of the majority, but the international standard of freedom of thought, conscience, and religion.

With respect to thought, conscience, and belief, the state's goal should not be to avoid discriminating—though such a goal is an appropriate starting point—but actively to promote tolerance and respect. The 1989 Vienna Concluding Document of the Conference on Security and Cooperation in Europe, of which the Russian Confederation is a participating state, directs govern-

---

[48] Ibid.

[49] Ibid., 18.

[50] "General Comment Adopted by the Human Rights Committee under Article 40, Paragraph 4, of the International Covenant on Civil and Political Rights," ICCPR/C/21/Rev.1/Add.4 (Sept. 27, 1993), Addendum, General Comment No. 22 (48) (art. 18), art. 9 [hereafter "General Comment"]. The Committee further explained that "the concept of morals derives from many social, philosophical and religious traditions; consequently, limitations on the freedom to manifest a religion or belief for the purpose of protecting morals must be based on principles not deriving exclusively from a single tradition." Ibid., art. 8.

[51] Ibid., art 2.

ments to "foster a climate of mutual tolerance and respect between believers of different communities as well as between believers and non-believers."[52] The 1997 Law fails to satisfy these standards of the ECHR, ICCPR, and the Vienna Concluding Document in at least three distinct ways.[53]

First, by involving the state in the process of making substantive determinations about the comparative rights of religious associations, the 1997 Law infringes on the freedom of religion. Perhaps the most obvious human rights norm pertaining to religion and conscience is that the state should avoid becoming entangled in making substantive judgments about the comparative merits of belief systems.[54] In the *Manoussakis* Case, the European Court of Human Rights held that:

> The right to freedom of religion as guaranteed under the Convention excludes any discretion on the part of the State to determine whether religious beliefs or the means used to express such beliefs are legitimate. [Administrative regulations on religious associations are permissible only] to verify whether the formal conditions laid down in [registration laws] are satisfied.[55]

The 1997 Law places the state between the people and their right to engage in religious activities.

Second, the 1997 Law infringes on the ability of religious associations to engage in practical activities that further their religious mission. The Law imposes a series of limitations on the rights of religious groups to own property, churches, educational and charitable institutions, and to obtain juridical personality. Such limitations on the practical ability of religions to operate in the modern world violate human rights norms. The 1981 United Nations Declaration on the Elimination of All Forms of Intolerance and of Discrimination Based on Religion or Belief states that religious groups have the right to "worship or assemble in connexion with a religion or belief, and to establish and maintain places for these purposes."[56] The ability to use property is not a

---

[52] Conference on Security and Co-operation in Europe: Concluding Document from the Vienna Meeting (Nov. 4, 1986–Jan. 17, 1989), art. 16b, *International Legal Materials* 28: 527 [hereafter "Vienna Concluding Document"].

[53] The *forum internum* appears to be essentially protected by the 1997 Law. The 1997 law appears not to infringe on the right to "hold" a belief *strictu sensu*, but on the right to engage in activities that manifest those beliefs.

[54] Such a rule does not, of course, prevent the state from criminalizing genuinely antisocial behavior. The state may reasonably and neutrally enforce tax laws, kidnapping laws, and laws relating to assault and battery. The 1997 Law, of course, makes no reference to neutral standards for prohibiting criminal behavior, but moves toward prohibiting some religious activity on the sole basis that it is new to Russia.

[55] *Manoussakis,* slip op. 19.

[56] 1981 United Nations Declaration on the Elimination of All Forms of Intolerance and of Discrimination Based on Religion or Belief, adopted January 18, 1982, GA Res. 55, 36 U.N. GAOR Supp. (No. 51), U.N. Doc. A/RES/36/55 (1982), art. 6(a) [hereafter "1981 UN Declaration"].

luxury, but rather a necessary and an integral aspect of many associations' activities. All religious groups, including the Russian Orthodox Church, would reasonably believe that it is essential for the effectiveness of their operations to be able to own churches, buildings, schools, and equipment. Freedom of religion thus includes not only the right to worship, but also "includes acts integral to the conduct by religious groups of their basic affairs, such as, *inter alia*, the freedom to choose their religious leaders, priests and teachers, the freedom to establish seminaries or religious schools and the freedom to prepare and distribute religious texts or publications."[57]

Third, the 1997 Law infringes on the right to receive and to exchange religious information with fellow believers.[58] Under human rights law, religious groups have the right to the free exchange and distribution of religious materials and to correspond with fellow believers in foreign lands.[59] The right to disseminate information is contained in the Russian Constitution, which provides for the right "to freely choose, hold and propagate religious or other beliefs."[60] The UN Human Rights Committee similarly identifies a right, under ICCPR Article 18, for religious groups to "prepare and distribute religious texts or publications."[61] The Vienna Concluding Document underscores the need to "respect the right of individual believers and communities of believers to acquire, possess, and use sacred books, religious publications in the language of their choice and other articles and materials related to the practice of religion or belief."[62] This includes the right of "religious faiths, institutions and organizations to produce and import and disseminate religious publications and materials."[63] Under the 1997 Law, however, only religious organizations are permitted to engage in international correspondence: "Religious organizations have the exclusive right to invite foreign citizens for professional purposes, including preaching and religious activity in the said organizations in accordance with federal laws."[64]

---

[57] General Comment, art. 4.

[58] The European Court would extend this right to communicate with fellow believers to nonbelievers as well. "[F]reedom to manifest one's religion . . . includes in principle the right to try to convince one's neighbour, for example through 'teaching.' . . . [Without the right to try to convince one's neighbor, the] 'freedom to change [one's] religion or belief', enshrined in Article 9, would be likely to remain a dead letter." *Kokkinakis v. Greece*, 260 Eur. Ct. H.R. (Ser. A), 17 (1993).

[59] There is a right to "establish and maintain communications with individuals and communities in matters of religion and belief at the national and international levels." 1981 UN Declaration, art. 6(i).

[60] Konst. RF, art. 28.

[61] General Comment, art. 4.

[62] Vienna Concluding Document, art. 16.9.

[63] Ibid., art. 16.10.

[64] 1997 Law, art. 20.2.

FREEDOM OF EXPRESSION

The Russian Constitution, the ECHR, and the ICCPR contain similar language protecting freedom of expression.

Freedom of Expression Guarantee Clauses

Russian Constitution	ECHR	ICCPR
Article 29 1. Everyone shall have the right to freedom of thought and speech. 4. Everyone shall have the right to seek, get, transfer, produce and disseminate information by any lawful means. The list of information constituting the state secret shall be established by the federal law.	*Article 10.1* Everyone has the right to freedom of expression. This right shall include freedom to hold opinions and to receive and impart information and ideas without interference by public authority and regardless of frontiers.	*Article 19.2* Everyone shall have the right to freedom of expression; this right shall include freedom to seek, receive and impart information and ideas of all kinds, regardless of frontiers, either orally, in writing or in print, in the form of art, or through any other media of his choice.

Freedom of Expression Limitations Clauses

Russian Constitution	ECHR	ICCPR
Article 55.3 Human and civil rights and liberties may be restricted by the federal law only to the extent required for the protection of the fundamentals of the constitutional system, morality, health, rights and lawful interests of other persons, for ensuring the defense of the country and the security of the state.	*Article 10.2* The exercise of these freedoms, since it carries with it duties and responsibilities, may be subject to such formalities, conditions, restrictions or penalties as are prescribed by law and are necessary in a democratic society, in the interests of national security, territorial integrity or public safety, for the prevention of disorder or crime, for the protection of health or morals, for the protection of the reputation or rights of others, for preventing the disclosure of information received in confidence, or for maintaining the authority and impartiality of the judiciary.	*Article 19.3* The exercise of the rights provided for in paragraph 2 of this article carries with it special duties and responsibilities. It may therefore be subject to certain restrictions, but these shall only be such as are provided by law and are necessary: (a) For respect of the rights or reputations of others; (b) For the protection of national security or of public order, or of public health or morals.

Freedom of religion, the subject of the preceding section, is commonly understood to be a special case of the broader right to freedom of expression. In the view of one commentator, "[p]ublic freedom of religion and belief thus normally represents a subcase of freedom of expression."[65] Accordingly, the rationale offered above with respect to freedom of religion applies, *mutatis mutandis*, to freedom of expression. The European Court of Human Rights has held that freedom of expression is a critical and sensitive right, particularly in a democracy.

> Freedom of expression constitutes one of the essential foundations of a democratic society and one of the basic conditions for its progress and each individual's self-fulfilment. . . . [I]t is applicable not only to "information" or "ideas" that are favourably received or regarded as inoffensive or as a matter of indifference, but also to those that offend, shock or disturb; such are the demands of that pluralism, tolerance and broadmindedness without which there is no "democratic society."[66]

The freedom of expression articles not only protect the right to express one's viewpoint, but they also explicitly include the right to receive information. Thus, it would appear to be a separate and independent infringement on human rights if a state were to restrict the dissemination of ideas on the grounds that such ideas are "foreign" or "alien," or that they would "disturb the State or any sector of the population."[67] Thus, "the right to freedom to receive information basically prohibits a Government from restricting a person from receiving information that others wish or may be willing to impart to him."[68]

The provisions of the 1997 Law that restrict the communication and receipt of information infringe on this additional aspect of freedom of expression.

FREEDOM OF ASSOCIATION

Article 30.1 of the Russian Constitution, like the parallel provisions of the ECHR and the ICCPR, provides for the rights of freedom of association.

The scope of freedom of association is not well developed in international human rights law. To the extent that the freedom of association in the Constitution, the ECHR, and the ICCPR are construed to guarantee little more than

[65] Manfred Nowak, *U.N. Covenant on Civil and Political Rights: CCPR Commentary* (Arlington, Va., 1993), 320.

[66] *Vogt v. Germany*, 323 Eur. Ct. H.R. (Ser. A), 25 (1995) (finding violation of ECHR articles 10 and 11).

[67] *Handyside v. United Kingdom*, 24 Eur. Ct. H.R. (Ser. A), 23 (1976). It should be noted that the freedom of religion clause of the Russian Constitution (Konst. RF, art. 28), unlike the ECHR and the ICCPR, explicitly guarantees the freedom to propagate *religious* information.

[68] *Leander v. Sweden*, 116 Eur. Ct. H.R. (Ser. A), 29 (1987).

Freedom of Association Guarantee Clauses

Russian Constitution	ECHR	ICCPR
Article 30.1 Everyone shall have the right to association....The freedom of public associations['] activities shall be guaranteed.	*Article 11.1* Everyone has the right to freedom of peaceful assembly and to freedom of association with others.	*Article 22.1* Everyone shall have the right to freedom of association with others.

Freedom of Association Limitations Clauses

Russian Constitution	ECHR	ICCPR
Article 55.3 Human and civil rights and liberties may be restricted by the federal law only to the extent required for the protection of the fundamentals of the constitutional system, morality, health, rights and lawful interests of other persons, for ensuring the defense of the country and the security of the state.	*Article 11.2* No restrictions shall be placed on the exercise of these rights other than such as are prescribed by law and are necessary in a democratic society in the interests of national security or public safety, for the prevention of disorder or crime, for the protection of health or morals or for the protection of the rights and freedoms of others.	*Article 22.2* No restrictions may be placed on the exercise of this right other than those which are prescribed by law and which are necessary in a democratic society in the interests of national security or public safety, public order, the protection of public health or morals or the protection of the rights and freedoms of others.

the right of people to meet together, the 1997 Law would seem not to conflict with this modest standard.

However, to the extent that freedom of association implies more than the right to associate informally, the 1997 Law encounters difficulties. The European Court has, for example, identified a cognizable right of a minority whose freedom of association had been restricted by a majority of trade union members.

> [P]luralism, tolerance and broadmindedness are hallmarks of a "democratic society." Although individual interests must on occasion be subordinated to those of a group, democracy does not simply mean that the views of a majority must always prevail: a balance must be achieved which ensures the fair and proper treatment of minorities and avoids any abuse of a dominant position.[69]

---

[69] *Young, James and Webster v. United Kingdom*, 44 Eur. Ct. H.R. (Ser. A), 21 (1981).

Majorities *qua* majorities must act within the limits imposed by the European Convention.

A significant issue related to freedom of association that has not been considered fully by international tribunals is the extent to which associations may have an inherent right to obtain juridical (or legal) personality. The texts of the Russian Constitution, the ECHR, and the ICCPR do not, in and of themselves, speak directly to the question of whether freedom of association necessarily implies the right of associations to obtain juridical personality. The ability to obtain juridical personality is certainly important for any association that seeks, in the name of the association rather than in the names of its individual members, to buy or rent real property, to contract for goods and services, or to obtain tax-exempt status. For religious associations that wish to own or rent churches, cathedrals, mosques, buildings, or temples, the right to obtain juridical personality may be essential for effectively carrying out their mission. Professor Manfred Nowak has opined that the ICCPR implicitly guarantees the right of associations to obtain juridical personality. He asserts that "[b]ecause groups of persons usually seek to pursue their longer-term interests in a legally recognized form (usually as juridical persons), States Parties [to the ICCPR] are also under a *positive duty* to provide the legal framework for founding juridical persons."[70]

To the extent that the Russian Constitution, international law, or other municipal laws of the Russian Federation are construed to create a right for associations to obtain legal personality, the 1997 Law violates that right.[71] Unlike the 1990 Law, which permitted all religious associations to obtain juridical personality, the 1997 Law permits only privileged religious organizations to obtain this status.[72] Although it arguably is essential that religious entities be permitted to obtain juridical personality in order to take advantage of other rights guaranteed them under human rights law, it is not evident that such a right heretofore has been recognized.

---

[70] Nowak, *CCPR Commentary*, 387.

[71] The Russian Civil Code also suggests that associations may have the right to form and become juridical persons. "Legal persons which are non-commercial organizations may be created in the form of consumer cooperatives, societal or religious organizations (or associations)." Grazhdanskii Kodeks RF, art. 50.3. Also, like the Constitution, the Civil Code has supremacy over other statutes, including those that are later enacted: "Norms of civil law contained in other statutes *must conform to the present Code.*" Ibid., art. 3.2 (emphasis added).

In Russia, the rules governing juridical persons are set forth in the Civil Code of the Russian Federation. Ibid., arts. 48-65. The Civil Code contemplates that there shall be a Law on the Registration of Juridical Persons. See ibid., art. 51.1. See also the 1990 Law on Law on Public [Social] Associations—which apparently excludes religious organizations from its scope. For discussion of this issue, see F. J. M. Feldbrugge, *Russian Law: The End of the Soviet System and the Role of Law* (Dordrecht, 1993), 307-8.

[72] 1997 Law, arts. 8.1, 7.1.

THE INFRINGEMENTS OF THE 1997 LAW
ON PROTECTED RIGHTS ARE NOT JUSTIFIABLE

The first phase in the analysis of a possible violation of a human rights convention focuses on the question whether there has been an infringement of a protected right, such as the right of equality or one of the substantive rights of freedom of religion, expression, or association. Once it is shown that there has been an actual interference with a substantive right of freedom of religion, expression, or association, the analysis shifts to the question whether such interference is justifiable under the "limitations clauses" of the respective human rights conventions.[73] Although phrased somewhat differently, the limitations clauses provide similar grounds on which governments may legitimately restrict the exercise of rights. In general, governments are permitted to restrict the exercise of rights if such restrictions are necessary to promote public health and safety, or to protect the security of the state.

The most authoritative international analysis of limitations clauses is found in the jurisprudence of the European Court. The European Court employs a three-part analysis to determine whether a government's infringement of the freedoms of religion, expression, and association is permissible under its limitations clause. First, the Court determines whether the activity is "prescribed by law." Second, the Court determines whether the government had a "legitimate aim" in restricting the activity. Third, the Court decides whether the restriction is of a type that is "necessary in a democratic society."[74] The European Court has generally been deferential to the justifications advanced by member states with regard to the first two parts of the analysis. It is only with regard to the third part—the question whether the limitation is "necessary in a democratic society"—that the European Court has exercised its "supervisory

---

[73] The permissible limitations are enumerated in the second clauses of Articles 9, 10, and 11 of the ECHR and the second clauses of Articles 18, 19, and 22 of the ICCPR. The limitations clause for the Russian Constitution is Article 55.3. The language of the limitations clauses of the ECHR and the ICCPR varies somewhat with respect to the different rights at issue.

[74] See, e.g., *Manoussakis*, slip op. 15-20 (finding a violation of art. 9); *Kokkinakis*, 17 (finding violation of art. 9); *Vogt*, 23-30 (finding violation of art. 10); *Open Door and Dublin Well Woman v. Ireland*, 246 Eur. Ct. H.R. (Ser. A), 27-32 (1992) (finding violation of art. 11); *Vogt*, 31 (finding violation of art. 11).

Article 55.3 of the Russian Constitution does not employ the first two of these three terms. With respect to the third term, the Constitution provides that legitimate restrictions on the exercise of protected rights are permissible "only to the extent required for the protection of" certain specified interests. Konst. RF, art. 55.3 (1993). Although the ICCPR requires that restrictions on the freedom of association be "necessary in a democratic society," the restrictions on religion and expression may be imposed only to the extent that they are "necessary" to protect public order, morals, or other identified grounds.

jurisdiction" over member states in a meaningful way.[75] The three parts of the Court's analysis are considered below. Although there is no limitations clause per se for the equality guarantees of the ECHR, the European Court has developed similar guidelines for evaluating the legitimacy of infringements of Article 14 of the European Convention.[76] Because the equality analysis is quite similar, the analysis below focuses exclusively on the limitations clauses of the substantive rights.

"PRESCRIBED BY LAW"

Before a government may lawfully impose a limitation on the freedoms of religion, expression, or association under the ECHR, it must be able to show that such a limitation is "prescribed by law."[77] The European Court has interpreted this peculiar phraseology to mean that the law has been made accessible to the public (usually by publication in an official gazette), and that the application of the law to the case at hand was foreseeable.[78] The author is aware of only one case in which the European Court has struck down any law based upon the "prescribed by law element," and no case that related specifically to Articles 9, 10, or 11.[79] Unless the 1997 Law is actually applied in some way that is now unforeseeable, the European Court would likely find that it passes muster under this first inquiry.

"LEGITIMATE AIM"

The language of the ECHR does not explicitly require governments to have a "legitimate aim" for their laws, regulations, and actions that infringe upon the

---

[75] *Vogt*, 26.

[76] See, e.g., *Darby v. Sweden*, 187 Eur. Ct. H.R. (Ser. A), 12 (1990); *Karlheinz Schmidt v. Germany*, 291 Eur. Ct. H.R. (Ser. A), 33 (1994); *Stjerna v. Finland*, 299 Eur. Ct. H.R. (Ser. A), 63 (1994); *Hoffmann*, 59; *Observer and Guardian v. United Kingdom*, 216 Eur. Ct. H.R. (Ser. A.), 35; *Sunday Times v. United Kingdom* (No. 2), 217 Eur. Ct. H.R. (Ser. A), 32 (1991); *Fredin v. Sweden*, 192 Eur. Ct. H.R. (Ser. A), 19 (1991).

[77] See ECHR, arts. 9.2, 10.2, 11.2.

[78] *Müller and Others v. Switzerland*, 133 Eur. Ct. H.R. (Ser. A), 20 (1988).

[79] There has been one recent religion case where the Court hinted that it might have been prepared to rule against a law on the basis of the "prescribed by law" element, but it withheld judgment because the law was faulted on other grounds. *Manoussakis*, slip op. 15-16. In *Herczegfalvy v. Austria*, 244 Eur. Ct. H.R. (Ser. A), 27-28 (1992), the government failed to satisfy the "prescribed by law" inquiry on the grounds of a lack of foreseeability. In an Article 9 case, the European Commission found that the government failed to satisfy the "prescribed by law" element, although the European Court effectively reversed the Commission's decision. See *Kalaç v. Turkey*, Eur. Ct. H.R. (Ser. A), No. 61/1996/680/870, slip op. 9-10 (July 1, 1997).

exercise of the rights of religion, expression, and association. Nevertheless, the European Court has held that such a requirement is implicit in the limitations clauses of the ECHR. The Court thus requires governments, whenever they take actions that infringe on human rights, to have done so in furtherance of one of the "legitimate aims" that are specified in the limitations clauses. The chart below identifies the "legitimate aims" that are included in the limitations clauses of the Constitution, the ECHR, and the ICCPR.

"Legitimate Aims" for Which Governments May Restrict Fundamental Rights

Russian Constitution	ECHR	ICCPR
Thought, Conscience, and Religion		
Protect the constitutional system	Public health, safety, order, or morality	Public health, safety, order, or morality
Public health and morality	Rights and freedoms of others	Rights and freedoms of others
Rights and interests of others		
Security and defense of the state		
Association		
Protect the constitutional system	National security	National security
Public health and morality	Public health, safety, or morality	Public health, safety, order, or morality
Rights and interests of others	Prevention of disorder or crime	Rights and freedoms of others
Security and defense of the state	Rights and freedoms of others	
Expression		
Protect the constitutional system	National security or territorial integrity	Rights and reputations of others
Public health and morality	Public health, safety, or morality	Protection of national security
Rights and interests of others	Prevention of disorder or crime	Public health, safety, or morality
Security and defense of the state	Reputation or rights of others	
	Confidential information	
	Authority and impartiality of the judiciary	

Although the European Court formally requires governments to have a "legitimate aim" whenever they take actions that infringe on guaranteed rights, the European Court nevertheless has been extremely deferential to member states. With respect to cases arising under Articles 9, 10, and 11 of the ECHR, this author is aware of no case in which the European Court found that a government's purported "legitimate aim" failed to find sufficient support in the limitations clauses. The Court in the *Manoussakis* Case came closest to challenging a governmental action based upon the possible absence of a legitimate aim, but the Court failed to do so, finding that there was a sufficient justification for maintaining public order.[80] Under the "legitimate aim" component, the European Court has thus far required only that governments be able to articulate a possible legitimate basis for an action that infringes on the enumerated rights. The Court has not inquired into whether governments' stated "aims" were merely pretextual or, indeed, whether they were even plausible. Although the European Court has not yet used the "legitimate aim" requirement to subject any legislation to meaningful scrutiny, such a requirement nevertheless ought to be taken seriously.

The "legitimate aims" that are identified in the limitations clauses are quite vague and, depending on how they are interpreted, could be used to justify even the most repressive governmental actions. For example, a permanent twenty-four-hour curfew might be justified as promoting "order." A ban on all public meetings might be justified as a means of promoting "public health" by reducing the spread of communicable diseases. A state might impose strict dress standards as a means of promoting morality. To the extent that the "legitimate aim" requirement of the limitations clause is taken seriously, however, it is appropriate to consider whether the 1997 Law was motivated by legitimate aims. Unfortunately, most of the official negotiations and discussions of the proposals preceding the adoption of the 1997 Law took place behind closed doors and in secret. The 1997 Law was, however, promoted principally by a coalition of supporters of the Russian Orthodox Church, as well as by Russian nationalists, and current and former communists.[81]

As early as 1993, the Russian Orthodox Church began actively to promote legislation designed to curtail the religious activities of "new" religions and missionaries. These efforts led to the passage of restrictive legislation by the Duma in 1993, although such measures ultimately were vetoed by President Yeltsin.[82] The Russian Orthodox Church was sharply critical of his veto and

---

[80] *Manoussakis*, slip op. 16.

[81] "Russian Orthodox Church Welcomes Passage of Law," *RFE/RL Newsline* 1 (Sept. 22, 1997): No. 122, available at <www.rferl.org/newsline/1997/09/220997.html>.

[82] For discussions of the 1993 bills, see Harold J. Berman, "Religious Human Rights in Russia at a Time of Tumultuous Transition: A Historical Theory," in Johan D. van der Vyver and John Witte Jr., eds., *Religious Human Rights in Global Perspective: Legal Perspectives* (The Hague, 1996), 297-99. See also W. Cole Durham et al., "The Future of Religious Liberty in Russia: Report of the De Burght Conference

vowed to press on in its efforts. In December 1996, the Duma sent a message to President Yeltsin informing him that it believed that new religious cults were interfering with the health of Russians.[83] By the late spring of 1997, the Duma passed a new piece of legislation on religious associations, but it too was vetoed by President Yeltsin.[84] In his veto message, Yeltsin identified dozens of provisions of the bill that ran afoul of the Russian Constitution and international human rights conventions.[85] After a series of largely secret negotiations during the summer and early fall of 1997, Yeltsin and the Duma drafted "compromise" legislation that, for all practical purposes, tracked closely the bill he had vetoed only two months earlier. The new bill failed to address the many provisions that had only recently been criticized by President Yeltsin as being unconstitutional and in violation of international human rights norms.

There appear to have been two intertwined rationales that prompted enactment of the 1997 Law. First, the traditional churches in Russia witnessed what they perceived to be an onslaught of foreign missionaries who arrived with, relatively speaking, significant financial resources and abilities to promote their missionary and proselytizing activities. Second, it was perceived that some of the new religious groups were cults that, like Aum Shinrikyo in Japan, were capable of murder, mass suicide, and brainwashing. These two rationales were blended in pronouncements like that of the Council of Bishops of the Russian Orthodox Church. The Council stated:

> We express our concern in connection with the continuing proselytising activity of protestant false missionaries in Russia and other countries of the CIS. . . . The council is deeply concerned by the growth of organised pseudo-Christian and pseudo-religious sects, of neo-pagan communities, occultists and devil worshipers. . . . The council is extremely troubled by the anti-Orthodox campaign which is being waged by the followers of these pseudo-religious organisations and their protectors. . . . [T]he leaders of these totalitarian sects are in fact depriving their followers of these rights [of freedom of conscience] and reacting aggressively to any criticism of their activity. Those who attempt to oppose them are subjected to cruel persecution by the sect leaders and their highly-placed protec-

on Pending Russian Legislation Restricting Religious Liberty," *Emory International Law Review* 8 (1994): 1.

[83] "Russia: Duma Appeal on Dangerous Religious Sects," *Moscow Rossiyskaya Gazeta* (Dec. 28, 1996): 4, translated in *FBIS Daily Report* (March 14, 1997).

[84] In the interim, the U.S. Senate passed a resolution threatening to cut off $200 million in aid to Russia if the bill were enacted into law. It was the opinion of many that this threat by the U.S. Congress was counterproductive and made some of the participants more intransigent. See, e.g., Georgiy Bovt, "Only Established Faiths Being Allowed into Temple. President Has Outflanked Everybody in Order to Satisfy Majority," *Moscow Segodnya* (Sept. 27, 1997): 3.

[85] "Russia: Yeltsin Details Objections to Religion Law," *Moscow Rossiyskiye Vesti* (July 25, 1997): 2, translated in *FBIS Daily Report* (July 28, 1997).

tors, including intimidation, psychological pressure, the gathering of incriminating information, slander and repeated searches of their property.[86]

Patriarch Aleksii strongly urged new legislation. He praised the new law because it would remove "destructive totalitarian sects" and would "streamline the activities of foreign sects and quasi-missionaries."[87] He asserted that "Russian law should recognize 'our own traditions and history' . . . and that proselytizing should be banned because it attempts to 'entice people who profess the religion of their ancestors into a different faith.'"[88] Aleksii characterized the new legislation as accomplishing nothing more than protecting the human rights of Russians:

> In seeking to limit this incursion of missionary activity we are often accused of violating the right to freedom of conscience and the restriction of individual rights. But freedom does not mean general license. . . . [T]he aggressive imposition by foreign missionaries of views and principles which come from a religious and cultural environment which is strange to us, is in fact a violation of both religious and civil rights.[89]

If these words are to be taken seriously—and not merely as propaganda—they suggest that the aim behind the 1997 Law was to protect Russian culture from well-financed and unprincipled religious missionaries who engage in deceptive practices to win souls. To the extent that a law were enacted to ameliorate such problems—psychological manipulation, harassment, and bribery—it might indeed have an "objective justification" and a "legitimate aim."

These purported rationales are, however, undercut by an examination of the 1997 Law itself. It contains no provisions addressing abusive proselytizing activities, religious kidnapping, murder, suicides, brainwashing, or "totalitarian practices." These ostensible reasons for enacting the law are not addressed anywhere in the legislation. The 1997 Law does not even refer to these practices; rather, it restricts the activities of all religious groups that have not been active in Russia during the past fifteen years. The rationales offered in support of the 1997 Law appear to be pretexts to discriminate against all religious activities that, in the eyes of the government, appear to be new to the Russian soil.

---

[86] Article no. 33 of the Resolution: "On the Specific Issues of the Internal and External Activity of the Church, Adopted by the Council of Bishops of the Russian Orthodox Church," *Pravoslavnaya Moskva* 7/103 (March 1997): 11.

[87] "Russian Orthodox Church Welcomes Passage of Law."

[88] "Patriarch against 'North American Norms,'" *RFE/RL Newsline* 1 (Aug. 28, 1997): No. 105, available at <www.rferl.org/newsline/1997/08/280897.html>.

[89] Report of Patriarch Aleksii II to the Bishop's Council in Moscow, "Interconfessional and Inter-faith Relations. Participation in the Activity of International Christian Organizations," *Pravoslavnaya Moskva* 7/103 (March 1997): 4.

The government's reason for enacting the 1997 Law was not to provide a regulatory scheme for registering religious associations—that had already been accomplished by the 1990 Law. The true purpose of the 1997 Law was to undercut the status of preexisting religious associations, to undercut missionary activities, to restrict dissemination of information about religion, and to buttress the activities of the Russian Orthodox Church (and other "traditional" churches of Russia). To the extent that the "legitimate aim" component of the limitations clause test is taken seriously, the 1997 Law fails to promote a legitimate aim.

THE "NECESSARY" (OR "PROPORTIONATE") COMPONENT

The ECHR, the ICCPR, and the Russian Constitution provide that governmental restrictions on the exercise of rights may be imposed only when certain specified conditions are met. The freedom of religion, expression, and association provisions of the ECHR, as well as the freedom of association guarantee of the ICCPR, permit restrictions only when they are *"necessary in a democratic society"* to further one of the "legitimate aims" identified above.[90] With respect to the ICCPR's guarantees of freedoms of religion and expression, the limitations clauses permit restrictions that are "necessary" to further legitimate aims without imposing any requirement related to democratic societies.[91] Similarly, the Russian Constitution, albeit in somewhat different terms, permits restrictions on the exercise of rights "only to the extent required for the protection" of the specified interests.[92] By using the terms "only to the extent required" and "necessary," the Constitution and the international conventions prevent the Russian Federation from enacting laws that unnecessarily restrict protected freedoms—regardless of the purpose or benefits of the laws.

The principal public justification for the 1997 Law, given by its supporters, was to restrict the activities of "destructive" and "totalitarian" sects. Thus, to the extent that the 1997 Law had a legitimate purpose, it would presumably have been to restrain unscrupulous groups from employing techniques such as bribery and psychological manipulation to gain converts. Additionally, it might have had the legitimate aim of ensuring that religious groups would be responsible and comply with established criminal and civil law.

Even if we assume that the government had a legitimate purpose in restricting the activities of "destructive" cults, it is nevertheless clear that the 1997 Law indiscriminately penalizes all new religious groups—regardless of whether they proselytize, practice brainwashing, or simply wish to correspond with fellow communicants who live abroad. If the justification of the law is that it

---

[90] ECHR, arts. 9.2, 10.2, 11.2; ICCPR, art. 22(2) (emphasis added).

[91] In other words, the restrictions on religion and expression in the ICCPR need not be of a type that "democratic societies" impose, though the restrictions nevertheless must be necessary for the furtherance of the legitimate aims.

[92] Konst. RF, art. 55.3.

will restrict the activities of "destructive" and "totalitarian sects," then the law should be narrowly tailored to apply to *totalitarian* sects, not to *new* sects or to *foreign* sects. The 1997 Law contains no provisions whatsoever that establish criteria for identifying religions that are harmful to health, welfare, or morals—unless one assumes that the new and the foreign are, by definition, "harmful." The 1997 Law, in fact, appears to be motivated by the fear of the new and the different, motivations that are not cognizable under international human rights law. Thus, even to the extent that some new religions are indeed engaging in dangerous and immoral practices, the remedies of the 1997 Law are not proportional to the perceived harms.

CONCLUSION

Human rights law presupposes that governments—whether democracies or dictatorships—should not employ political power to infringe on universally recognized rights. It also recognizes that political majorities will attempt to seize the instrumentalities of power to further their interests at the expense of minorities. Under Communism, the Soviet State used its political powers to oppress religious believers. The 1990 Law provided a welcome and dramatic change of direction from state control over religious life. With the enactment of the 1997 Law, however, Russia has taken a significant step backward to the era when the state interfered with the ability of both citizens and non-citizens to practice the religion of their choice.

14.

FREEDOM OF RELIGION IN RUSSIA

An Amicus Brief for the Defendant

———————◆———————

Harold J. Berman

I would like to offer a defense of the Patriarchate's support of substantial privileges for itself and other so-called traditional religious denominations that lived under Soviet repression and its support of restrictions upon proselytism by religious associations from outside of Russia. In presenting what may be called an amicus brief for the defendant, however, I do not want to be understood as resting its case primarily on law. The essence of its position is founded on what is called in the Gospel of St. John grace and truth, the grace and truth that was given by Jesus Christ. The Moscow Patriarchate respects the rights of others, including their legal rights, but it subordinates them to divine duties, and especially now to the duty to help to restore the spiritual identity of the Russian people at this time of crisis when the very soul of the Russian people is in danger of being lost. In the words of a representative of the Patriarchate, "Of course we do not want to violate international law or our own Constitution or principles of human rights. But we hope that those legal and moral norms can be adapted to meet the acute spiritual crisis that now confronts the Russian Church."[1]

Reference may also be made in this context to the statement of the Russian Orthodox theologian Sergei Bulgakov: "Russian society," Bulgakov wrote in 1909, "exhausted by previous exertion and failures, finds itself in [a] state [of] spiritual stupor, despondency."[2] This was said four years after the 1905 Revolution and eight years before the Bolshevik Revolution, and if Bulgakov's words

---

An earlier version of this chapter first appeared in *Emory International Law Review* 12 (1998): 313-40.

[1] Interview with Archimandrite Joseph Poustoooutoff, Moscow (1994).

[2] Quoted in Mark Elliott and Anita Deyneka, chap. 11 herein.

ring as true today as when they were uttered, as Elliott and Deyneka contend, then we must beware that another upheaval does not overtake the Russian people during the coming years.

The Moscow Patriarchate believes, and a great many—perhaps most—Russians also believe, that the cure for Russia's spiritual crisis does not lie in the conversion of Russians to foreign religious faiths, whether Protestant or Catholic, but in the strengthening of the Russian Orthodox faith, which is the principal traditional faith of the Russian people.

The close connection between the Russian people, the *narod*, the nation, on the one hand, and Russian Orthodox Christianity, on the other, withstood for seventy years the massive attack by the Soviet regime upon all forms of religious belief. The story of that connection is embodied in Russian literature and art and, despite all counter-pressures, has been retold to successive generations of Soviet children by their grandmothers. Major events of that story include the conversion to Christianity in 988 of Prince Vladimir and the people of Kievan Rus, the role of great saints such as Alexander Nevsky and Sergius of Radonezh in the forging of the Russian character and in the resistance to invasions of Roman Catholic Crusaders from the West and Mongols from the East, the martyrdom of Metropolitan Benjamin for standing up against Ivan the Terrible, and the great novels of Christian writers like Dostoyevsky and Tolstoy. "Do not forget that the true Russia," a Soviet admiral whose vessel was in British waters in World War II said privately to an English interpreter of Russian extraction, "is the Russia of St. Sergius and Dostoyevsky." Thus, the spiritual argument is linked with a historical argument: the spiritual identity of Russia is founded on the historical role of the Russian Church in forging the Russian character and giving the nation its sense of community and common purpose.

Specifically, then, the issue addressed here is whether the establishment of a privileged position for the Russian Orthodox Church and the imposition of substantial restrictions on activities of foreign missionaries, as provided in the law enacted by the Russian Parliament in 1997 and signed by President Yeltsin, is a violation of the internationally accepted human right of religious freedom, or whether, on the contrary, the internationally accepted right of religious freedom, as applied to Russia, must be qualified to take account of Russia's present spiritual crisis viewed in the light of Russia's historical experience.

To resolve this issue it is necessary to consider, in the first instance, the history of Church-State relations in Russia in the pre-Soviet and Soviet periods as well as in the present post-Soviet period.

THE PRE-SOVIET PERIOD

Prior to the Bolshevik Revolution of November 1917, the Russian Orthodox Church was the established church of the Russian Empire, and the Tsar was its head. The Empire itself, however, embraced many different ethnic and religious cultures, each of which was allowed to have a degree of autonomy. Finland, ceded by Sweden in the early eighteenth century, was largely Protestant, as were the Baltic provinces of Latvia and Estonia. Poland, ceded by the Congress of Vienna in the early nineteenth century, was largely Roman Catholic, as was the Baltic province of Lithuania. The Central Asian regions, originally inherited from the Mongols, were largely Muslim. A large number of ethnic Germans, originally invited by Catherine the Great to settle in the Volga region of Russia on condition that they not intermarry with Russians, remained Lutheran. The vast majority of the five-and-a-half million Russian Jews were required to live in the Pale of Settlement stretching from Riga to Odessa and from Polish Silesia to Kiev. Ethnic Russians, who constituted most of the Empire's population, and who governed all its territories, were largely Russian Orthodox, but a substantial minority adhered to the schismatic Church of the Old Believers, and a smaller number adhered to sectarian churches (Dukhobors, Molokane, and Stundists). Other ethnic-territorial Orthodox churches within the Empire included the autocephalous Georgian Orthodox Church and the Armenian Orthodox Church. Although in the early twentieth century some ethnic Russians became converts to Roman Catholicism and to foreign Protestant sects (such as the Baptists), and although there were some converts to Russian Orthodoxy among Jews and other ethnic minorities, the religious map of the Empire coincided to a considerable extent with the ethnic map. It is, indeed, a tenet of traditional Russian Orthodox theology, and of Eastern Orthodox Christianity generally, that religious affiliation is closely connected with ethnicity and, to a lesser extent, with territory—with blood and with soil.

Only in the early twentieth century, and especially after the 1905 Revolution, both the supremacy of Russian Orthodoxy and the subordination of the Russian Orthodox Church to the Tsar slowly began to be challenged. In 1905 a Law on Tolerance, issued by the Tsar, granted Russians the right to depart from Orthodoxy, the right of parents who departed from Orthodoxy to raise their children in a new religion, the right of persons previously considered Orthodox against their will not to be so classified, and the right of people raising abandoned children to baptize them according to their own faith. The law also gave new rights to Old Believers and Christian sectarians, including the right to have houses of worship, the right to own property, and the right to organize their own elementary schools that would provide religious instruction. Also important in the 1905 Law on Toleration were provisions extending to adherents of foreign Christian denominations the right to build churches and prayer houses and to provide religious education for children.[3] These pro-

---

[3] Ob ukreplenii nachal' veroterpimosti (On the Strengthening of Principles of Religious Tolerance), *Polnoe Sobranie Zakonov Rossiiskoi Imperii*, 3d series, v. 25, no. 26126 (1905), arts. I (4), II, IX.

visions reduced substantially the effect of earlier prohibitions against missionary activity by foreigners.[4]

Developments after 1905 also led to slightly greater freedom of the Russian
Orthodox Church from control by the Tsar and by the Holy Synod, a lay body
created in 1721 by Peter the Great to govern the Church. In the first two
decades of the twentieth century there was a movement within the Church to
restore the Moscow Patriarchate, which Peter had abolished in 1700. After
the abdication of the Tsar in February 1917 and the establishment of the Pro-
visional Government, the first All-Russian Church Council was called. It was
convened in August 1917 and on November 5 it elected a Patriarch.[5] Two
days later Lenin and his Bolshevik Party seized power and, in effect, proclaimed
the establishment of an atheist state.

THE SOVIET PERIOD, 1917-1987

Soviet atheism was derived in part from Marxist theory, but for Marx atheism
was primarily a philosophical tenet, an inference drawn from his theory of
historical materialism, whereas for Lenin and his Russian followers atheism
was a militant faith, a revolt against God, with deep roots in Russian anar-
chism. Lenin could have repeated what the nineteenth-century Russian revolutionary Bakunin had said: "If God really existed, he would have to be destroyed." Leninist atheism was not only something to be believed but also
something to be believed *in*, something to be practiced in one's daily life. It
rested on the passionate conviction—of which Lenin, not Marx, was the great
apostle, and which was more Russian than Western—that humanity is master
of its own destiny and by its own power can construct a paradise on earth. For
the Russian Communist Party, which Lenin created, atheism represented man's
power to do by himself, by his own intellect and will, through collective action, what Russian Christianity had taught that only God can do, namely,
create a universal peace in human hearts.

For seventy years, from the Bolshevik Revolution to the closing years of the
Gorbachev regime, militant atheism was the official religion, one might say, of
the Soviet Union, and the Communist Party was, in effect, the established church.

---

[4] An 1896 law provided that "only the ruling Orthodox Church has the right to
persuade followers of other Christian confessions and other faiths to accept its teachings concerning faith." Persons of other Christian confessions and faiths were declared to be subject to criminal punishments if they "encroached upon the convictions of conscience of those not belonging to their religion." Svod uchrezhdenii i
ustavov upravleniia dukhovnykh del inostrannykh ispovedanii khristianskikh i
inovernekh (Collection of Institutions and Statutes of Administration of the Spiritual
Affairs of Foreign Confessions of Christians and Other Believers), *Svod Zakonov
Rossiiskoi Imperii*, v. XI, part 1 (1896), art. IV.

[5] See Timothy Ware, *The Orthodox Church* (Baltimore, 1964), 137-38.

It was an avowed task of the Soviet state, led by the Communist Party, to root out from the minds and hearts of the Soviet people all belief systems other than Marxism-Leninism. This was surely the most massive and the most powerful assault on traditional religious faith ever launched in the history of humankind.[6]

The policy of the Soviet government toward religion was laid down in the first law on the subject, in January 1918, called "On the Separation of the Church from the State and of the School from the Church." To American ears, the title sounds harmless enough, but when the Soviets said "separation" they really meant it! In principle, the state would not give the slightest support whatsoever to the Church, and the Church was forbidden to engage in activities which were within the sphere of responsibilities of the state. This had a special meaning in a socialist system of the Soviet type, in which State and Party swallowed up civil society. Churches, mosques, and synagogues were deprived of almost all activities except the conduct of worship services. Moreover, schools were not merely to avoid the teaching of religion; they were actively to promote the teaching of atheism.

These doctrines were spelled out in a 1929 law that remained the basic legislation on the subject until the Gorbachev reforms of the late 1980s. There was freedom of religious worship, but churches were forbidden to give any material aid to their members or charity of any kind, or to hold any special meetings for children, youth, or women, or general meetings for religious study, recreation, or any similar purpose; or to open libraries or to keep any books other than those necessary for the performance of worship services. The formula of the 1929 law was repeated in the 1936 Constitution and again in the 1977 Constitution: freedom of religious worship and freedom of atheist propaganda—meaning (1) no freedom of religious teaching outside of the worship service itself, plus (2) a vigorous campaign in the schools, in the press, and in special meetings organized by atheist agitators to convince people of the folly of religious beliefs. Moreover, since the Party was avowedly atheist, and Party membership was a prerequisite for most offices, open religious believers were generally deprived of any possibility of advancement in most secular professional careers.

The 1960 Criminal Code of the Russian Republic imposed a fine for violating laws of separation of the church from the state and of the school from the church, and, for repeated violations, deprivation of freedom up to three years.[7]

---

[6] For sources of data presented in the following paragraphs concerning Soviet restrictions of religious freedom, see generally Ware, *The Orthodox Church*; see also Paul Anderson, *People, Church, and State in Modern Russia* (London, 1944); Harold J. Berman, "Atheism and Christianity in Soviet Russia," in *Freedom and Faith: The Impact of Law on Religious Liberty*, ed. Lynn R. Buzzard (Westchester, Ill., 1982), 127-43, reprinted in Harold J. Berman, *Faith and Order: The Reconciliation of Law and Religion* (Atlanta, 1993), 355-65.

[7] Ugolovnyi Kodeks (Criminal Code), art. 142 (RSFSR), translated in Harold J. Berman and James W. Spindler, *Soviet Criminal Law and Procedure: The RSFSR Codes* (Cambridge, 1972).

Violations included organizing religious assemblies and processions, organizing religious instruction for minors, and preparing written materials calling for such activities. Other types of religious activities were subject to more severe sanctions: leaders and active participants in religious groups that caused damage to the health of citizens or violated personal rights, or that tried to persuade citizens not to participate in social activities or to perform duties of citizenship, or that drew minors into such groups, were punishable by deprivation of freedom up to five years.[8] This provision was directed primarily against Evangelical-Baptists, Jehovah's Witnesses, Pentecostals, and other sects.

These articles of the Criminal Code were enacted as part of the severe antireligious campaign launched under Khrushchev in the early 1960s, when an estimated fourteen thousand Russian Orthodox churches—two-thirds of the total number in the entire Soviet Union—were closed, together with five of the eight institutions for training priests, and the independence of the priesthood was curtailed both nationally and locally. Similar attacks were made against other religious communities. The antireligious campaign ended with Brezhnev's accession to power in 1964. Nevertheless, the rights of believers that were taken away in the Khrushchev period were not restored. The closed churches, monasteries, and seminaries remained closed. Parents who baptized their children had to register, and could then be subjected to harassment. Practical impediments were placed in the way of church weddings. Sermons were strictly controlled.

Notwithstanding this massive effort to suppress traditional religious belief, or perhaps partly because of it, there was, in fact, a strengthening of Christian faith. Christianity not only survived the assault upon it but was purged and purified by it. Despite Soviet official claims to the contrary, and the superficial impressions of Western tourists, religion did not die out in Soviet Russia. And it was not only the aged who clung to religious faith. It is possible, and even likely, that among the Russian half of the Soviet population a majority of the adults were Christian. Indeed, in the 1970s and 1980s there was a substantial turn to Christianity among students and other young people. In the 1970s Soviet writers themselves estimated the number of believers at 20 percent of the total Soviet population—about fifty million. Competent non-Soviet observers said 40 percent or more.

What has been described thus far is the elemental confrontation of two fundamental faiths, Christianity and atheism, a confrontation that existed in the Soviet Union for seventy years. One was a faith in man's power to raise himself, by his own collective reason and will, to a political order of power and wealth, and ultimately to a utopian social order of universal peace and brotherhood. The other was a faith in God's merciful forgiveness of human weakness and selfishness and in God's offer of redemption from suffering and death to all who follow the example of Jesus Christ. Both these faiths showed an extraordinary capacity to survive in the Soviet Union, despite frequent betrayal by their adherents.

---

[8] Ibid., art. 227.

In 1990 Aleksii II, Patriarch of Moscow and Russia, defended the hierarchs of the Russian Orthodox Church against the charge of subservience to Communism in the past, saying that the only alternative would have been to expose their flock to the danger of destruction. "The Church," he said, "with its many millions of members, cannot descend into the catacombs in a totalitarian state. We sinned. But . . . [f]or the sake of the people, for the sake of preventing [many] millions of people from departing this life for good." In order to save those who have remained faithful, he said, "the hierarchs of the Church took a sin upon their souls, the sin of silence, the sin of nontruth. And we have always done penance before God for this."[9]

He then added something which is significant for an understanding of Russian Orthodox Christianity today. "Our refusal to take the Church down into the catacombs," he said, "bore an even more intense spiritual fruit. We members of the Russian Orthodox Church did not cultivate in ourselves hate and a thirst for revenge. I fear that a catacombs psychology would have driven us precisely to this."[10]

It should be noted that although the Russian Orthodox Church—and other religious bodies in Russia—sinned, perhaps *had* to sin, in their submission to the Soviet State and Communist Party, nevertheless in proclaiming the existence of God in their worship services, they, with the other registered churches, constituted for seventy years the one and only voice of public dissent from a fundamental tenet of Marxist-Leninist doctrine.

Moreover, under Communism the Russian Orthodox Church preserved for the future the heritage of the Russian past. The liturgy, with its Church Slavonic prayers and chants, its icons and candles, its Tschaikovsky masses, and, above all, its invocation of a higher world of angels and saints, represented a Russian vision which transcended the secular utopia of Communism. I recall hearing a sermon in Leningrad, at the height of the Khrushchev antireligious campaign, in which the priest read from the Bible the story of Joseph's interpretation of Pharaoh's dream of the seven sleek and fat cows eaten up by the seven lean and ugly cows, and the seven full and ripe ears of corn swallowed up by the seven meager and scorched ears. The priest told the congregation—two thousand devout parishioners at a weekly Wednesday evening service: "The Russian Church is now living through the seven lean years, but we have all the riches of the past to sustain us."

THE GORBACHEV REFORMS

The Gorbachev political reforms of the late 1980s, including the introduction of freedom of speech and the end of the one-party system, were accompanied by a movement to restore freedom of religion. In 1988, the Soviet state itself

---

[9] See Berman, *Faith and Order*, 397.
[10] Ibid.

celebrated the 1000th anniversary of the introduction of Christianity into Russia. In December 1988, President Gorbachev, in an important speech to the General Assembly of the United Nations, promised that new Soviet legislation on freedom of conscience would meet "the highest [international legal] standards."[11] In 1989, the new popularly elected USSR Congress of People's Deputies included clergy among its members as well as lay persons previously persecuted for religious activities. After widespread discussion, new laws on freedom of religion and the rights of religious organizations were enacted in 1990 both in the USSR and in the Russian Soviet Federated Socialist Republic (RSFSR).

The USSR law of October 1, 1990, entitled "On Freedom of Conscience and [on] Religious Organizations,"[12] declared in Section I ("General Provisions") that "every citizen . . . shall have the right, individually or in conjunction with others, to profess any religion or not to profess any, and to express and disseminate convictions associated with his relationship to religion"[13]; that the exercise of such freedom shall be subject only to restrictions that are "compatible with the international commitments of the USSR"[14]; that "all religions and denominations are equal under the law"[15]; that there shall be "separation of church (religious organizations) from the state" but that "clergy of religious organizations shall have the right to participate in political life on an equal footing with all citizens" and "the state shall facilitate the establishment of relations of mutual toleration and respect between citizens who profess a religion and those who do not profess one"[16]; and that "religious organizations whose charters (or statutes) are registered in accordance with established procedure shall have the right . . . to create educational institutions and groups for the religious education of children and adults."[17]

These provisions constituted a complete repudiation of fundamental tenets of Leninist theory and a complete reversal of more than seventy years of Soviet policy. In Chapter II of the law, however, entitled "Religious Organizations,"

---

[11] "The Gorbachev Visit; Excerpts From Speech to U.N. on Major Soviet Military Cuts," *New York Times* (December 8, 1988): A16.

[12] O svobode sovesti i religioznykh organizatsiiakh (On Freedom of Conscience and [on] Religious Organizations), *Vedomosti SSSR*, Issue No. 41, Item No. 813 (1990) [hereafter "1990 USSR Law"]. In the Russian text, the first word of the law, "O" (meaning "on" or "concerning"), only appears once, but because "Religious Organizations" in Russian appears in the prepositional case an additional "on" should be included in the English translation to avoid the erroneous implication that the law concerns freedom, as contrasted with regulation, of religious organizations. English translations of the law that differ slightly from the one offered above appear in Igor Troyanovsky, ed., *Religion in the Soviet Republics* (San Francisco, 1992), 23, and *Journal of Church and State* 33 (1991): 191-201.

[13] Ibid., art. 3.

[14] Ibid.

[15] Ibid., art. 5.

[16] Ibid.

[17] Ibid., art. 6.

some state controls were preserved. Although citizens were permitted freely, and without informing state agencies, to form "religious societies"—apparently meaning congregations—"for the joint profession of faith and the satisfaction of other religious needs," other types of religious organizations, including religious centers and administrations as well as monasteries, brotherhoods, missions, and educational institutions founded by such centers and administrations, were required to submit their charters for registration by the Soviet executive committee—in effect, the government—in the locality in which they were situated.[18] Such charters were to contain detailed information concerning the nature and structure of the religious organization, its property, its powers, special features of its activity, and related matters.[19] Registration gave the religious organization the character of a legal entity, with capacity to own property and to enter into contracts.[20] A decision by the Soviet executive committee to refuse to register the religious organization, or a failure to register it within one month, could be appealed to the courts.[21] Nothing was said in the 1990 USSR law, however, about the grounds on which the courts were to reverse such a decision.

State supervision was also to be exercised, under the 1990 USSR law, by a USSR state agency for religious affairs, to be formed by the USSR Council of Ministers. Similar agencies were to be formed in the various republics of the USSR. The USSR agency was to be "a center for information, consultation, and expert review," and its stated purposes were entirely benign; nevertheless, its powers were not defined, and its denomination as "USSR state agency for religious affairs"[22] was an ominous reminder of the former USSR Council for Religious Affairs, which for decades had enforced the harsh antireligious legislation of the pre-Gorbachev era.

The 1990 USSR law concluded with the provision that "[i]f an international treaty to which the USSR is a party establishes rules other than those contained in legislation on freedom of conscience and on religious organizations, the rules of the international treaty shall apply."[23] Since the USSR was a party to the International Covenant on Civil and Political Rights, this provision was an important step toward realization of the goal set by President Gorbachev in his 1988 speech to the United Nations. The 1990 USSR law did not go so far, however, as to provide for conformity with international agreements of the USSR that fell short of being treaties. Perhaps the most important such agreement was the so-called Concluding Document of the Vienna Follow-Up Meeting of the participants in the 1975 Helsinki Final Act.[24] That

---

[18] Ibid., art. 14.

[19] Ibid., art. 12.

[20] Ibid., art. 13.

[21] Ibid., art. 15.

[22] Ibid., art. 29.

[23] Ibid., art. 31.

[24] Concluding Document of the Vienna Follow-Up Meeting, reprinted by U.S. Commission on Security and Cooperation in Europe (January 1989).

document, signed in January 1989, represented a consensus of the signatories concerning the meaning of freedom of religion in international law.[25] It went far beyond preexisting international treaties in specifying religious rights. The head of the Soviet delegation to the Vienna Meeting later stated that "the Vienna agreements were not imposed on us from the outside; they were the goals that the USSR has itself set, they are what our society required."[26] It is possible that an oblique reference to the Vienna Concluding Document is made in the provision of Article 3 of the USSR law, which might be translated to provide that only such restrictions on freedom of conscience shall be permitted as are "compatible with the international *commitments* of the USSR."[27]

The RSFSR law enacted on October 25, 1990, which was repealed in 1997, repeated many of the provisions of the USSR law but went considerably farther in its protection of religious freedom. In contrast to the USSR law, it is entitled "On Freedom of Religion," a phrase that is broader than "freedom of conscience," implying freedom to give expression to one's religious beliefs through the activities of religious organizations.[28] This is borne out in Article 1 of the 1990 RSFSR law, which stated that the purpose of the law is to secure "observance . . . of the principles of freedom of conscience . . . as well as realization of the right of citizens to exercise that freedom." The 1990 RSFSR law also stated in the Preamble that freedom of religion is an "inalienable right of citizens of the RSFSR guaranteed by the Constitution of the RSFSR and by international obligations of the Russian Federation," and that "[t]he present law proceeds from principles contained in international agreements and conventions providing that freedom to have religious or atheist convictions and to engage in actions corresponding to such convictions is subject only to limitations established by law and necessary for the security of the rights and freedoms of other persons." The use of the word "agreements" instead of "treaties" was undoubtedly intended to include the Vienna Concluding Document, which stresses not only the right to hold religious convictions but also the right to engage in actions corresponding to such convictions.

The 1990 RSFSR law also went beyond the USSR law in providing explicitly that not only citizens but also foreigners and stateless persons "may exer-

---

[25] Ibid., ¶¶ 11, 16-17.

[26] Harold J. Berman, Erwin N. Griswold, and Frank C. Newman, "Draft USSR Law on Freedom of Conscience, with Commentary," *Harvard Human Rights Journal* 3 (1990): 137, 138 (article-by-article critique of the draft 1990 USSR Law). The critique was studied by Soviet specialists involved in the legislative process; it seems to have affected only slightly, if at all, the final version of the 1990 USSR Law, but some of its recommendations were included in the 1990 Law of the RSFSR on Freedom of Religion.

[27] 1990 USSR law (emphasis added).

[28] O svobode veroispovedanii (On Freedom of Religion), *Vedomosti RSFSR*, Issue No. 21, Item No. 267-1, at 240 (1990) [hereafter "RSFSR Law"]. The Russian word *veroispovedanie*, translated here as "religion," means literally "profession of faith," whereas the Russian word *sovest'*, meaning "conscience," refers to the inner belief rather than the outer profession of the belief.

cise the right to freedom of religion individually as well as jointly through creation of appropriate social associations."[29] Such associations, whether of citizens or of non-citizens, were only required to register their charters if they wished to have the rights of a legal person. Moreover, in contrast to the registration requirements of the USSR law, the charter was to be registered not by the local Soviet executive committee but by the Russian Ministry of Justice, which could refuse to register the charter "only if its contents contradict the requirements of the present Law and other legislative acts of the RSFSR."[30] As under the USSR law, the refusal to register the charter of a religious association could be appealed to a court; however, in contrast to the USSR law, the 1990 RSFSR law did not leave the decision to the discretion of the court but required the court to decide on the basis of "the present Law and other legislative acts of the RSFSR." It should be noted, however, that the Russian conception of "legislative acts" is a broad one, including regulations of administrative bodies, and only in recent years has such delegated legislative power begun to come under strict scrutiny to ensure that it is exercised in conformity with statutory law.

THE VETOED LAW OF 1993
AND THE ENACTED LAW OF 1997

The 1990 USSR Law on Freedom of Conscience and on Religious Organizations expired on December 8, 1991, with the expiration of the Soviet Union, leaving in force in Russia the 1990 RSFSR Law on Freedom of Religion. In July 1993, however, the Russian Parliament (still officially named Supreme

---

[29] Ibid., art. 4

[30] Ibid., art. 20. As of September 1, 1993 a total of 9,489 religious associations were registered under the RSFSR Law. Of that number, the following religious denominations were most numerous: Russian Orthodox Church (5,019), Muslim (2,639), Pentecostal (165), Christian Nondenominational associations (137), Seventh-day Adventist (130), Old Believers (121), Roman Catholic (90), Lutheran (86), Charismatic (73), Hare Krishna (68), Russian Orthodox Free Church (64), Buddhist (59), Evangelical Christian Baptist (49), Evangelical Christians (49), Jewish (48). In addition there were 21 Methodist associations, 41 Presbyterian, 47 Jehovah's Witnesses, 3 Mormon, and 1 Unification Church (Moon). The types of associations registered include religious centers, congregations, monasteries, convents, religious educational centers, nursing centers, and missions. A. I. Kudryavtsev and A. O. Protopopov, eds., *Zakonodatel'stvo Rossiiskoi Federatsii O Svobode Sovesti, Veroispovedaniia I Religioznykh Ob"edineniiakh* (Legislation of the Russian Federation on Freedom of Conscience, Religion, and (on) Religious Organizations) (1994), 100-103. However, the number of foreign religious organizations that registered was only a small percentage of the dozens of foreign religious organizations that carried out missions and the thousands of foreign missionaries that were active in Russia. See Pamela Meadows, "Missionaries to the Former Soviet Union and East Central Europe: The Twenty Largest Sending Agencies," *East-West Church and Ministry Report* 3 (1995): 10.

Soviet) passed a new comprehensive law entitled "On the Introduction of Changes and Additions to the RSFSR Law on Freedom of Religion."[31] That law was returned to the Chairman of the Supreme Soviet by President Yeltsin, unsigned.[32] It was reenacted by the Supreme Soviet, with minor changes, in August 1993, but again vetoed, in effect, since it was not signed by the president prior to his dissolution of the Parliament in September 1993.

Although the vetoed law of August 1993, like the July law, was called "A Law on Changes and Additions to the [1990] RSFSR Law on Freedom of Religion," and was often referred to in English and American publications as an "Amendment" to the 1990 law, it was, in fact, an entirely new version of that law, repeating many of its provisions but subtracting some and adding others.[33] The main additions were provisions granting special rights to "traditional confessions" and sharply restricting the rights of foreign religious associations.

Article 10 of the 1990 RSFSR law, which provided in the strongest terms for equal treatment of all religions and all religious associations, was removed from the August 1993 version, and a new paragraph was inserted in Article 8 requiring the state to "render support" to "the traditional confessions of the Russian Federation."[34] These were defined as "those religious organizations whose activity preserves and develops the historical traditions and customs, national-cultural originality, art, and other cultural heritage of the peoples of the Russian federation." Which denominations would constitute "traditional confessions" was not indicated.

Foreign missionary activity was expressly prohibited by Article 21 of the August 1993 version, and invitations to foreign citizens and stateless persons for "professional religious work" were subject to approval by state agencies only after strict scrutiny.[35] Moreover, foreign religious organizations whose charters were not registered before October 25, 1990 (the date of enactment of the 1990 law), were required to wait up to twelve months while their applications for such registration were being considered—during which time they could not function as legal entities.[36] This would have meant that many existing foreign reli-

---

[31] David Filipov and Pyotr Zhuravlyov, "Parliament Puts Limits on Foreign Churches," *Moscow Times* (July 15, 1993): 1.

[32] Yeltsin's letter to Ruslan Khasbulatov sharply criticized the law, emphasizing that it violated both the Russian Constitution and international treaties to which Russia adheres. The letter was especially critical of provisions that discriminated against nontraditional confessions. See W. Cole Durham et al., "The Future of Religious Liberty in Russia," *Emory International Law Review* 8 (1994): 1, 47-61.

[33] For a translation of the vetoed 1993 law, see *Emory International Law Review* 8 (1994): 47-61.

[34] Ibid., art. 8.

[35] "Professional religious work" is defined in Article 14 as "activity conducted specifically for the purpose of meeting religious needs of believers, which includes making contracts, holding a position in a religious organization and carrying out decision-making functions over believers." Ibid., art. 14.

[36] Ibid., art. 16.

gious organizations in Russia would have had to discontinue their property, contract, and other civil-law relationships and activities, at least temporarily.

Foreigners and stateless persons were still permitted, under the aborted 1993 law, to form religious groups and to conduct worship and other religious activities, but they were to inform in advance the agencies of internal affairs of the measures to be taken in these regards. It was further provided that "agencies of justice and of internal affairs shall have the right to demand from [the organizers of such groups] information concerning the particulars of their religious activity and to control their observance of legislation."[37]

In 1995, revisions of the law on religion again came under consideration in the lower house of the new Russian Parliament, now called the State Duma, which was elected in December 1993, at the same time as the adoption of the new Constitution of the renamed "Russian Federation," or "Russia"—without the "Soviet" and without the "Socialist." A proposed bill submitted in May 1995 by Deputy V. A. Lisichkin, a member of the ultranationalist party headed by Vladimir Zhirinovsky, did not survive the required review by the Committee for the Affairs of Social Associations and Religious Organizations. The proposed bill declared the Russian Orthodox Church to be "the church of the majority in the Russian Federation" and authorized the government to conclude "partnership agreements" with Russia's "traditional" religions, identified as Orthodoxy, Islam, Judaism, and Buddhism. It also placed substantial restrictions on the registration of foreign religious associations and on their missionary activities.[38]

Later in 1995 the government sponsored a bill which expressly reasserted the equality of all religious organizations and stated that "[t]he establishing of any privileges for one or more religious organizations shall be prohibited." The bill strongly reaffirmed the secular character of the Russian state, ensured the secular nature of education in state and municipal educational institutions, prohibited the performance of public religious rites or ceremonies in connection with the activity of state agencies, and forbade religious organizations from fulfilling the functions of state agencies or agencies of local self-government and from participating in the activities of political movements or parties or providing them with material or any other kind of assistance. It also recognized the right of registration of religious organizations whose higher-level agency or headquarters is situated outside the borders of the Russian Federation.

The government-sponsored bill was strongly opposed, and ultimately defeated, by supporters of the hierarchy of the Russian Orthodox Church, which is, indeed, the church of the great majority—70 percent, according to its own estimates—of the Russian people.

The 1997 Law on Freedom of Conscience and on Religious Organizations is basically the same as the vetoed 1993 law—in some respects even more

---

[37] Ibid.

[38] A copy of an English translation of the proposed bill ("draft law") of Academician Lisichkin is on file with the author.

restrictive with respect to foreign missionaries. The main difference is that, after some hesitation, President Yeltsin signed it. It is discussed at length by others and needs little further elaboration here.[39] It may be noted only that it does give a privileged position not only to Russian Orthodoxy but also to three other "traditional religions" that survived repression in the Soviet period: the previously registered "Christianity," Islam, and Judaism. Admittedly, however, the mutual toleration of certain faiths does not meet the goal of absolute religious freedom that is proclaimed in the international law of human rights. The position of the Moscow Patriarchate is that during the critical and even catastrophic transition that is now taking place in Russia[40]—from a one-party political system to a multi-party democracy, from a monolithic belief system to ideological pluralism, and from a system of planned economy to a market economy—the recognized international legal principle of cultural accommodation permits it to support legislation which gives the so-called traditional religions a preferred position and a right to special support by the state.

IN DEFENSE OF THE MOSCOW PATRIARCHATE

With respect to the severe restrictions upon proselytism by foreign churches, the Moscow Patriarchate starts not from a legal but from a religious position, namely, that proselytizing of Russian Christians by foreign Christians is itself anti-Christian. The Patriarch has quoted, in that connection, the Epistle of St. Paul to the Romans, in which the apostle said: "It is my ambition to bring the gospel to places where the very name of Christ has not been heard, for I do not want to build on another man's foundation" (Rom 15:20). St. Paul added that that is why he had not previously come to the Romans, but that he planned to visit them as he was traveling on his way to Spain. So the Moscow Patriarchate welcomes friendly visits by Christians of other denominations from other countries, but opposes their proselytism of Russian Christians.

---

[39] See W. Cole Durham Jr. and Lauren B. Homer, "Russia's 1997 Law on Freedom of Conscience and on Religious Associations: An Analytical Appraisal," *Emory International Law Review* 12 (1998): 101-246. See also chapters by Homer and Uzzell, Gunn, and Witte herein.

[40] The Russian Independent Institute for Social and Nationality-Related Problems polled 2,200 people aged 18 and over in a Russia-wide sociological survey in September 1997. The results showed Russians' views to be deeply pessimistic. Situations that were surveyed and the percentages of the Russian population that consider each situation as "critical or catastrophic" are as follows: industry, 92%; crime-fighting, 91.6%; Russian Army, 87.3%; agriculture, 87.2%; ecology, 84.2%; employment, 83.6%; spirituality and morals, 82%; health care, 81.6%; housing, 78.3%; power, 78.1%; culture and science, 77%; education, 76.2%; price formation, 75.7%; and relations between nationalities, 69.4%. See *Current Digest of the Post-Soviet Press* 49/41 (1997): 2.

A Theological Defense

It is sometimes said by foreign missionaries that it is not their purpose to convert Russian Christians to a different branch of the Christian Church but rather to convert Russian atheists to Christianity. To this, the Moscow Patriarchate makes two responses. First, it takes the position that the Russian Church is the church of all who were baptized in it, including those who are now not believers. Since even under Soviet atheist rule, most Russian infants were baptized in the Russian Orthodox Church—often brought to church for that purpose by their grandmothers—the foreign missionaries who would convert them to a non-Orthodox faith, and perhaps re-baptize them, are offending against a Russian Orthodox theological doctrine concerning the efficacy of the sacrament of baptism. "Their roots," it is said of all baptized Russians by Russian Orthodox Church leaders, "are Orthodox. It is our task to return them to Orthodoxy."[41]

A second response of the Patriarchate is that the foreign missionaries are engaging in unfair competition. They have a distinct advantage over the Russian Orthodox clergy, who have had virtually no experience in missionary activity, which was strictly prohibited under the Soviet regime: the Church could hold worship services for believers and perform sacraments but was prohibited from engaging in any other religious activities. Only now has the Russian Orthodox Church begun to train clergy to conduct missionary activities among nonbelievers. Moreover, foreign missionaries often exploit this advantage by giving material benefits to their congregations—food and clothing as well as bibles and other religious literature—which the Russian Church cannot afford to give. They also pour large sums of money into evangelization, paying for billboard advertisements and television programs featuring American preachers and hiring stadiums to spread their message—all of which, again, are beyond the means of the Russian Orthodox Church.

In addition, by no means are all foreign missions in Russia benign in their influence. Together with such cults as the Moonies and the Hare Krishnas, Russia has suffered an influx of quite wild and even suicidal religions that have done great harm, especially among young people. Russian Church leaders say that the United States, with its two hundred years of democratic pluralism, can tolerate and assimilate such groups.[42] "We are only beginning our democracy," they say. "Today your pluralism would destroy us."

---

[41] Interview with Archimandrite Joseph Poustoooutoff.

[42] A resolution adopted by the Council of Bishops of the Russian Orthodox Church in February 1997 states:

> The Council is deeply concerned by the growth of organised pseudo-Christian and pseudo-religious sects, of neo-pagan communities, occultists and devil worshipers in the CIS and the Baltic States. . . . We acknowledge that the right of each person to freedom of conscience and religion should be respected, but the leaders of these totalitarian sects are in fact depriving their followers of these rights. . . . Those who attempt to oppose them are subjected to cruel persecution by the sect leaders and their highly placed protectors, including intimidation, psychological pressure, the gathering of incriminating information, slander and repeated searches of their property.

"On the Specific Issues of the Internal and External Activity of the Church," section 35, *Pravoslavnaia Moskva* (Orthodox Moscow), no. 7 (103) (March 1997): 11.

A HISTORICAL DEFENSE

A basic law must reflect not only the political will of those who drafted it and those who adopted it, and not only the moral values that are expressed in it, but also the historical experience of the society whose law it is—its memories of the past and its anticipations of the future. Even a constitution adopted by popular referendum must be interpreted in the light of such historical experience.[43] Indeed, if the historical experience of a people with respect to a matter is sufficiently important that it constitutes a foundation of the constitution itself, then it may even justify departure from the ordinary meaning of the words of particular constitutional norms. Such a historical argument receives some support in the Russian Constitution itself, which provides that "[h]uman and civil rights and freedoms may be restricted by federal law only to the extent necessary for upholding the foundations of the constitutional system, morality, or the health, [and] rights and lawful interests of other persons, or for ensuring the defense of the country and state security."[44]

It is such a historical argument—that the constitutional system itself is founded on the heritage of the Russian people, including its religious heritage—that the Moscow Patriarchate invoked in urging the passage of the 1997 law and in subsequently defending it. This argument must be taken seriously if religious peace is ultimately to be established between foreign Christians living in Russia and the Russian Orthodox Church as well as between the Russian Orthodox Church and other Russian churches that are striving, each in its own way, to restore spiritual health to the tormented Russian soul.

It is particularly important that foreigners come to understand the religious basis for the opposition of the Moscow Patriarchate to the thousands of foreign missionaries, chiefly American, who flocked into Russia in the early 1990s, and who in the years from 1993 to 1997 mobilized widespread support abroad for their vigorous protests against Russian Orthodox efforts to restrict their activities. The heart of its opposition is its belief that the Russian Orthodox Church is the church of the Russian people, that is, the Russian *narod*, the people viewed as a single collective entity, a nation.

It is difficult for most Western Christians to accept, or even to understand, the belief in ethnic Christian churches. In the Western Christian tradition, now embodied in secular constitutional law in most countries and adopted by the human rights covenants, religious freedom is conceived primarily in terms of the religious faith of the individual believer, including his or her right to mani-

---

[43] It was reported that of those eligible (106 million), 54.8% voted on December 12, 1993. Of those that voted, 58.4% (32.9 million) voted in favor of the Constitution. See "Election Results Updated (But Still Not Final)," *Current Digest of the Post-Soviet Press* 45/51 (1993): 7.

[44] Konstitutsiia RF (Constitution of the Russian Federation), art. 55 (1993), translated in *Constitution of the Russian Federation*, ed. Vladimir V. Belyakov and Walter J. Raymond (Lawrenceville, Va., 1994).

fest that faith in collective bodies that are conceived to be voluntary associations. The most vivid contrary example of a collective faith of an ethnic culture is the Judaic faith of the Hebrew people. An ethnic Jew may not be religious, but Judaism is considered by most Jews, whether or not they are religious, to be the indigenous religious faith of the Jewish people, *am Yisroel*, the Jewish *Volk*.

In 1994, in a two-hour conversation on these matters with Archimandrite Joseph Poustooutoff of the Department of External Church Relations of the Moscow Patriarchate, I mentioned that in the religious worship services conducted by foreign Christian evangelical missionaries in Russia that I had attended there was nothing antagonistic to Russian Orthodoxy. I said that they bring the Bible to Russians previously ignorant of it, and their sermons reflect a simple belief in Christian faith, hope, and love, and a doctrine of salvation that is somewhat different from the Russian Orthodox doctrine but not incompatible with it. He replied: "That is fine, but it would be better if at the end of the sermon your preachers would tell the Russians in the congregation that they can also find these same truths in their own Russian Orthodox Church."

The historical argument of the leaders of the Russian Orthodox Church against proselytism from abroad goes much deeper, however, than nationalism or traditionalism. It is a historical argument that is directed not only to the past but also to the present and future. To quote Archimandrite Poustooutoff again:

The changes now taking place in Russia require a new post-Soviet psychology among the people. For three generations people have been brought up on a simple monolithic ideology that is now repudiated. The belief in Soviet superiority is gone. The belief in progress toward a bright future is gone. The people, the *narod*, feels lost.

The foreign evangelical missionaries know that there is a spiritual crisis but they do not understand it. In fact, they are offering to the people another simple solution. Like the Communists, they offer salvation in return for a commitment which requires little effort. "Just believe, and you will be saved." This reinforces the old psychology, in which simple slogans were offered in return for immediate minimum rewards but great rewards in the future. Russian Orthodoxy is more complex and more difficult. It teaches not rewards but sacrifice. It teaches the positive value of suffering. Its spiritual demands are great.

In the past, whenever there has been a spiritual crisis of this intensity, the *narod* has turned to the Russian Church. That was true at the time of the Napoleonic Wars. It was true in the First World War. It was true even under Stalin in the Second World War. Now we are in a comparable crisis. Moreover, both the nationalists on the right and the radical democrats on the left can be reconciled on this point, namely, that to meet our spiritual crisis it is important that a strong role be played not only by the

Russian Orthodox Church but also by other traditional Russian confessions that have been tested by repression for seventy years and that have forged a fraternal relationship with each other.[45]

It is easy for foreigners as well as for non-Orthodox Russians to attribute the effort of the Moscow Patriarchate to make the Russian Orthodox Church an established church and to restrict foreign proselytism simply to its desire for power. There is, indeed, as James Billington, Librarian of Congress and distinguished historian of Russia, has recently said, "a battle within the Russian religious tradition between the recovery of its more inwardly spiritual, locally based, and communally participatory dimension, on the one hand, and the reassertion of a more familiar imperial, autocratic dimension, on the other—the tendency referred to as Orthodoxy without Christianity."[46] But that battle is being waged not only within the Russian religious tradition as a whole but also within the Patriarchate itself, and responses to the policies of the Patriarchate should be directed to the support of its "inwardly spiritual, locally based, and communally participatory dimension." Foreign Christians who go to Russia should make it their mission not to compete with the Russian Orthodox Church but to cooperate with it in an ecumenical spirit.

Not only Russia but also America has "an immense stake," in Billington's words, "in the outcome of the battle" now taking place within the Russian Church between an inwardly spiritual Christian Orthodoxy and a political Orthodoxy that seeks power. He stresses the geopolitical dangers that would confront America if a hostile authoritarian power, with nuclear capability, gained control over the great Eurasian landmass. He notes in addition that America, which is now seen by many Russians as a model, will itself be the object of opprobrium if the Russian experiment in freedom fails. "America cannot control the outcome," he states, "but should at least recognize that perhaps the decisive element in the process will be the way the Russian people come to grips with perhaps the greatest Christian martyrology of the twentieth century (during the first five decades of Soviet rule) and the century's largest mass conversion to Christianity during this last decade."[47]

CONCLUSION

In a society like the Russian society today, which has undergone, on the one hand, a sudden and substantial enlargement of human rights, including religious human rights, and, on the other hand, revolutionary economic, political, and

---

[45] Interview with Archimandrite Joseph Poustooutoff.

[46] James T. Billington, "The West's Stake in Russia's Future," *Orbis* 41 (1997): 545, 552. See also his chapter herein.

[47] Ibid.

spiritual changes—at such a time and in such a society the arguments of the Moscow Patriarchate deserve to be carefully and sympathetically considered.

Indeed, one may conclude that the ultimate resolution of the intense inter-church, interdenominational conflicts that will continue to exist in Russia, both among citizens of Russia and between Russians and foreigners, must be undertaken not at the level of legislation but at the level of dialogue and nego-tiation among all the conflicting groups. There is a strong but almost untrans-latable word for this in the tradition of Russian Orthodoxy: *sobornost'*, conciliarity, collectivity, or perhaps, to coin a new word, "communification," a bringing of diverse groups together into community through the power of speech, and indeed, the power of prayer. Surely all the bitterly contending religious groups, domestic and foreign, traditional or not, should seek divine guidance in reconciling their differences.

15.

FEDERAL AND PROVINCIAL RELIGIOUS FREEDOM LAWS IN RUSSIA

A Struggle for and against Federalism and the Rule of Law

———————◆———————

Lauren B. Homer and Lawrence A. Uzzell

INTRODUCTION

This chapter examines legislation enacted or proposed between 1993 and 1996 in more than one-third of the eighty-nine political subdivisions of the Russian Federation ("RF" or "Russia").[1] These laws seek to regulate and restrict the activities of religious workers and religious organizations in spreading their faiths, particularly if they are part of "foreign" or "nontraditional" religions. In many respects, they are inconsistent on their face with the provisions of the RF Constitution and with both the 1990 and 1997 RF federal laws, which regulate religious freedom and religious organizations and purport to preempt inconsistent local laws.

Nonetheless, only one of these laws has been judicially challenged—that of the Udmurt Republic. It was invalidated in an excellent opinion by its Supreme Court in March 1997. No other regional or federal court has as yet considered the validity of these laws, although the federal Ministry of Justice has issued a report stating that many are, in its opinion, unconstitutional.[2] The sole federal

---

This chapter is an excerpt and update of the authors' article that appeared in *Emory International Law Review* 12 (1998): 247-312.

[1] These "subdivisions" of the RF include its constituent republics, territories (*krai*), regions (*oblasts*), and cities.

[2] "An investigation conducted by the Ministry of Justice has shown that many of the 27 regional laws in the area of religious rights and human freedoms do not accord with the constitution and federal legislation." Press Conference of Minister of Justice Pavel Krashennikov, May 25, 1998, trans. P. D. Steeves at <www.stetson.edu/~psteeves/relnews/>.

lawsuit was a challenge to the laws of the Tula and Tyumen Republics, brought before the RF Constitutional Court in late 1995 by ninety State Duma deputies. However, it was dismissed for lack of jurisdiction after some of the deputies withdrew from the case. There have been virtually no other attempts by the central government, religious groups, or courts to nullify these laws.

Some thought that the September 1997 RF federal law "On Freedom of Conscience and on Religious Associations"[3] (the "1997 Law"), which contains restrictions on activities of foreign religious workers and newer religious associations, would lead the regions to abandon their own regulations. This has not proven true. The mere passage of the 1997 Law, which was intended to be more restrictive than it turned out to be, coupled with the lack of federal intervention concerning the regional laws, has also caused many regional administrations to conclude that they can act arbitrarily and with impunity in dealing with religious minorities and newer religious organizations.

Further, while the central government has attempted to limit the negative impact of the 1997 Law through generous interpretations and unofficial instructions to ignore its most unconstitutional features, local authorities have tended to read it literally or even more severely than its terms permit. Thus, it appears likely that regional laws and unreasonable regional enforcement of the 1997 Law will continue to present practical and legal challenges to religious freedom in many parts of Russia for years to come.

REGIONAL LEGISLATION OF RELIGION

The new regional laws on religion are part of a broader historical conflict between forces of centralization and the urge for regional autonomy. For centuries, the Russian Empire and the Soviet Union attempted to control all aspects of life, including religious belief, from the center in order to preserve political uniformity and stability in the world's largest nation. However, uniformity is hard to achieve in a country as vast as Russia. Stretching from the Arctic Circle to the Caspian Sea and from the Baltic Sea to the Sea of Japan, Russia spans eleven time zones. Within these expansive boundaries there exist multitudinous regions, provinces, and cities as well as hundreds of ethnic groups, languages, and religious traditions, not to mention divergent economic and strategic interests.[4] Thus, historically, attempts by the center to standardize

---

[3] Russian Federation Law on the Freedom of Conscience and on Religious Associations, Federal Law No. 125-FZ (September 26, 1997), trans. Lawrence A. Uzzell in *Emory International Law Review* 12 (1998): 657-80 [hereafter "1997 Law"]. The law became effective upon its publication on October 1, 1997.

[4] Russia has historically included followers of all of the world's great religions— Christianity, Judaism, Islam, Buddhism, as well as deeply rooted traditional religions, including shamanism, nature worship, folk beliefs, the occult, paganism, and syncretic religious systems. See chapter 4 by Aleksandr Shchipkov and chapter 9 by Sergei Filatov herein.

beliefs have been stoutly resisted in the regions, sometimes militarily, but more often through bureaucratic intransigence, corruption, or covert resistance.

Tensions between federal and local government powers and authority have risen to the forefront of Russian politics since 1992, following the dissolution of the Soviet Union and the disintegration of central political, military, police, and civil government power. The same factors, coupled with changing economic and social conditions and the wholesale rewriting of national laws, have turned today's Russia into a largely lawless state and one in which a "war of laws" is carried out between the center and the regions. Legal conflicts between regional and federal laws occur in all areas of life—local governments refuse to pay tax revenues to the center, declare themselves free-trade zones governed by a separate set of laws, and so forth. To a great extent, the regions are succeeding in flouting the central government's authority.[5] The success of the small Chechnya region in freeing itself of federal government control is only the most dramatic example, and one in which religious factors played a major role. The same Ministry of Justice report that noted that local religion laws were inconsistent with federal standards stated that one quarter of 3,089 current regulations of the subjects of the RF analyzed by legal experts were found to be unconstitutional. Yet the central government clearly lacks the will and the resources to do anything about its increasingly tumultuous relationship with the regions.

THE DELUGE OF REGIONAL LAWS

Local authorities in the regions, not waiting for central government lawmakers to act, took matters into their own hands and promptly enacted or considered legal action to address what they saw as a disorderly situation, what some called a "missionary invasion." From 1993 to 1997, more than one-third of Russia's eighty-nine provincial governments[6] adopted laws or executive decrees shrinking the rights of foreign religious organizations, religious minorities, and even major religious organizations.

The earliest documented attempt occurred in the City of Kazan in Tatarstan in 1993. An ordinance of its mayor—"On the Activities of Representatives of Individual Religious Confessions in the City of Kazan"—addressed "[f]oreign representatives of charismatic Protestant communities . . . [as] prompting pro-

---

[5] The dissolution of the USSR itself resulted from a decision by President Yeltsin to let the outlying regions go their own way as a means of consolidating his control over the Russian Federation. The last five years have seen a host of compromises with regional interests by federal authorities on issues from tax collection to local autonomy. See J. Helmer, "Russian Regions Pressure Kremlin into Policy Shift," *Radio Free Europe/Radio Liberty Broadcast* (November 7, 1997) (reporting thirty-seven "treaties" between the Kremlin and Russian regions on tax collection and other issues).

[6] There are only eighty-eight if secessionist Chechnya is excluded.

tests from residents."[7] In September 1994, there were recommendations to ban "totalitarian charismatic religious sects" in the Republic of Tatarstan.[8] One of the earliest of the new regional laws was enacted in late 1994 by the Tula region, 120 miles south of Moscow. It became a model for other regions. The enactment of regional laws accelerated in 1996, and they became increasingly restrictive, discriminatory, and violative of federal law.

How many such laws have been passed altogether? It is impossible to get a precise current figure. There is no centralized database with information on all regional laws. In addition, there is a lack of full-fledged *glasnost* in the provincial governments. Rule-making still sometimes takes place by informal and under-reported means. For example, several sources in Ulyanovsk, on the Volga 450 miles southeast of Moscow, told Keston News Service that the regional government there had issued a Soviet-style, secret order to its own bureaucrats instructing them not to rent public auditoriums to Pentecostals and other minorities. However, the order has never been published. Arbitrary closings of churches occurred in Moscow in 1997, despite the absence of any published law, on grounds that public buildings could no longer be rented to religious groups. A law on foreign missionaries in the Kostroma region, discussed below, was unpublished, and local authorities refused to give a copy of it to a Keston News Service reporter.

Viktor Kalinin, chief legal advisor to Patriarch Aleksii II—and a former official of the Soviet-era Council for Religious Affairs—told Keston in an October 1996 interview that the total number of provincial laws or executive orders was about twenty-five. In December 1996, Yuri Zuyev, dean of the religion department of the Academy of State Service in Moscow, told Keston that the total had reached about thirty. A report by the Minister of Justice in May 1998, however, identified only twenty-seven such laws. The authors have reviewed a representative sampling of regional laws, decrees, and regulations from twenty-four Russian regions and cities.[9]

In reading of these events and the texts of these provincial laws, one must recall the provisions of the Russian Constitution discussed in other chapters

---

[7] Lev Levinson, "Local Law as a Means of Destroying Federal Law?" *Religion & Law* 1 (1996): 1, 4.

[8] Ibid.

[9] These include both enacted and draft laws, decrees, and regulations from the following Russian political subdivisions: Arkhangelsk, Bashkortostan, Buryatia, Daghestan, Ekaterinberg, Kalmykia, Komi, Kostroma, Kurgan, Moscow, Murmansk, Perm, Primorsk, Ryazan, Sakhalin, Sverdlovsk, St. Petersburg, Tatarstan, Tula, Tuva, Tver, Tyumen, Udmurtia, and Yaroslavl. Lev Levinson, a prominent activist in the religious freedom area, reported laws or decrees in the Khabarovsk region, the Khanty-Masi Autonomous Region, Tatarstan, the City of Kazan, the Kaliningrad Region, and the Chuvash Region. See Levinson, "Local Law." See generally G. P. Yakunin and V. Polosin, "Federal Authorities and Freedom of Conscience" (unpublished manuscript, 1996), which reports on various regional laws and problems experienced by minority religions in a large number of provincial towns and cities.

herein, which ostensibly guarantee to every person in the territory of Russia the right to practice and publicly proclaim his or her religious beliefs, and which ostensibly ensure that all faiths will have equal legal rights and treatment from the state. Even the most tortured logic would not suffice to reconcile the new provincial laws with these constitutional guarantees. Indeed, the laws' authors have not even attempted such a feat, but have simply proceeded as if these provisions of the constitution did not exist.

CHARACTERISTICS OF THE REGIONAL LAWS

Although the regional laws vary widely, many of them share common provisions and characteristics. Indeed, it is known that local legislatures in some cases draw considerable guidance from laws already enacted elsewhere. This section discusses some of the more frequently seen provisions and approaches in the regional laws.

"Accreditation" or Registration Is a Prerequisite to Religious Activity

The laws all require annual registration or "accreditation" of both religious organizations and of individual religious workers with local authorities, often in addition to registration under the federal 1997 Law. Accreditation involves issuance of a sort of "license" before engaging in various forms of religious expression or group activities. For the applicant, this process entails filing detailed documents, paying significant application fees, and undergoing a substantial review of the beliefs and activities of the applicant. The review can take one or more months. Religious activities by unaccredited groups or individuals are prohibited. Violators may be prosecuted criminally. In effect, religious activities from small home Bible studies, to personal sharing of beliefs with a friend, to group religious services, large-scale evangelism, and public distribution of religious literature all require advance approval by local authorities under these laws.

Most demand accreditation even for groups already legally registered with the federal Ministry of Justice. Only an occasional law, such as the Ryazan law, gives automatic accreditation to such organizations. Other areas impose duplicative, costly, and often inconsistent standards—for example, barring activities by types of groups that are registered with federal authorities, such as Charismatic Christians. Further, regional laws typically require applications for accreditation by each individual religious worker or evangelist, even if their religious organizations are registered and accredited in the region. The laws thus add a level of regulation not foreseen by the federal law.

Monitoring and Restriction of Religious Beliefs

Virtually all of the laws provide for investigations of the beliefs and activities of groups and individuals seeking accreditation before the groups may legally operate. The accreditation process thus presents an obvious opportunity for the authorities to ban disfavored groups.

Expert committees are to be formed to decide whether "new" faiths are acceptable. Further, the laws contain a list of activities and type of beliefs, which varies from region to region, that are cause for closing down religious organizations or withholding or revoking accreditation. Many laws list types of religious activities, beliefs, or even faiths that cannot operate in their regions.

Discrimination against "Foreign" Religions and Special Surveillance of Foreign Citizens

Most of the laws apply only to foreign citizens or organizations. However, even residents of other Russian regions may be considered foreigners under some of the laws. Also, if religions originated abroad, even if they are run by local citizens or have existed for hundreds of years in Russia, they may be termed "foreign." On the other hand, "traditional" Russian religions or specific faiths are often specifically exempted from the laws' operation.

Many of the laws additionally order existing or new regulatory bodies to investigate and review visas of foreigners engaged in religious activities and to order them to leave if their religious activities are inconsistent with their visa status. Some provide for wholesale investigation of foreign students or workers to see if they are engaged in religious activities.

The emphasis on restricting foreigners and foreign-based groups is founded in longstanding Russian xenophobia and a refusal to acknowledge constitutional and statutory provisions that give foreigners and people without citizenship the same rights as Russian citizens.[10] This is of particular concern given the fact that over twenty million persons are believed to be living in Russia without citizenship, due to post-Soviet migration. Moreover, the 1997 Law allows foreign citizens with valid visas, based on invitations from registered religious organizations, to work in Russia as "professional" religious workers, without further investigation of their personal background or beliefs.

Limits on Use of Public Forums and on Religious Speech

Many of the laws ban religious groups, especially foreign ones, from using public buildings and forums, including schools, theaters, stadiums, and radio and television stations—even if the groups have been accredited under local law. Some also limit certain activities, such as children's ministry and publication or dissemination of literature, to certain locations, such as the main office of the ministry organization. Use of public forums for religious activities has been routine since 1992 and is critical, as the vast majority of new congregations have nowhere else to meet.

---

[10] See, e.g., Yakunin and Polosin, "Federal Authorities," 19. Yakunin and Polosin quote the Preamble to the 1993 City of Kazan Resolution, which states that "visits of foreign representatives of Protestant charismatic organizations continue. They view our city as an open field for missionary work and are conducting a propaganda of their views without taking into account the national and religious traditions which have formed over the centuries."

Creation of New Regulatory Agencies on Religion

In addition to their restrictive content, the laws are also troubling in their mode of adoption and promulgation. Most of the laws create new organizations, similar to the Soviet-era Councils for Religious Affairs, to monitor religious organizations and workers and their beliefs and activities.

Violations of the Rule of Law

Many of the laws and decrees are secret or unpublished. Nonetheless, they are used to limit rights of religious organizations. Some laws are implemented selectively, while others are enacted but not enforced.

The provincial laws appear to be inconsistent with the expansive provisions in the RF Constitution, which give freedom to practice and articulate one's religious beliefs to all persons. They effectively silence traveling preachers and evangelists, whether visiting from abroad or from other parts of Russia, because the application process takes longer than the usual visit. Even Patriarch Aleksii II of the Russian Orthodox Church needs accreditation from local authorities before engaging in religious services, if he visits regions such as Udmurtia.

The local laws are also inconsistent with both the 1990 and 1997 RF Laws, which contain no provisions requiring state approval before engaging in religious speech or group activities.[11] Indeed, the 1997 Law specifically permits religious activities by unregistered religious groups, including "worship services, religious rituals and ceremonies, and also the teaching of religion and religious upbringing of their followers."[12] The rights of these religious groups, composed of ten or more citizens, can be restrained only if they violate certain standards in the 1997 Law, which are certainly not based on whether they are "traditional" or part of a listed group of faiths.

The rules permitting refusal of accreditation and religious speech based on the content of beliefs offend Article 28 of the RF Constitution, which protects all faiths that offer their beliefs to nonmembers. Indeed, they are redolent of the anti-proselytism laws of the Soviet period.

The process is also expensive, erecting barriers to activities for many individual Russian believers. Since "taking the Gospel to all the world" is a central tenet of Christian belief and indeed was the basis for Christianization of the eastern Slavs by itinerant missionaries from the ninth century onward, the requirements of application, waiting, and approval oppose the core doctrine

---

[11] Russia's first post-Soviet federal law on religious freedom was the 1990 "On Freedom of Conscience." Law of the Russian Soviet Federative Socialist Republic on Freedom of Worship (October 25, 1990), trans. in Igor Troyanovsky, ed., *Religion in the Soviet Republics* (San Francisco, 1991), 31 [hereafter "1990 Law"]. See further discussion in chapter 14 by Harold J. Berman and the Introduction by John Witte Jr. herein.

[12] 1997 Law, ch. II, art. 7.

of this and most other faiths. These provisions were in direct conflict with the 1990 Law, when most were enacted, and remain in conflict with the 1997 Law. Both give all religious groups the right to operate without registration, enable religious activities to occur in a variety of public places, and allow children to exercise independent decisions about participation in religious activities.[13] Their focus on foreigners was totally inconsistent with both the 1990 Law and the 1993 RF Constitution, which give all persons, including foreigners, rights equal to those of citizens. The situation under the 1997 Law is more complex, in that it does require visa invitations from registered Russian religious organizations prior to professional religious activity.[14] However, arguably other types of religious activity are not subject to these same strictures. Further, once such an invitation is issued, subjecting the individual to further examination is inconsistent with the federal law.

These provisions, moreover, reflect an ominous reversion to other Soviet principles. Anything religious must be strictly controlled; whatever is not expressly permitted is forbidden. Instead of regarding religious practice as a fundamental human right, it is treated like flying an airplane or performing surgery: an activity to be allowed only under detailed supervision, inspection, regulation, and licensing by the state.

EXAMPLES OF REGIONAL LAWS

The 1994 Tula Law, which served as a model for many other regions, applies only to "foreign organizations, representations, and representatives coming to the region." It does not define the term "foreign" but implies that it applies to groups that are part of an organization that is legally established in another country.[15] It requires such groups to undergo an "accreditation" procedure, involving submission of an application that includes authenticated copies of documents from its home country, information on the proposed activity and structure of the group, and payment of a fee of twenty times the legal minimum wage.[16]

In Tula, accredited groups obtain only the rights of "representations," which do not have most of the rights of a legal entity.[17] They can be shut down for misstatements in the application or if their activity "entails incitement of national, racial, or religious dissension, harm to health of citizens, other encroachments on their person and rights, the performance of other illegal actions or violations of legislation."[18] The law requires that their activities be held "pre-

---

[13] 1990 Law, arts. 4, 9, 22.
[14] 1997 Law, ch. III, art. 20.2.
[15] Law of the Tula Region, "On Missionary (Religious) Activity on the Territory of the Tula Region," art. 1 (November 24, 1994), trans. as Appendix C, *Emory International Law Review* 12 (1998): 693-700 [hereafter "Tula Law"].
[16] Ibid., arts. 6, 7, 9.
[17] Ibid., art. 2.
[18] Ibid., art. 15.

dominantly . . . in places designated for religious purposes," and they may "address minors . . . only according to their desire and upon receiving written permission from their parent or guardian."[19]

A typical later law is that of the Kurgan region, adopted in January 1996. It also deals only with foreign groups, stating that it applies to "foreign religious missions," defined as "a group of foreign citizens, representing a religious organization, which has come to the region for the purpose of spreading its dogma."[20] Both missionary organizations and individual missionaries are covered by the law. Its provisions do not apply "to religious organizations registered in the Russian Federation." Foreign-based groups thus can avoid the impact of the law by setting up their own registered Russian organizations.

The law requires formal registration with the local branch of the Ministry of Justice prior to engaging in any missionary activities, which are not defined.[21] Applicants must submit (either directly or through a local inviting organization) an application, copies of their articles of incorporation and certificate of good standing from their home country (complete with appropriate authentication documents), a passport, and a Russian entry visa.[22] Consideration can take ten to forty days and a fee of ten times the minimum monthly wage must be provided.[23] If the application is granted, a certificate of registration is issued, permitting the pursuit of missionary activities for one year. Registration can be extended for consecutive years without payment of a fee, if no violations have occurred.[24]

Registration can be "annulled" for a variety of reasons that make clear the nature of local concerns in the Kurgan region about foreign missionaries. Annulment may occur

> if the mission (missionary) employs in its activity illegal measures of coercion, or preaches war, violence, or misanthropy (hatred) . . . causes harm to the physical, psychological, or moral health of people, including the use of narcotics or other mind altering substances, conducts lecherous acts, performs acts which violate social morality, or if activity entails infringement on the rights or personal freedoms of citizens; . . . if the mission (missionary) incites citizens to refuse to fulfill legal duties or family commitments or to perform other illegal acts, including the disposal of common property or private property in a manner harmful to the interests of family members or disabled persons.[25]

---

[19] Ibid., art. 18.

[20] Kurgan Region Law, "On Missionary Activity by Foreign Religious Missions (Missionaries) on the Territory of Kurgan Region," art. 2.1 (January 5, 1996), trans. Felix Corley at <www.law.emory.edu/EILR/special/kur.html>.

[21] Ibid., art. 5.8.

[22] Ibid., arts. 5.1, 5.2.

[23] Ibid., arts. 5.3, 5.4.

[24] Ibid., arts. 5.5, 5.6.

[25] Ibid., art. 7.1.

The Decree of the Governor of the Sakhalin Region (No. 315, July 4, 1996) is also entirely focused on foreign religious groups. It bars "missionary religious activity" in state, municipal, or other educational institutions and also bars "[r]ental of buildings and structures of state or municipal educational institutions, medical facilities, homes for the elderly or invalids, children's homes or boarding schools . . . for the conducting of worship services, religious rites and ceremonies."[26] The latter are venues typically used by newer religious groups in eastern Russia, where buildings dedicated to religious use are scarce.

The Sakhalin decree also creates special procedures for reviewing and issuing visas to religious workers and foreign students. Moreover, it ordered an analysis of the activities of foreign religious groups, and "upon the ascertaining of facts," it authorizes the government to take measures, "up to the annulment of their certificate of accreditation."[27] In other words, if religious groups are found to be objectionable by local authorities, however deeply held and valid their religious beliefs, they can be shut down. If foreign students use their spare time to engage in religious work, they risk being thrown out of the local university and being deported.

The focus on foreigners is also found in the 1996 law of the Tyumen (Tumen) region, about thirteen hundred miles east of Moscow, which defines a missionary as "a representative of a foreign religious organization," and states that its provisions do not apply to domestic religious groups.[28] The 1995 executive order of Tver region, ninety miles northwest of Moscow, requires registration only for religious groups which are "structural subunits of foreign religious organizations located outside the borders of the Russian Federation."[29] The Tver executive order also states that these groups cannot receive free transfers of property from the state for use for church buildings.[30] In point of fact, under Russian law, foreign corporations may not own property at all, unless they set up a local legal entity. However, the term "structural subunit" may go beyond this distinction.

This language in the Tver executive order and language focusing on the nationality of religious workers in other laws will have adverse consequences even for groups with registered Russian organizations and strong, longstanding support from Russian citizens. For example, Roman Catholic parishes are tech-

---

[26] "On the Regulation of Missionary Activity of Various Religious Confessions on the Territory of the Sakhalin Region," Decree No. 315, art. 8 (July 4, 1996), trans. Keston Institute at <www.law.emory.edu/EILR/special/sak.html>.

[27] Ibid., art. 6.

[28] Law of the Tyumen Region, "On the Missionary Activity of the Foreign Religious Missions (Missionaries) on the Territory of the Tyumen Region," art. 3 (May 26, 1996), trans. Keston Institute at <www.law.emory.edu/EILR/special/tyu.html>.

[29] Decree of the Legislative Assembly of the Tver Region, "On Religious Associations Constituting Structural Subdivisions of Foreign Religious Organizations Which Are outside the Jurisdiction of the Russian Federation" (February 21, 1995), trans. Felix Corley, Appendix D, *Emory International Law Review* 12 (1998): 701-2.

[30] Ibid., art. 2.

nically "subunits" of a foreign organization, under the spiritual and administrative authority of the Vatican, even though the Catholic Church is legally registered in Russia. Thus, it could be barred from receiving back church property under the Tver order, in violation of the anti-discrimination provisions of both the RF Constitution and the 1997 Law. Also, most Catholic clergy in Russia, as well as many Orthodox, Baptist, other Protestant, and Jewish clergy, are at present non-Russians. This is an inevitable result of the virtual eradication of seminaries for the training of indigenous priests and clergy during the Soviet era.

Most regional laws treat Catholic parish priests, and other foreign clergy, as "foreign missionaries," even though they work for a registered Russian organization and most of their flocks are Russian citizens of Catholic ancestry. In fact, Belgorod region, about four hundred miles south of Moscow, did just that to Fr. Joseph Gonchaga in February 1997. They thus must be accredited, in addition to central government visa restrictions and requirements of official invitations for these workers under the 1997 Law. This creates obvious legal and practical challenges for their congregations, which often have to pay for burdensome annual accreditation in addition to frequent foreign travel to renew visas (as often as every three months) and put up with vacant pulpits. All Russian congregations and citizens that rely on foreign clergy and that take their spiritual direction from abroad are adversely affected by the multiple regulatory burdens these laws create and are unconstitutionally hindered in their free exercise of religious belief.

However, not all of the regional laws focus on the "foreign" element in missionary work. Some betray a more pervasive antireligious bias, possibly based on a desire to seem fair, regulating all religious organizations and workers. For example, a proposed law in the City of St. Petersburg, as drafted in March 1996, defined "missionary activity" as "religious, educational, charitable, informative, cultural, property, financial and other activities carried out ... with the purpose of studying, propagating and disseminating *any beliefs* among people."[31] Thus, all Russian Orthodox priests, as well as all propagators of doctrines such as atheism, were required to apply for and receive accreditation before engaging in their work. Indeed, by these standards, any committed member of any Christian confession which takes Matthew 28:19[32] seriously would be a "missionary," whether a Russian or a foreigner, an ordained cleric or a layperson. Notably, this law was twice rejected by Mayor Anatoly Sobchak, on grounds it exceeded the authority of the St. Petersburg city council. Sobchak referred specifically to Article 71 of the RF Constitution.

Two enacted regional laws apply to all religious workers: the Perm law, which was adopted at the direct suggestion of Patriarch Aleksii II, and the very

---

[31] Law of St. Petersburg, "On the Accreditation of Organizations and Citizens Carrying Out Missionary Activity in St. Petersburg," art. 1 (March 15, 1996) (emphasis added), trans. Felix Corley at <www.law.emory.edu/EILR/special/stp.html>.

[32] "Go ye therefore, and teach all nations, baptizing them in the name of the Father, and of the Son, and of the Holy Ghost."

similar law of the Udmurt Republic. Each specifically includes both RF citizens and all others who engage in "missionary activities" in the scope of its accreditation requirements.

The Perm law says that

> the subjects of missionary activity are missionaries of religious organizations of the Russian Federation. Foreign missionaries (missions) are people without Russian citizenship or individuals without citizenship, who have come to the Perm region with the purpose of performing missionary, charitable or other activity. . . . *Missionary activity in any form, conducted on the territory of the Perm region is to be accredited.*[33]

Although all types of believers are included in the Perm Law, it singles out foreigners and citizens of other former Soviet republics for particularly negative treatment. It requires that they have an invitation from a local religious organization that has been approved in advance by local governing bodies or by the regional administration.[34] Even Russian groups from other parts of the Russian Federation must have invitations from local bodies before they may engage in missionary activities, although these invitations do not need advance government approval.[35]

The Udmurt Law applies equally to Russians and non-Russians, defining "missionary activity" broadly as "dissemination of religious teaching among adherents of different faiths, as well as among nonbelieving citizens, with the aim of attracting them into religious formations . . . by various methods: the conducting of propagandistic/educational work, the organization of collective divine worship, religious rites and ceremonies, individual work and other forms of activities."[36] It forbade "missionaries" to engage in "missionary activities" unless they were specifically accredited by the republican government, for which accreditation they were to pay a fee and apply for re-accreditation every year. The persons subject to registration prior to engaging in mission activity included "foreign citizens, persons without citizenship, citizens of the former USSR not being citizens of the Russian Federation, and citizens of the Russian Federation from other regions of the country."[37]

In a variation on the approach of Perm and Udmurtia of applying their laws to all religions, some regional laws apply to all missionary activity but

---

[33] Law of the Perm Region, "On the Procedure for Conducting Missionary Activity on the Territory of the Perm Region" (emphasis added) [hereafter "Perm Law"]. See also Law of the Udmurt Republic on Missionary Activity on the Territory of the Udmurt Republic, art. 2 (May 28, 1996), trans. Felix Corley, Appendix E, *Emory International Law Review* 12 (1998): 703-14 [hereafter "Udmurt Law"].

[34] Perm Law, art. 3.

[35] Ibid.

[36] Udmurt Law, art. 1.

[37] Ibid., art. 12.

exempt certain religious faiths from their application. The exemptions usually apply to groups that are "traditional" for the region. Oddly, these exemptions operate regardless of whether the groups have "foreign" origins.

For example, in Sverdlovsk, home region of President Yeltsin, the regional law on religious missionary activity states:

> The application of this law extends to all religious associations which conduct missionary activities on the territory of Sverdlovsk Region, except for the Russian Orthodox Church, congregations of Orthodox Old Believers, the Spiritual Directorate of Muslims, the Roman Catholic Church, the Evangelical Lutheran Church, and Jewish religious organizations.[38]

Ironically, even if these associations are foreign-sponsored Lutheran, Muslim, or Jewish groups, they are not included in the operation of the law. However, all others, including Russian-based groups with hundreds or even thousands of years of historic activity in Russia must be accredited—for example, Baptists, Pentecostals, and Buddhists.

The groups to be exempted vary from region to region, according to the range of traditional faiths practiced in each particular region. For example, in Murmansk, exemptions are granted only to "the Russian Orthodox Church, the Orthodox Old-Believer community and the Spiritual Administration of Muslims."[39] Russian Baptists, Pentecostals, Catholics, and all other groups, even native religions of Murmansk, must be accredited. In Buryatia, a resurgence of pre-Christian shamanism and nature worship has led to the inclusion of these religions in the privileged categories.

Other regional laws do not focus on the national origins of the faiths, but distinguish between "sects," which are regulated, and "traditional religions," which are not. The Ryazan Law, for example, provides for review of religious beliefs by both the Ministry of Justice and an "expert-consultative council for religious affairs of the administration of the Ryazan Region." A "religious sect" is defined as a "religious association of citizens for joint confession and dissemination of a dogma, differing from the teaching of traditional religions." "Traditional religions" are defined as "a religion, historically accepted by a large part of the population living in a concrete territory."[40] "Sects" are required to provide information in their applications about "how [their doctrines]

---

[38] Sverdlovsk Regional Law, "On the Execution of Missionary Activity on the Territory of the Sverdlovsk Region," art. 1 (October 10, 1996).

[39] Law of the Murmansk Region, "On the Conducting of Missionary (Religious) Activity on the Territory of Murmansk Region," art. 2, trans. Felix Corley at <www.law.emory.edu/EILR/special/mur.html>.

[40] Law of the Ryazan Region, "On the Regulation of the Activities of Religious Sects and Healers on the Territory of the Ryazan Region," art. 1 [hereafter "Ryazan Law"].

diffe[r] from traditional religions, reasons and purposes for the founding of the organization, statement of dogma, history, description of foreseen leadership and number of members, forms and methods of attracting new members, any kind of required attitude toward traditional religions for members of the sect."[41] Thus, if Methodists were active in Ryazan before the Russian revolution, but Baptists were not, the latter would have to go through these additional procedures, while the former would not.

A similar provision is found in the law of the Arkhangelsk region, in the northernmost parts of Russia, bordering the White Sea, seven hundred miles north of Moscow.[42] The Arkhangelsk legislation, enacted in January 1997, is one of the most recent provincial laws. It is also perhaps the most repressive. It therefore illustrates what may be a trend in regional legislatures toward even greater restrictions on religious liberty. The Arkhangelsk law targets "sects" for regulation, while exempting from regulation all "traditional religions,"[43] which are defined as those "historically accepted by a large part of the population" in the region.[44] Indeed, the Arkhangelsk law goes so far as openly to consign minority faiths to second-class status.[45] In Soviet style, the Arkhangelsk law also denies believers in "nontraditional" faiths the basic right to proclaim and practice their faith except in tightly restricted, and presumably invisible, places. It defines as a "missionary," subject to special licensing and regulations, anyone "carrying out religious, religious educational, or charitable activities outside the walls of a religious congregation."[46] Article 5 of the new law also forbids "sects" and "foreign religious organizations" from requesting donations of any kind of property, including cash.[47]

The very notion of requiring a historical pedigree for religious faiths seems altogether strained in Arkhangelsk, if not ridiculous. There, the Soviet regime converted centuries-old Orthodox monasteries into some of the country's most brutal penal institutions for prisoners, including prisoners of conscience. It might have been expected that the Arkhangelsk law would be applied in a benign fashion to groups such as the Russian Pentecostals, who have existed in Russia for over one hundred years. The Pentecostals were mercilessly perse-

---

[41] Ibid., art. 4(a).

[42] Regional Law of Arkhangelsk, "On the Regulation of the Activity of Religious Sects, Representations (Branches) of Foreign Religious Organizations, and Individual Preachers and Missionaries on the Territory of Arkhangelsk Region" (January 30, 1997), trans. Felix Corley, Appendix B, *Emory International Law Review* 12 (1998): 681-92.

[43] Ibid., arts. 1, 2.

[44] Ibid., art. 2.

[45] See, e.g., ibid., art. 7 (requiring all "preachers, missionaries, religious sects and representations of foreign religious organizations" to undergo regular "expert examination").

[46] Ibid., art. 2.

[47] Ibid., art. 5.

cuted during the Soviet period and were only allowed to register in the early days of *perestroika*.

However, in a May 1997 conversation with Keston, pastor Nikolai Makuyed of Russia's Pentecostal Union said that the new law in Arkhangelsk was being vigorously enforced against his church, despite its local registration and membership in a centralized organization registered with the RF Ministry of Justice. Following its enactment, he said, the Arkhangelsk congregations of his Union had been forbidden to rent meeting spaces, even in private flats, unless they receive accreditation, for which they must pay a fee equal to fifty times the monthly minimum wage. One congregation had been expelled from the Arkhangelsk hall that it had been renting. Thus, the term "traditional" in this regulation means something other than religious groups that have historically existed in Russia.

This treatment of Russian Pentecostals is clearly in violation of the RF Constitution, and even of the 1997 Law, which limits the rights of groups not registered during the Soviet period, but still gives all Russian religious groups the right to meet and worship, without prior government approval, and all registered organizations the right to receive donations, rent or own property, and to promulgate their faiths in a variety of forums.

In a handful of regions, including Kalmykia, Chechnya, and Tatarstan, local governments have gone so far as to *ban* some or all but a handful of religions. Thus, even religious organizations registered at the federal level may not have congregations in these regions, according to their local laws, in clear violation of the RF Constitution and the 1997 Law. These laws employ different language to define the range of groups they intend to restrict. Frequently, these definitions appear vague. For example, the Ryazan law completely bans activities of "totalitarian sects," a term not defined in the law. In the Republic of Kalmykia, the governor issued a decree in 1993, as yet still on the books, identifying Buddhism, Islam, and Russian Orthodoxy as the only legal religions in his republic. He also set himself up as a sort of deity and head of his own interfaith synod. However, this did not stop him from founding, on his own initiative, a Catholic Church.[48]

Virtually all of the Russian provincial laws provide grounds for stopping the activities of religious organizations and individual believers, or imposing penalties or fines, based on the content of their religious beliefs and statements. Provisions to this effect from the law of the Kurgan region are quoted above. Another example is the Ryazan law, which bars or annuls registration or activities, that

a) violate public safety and order; b) preach war, violence, misanthropy (hatred), enmity toward traditional religions, ideas of religious superiority, incite in their members hostility toward their own culture, government, national customs, arouse social, racial, national, or religious

---

[48] Interview with Father V. Chaplin (October 9, 1997).

dissension; c) contradict in their activities generally conventional norms of public morals; d) mislead citizens by hiding the character and goals of their activity, or also perform other illegal activities, in violation of the legislation of the Russian Federation and the Ryazan Region.[49]

Provisions of this type frequently are extremely vague and vary from region to region. They give the authorities wide discretion to investigate the content of religious speech, including both core doctrines and the contents of particular sermons. These provisions could readily be used to close down or deny accreditation to churches that periodically engage in what they believe to be prophetic witness but which the authorities might label as "promoting disobedience to state authorities" or "igniting religious dissension." As examples, public criticism of Russian government activities such as bombing civilian populations in Chechnya or even the new 1997 Law could be regarded as preaching hostility toward the government. Public disagreement about religious practices, such as the Russian Orthodox veneration of icons or healing prayer and manifestation of spiritual gifts among Charismatic Christians could also fall into these categories. These are common points of interest and disagreement among religious believers. Indeed, they often are the subject of forceful religious dissension among Christian believers in many nations.

Phrases banning teaching that "harms mental or moral health" or "creates obstacles to general education" can and have been used against groups that believe in healing prayer, bar their members from receiving blood transfusions, or call for special forms of nonpublic education. Bars to groups that "encourage citizens to refuse to carry out their civic or family obligations" could be used against religious groups which promote pacifism, celibacy, or the monastic life.

Bans on preaching "ideas of religious superiority" or "religious dissension" could apply to virtually all traditional faiths, many of which argue that their truth claims are superior to others. The Orthodox Church, for example, teaches that it is superior to all other Christian faiths, but the forceful statements of its priests accusing other denominations of being instruments of the devil are hardly likely to lead to imposition of penalties under these laws.

Moreover, the fundamental truth claims of most faiths are inherently hostile to other belief systems. Thus, these anti-dissension provisions could be the basis of stopping the promulgation of basic doctrine. If they are applied to ban all religious teaching that conflicts with the tenets of other faiths or denominations, these rules could quickly ignite even more religious tensions. Moreover, such restrictions would plainly violate the Russian Constitution and even the 1997 Law, which protect the promulgation of one's own faith.

Like the requirements for licensing the so-called missionaries, these provisions are likely to be enforced selectively, not against the Orthodox but only against those religious groups which lack political connections. Recent devel-

---

[49] Ryazan Law, art. 4.3.

opments in the form of agreements between the Ministry of Health and the Russian Orthodox Church on providing mental-health treatment for "victims" of foreign sects only highlight the dangers which these provisions present.[50]

The regional laws conflict with federal laws by limiting even accredited groups and ones registered with the Ministry of Justice in the place and manner of their religious activities. Some laws limit the right to distribute or sell religious literature to the organization's legal address and place of worship.[51] This means, for example, a bar on street distribution of literature, a practice common in recent years, and even selling one's books through local bookstores or street kiosks. Laws like that in Ryazan bar accredited groups from activities "near" educational and children's establishments, places of worship for traditional religions, and centers of pilgrimage.[52]

Presumably, these rules could be used to legalize current practices, such as refusing building permits to a new Baptist church where the plot involved is felt to be too close to an existing Orthodox church. The Ryazan Law also bars "seances of mass healing," particularly those involving the mass media.[53] While the term "seances of mass healing" is fairly obscure, this language could presumably be used to ban televised healing services. These have become a sticky issue in some regions. For example, a charismatic church in the Yaroslavl region was almost shut down for teaching about healing prayer, even though miraculous healing, including healings based on special icons or holy wells, is a basic doctrine of Orthodoxy as well.

The regional laws are justified on grounds that there is a gap in the federal legislation that does not provide for giving local governments notification of and control over these activities. There are no comparable laws for Pepsi Cola salesmen, however. The accreditation requirement will clearly eliminate preaching by foreign visitors or even visitors from other parts of Russia. Whether the speaker is Billy Graham or the Ecumenical Patriarch Bartholomew, he must submit an application, including his passport and visa. The waiting period after this application is submitted may then extend anywhere from ten days to six months. Moreover, once they obtain the right to speak, speakers may find themselves unable to do so in any public space other than a local forest, due to restrictions in local laws on renting facilities. This actually happened to a church in the Moscow region which was deprived of a previously rented hall as a worship facility. A government official reportedly told members they could simply meet outside, in the Moscow winter, in a local park.

There is already evidence of selective enforcement in the allocation of real estate to religious groups. In this area, religious freedom is intimately connected with economic freedom: when the state has an effective monopoly of ownership, it almost always will use that monopoly to favor some groups

---

[50] See Yakunin and Polosin, "Federal Authorities," 7.
[51] Ryazan Law, arts. 4.2, 6.
[52] Ibid.
[53] Ibid.

(both religious and nonreligious) and disfavor others. That is precisely the situation in most of provincial Russia, where the authorities still control nearly all places suitable for large worship services or other public gatherings, such as the "houses of culture," "palaces of sport," and movie theaters built during the Soviet period. Indeed, the right to hold religious services is meaningless if there is no place in which to do so.

In recent years it has become common practice for local authorities to order the directors of such institutions not to rent them to Baptists, Adventists, or other minority congregations, even at times such as Sunday mornings when these buildings would otherwise be vacant. An official in Irkutsk region, in Siberia, three thousand miles east of Moscow, told Keston in October 1996 that he was drawing up plans to forbid all religious activities in all regional or municipal institutions of culture, education, and sport—even though he admitted that many of these buildings are regularly rented out for events such as rock concerts. Udmurtia tried to go even further, formally banning all "missionary activities," even in sport halls or school buildings. The broad language of this ban could extend even to restriction of "missionary activities" on private property. Many non-Orthodox groups have found it extremely difficult to obtain permits to build new churches, even when land has been given to them for that purpose by local authorities. They are often told that they will be permitted only in locations so remote as to be inaccessible by foot and public transportation. In a country in which most still lack private automobiles, this is a significant hardship.

Regulations for the City of Moscow issued on August 19, 1997, created a new Committee for Relations between the Moscow City Government and Religious Organizations. This committee is charged with performing specialized analyses of religious organizations' activities and beliefs within the city. City agencies are then to develop new regulations concerning construction, renting, and use of buildings and land for religious purposes.[54] In the wake of this new regulation, there have been several reports that organizations with leases of city property have been told that they can no longer use them for religious meetings.

The law in the Tula region applies only to foreign religious organizations and to missionary activity. It states, among other things, that they can meet only following accreditation and only in buildings set aside for religious use.[55] However, the region has seen a refusal to rent public buildings, even to nationally registered Russian religious organizations, including Adventist and Catholic groups. At the same time, the government, using public funds, has erected a

---

[54] Moscow City Regulation No. 642-PM, "On Measures for Perfecting the Relationships between the Moscow City Government and Religious Organizations in the City and for Regulating the Activities of Pseudo-Religious Organizations" (August 19, 1997), arts. 1, 5, trans. Lawrence A. Uzzell at <www.law.emory.edu/EILR/special/mos.html>.

[55] See Tula Law, arts. 1, 18.

new church building for the Orthodox.[56] This clearly constitutes discrimination based on religious belief, if not an outright establishment of the Orthodox faith, in violation of RF constitutional and statutory protections. It also operates to make second-class citizens of certain types of religious believers, especially of Protestant, Old Believer, and other minority confessions, which in many towns do not have historic, pre-1917 church buildings of their own because they were not allowed to hold property during most of the Czarist era or because their buildings were simply destroyed by the Bolsheviks.

Most troubling is that enforcement of the new regional laws is committed to the discretion of newly created (or newly reopened) local bureaucracies, operating under various names. In Udmurtia, the relevant local bureaucracy is the Expert Consultative Council for Cooperation with Religious Associations. In Sverdlovsk region it is the Expert Consultative Council on Questions of Freedom of Conscience and Creeds. And in Moscow, it is called Committee for Relations between the Moscow Government and Religious Organizations. But whatever their names, all of these new committees share a key common characteristic: all are new organizations specifically assigned to investigate the doctrines and bona fides of new religious groups. For example, the new Sverdlovsk council is explicitly authorized to evaluate the character of a religious group's religious doctrines, rituals, and relations to Russian cultural traditions; to analyze "the social psychological consequences" of the group's activities; and to gather information and opinions on it from other organizations and from private individuals in order to decide whether it should be registered.

In the Soviet period, similar surveillance and regulation was carried out by a system of federally administered Councils for Religious Affairs. The CRA system was abolished by a 1990 Soviet law on religious freedom. The 1990 Law also strictly prohibited re-creation of similar structures. It stated that "[e]xecutive or administrative organs of state authority and state job positions specifically intended to resolve issues related to the exercise of citizens rights to freedom of *religion may not be instituted* on the territory of [Russia]."[57] Unfortunately, those prohibitions were deleted from the 1997 Law. Instead, the 1997 Law provides for creation of special administrative structures and expert councils to evaluate the content of religious beliefs.

The official responsible for registration of religious organizations in the Federal Ministry of Justice informed officials of the U.S. Helsinki Commission in September 1997 that the old CRAs were actually reconstituted and active in three Russian regions—Tatarstan, Bashkortostan, and Daghestan—in September 1997. These are all regions with predominant non-Christian religious traditions that have experienced repressive legislation and extra-legal actions against minorities in recent years. On December 17, 1997, the RF State Duma asked Prime Minister Chernomyrdin to form a new federal agency for religion

---

[56] See Sergei Filatov, Aleksandr Shchipkov, and Lawrence A. Uzzell, "Tula Cracks Down on Religious Minorities," *Keston News Service* 496 (May 1, 1996).

[57] 1990 Law, art. 8 (emphasis added).

to oversee the implementation of the 1997 Law on freedom of conscience and religious organizations.[58] The Duma said that the new agency should monitor compliance with the new law, particularly by "destructive sects and pseudo-religious organizations."[59]

Many of the new regional structures are direct or indirect successors to the old local offices of the Council for Religious Affairs, with antireligious bureaucrats still in power. Quite often, the officials of the new bodies have rich experience in church-state relations as former employees of the Soviet-era Council for Religious Affairs, which worked closely with the KGB to suppress independent religious activity in the interests of the totalitarian atheist state.

Officials who formerly served the supposedly defunct Council for Religious Affairs now hold key posts shaping church-state relations not only in these provincial agencies but also in the federal government, and even in the Orthodox Patriarchate of Moscow. With remarkable effrontery, they protest when commentators mention its numerous past ties to the KGB. It is as if former Gestapo officials had formed policy on treatment of local non-German ethnic populations immediately after the end of the Second World War.

These officials can be expected to act in a discriminatory or even uniformly antireligious manner in the absence of retraining regarding the new legal climate. However, limited judicial resources, a scarcity of human-rights and religious-freedom lawyers, fear on the part of minority groups, and lack of tracking mechanisms—as well as Russia's vast size and complex legal and regulatory structure—mean that administrative fiat and harassment will be hard to overcome. In the short run, these new laws mean that local officials can readily squelch religious freedom for disfavored groups and individuals.

It is also inevitable that the secular authorities will use their powers of licensing and regulating churches to advance or to protect their own political or financial interests. Russia has an almost uninterrupted, three-century habit of treating clergymen as if they were civil servants whose first loyalty is to the state rather than to God.[60]

THE NEW LAWS AT WORK: TWO CASE STUDIES

In travels from St. Petersburg to eastern Siberia, Keston has found that practices vary widely and unpredictably from one province to another. In human rights, as in economic reform and other areas, Russia—for millennia one of history's most hypercentralized and totalitarian states—is turning into a real rather than just a nominal federation. In the long run, this development may be positive, despite the anarchic way in which it is happening and despite the fact that currently most of the provincial governments are still dominated by

---

[58] "Newsline," *Radio Free Europe/Radio Liberty Broadcast* (December 18, 1997).

[59] Ibid.

[60] Ironically, this habit is based not on classic Byzantine Orthodoxy but was imported by Czar Peter I from Lutheran Sweden.

old-guard apparatchiks. Indeed, to this point, the only way humankind has found to govern a continental-sized polity like Russia as a truly free country is to organize it as a decentralized federation, as the examples of the United States and Canada attest.

On the one hand, Russian officials have boldly chosen to ignore the Constitution and other laws in enacting ordinances like those described above and in arbitrary and discriminatory actions against religious minorities. Some enforce these and other laws which violate human rights in an even more repressive fashion than the texts themselves would seem to require. Paradoxically, however, the lawless character of the political culture in which these officials now operate is not always harmful to religious freedom. Some provinces are not actually enforcing the laws that they have enacted. Others have thus far not adopted repressive laws and indeed show every sign of openness to new religious groups and to the rule of law, an openness that will likely mitigate the impact of the repressive federal legislation.

These circumstances lead to some localized situations in which concrete practice is less authoritarian than the new laws on the books. Thus, a strict legal analysis of statutory texts is a more limited tool in Russia than it would be in the West for understanding the real state of religious freedom. It is far more important to observe at close hand how these statutes are actually being implemented.

The Tula region is one of those provinces where concrete practice is more repressive than formal law. Tula's case is especially interesting for several reasons. This region's statute, adopted in November 1994, was the very first of the new provincial laws on church-state relations. Paradoxically, its most active advocate was not a Stalinist reactionary but Nikolai Sevriugin, then regional governor, who was generally seen as pro-reform, at least on economic issues. Sevriugin continued to be a member of former prime minister Yegor Gaidar's pro-reform political party even after that party lost the 1993 parliamentary election.

The Tula Law is also significant because it has been widely circulated as a model for other provinces and even for federal legislation. For example, legislation adopted in the Tyumen region on May 26, 1995, tracked the Tula Law in many details. In the summer of 1995, a Keston representative observed deputies in the Russian Duma, the national legislature, sharing photocopies of the Tula Law with each other. Later in 1995, the Keston News Service visited the Kostroma region, on the upper Volga about 250 miles northeast of Moscow. After considerable difficulty, Keston obtained a copy of draft legislation which had been proposed to the Kostroma regional Duma by the local Orthodox clergy. It turned out to be identical to the Tula region's text, although the language actually adopted via executive order in Kostroma was not as repressive.

As described above, a core, not incidental, feature of Tula's law is discrimination against religious organizations that are foreign in their legal status (or place of incorporation). The law states that it is aimed only at "foreign organizations, representative bodies and representatives."[61] It also states that

---

[61] Tula Law, art. 1.

"unaccredited foreign organizations may not open representative bodies in the region."[62] The law is clearly only aimed at these groups when they have not registered sister organizations in Russia because only foreign organizations have any reason to open representations under Russian law. The Tula Law contradicts both the 1990 and 1997 RF federal laws by providing that accreditation is a mandatory condition for any religious activity. Under the federal laws, accreditation is required not for all activities, but only as a permissive condition for groups that desire to have certain legal rights, such as the rights to hold property corporately, to maintain a corporate bank account, or to hire employees. This is a key problem because Russia has thousands of domestic religious congregations, such as those of the *initsiativniki*, a dissident Baptist sect, which refuse on principle to register with the state. The provisions in the 1990 and 1997 Laws on activities by unregistered groups were intended to protect them.

Empowered to grant or deny accreditation is the Tula region government's plenipotentiary (*upolnomochenny*) on religious questions. The very title is strikingly similar to that of the heads of the old Council for Religious Affairs. This official is the gatekeeper who decides whether representatives of foreign religious groups will get permission (*razresheniye*, a word which appears several times in the statute) to exercise what the 1993 constitution declared to be a fundamental and inalienable right.

The law states that a "foreign" church may invite visiting missionaries. However, such short-term visitors may conduct their activities in the region only "after agreement on their program with the accrediting body."[63] Thus, if a foreign religious leader, even one with international renown such as the late Mother Teresa, is invited to Tula and arrives with a valid religious worker visa and wants to preach or lead a prayer meeting in Tula, local authorities can veto the planned activities purely at their own discretion.

A unique feature of the Tula region is that it is the most important center of the Seventh-day Adventist movement in the entire Russian Federation. The region's capital has a radio studio in which the Adventists record programs which are broadcast across Eurasia by contract with the Russian state radio company. The small country town of Zaokski, on the Oka River north of Tula City, houses a divinity school which trains future Adventist pastors from all over the former Soviet Union. Significantly, neither the radio program nor the divinity school—both of which are highly visible, have numerous international connections, and bring revenues into the local economy—has suffered harassment under the new regional law. Those Adventists who have experienced harassment are the rank and file, local congregations which consist entirely of indigenous Russian citizens, even though neither they nor their organization can be considered "foreign" under the Tula Law. The Seventh-day Adventists were registered prior to and throughout the Soviet period, although they were persecuted greatly.

---

[62] Ibid.
[63] Ibid.

Tula Adventist pastor Pavel Zubkov told Keston in March 1996 about two such episodes. The first took place in the spring of 1995, when the Adventists tried to hold a public meeting in the town of Novomoskovsk. Zubkov discovered that all the posters advertising the meeting had been taken down, apparently because the town's Orthodox pastor had put pressure on the mayor to prevent the meeting. The Adventists then appealed to the regional plenipotentiary on religious affairs, Igor Shelopayev, who told them that they would have to get the consent of the local Orthodox priest before they could proceed with their plans. "As far as I know," Zubkov told Keston, "since then no Protestants have been able to rent halls in that city."

The second episode took place in early 1996, in the city of Yefremov. Having learned from their experience in Novomoskovsk, the local Adventist leaders approached Shelopayev beforehand, asking him if the new regional law would allow a meeting in Yefremov, which they said would be "interconfessional." The plenipotentiary again directed them to negotiate with the local Orthodox priest. Once it became clear that the priest was opposed to such a meeting, the town's mayor told the Adventists that, although he would like to help them, he was powerless to do so. He recommended that, instead of the house of culture, which they had been trying to rent for their meeting, they find a private home—preferably an inconspicuous one on the outskirts of town.

Both these episodes are in keeping with a warning that the Adventists received from Shelopayev in early 1996. According to Petr Kulakov, director of the Adventist radio studio in Tula, the plenipotentiary told him then that Adventist and other non-Orthodox congregations would soon have to stop using houses of culture and other public buildings for their worship services.

Roman Catholics have also come under pressure in Tula. A group of Catholic lay activists told Keston that the College of St. Bonaventure, founded by members of the lone Catholic parish in the region's capital, was finding it increasingly difficult to get even a meeting place. One instructor, Avgustin Manko, said that he was warned that if he continued to "preach Catholic doctrine" he would lose his teaching post at a nearby secular university. He said that the university's dean told him that officers of the ex-KGB had demanded that the college be closed.

When Keston met directly with plenipotentiary Shelopayev to ask him about religious freedom in Tula region, he denied that there had been any discrimination or even complaints of alleged discrimination. "There are equal conditions for all confessions" in the region, he said. On the region's new law, he said that "experience has shown that there is nothing wrong with the new system. There have been no protests, nobody says he has been oppressed." But Shelopayev expressed a different view to a visiting scholar from the Russian Academy of Sciences, acknowledging that state officials "give preference to the Russian Orthodox Church" for the sake of "stability." Shelopayev told Keston that foreign missionaries had "discredited" the very idea of missionary activity because of their frequent ignorance of Russia's history and culture and of the Russian language. "Their own lack of professionalism and lack of respect for the Russian people is what has created the problem," he said. Keston asked whether he believes that freedom of speech should be available only to those with high culture and good manners. The plenipotentiary changed the subject. More significantly, the problems experienced by the Adventist and Catholic churches involve Russians, albeit those who have chosen to embrace religions with only one hundred, as opposed to one thousand, years of historic existence in Russia.

The Roman Catholic activists told Keston that what matters more than the formal provisions of the regional law is the Tula authorities' position that everyone other than the Orthodox is inferior. The law, they said, is important mainly as a symbol of that position. The authorities' behavior toward the Adventists clearly confirms this view. The region's Adventist institutions are all led by Russians—some of whose families have been Adventist for several generations—even though they preach doctrines formulated in America, just as the Russian Orthodox Church preaches doctrines imported from Constantinople. If the Russian Federation were a truly law-governed state and the Tula region a law-governed province, the regional statute aimed explicitly at foreigners would be irrelevant to such a group. But in practice the law has served as a signal to Tula's own regional and municipal officials, assuring them that they are free to crack down on minority confessions regardless of their members' nationality.

The new regulations in Kostroma region may be a signal of a different kind—that regional laws may sometimes be a way for the region's secular authorities to appease its Orthodox clergy without actually doing anything serious to restrict the activities of non-Orthodox believers. Though the lack of true *glasnost* in Kostroma makes it difficult even to get the full official text of the region's May 1995 executive order on church-state relations, much less a candid explanation of the regional authorities' motives, at least two points are clear. First, the new order (*postanovleniye*) clearly contradicts the 1990 federal law and 1993 constitution. Second, the order is not being enforced at all in practice; as far as Kostroma's religious minorities are concerned, it might as well not exist.

Kostroma's enacted executive order is much shorter and milder than the law in Tula, although an interim draft of the Kostroma regional Duma followed it to the letter. Several of its provisions are apparently aimed solely at "extrasensory" charlatans who claim to practice "mass healing." To these "charlatans," the law denies access to public auditoriums and the mass media. There is some basis for this restriction. Fraudulent "mass healings" and other types of religious "performance" have led to deception and fleecing of the unsuspecting in Russia, just as in the United States. Unfortunately, the Kostroma rules were not drafted in such a way as to draw a clear distinction between such healing entrepreneurs and bona fide clergymen and believers who simply pray for the sick as part of their overall ministry.

A more serious violation of the RF Constitution and laws is found in Point Four of the executive order, which instructs the local police to stop foreign missionaries from distributing publications which promote "negative attitudes towards history and culture" or which "distort or violate the universal principles and norms of civilized society." It is impossible to understand what types of publications the authors of this order had in mind.

In October 1995, two representatives of the Keston Institute visited Mikhail Kuznetsov, the Kostroma regional government's specialist on relations with religious groups, to discuss the religious situation in the region. Kuznetsov in the Soviet era served as plenipotentiary for the Council for Religious Affairs in the region. He told Keston that none of the Western missionaries in Kostroma had complained about the new executive order, but under questioning, he admitted that he had never shown any of them the text, either before it was formally adopted or since. When asked for a copy, he replied that the text was available only to state officials, not to journalists or other members of the general public. Keston noted that the 1993 Russian Constitution requires that all laws be published. Kuznetsov insisted that the document in question was not a law (*zakon*), but an executive order (*postanovleniye*) and thus exempt from the operation of that constitutional provision. Keston asked: "How can people be expected to obey an edict which they have never been allowed to read?" Eventually Kuznetsov agreed to let the Keston representatives look at a handwritten document which he said was a copy of the order. However, that turned out to be not entirely accurate, as Keston found later after obtaining the full text of the executive order through other channels. But the document in Kuznetsov's office did include most of the controversial Point Four.

Keston suggested to the plenipotentiary that Orthodox icons are a fundamental part of Russian "history and culture," and asked who would decide whether a Protestant tract calling icons unscriptural would fall under Point Four's prohibition. He answered that the decision would be made by lawyers in the region's Administration of Justice. He added, "I personally think that this point was probably not necessary." Keston asked, "Doesn't it contradict the provisions in the federal constitution on freedom of speech?" "Maybe," Kuznetsov replied. "It's better to let each congregation go about its business." Yet despite his willingness to back down when challenged on this and other points, he showed no sign of being ready to call for the executive order's withdrawal or revision.

As soon as the executive order was issued, four months before Keston's visit to Kostroma, a local Russian journalist learned about it. As part of an article for the *Kostromskiye Vedomosti* newspaper, which is controlled by the more pro-reform Kostroma city government rather than by the regional authorities, the Russian journalist sought out various Western Protestant missionaries to find out what effect the new policy was having on them. To his surprise, it turned out that the missionaries had never even heard of the executive order and that they were continuing to distribute their tracts in public with no interference from the police. Indeed, they were experiencing no repression whatsoever. "The whole thing was news to them," the journalist told Keston. When Keston made its own calls to missionaries in October, the response was the same. One American pastor said that his congregation's worship services and educational programs had remained completely undisturbed;

the only reason he knew that such an executive order even existed was his conversation with the Russian journalist four months earlier.

Kostroma is not unique. Several months after the Sverdlovsk region adopted its harsh new law in November 1996, local sources told Keston that regional officials were virtually ignoring it because they considered it unenforceable, unconstitutional, or both. But, unfortunately, Tula seems to be more typical. In 1996 visits to the Irkutsk region, the Sakha republic (about five thousand miles east of Moscow), Ulyanovsk region and the Tatarstan republic (about five hundred miles east of Moscow), Keston found great variety in practice with Sakha having the most religious freedom and Ulyanovsk the least but in every case concrete practice was less free than the formal laws on the books.

THE IMPACT AND INTERPRETATION OF THE 1997 LAW IN THE REGIONS

The adoption of the 1997 Law should have put a stop to most disputes in the regions, clarifying treatment of foreigners, foreign religious organizations, and newer religious organizations. It temporarily froze registration for the period October 1997 to March 1998, when implementing regulations were promulgated. It gave currently registered organizations until December 31, 1999, to re-register.

The 1997 Law has its own set of problems, however. Specifically, it sets out a scheme of reduced rights for religious organizations and unregistered religious groups that have not "existed" in Russia for at least fifteen years. In particular, the law says that organizations that cannot make this showing may not issue invitations to foreign religious workers, work in schools and other public institutions, or engage in various other activities.[64] Further, central government authorities have issued an "instruction" to all levels of the Ministry of Justice, including regional and local divisions, to ignore the fifteen-year rule with regard to organizations that were legally registered before the 1997 Law was adopted.

Nonetheless, there has been a rash of new reports of actions in the regions that are inconsistent with the provisions of the law, that interpret the law inconsistently with the central Ministry of Justice instruction, or that go far beyond the terms of the law in discriminating against disfavored groups. Some local governments, for example, tried to shut down currently registered organizations immediately following adoption of the new law, even though it gave them until December 1999 to re-register.

For example, a Russian Lutheran congregation in the Republic of Khakassia was told on the date the statute was signed into law by President Yeltsin that it was closed because of the new law. Yet this congregation was Russian, was locally registered, and had until December 1999 to re-register. Moreover, the implementing regulations had not yet been released, and the law requires a court hearing prior to dissolution of a religious organization. Following pro-

---

[64] 1997 Law, art. 27.3.

tests and a series of telephone calls from Moscow, the local Ministry of Justice rescinded its order canceling the Lutheran group's registration in late 1997. Yet the provincial government's advisor on church-state relations stated that he would continue to work to close the church.

Within the next several months, the pastor of the Lutheran Church reported that all the signatories to the registration application received several personal visits from the local police and from the more feared FSB (formerly the KGB) asking why they had agreed to sponsor this religious group. Another action was brought to close the church and was dismissed because it was procedurally flawed, being brought in a court that lacked jurisdiction over this type of dispute. Further actual and threatened actions have occurred, all because the church receives some support from American Lutheran organizations.

Local authorities also attempted to stop activities by a Pentecostal congregation of an evangelistic nature in local children's homes.[65] The provincial government's adviser on church-state relations, Nikolai Volkov, in a January 1998 radio interview, called the *Proslavleniye* ("glorification") church one of the "destructive cults or totalitarian sects" which "turn people into bio-robots." He told listeners that under the new law the church will be forced to close all its educational institutions and forbidden to obtain or distribute religious literature. But he added that it is impossible to close the church altogether—"unfortunately." Asked how "non-traditional religions" had come to appear in Russia, Volkov replied: "America—a sewage ditch—when it was created all sorts of rabble thronged there, and Protestantism and all sorts of non-traditional religions arose there." In fact, the *Proslavleniye* church is affiliated with the *Slovo Zhizni* ("Word of Life") movement based in Sweden. The original homeland of Protestantism, is, of course, in Western Europe.

The same official has expressed the view that only two religions are "respectable": Orthodox Christianity and Roman Catholicism.[66] Volkov said his goal is to promote a policy of "protectionism of the religions which are traditional in Khakassia," shielding them against competition from newcomers. (However, he has gone so far as to tell the pastor of the *Proslavleniye* church to suspend the practice of speaking in tongues.) Asked by Keston News Service which confessions should be considered "traditional" in this province, he listed the Orthodox Christians, Old Believers, Roman Catholics, Lutherans, Baptists, Pentecostals, Jehovah's Witnesses, Molokans (a small, Protestant-like offshoot of Orthodoxy), Jews, and Muslims.

Given this list, his reasoning for attacking both a Lutheran and a Pentecostal church likely has more to do with their foreign connections and relative affluence than real religious motivations. At the same time, Catholic congregations are left alone, although they should be treated in the same manner, given Volkov's interpretation of the new law. In dealings with the Lutheran and Pentecostal congregations, this official clearly intends to read the 1997

---

[65] *Keston News Service* (March 13, 1998); *Keston News Service* (March 20, 1998).
[66] *Keston News Service* (March 20, 1998); *Keston News Service* (March 17, 1998).

Law literally and to act as if Article 27.3 is in effect until the congregations reregister and prove either fifteen years of existence in Russia or membership in a centralized religious organization. These cases plainly demonstrate the power of local officials to harass disfavored groups. Although both organizations have hired lawyers and succeeded in defeating Volkov's efforts to stop their activities, this is a major drain on their energies and resources, and central government officials have been able to exert little influence over the situation.

A widely publicized case in Kahbarovsk involved the abrupt deportation of Dan Pollard, an American pastor of a registered, independent Baptist congregation. There again, the local official interpreted Article 27.3 to be fully effective and thus stated that the congregation had no right to give a visa invitation to a foreign religious worker.

There have been many other examples of local harassment of newer or disfavored groups since the enactment of the new law. For example, in November 1997, a Pentecostal congregation was expelled from a schoolroom which it had been renting for evening and Sunday worship services in Izmailovsky, just south of Moscow, and was forced to meet in the flats of its members. The congregation is a member of the Union of Christians of the Evangelical Faith-Pentecostals, which is registered as a centralized religious organization. There were reports of behind-the-scenes pressure from the Orthodox Church.

Other incidents have been reported in the Moscow *oblast*, the region surrounding but not including the City of Moscow, ranging from arrests of pastors visiting from the center of the city in private flats to termination of long-term leases. Yuri Vlasov, head of the Directorate of Justice of the Moscow *oblast*, told Keston News Service on November 18, 1997, that a congregation founded less than fifteen years ago and not registered as of October 1997 will not be eligible for any form of registration. He said that he plans to withhold registration from congregations which functioned quasi-legally or illegally under the pre-*glasnost* Soviet regime, and that such congregations will be able to receive registration only by filing and winning court cases.

There have been numerous incidents of harassment and threats against religious groups throughout other parts of Russia. The most frequent victims are the pastors and congregants of Russian-led churches, rather than foreigners with better connections. It appears that each must seek legal counsel and other forms of redress and that it will be a lengthy process for the regions to become informed about and willing to comply with the central government's interpretation of the new law.

Of the 14,688 religious organizations registered in the RF as of January 1, 1997, over 3,000 are not affiliated with the Moscow Patriarchate, Islam, Buddhism, or Judaism. The vast majority of these organizations appears to be registered as local and not as centralized organizations. If a significant percentage is subjected to similar arbitrary tactics by regional officials in the wake of the perception of a crackdown on belief caused by the new law, there will be an avalanche of complaints requiring administrative or legal intervention.

TWO LEGAL CHALLENGES TO THE LOCAL ORDINANCES

The past two years have seen two significant court challenges to the patently illegal and unconstitutional aspects of the regional laws. One, a challenge to the laws of Tula and Tyumen in the RF Constitutional Court, was brought by members of the national Duma. Although it ultimately failed, the mere fact that ninety national leaders supported the appeal points to the existence in Russia of a principled, well-informed lobby for religious human rights. The other challenge may be even more significant, as it resulted in the overturning—by an exceptionally well-reasoned opinion—of an oppressive Udmurt Law by the regional court in Udmurtia.

THE FAILED CONSTITUTIONAL CHALLENGE TO THE LAWS OF TULA AND TYUMEN

In a typical example of the surreal nature of law and justice in today's Russia, federal officials in Moscow, while freely admitting that these provincial laws are unconstitutional, make little effort to counter them. As of early 1997, not one provincial official had been significantly penalized, pressured, or criticized by the central executive branch authorities for enacting or enforcing such laws. For example, in response to a complaint from the United States Embassy concerning the impending closure of the Evangelical Lutheran Mission in Khakassia, the office of Prime Minister Victor Chernomyrdin stated that it was wholly illegal under the new RF law. Yet officials in the office stated that there was nothing they could do about it. Notwithstanding that disclaimer, however, telephone calls were apparently placed to the region from Moscow and the threat was withdrawn, which shows that "telephone justice" may still have some advantages in the current lawlessness of the regions. In a private conversation with an official in the Ministry of Justice about this problem, one of the authors was told that courts in the regions often do not meet for scheduled criminal proceedings due to a lack of heating or even of paper to record proceedings. Thus, threatened imposition of laws affecting religious minorities are not a high federal law enforcement priority.

A document prepared by former Duma deputies and religious freedom experts Gleb Yakunin and Vyacheslav Polosin in late 1996 detailed their 1995 efforts to address these issues. Along with Deputy Valery Borshchov, still deputy chair of the Duma's Committee on Public and Religious Organizations, Yakunin and Polosin used a letter-writing campaign and other pressures to call attention to the new repressive laws in Tula and Tyumen.[67] Their activities led to the filing of the lawsuit in the RF Constitutional Court in December 1995 challenging the Tula and Tyumen laws.

---

[67] Yakunin and Polosin, "Federal Authorities."

They note that the justification for the local laws is a "gap" in federal legislation in the area of keeping track of missionary work in the regions and of individual foreign missionaries, requiring accreditation.[68] Also, local authorities believe that protests from local residents and clergy require taking such steps as refusing access to public buildings, allowing only "pre-cleared" preachers to speak, and reducing access to children, schools, media, advertising, and other public forums. Following failed appeals from federal deputies to the Prosecutor General's Office in Tula to intervene, the law was challenged in a direct appeal to the RF Constitutional Court in early December 1995. The appeal was signed by ninety deputies of the RF Duma, as required by the regulations of the Constitutional Court. (Appeals also may be brought by organizations affected by a law.) The Tyumen Law was also challenged in the same appeal.[69] Many of the Duma deputies were not re-elected during the 1995 Duma elections later that month,[70] however, and the case was dismissed for lack of standing after two of the deputies withdrew their names.[71]

Nonetheless, Polosin and Yakunin maintain that the efforts of the deputies have borne "some fruit." The deputy prosecutor general of the RF wrote a letter to the Duma stating that the unequal treatment of foreign missionaries and organizations in the Tyumen law was unlawful, as was the fee. The letter led to the modification of the law, as described above. Polosin and Yakunin reported that they also persuaded the prosecutor general to intervene in the Khabarovsk Territory on the fee issue—although this initiative was ultimately rejected by local deputies—and in the Tula, Kaliningrad, and Tver regions.[72]

THE SUCCESSFUL CHALLENGE TO THE UDMURT LAW

A unique and fully successful challenge was mounted against the law of the Udmurt Republic by a group of Russian citizens who are members of various churches of Evangelical Christians in various towns in the region. These churches are part of a centralized Russian Pentecostal Union, but trace their roots to a U.S. branch of the Assemblies of God. Their leadership was jailed during the Soviet period, and they had been refused the right to register until after the 1990 Law was enacted. At least one of the churches was registered with the Udmurt Republic in accordance with the 1990 Law, and its charter stated that one of its goals was missionary activity. Other plaintiffs explained that disseminating the gospel and seeking new converts were essential elements of their Christian faith. The case and its outcome are all the more remarkable because the union lacked funds to transport a lawyer to Ishevsk or

---

[68] Ibid., 17-18.

[69] Ibid., 26.

[70] Ibid., 23, 26.

[71] Direct appeals to the RF Constitutional Court require the signatures of ninety Duma deputies. Many of the signers of the appeal lost their seats in 1995.

[72] Yakunin and Polosin, "Federal Authorities," 23-24.

to hire a local lawyer. The plaintiffs were reduced to handling the case pro se, with legal counsel coming only by telephone from attorneys based in Moscow.

The seven complainants appealed to the Supreme Court of the Udmurt Republic, based on evidence of events that quickly followed the entering into force of the Udmurt Law on August 28, 1996, following its May 26, 1996, adoption.[73] In sum, in a set of circumstances directly applying the essence of the law, two church members were arrested for lack of accreditation and for lacking an Udmurt residence permit when they attempted to conduct missionary activity in an Udmurt village.[74] They were forced to pay a fine of 75,900 rubles, and their church was later required to pay a fee of 759,000 rubles (approximately $152) in order to attain accreditation and stay out of trouble with local police.[75] Other churches suffered immediate cancellations of rental agreements and expulsion from cultural centers and other buildings previously used for religious services, resulting in closure of public places of worship and a Sunday School.[76]

This was followed by various forms of official harassment. Local governments began refusing to rent buildings to religious groups. Believers inclined to engage in proselytism had reason to fear fines and other punishment. In at least one case, authorities arrested a couple merely for holding a prayer meeting in their own apartment. In short, while purporting to affect only missionary and proselytizing activities by Russian citizens, the law also brought about the virtual cessation of activities of fully registered religious organization with rights under the 1990 Law.[77]

The complainants maintained that the Udmurt Law was unconstitutional on several grounds. First, they argued that it usurped an area of regulation within the exclusive jurisdiction of the Russian Federation, under Article 71 of the Constitution. Second, they alleged that the law was in conflict with the 1990 federal law, which provided comprehensively for regulation of religious activities. Third, they asserted that it constituted an unconstitutional restraint on receiving and disseminating religious beliefs. (In this regard, they also argued that the Udmurt Law violated the 1990 Law, as well as Russia's international human-rights commitments.) Finally, the complainants argued that the law transgressed the Constitution in that it discriminated against Russian citizens who were not residents of the Udmurt region.[78]

---

[73] Case of Mashgatova Svetlana Pavlovna et al. concerning the Law of the Udmurt Republic "On Missionary Activity on the Territory of the Udmurt Republic" (Supreme Court of the Udmurt ASSR, Collegium for Civil Cases (March 5, 1997), trans. as Appendix F, *Emory International Law Review* 12 (1998): 715-38 [hereafter "Udmurt Opinion"].

[74] Ibid.

[75] Ibid.

[76] Ibid.

[77] Ibid.

[78] Ibid.

The position of the government was that the law arose from "objective need in connection with the significant activization of religious activity in the country and the spreading of nontraditional religions and missionary movements actively supported and financed from abroad and the necessity that had arisen of protecting citizens from the activity of totalitarian, destructive sects."[79] Their representatives stated that few religious groups had complained. They claimed that the law was permissive, not restrictive in nature; that it did not regulate the substance of missionary activity but only its limits; and that it was within the legal competence of the republic.[80] Testimony by a representative of the local passport and visa office was that there was no special federal visa regime for foreign religious workers, which is instead controlled at the level of visa invitations. The government also acknowledged that federal law did not support the requirement in the law that visitors register their visas and passports within twenty-four hours of arrival.[81]

The court agreed with virtually all of the plaintiffs' claims. In a sixteen-page statement of findings, the court significantly held that the Udmurt Law was in violation of the republic's constitutionally restricted competence. It found that Articles 14, 19, 28, 55.2, and 71 of the RF Constitution, comparable provisions in Articles 15, 17, and 28 of the Udmurt Republic's own Constitution, and the enactment of the 1990 Law operated to make regulation of the establishment of religious organizations and the religious activities of individuals a matter of exclusively federal jurisdiction, in terms of normative or positive law prescriptions. Effectively preempted by this federal legislation, the states are permitted only to protect and expand upon the federally created freedoms; they may not impose additional restrictions.

> [T]he court concludes that the resolution of questions connected with the implementation and realization of the constitutional right of the individual and citizen on the territory of Russia must be enacted in accordance with the RF Constitution and Federal Legislation, in particular with the RSFSR Law "On freedom of confession" and other federal laws. Subjects of the Russian Federation can adopt laws and other normative acts only on questions of the defense of the rights and freedoms of citizens. Normative acts adopted by subjects of the Russian Federation which contradict the RF Constitution and federal laws and restrict the right and freedom of citizens in the implementation and realization of constitutional rights are illegal.[82]

Analyzing the law appealed against by the citizens, the court concluded that the Law "On Missionary Activity on the Territory of the Udmurt Repub-

---

[79] Ibid.
[80] Ibid.
[81] Ibid.
[82] Ibid.

lic" prescribed a special system of legal regulation which violated the constitutional rights of citizens envisaged by Article 28 of the RF Constitution. In addition, the court concluded that the State Council of the Udmurt Republic, in adopting the law introducing a special system of legal regulation of missionary activity on the territory of Udmurtia, exceeded the competence of a subject of the Russian Federation.

This holding is itself sufficient to invalidate not only the Udmurt Law but the range of other local ordinances adopted by other subjects of the RF. In essence, it concludes, in a manner similar to U.S. decisions involving the "Supremacy Clause" of the United States Constitution, that once the federal government has undertaken to regulate an area, implementing an area of legislative competence entrusted to the federal government by the Constitution, this statute is not only controlling as against inconsistent local laws, but it usurps the entire area of statutory regulation of the matter at issue. Thus, once the RF government has undertaken to enact laws dealing with its areas of exclusive jurisdiction under Article 71 of the RF Constitution, local governments may act only further to safeguard citizens' rights or to implement the provisions of the federal law and may not enact their own regulatory schemes in the field.

Moreover, the court went on to deal with the substantive violations of the constitutional rights of freedom of conscience: to choose, hold, and disseminate religious beliefs.[83] It observed that "missionary activity is one of the forms of disseminating and professing a faith and thus an integral part of the right of the individual and the citizen to freedom of confession guaranteed in the RF Constitution."[84] It rejected the Udmurt Republic's claim that its law was valid because it granted rights to engage in missionary activity, stating that these rights were "an integral part of religious activity on the basis of the Constitutions of the RF and the Udmurt Republic." The court observed that Article 18 of the RF Constitution creates such rights directly; the validity of these rights does not depend upon any additional legislative confirmation, much less a legislative grant.[85]

The court further held that in forbidding the activity of non-accredited missionaries and in conditioning such activity on accreditation, Article 3 of the law "crudely violates" and restricts the rights of citizens to freedom of confession guaranteed in Articles 28 and 29 of the RF Constitution and the 1990 Law.[86] It held that limitations on the time for which missionary activity could be carried out (one year following accreditation) and requiring registration within twenty-four hours of arrival in Udmurtia were unlawful, with the former affecting "rights and freedoms of the individual [that] are inalienable and be-

---

[83] See Konstitutsiia RF (Constitution of the Russian Federation), arts. 3, 17.2 (1993), trans. in Vladimir V. Belyakov and Walter J. Raymond, eds., *Constitution of the Russian Federation* (Lawrenceville, Va., 1994) [hereafter "Konst. RF"].

[84] Udmurt Opinion.

[85] Ibid.

[86] Ibid.

long to everyone from birth," quoting Article 17.2 of the RF Constitution. It also found unconstitutional the provision conditioning the constitutional right to disseminate beliefs on "a norm for the period of consideration of the documents" and payment of a fee. The latter was also said to "crudely violate" the constitutional rights of citizens "as the implementation of the given constitutional right is subject to material dependency, which contradicts the Constitution of the RF and the Udmurt Republic which enshrine the principle that the rights and freedoms of citizens are valid directly." In other words, requiring citizens to pay in order to exercise a "self executing" constitutional right is itself unconstitutional.[87]

This aspect of the decision could be used to call into question all fees for registration of religious organizations, which were specifically not required under the 1990 Law but are a common feature of the regional regulations.[88] Likewise, the conclusion that a regulatory waiting period for government approval prior to engaging in religious speech is unconstitutional has major implications for the various waiting periods set forth in the new federal legislation, as well as in the various regional laws.

The court also went on to find that the limitation of places in which missionary activity could occur "significantly restricts the constitutional right of citizens to freedom of conscience and confession" and that "[t]he absolute ban on missionary activity in all public places . . . contradicts Art. 31 of the RF Constitution and part 5 of Art. 22 of the RF Law 'On freedom of confession.'"[89] Moreover, the court held that the restrictions on forms of missionary activity and the conditioning of dissemination of religious literature, holding of concerts, showing of films and videos, and the conducting of charitable activity on accreditation violated Articles 28 and 29 of the Constitution and Articles 15, 17, and 24 of the 1990 Law, all of which grant these rights irrespective of creation of legal entities.[90]

The court also invalidated the differential treatment of citizens from outside the Udmurt Republic in Article 14 of the Udmurt Law as violative of Article 6.2 of the RF Constitution, "which lays down that 'every citizen of the Russian Federation enjoys all rights and freedoms on its territory and holds equal obligations enshrined in the Constitution.'"[91]

The court also found that the provision in the law requiring reports on changes in personnel of missionary organizations was "not based on current

---

[87] See Konst. RF, art. 18. The court also found that the fee provisions contradict articles 20, 21, and 18 of the RF Law, "On the Principles of the Tax System of the Russian Federation," Federal Law No. 2118-1 of 27 (December 1992) (with subsequent amendments and additions).

[88] Some Russian commentators have concluded that they were as much a local government revenue device as a principled effort to bring "order" into the realm of religious life in Russia. See, e.g., Levinson, "Local Law," 6-7.

[89] Udmurt Opinion.

[90] Ibid.

[91] Ibid. (quoting Konst. RF, art. 6.2).

federal legislation," which required no such reporting. (Although the 1997 Law does require annual filing of reports, there is no requirement that personnel changes be reported within three days of their occurrence, as stipulated in the Udmurt Law.) It went further and found that the entire scheme of administrative regulation and fines for violations "crudely violates the constitutional rights of citizens, as the defense and regulation of the rights of citizens lies, according to Art. 71 of the Russian Constitution, within the competence of the Russian Federation."[92]

This decision is a truly stunning victory for religious-freedom activists in Russia. Although it applies only to a single Russian territory, the decision could not have been more legally or politically courageous. It cannot be treated as the product of a liberal region or political structure because it was vigorously defended in court by local officials.[93] Moreover, the breadth of its analysis and comprehensive invalidation of all of the key provisions of the legislation in the Udmurt Republic provide a blueprint for other regional courts that may be required to consider the same matters. The decision should serve as a model for the RF Constitutional Court, should that court have an opportunity to consider the regional laws or conflicts between the 1997 Law and the RF Constitution.

It is important for foreign observers to realize that the rule of law and the independence of the judiciary are very recent developments in Russia. The Udmurt decision is the equivalent of the U.S. Supreme Court's decision in *Marbury v. Madison*[94] in determining the scope of federal power versus state authority and the principle of judicial review of legislative and executive branch decisions in light of constitutional protections of citizens. The laws of the regions discussed in this chapter are, as the Udmurt Supreme Court held, unlawful and in conflict with the plainly stated rights granted by the RF Constitution and those of the regions and by federal law, even including the new version of the law "On Freedom of Conscience."

AN UNCERTAIN OUTLOOK

The great decision facing Russia now is whether both its government and its populace will be willing to submit to the high standards they have set for themselves in their governing documents and international agreements. In early 1997, the decision in the Udmurt Republic and other signs of hope at the provincial level gave some promise that the worst fears engendered by the new

---

[92] Ibid.

[93] The same court, at the same time, also invalidated other antidemocratic actions of the Udmurt government, whose governor had summarily dismissed the occupants of lower-level elective offices, including the mayor of Ishev, and replaced them with his own nominees.

[94] 5 U.S. (1 Cranch) 137 (1803).

regional laws might not be realized. During the first four months of 1997, the governor of St. Petersburg vetoed, for the second time, anti-missionary legislation passed by the city council; the administration of the Yaroslavl region dropped consideration of an especially harsh anti-missionary bill after receiving a withering critique drafted by Moscow's Institute of Law and Religion; and local officials refused to enforce an equally harsh, newly enacted law in the Sverdlovsk Region, partly because the respected adviser on church-state relations to the mayor of Yekaterinburg advised her colleagues that the law was unconstitutional. Later in 1997, the government of Khakassia lost two successive attempts unlawfully to close a registered church on the basis of the newly enacted federal law.

Although the Russian parliament abandoned the liberal 1990 Law by adopting the more restrictive 1997 Law in September 1997, it adopted the European Convention on Human Rights in March 1998, signaling its willingness to continue to move toward Western human-rights and religious-freedom standards. The only alternative is a return to the standards of the past, in which laws do not mean what they say and are subject to arbitrary implementation and the dictates of the majority (or at least the majority of those in power).

There is substantial evidence that federal and regional courts in Russia are rising to the challenge of establishing the rule of law through judicial decision. Further, bringing lawyers into the picture has resulted in positive outcomes in disputes with regional authorities in many instances. The struggle for uniform federal laws and for regional autonomy will continue for years to come.

The passage of the repressive new 1997 Law creates the tantalizing, but far from wholly satisfactory, possibility of a truly "federalist" solution to the problem of religious freedom in Russia. Before this law was passed, decentralization of policy-making on church-state relations seemed to mean the transfer of decision-making from a relatively tolerant and pro-reform national government to mostly intolerant and anti-reform provincial governments. But now that the national government has itself embraced more repressive legislation, a federalist scenario may offer hope for preserving and creating islands of freedom at the regional and local level if national backward movement continues. Just as some regions have managed to create local legal environments that favor free markets and development of small business, some regions may determine that religious freedom and equal treatment of citizens and of foreigners are in their best interests.

Decisions invalidating restrictive laws by local courts, such as that of Udmurtia; decisions by regulators not to enforce restrictive laws; and decisions by local legislatures not to enact them and to ignore repressive national legislation may mean that the rights of religious minorities will continue to vary widely from one region to another, much as they did in the United States during the late eighteenth and early nineteenth centuries.

This may give Russia a chance to see the results of different models of church-state relations and of religious freedom. While hardly the best result from the perspective of the rule of law and international treaties and agreements, the federalist scenario may now offer the best opportunity for letting Russians see for themselves which models of church-state relations work best. Church leaders will have a chance to see whether Orthodox church life actually turns out to be more vigorous in those provinces which rely on coercion rather than free competition as the organizing principle of church-state relations. It will be interesting to see whether extremist, pseudo-religious "cults" do less damage when driven underground than when open and visible. Ultimately people are persuaded to embrace freedom not by abstract argument but by their own experience.

We can conclude only by saying that the regional laws are symptomatic of the widespread malaise with the social, economic, and spiritual consequences of seventy-five years of totalitarian rule, followed by an anarchic path toward free markets and democracy. Their inconsistency with legal norms is clear. The real test of the will of the Russian people to submit to the rule of law will come in the near future as its courts and its citizens continue to evaluate these laws in light of those legal norms and to decide whether to obey them or to disregard them, in keeping with centuries of Russian tradition. Additionally, the willingness of provincial governments to conform their laws to federal standards will be part of the ongoing battle for a new federal-regional relationship.

Part Three

SIGNPOSTS FOR A NEW WAY

———◆———

16.

GUIDELINES
FOR AMERICAN MISSIONARIES
IN RUSSIA

Lawrence A. Uzzell

In religion, as in other areas of life, bad manners usually should not be out-lawed. Advocates of religious freedom correctly argue that the state should tolerate even boorish exercises of that freedom—if politicians and bureaucrats are given the power to curb religious activities which seem overly aggressive or obnoxious, eventually they will use that power to ban expressions of unpopu-lar religious views simply because they are unpopular. Nevertheless, bad man-ners remain bad manners.

Not only rudeness, but arrogance, provincialism, willful ignorance, ma-nipulative tactics which fall just barely short of outright fraud or bribery—all these forms of behavior should be repudiated by all serious missionaries, espe-cially by those who insist that such behavior should not be legally prohibited. Such a voluntary repudiation would be a logical corollary of the general prin-ciple that Christians in every walk of life should set for themselves higher standards than merely obeying the secular laws. Many nonbelievers accept that principle as well: Medical or legal practitioners, among others, are accus-tomed to voluntary codes of ethics which they pledge to observe as part of their commitment to the well-being of those whom they serve and to the integ-rity of their own profession.

A code of ethics is especially overdue for American Protestant missionaries in Russia. Presumably none of these missionaries would accept the abstract proposition that the end justifies the means. But they have failed to make clear, either to others or to themselves, what means are and are not acceptable to

324 • Lawrence A. Uzzell

advance their goals. What they need is what we all need when tempted by self-serving relativism: a precise, objective body of principles plus the will to enforce those principles on ourselves, even if it hurts.

What follows is one American's attempt to draft such a voluntary code of conduct, based on more than six years of personal experience in Russia combined with the wealth of vicarious information available to the Keston Institute. Comments from all affected, both missionaries and their potential converts, would be welcome. In the long run such a code of conduct can take root only if it grows out of dialogue.

First, missionaries should take the trouble to study the language, culture, and history of the people they are presuming to "save." More than a decade after the doors opened to foreign missionaries, all too often Protestants gather in Moscow for conferences where everything has to be translated into English because most of the Americans present do not know Russian. In effect, these missionaries are conveying the message that their Russian hosts should adapt to them rather than vice versa. Russia is a country where tens of millions of people have intensively studied English and other languages of Western countries which they never expect to visit, a country where some classic American authors are more widely read than they are by today's Americans. It is also a country with one of the greatest literary traditions in the world—a tradition which reached its peak only a century ago, so that its classics are still reasonably accessible even if one learns only contemporary Russian. For Americans to live for years on end in Russia without seriously studying the language is simply insulting.

One can master the Russian language but still be culturally illiterate. American missionaries who do not appreciate that the ancestors of today's Muscovites lived in a Christian country centuries before Columbus set sail are just as unqualified to serve in Russia as if they did not know the difference between St. Peter and St. Paul. The Americans who swept into Russia in the early 1990s as if it were a land of pagan savages who had never heard the Gospel bear a large share of the responsibility for the resentments and conflicts which followed. As one American Protestant with extensive experience in Russia told Keston, the Protestant cause would have fared better if America had sent only one-tenth as many missionaries to Russia, and if those missionaries had been ten times as well prepared.

What would one think of missionaries who set themselves the goal of spreading Protestantism in Latin America but who had never experienced a Roman Catholic Mass? Keston's experience suggests that such willful ignorance is not merely frequent, but typical among American Protestant missionaries in Moscow. Those who have sampled Orthodox Christian worship have usually done so only by listening to a few minutes of an untranslated service in Old Church Slavonic—roughly as accessible to foreigners, even those who have studied contemporary Russian, as an unadapted, unannotated performance of Shakespeare would be to a Russian.

The overwhelming majority of Americans live within a few hours' drive of an Orthodox parish which worships partly or entirely in English; visiting such a parish should be as much a part of any serious Christian's preparation for a trip to Russia as buying a guidebook. Those already in Russia can sample the Moscow outpost of the Orthodox Church in America—St. Katherine's Church, next to the Israeli Embassy. St. Katherine's has priests from America and England, an English-speaking Russian choir, and a bookstore which sells copies of the Orthodox Liturgy in Old Church Slavonic with parallel English translation. A few Protestant missionaries have dropped by, but not many.

Second, missionaries should avoid behaving as if the Gospel and the American way of life are identical. All too often American missionaries seem to assume that because America's economy and political system are more successful than Russia's, it automatically follows that America's religious customs are also superior. In 1996 Keston interviewed a former student at a Baptist seminary in Moscow who dropped out because the seminary's American sponsors wanted him to study English rather than Greek; he is now a Russian Orthodox priest. On another occasion Keston attended a U.S.-sponsored "prayer breakfast" at Moscow's luxurious Olympic Penta Hotel. Except for the translation into Russian, this gathering could have been taking place in the American Bible Belt; its organizers did not change even one nuance to accommodate Russian customs, even Protestant Russian customs. For example, they either did not know or did not care that Russian Baptists, like Russian Orthodox, stand rather than sit to pray.

Such unconscious (one hopes they are unconscious) assumptions of American cultural superiority reach their absurd extremes when impressionable young Russians begin to internalize them. Russian Christians, both Orthodox and Protestant, have complained to Keston about Russian students at U.S.-financed Protestant seminaries who have begun speaking Russian, their native language, with American-style intonations—somewhat like nineteenth-century Russian aristocrats infatuated with French.

To be fair, it was easy for both American and Russian Protestants to fall into such traps in the early 1990s. At a time when everything American was wildly and irrationally fashionable in Russia, Protestantism's strongest selling point was that it was seen as the religion of America. But when the pendulum began swinging the other way, the missionaries who rode that trend paid the price Christians usually pay when they hitch themselves to fleeting secular fads. Thus, in visits in the mid-1990s to provincial Russian cities such as Irkutsk, Keston found that Protestant congregations founded and run by American missionaries were shrinking while those headed by indigenous Russian pastors were still growing. It is now the enemies of Protestantism in Russia who continue to stress its American links—to the point that one old-style communist bureaucrat in Siberia even told a radio audience in early 1998 that Protestantism originated in the United States!

Third, missionaries should avoid behaving as if the only "enlightened" or "reformist" Orthodox Christians are those influenced by current Western trends. In the mid-1990s, a spokesman for the Moscow Patriarchate complained to Keston, justly, that Western Christians visiting Moscow often acted as if the city had only two Orthodox parishes worth visiting—the two most radical centers of innovations such as the use of contemporary language in worship. The tacit assumption of such Westerners seems to be that the only intellectually serious elements in Orthodoxy are those which mirror liberal, modernist Protestantism or Catholicism. Whether they realize it, they are practicing a form of chronological provincialism just as narrow as the geographical provincialism of those who assume that the only legitimate form of Christianity is that of America's Bible Belt. They convey to Russians the impression that they are interested in dialogue not with the mainstream of the Orthodox tradition but only with those Orthodox who are already most similar to themselves.

Such behavior is especially offensive, even if unintentionally so, when it takes the form of denying the Orthodox Church the right to define its own ecclesiastical and sacramental boundaries. Keston has repeatedly witnessed Western Christians in Moscow attempting to receive the Eucharist in Orthodox churches—as if the Orthodox Church had the same rules as many Western denominations which make their sacraments available to any baptized Christian regardless of his or her beliefs. Orthodox theology on such matters differs profoundly from contemporary Western theology; as one writer put it, from the Orthodox viewpoint inter-Communion without doctrinal accord is the equivalent of extramarital sex. When Westerners casually violate the canons of a Church of which they are not even members, they unwittingly reinforce the impression that they hold Orthodoxy in contempt.

Fourth, missionaries should not buy converts. In virtually every conversation which Keston has had on this subject with representatives of the Russian Orthodox Church, they have raised the issue of money. One deacon thought that Western economic expansion and "religious expansion" were intimately linked, as if McDonald's executives and Baptist preachers were all cogs in a single, monolithic organization. However ill-founded such views, Western missionaries should remember that what appears to them to be an incidental "extra," such as a free meal, looms quite large in the budget of a Russian whose monthly income is $100. The realities of the Russian economy are such that it is a perfectly rational investment of a nonbeliever's time to spend an hour listening to an American preacher in return for a Bible which he can then sell for the equivalent of half a day's pay. Giving a provincial Russian a free Bible as an inducement to attend a religious lecture or worship service is the equivalent of paying an American fifty dollars or so for that purpose; just as missionaries would not pay such bribes in America (at least one hopes they would not), they should not do so in Russia. There is nothing inherently wrong with giving away goods or services free of charge. But missionaries should make such items available to all who are in need, not just to participants in the missionaries' own programs.

That principle should be especially firm for charitable activities. Conditioned by Madison Avenue, American missionaries too easily forget that Christ said, "Take up thy cross and follow me," not "Take advantage of our new special offer." Free soup kitchens or food parcels should be targeted to all who are hungry, not just those willing to sit through Protestant sermons. Free English lessons should not be linked to conversion or to study programs intended to lead to conversion, as they were at an American evangelist's summer Bible-study program in a Volga town which Keston visited in 1996. The first question from the audience at the first lesson was, "Will there be a separate discussion group conducted entirely in English?" and the answer was "Yes." It was clear that a thirst for Protestantism was of less importance than learning English, at least for some of the participants.

Even more dubious is the practice of offering brand-new converts or prospective converts a lure that millions of Russians dream about: a free trip to America. No matter how well intentioned everyone on both sides, immersion in the American shopping-mall culture is not the best preparation for life back in the austere conditions of the Russian provinces. A trip to the United States can easily become just a holiday, shopping opportunity, or springboard for permanent emigration. With rare exceptions, American missionaries should not offer extended stays in the United States to schoolchildren, undergraduates, or others who have not already demonstrated a serious long-term commitment to Christian service in Russia. Even when it is clear that a student does have such a commitment, Americans should seriously assess whether they are offering an academic experience which is genuinely needed and definitely not available in Russia.

Fifth, missionaries should avoid sacrificing the needs of their Russian audience to the missionaries' own thirst for self-aggrandizement. In 1996 a Russian Protestant with a radio ministry told Keston that it was difficult to get his American partners to support the production of original Christian broadcasts in Russian rather than mere translations of programs designed for American audiences. What the Russian broadcaster wanted was programming scripted, produced, and performed by Russians for Russians—using literary and historical references familiar to Russians rather than Westerners. What the Americans wanted, he said, was the opportunity to boost their own image back home by boasting about how many Russians were hearing the same celebrity preachers familiar to the American broadcast audience.

The same phenomenon is repeated on a smaller scale when planeloads of short-term "missionary tourists" descend on Russia to film each other handing out Bibles in downtown Moscow before returning to their comfortable hotel rooms. A more edifying model is that of the young people—Catholic, Protestant, and Orthodox—who spend their summer vacations laboring to build or restore churches deep in the Russian hinterland.

Sixth, missionaries should be honest about identifying themselves. A Baptist or Methodist should call himself or herself just that, not a generic "Christian." To many Russians the words "Christian" and "Orthodox" are virtually synonymous, and Russian Orthodox clergy are understandably annoyed when their flocks end up at non-Orthodox gatherings because of this misunderstanding. Even independent missionaries who regard themselves as "non-denominational" and call themselves simply "Christian" in the West should go out of their way to make it clear that their activities in Russia are not connected with the Orthodox Church.

Keston has repeatedly heard complaints about groups which invite unsuspecting people to seminars which purport to be neutral forums for the study of various religious traditions, but which in fact are subtly designed to propagate the doctrines of a specific denomination. Deceptive tactics like this are especially indefensible when they are aimed at naive and impressionable audiences, such as schoolchildren.

Seventh, missionaries should avoid taking advantage of captive audiences. In 1998 Keston interviewed an American Protestant missionary who had visited a Russian prison camp to preach to convicted criminals. He described how one of the inmates had told the camp's commander that he did not want to attend the missionary's sermon—to which the commander replied that the prisoner had no choice, that he was being ordered to attend. The missionary told this story with obvious relish, suggesting a rather selective view of religious freedom. In the early 1990s other American missionaries sought, and often received, access to public schools to preach to the schoolchildren during regular school hours. Such brazen disregard for the rights of Russian parents who do not share Protestant beliefs helped provoke the reaction which has now brought excesses in the opposite direction, such as bans on renting classrooms to minority religious congregations even on Sundays when the schools are vacant.

Eighth, missionaries should avoid paying bribes. In 1997 a provincial official in Siberia described to Keston how Western missionary organizations had offered his predecessors and colleagues cash payments and free trips to Western Europe, and how some of these offers had been accepted. While such tactics may achieve their short-term objective of favorable treatment for the missionary's own organization, they amass an immense cost for believers in general. They encourage Russia's bureaucracy, already rife with corruption, to institutionalize the practice of setting up artificial barriers to normal religious life and then charging under-the-table fees for the selective removal of those barriers. The groups least able to afford such fees are the purely indigenous churches without wealthy foreign patrons—precisely those groups on which Russia's long-term spiritual future most depends. Close observers could not avoid noticing in 1998 that the then-new law on religion was being enforced more vigorously against domestic than against foreign religious bodies. If bribery becomes commonplace, this pattern is likely to become even more pronounced.

Even indirect bribes, such as "charitable" gifts to government agencies or "consulting fees" to well-connected "contractors," poison the moral and legal climate which honest people, and particularly Christian believers, should be trying to foster in Russia. All the arguments offered in defense of such practices amount to variations on the idea that the end justifies the means—a principle which no true Christian can accept. On a more pragmatic level, these practices risk the same outcome which has already been reached in the area of charitable shipments to Russia: Customs officials have become so rapacious in their demands for bribes that some of the groups most able and willing to help have now given up in disgust.

Ninth, missionaries should uphold and defend religious freedom for all, not just their own co-religionists. In August and September of 1997, key leaders of minority religious bodies in Russia allowed the secular authorities to draw them into a game of "divide and conquer," in which Kremlin officials met and negotiated separately with separate confessions. What had looked like a common front against repressive new legislation broke down when representatives of the two largest and most powerful minorities—the Roman Catholic Church and the Union of Evangelical Christians-Baptists—signaled their willingness to accept a "compromise" bill more threatening to the smaller minorities than to "centralized" structures such as the Catholics and the Baptist Union.

Such readiness to bargain away the liberties of others is not just wrong in principle but dangerous to the Catholics and Baptists themselves. Once the state has the power to classify some religious bodies as first class and others as second class, it is not difficult for its officials to change those classifications according to the political opportunities of the moment. Even clergy whose parishes have powerful international connections know that much of what they do, such as educational or publishing programs, is formally illegal under a strict interpretation of Russia's new law. That awareness creates a chilling effect on religious life and religious speech in general; for example, the mainstream Christian confessions have been far less vocal in Russia than in the West on issues such as abortion and capital punishment.

Tenth, American missionaries and human-rights activists should avoid demanding that every country should precisely imitate the current American model of church-state relations. Advocates of religious freedom are right when they insist that certain basic liberties are universal and should be respected by every state regardless of local circumstances. But there are many different ways to secure those liberties in practice. On various specific points, a law or regulation which most Americans would oppose in their own country might be perfectly acceptable elsewhere. One such point is the practice of formally establishing as an official state church that faith which is most closely identified with a specific national tradition—such as Anglicanism in England or Lutheranism in Norway.

Only the most provincial modern American—provincial both as an American and as a slave to modernity—would insist that the mere existence of such an established church is incompatible per se with freedom for dissenters and nonconformists. (Whether such established status is beneficial for the church itself is a separate question.) The radical Jacobin view, which insists on total separation of church and state—and which in practice usually turns into state hostility to religion—is almost as alien to the original American polity as to the Russian tradition. Only in the late twentieth century have U.S. court decisions, such as those concerning religion and education, driven God out of the "public square."

In theory, it is not difficult to imagine a Russia in which the constitution formally acknowledged the Orthodox Church as a bearer of cultural identity and moral legitimacy. Such a polity would give full protection to the rights of minority religions, but at the same time would be bathed in Orthodox symbolism as part of the Russian heritage. To implement such a theory Russia would have to amend its 1993 constitution, which states that the church is separate from the state. Such an amendment would have to be accompanied by amendments strengthening minority religious rights, since even the rights currently listed in the constitution have not been respected in practice. Far more important, both Orthodox and secular authorities would have to demonstrate the good will needed to make such a mild form of establishment actually work.

In fact, of course, the authorities have made no such effort to balance the rights of religious minorities and the special role of Orthodoxy within the rule of law. Instead they have continued the Soviet style of governing: reassuring everyone that they respect the freedoms guaranteed by the constitution and by international treaties while in practice simply ignoring these guarantees when convenient.

But that is no excuse for Americans to be equally chauvinistic. American missionaries, who claim to serve a kingdom not of this world, should be especially sensitive to the fact that their own homeland is now the world's greatest concentration of secular power—and therefore also the greatest potential source of arrogant, utopian abuses of such power. They should serve bravely but humbly.

17.

GUIDELINES
FOR FOREIGN MISSIONARIES
IN THE FORMER SOVIET UNION

——————◆——————

Anita Deyneka

The role of foreign Evangelical missionaries in Russia is controversial. Appreciated and applauded by many, they are criticized and condemned by others. Critics can be found among members of the Russian Orthodox Church, the Russian government, the Russian Protestant Church, and even among certain Western missionaries. Some Russians plead for more missionaries to come to their country. From the perspective of other nationals, the ideal foreign evangelist would not enter Russia at all. Anatoli Pchelintsev, director of the Institute of Religion and Law, an organization with extensive contacts with both national and foreign Christians of all confessions, asserts that "Russia still needs Western missionaries, but we need the right kind of help."[1]

Is there a profile of the ideal foreign missionary in Russia? Is such a paradigm possible to create? Does the nature of the evangelistic enterprise always engender controversy? Perhaps the most successful Evangelical missionaries are, by the criteria of their own definition of evangelism, more likely to be opposed by those who regard their actions as proselytism.

Ultimately, the only entirely trustworthy evaluation of past and future Evangelical missionary endeavors in Russia is divine. While this is not discernible with certainty by fallible followers of Christ, consensus from all sides does reveal certain attitudes and actions to be more desirable than others. Neither comprehensive nor infallible, the following suggestions, gleaned from many sources, are a step toward guidelines for foreign missionaries in Russia.

---

[1] Interview by Anita Deyneka with Anatoli Pchelintsev (July 1993), available in Russian Ministries Files, Wheaton, Illinois.

First, we must know and appreciate Russian culture. Paul Semenchuk, an American of Russian ancestry who has served thirty-five years as a missionary to Russians with Trans World Radio, urges Western ministers in Russia to honor the country's culture:

> We triumphantly invade Russia without any preparation, not having read one Russian book, not even one book about Russia. We need to read their classical writers and poets if we want to understand Russians . . . because of its peculiar past, the Russian personality is exceptionally complex. We will never reach the soul of the Slav if we don't familiarize ourselves with their history, literature, art. . . . Knowing and somewhat understanding Russian history is one thing; knowing and understanding Russian current events is no less essential. . . . But there is no quick fix. . . . Cultural assimilation takes time. I need on-site, hands-on experience. I have to grow into it. It has to grow on me. . . . I get it by caring, curiosity, observation, scrutiny, questioning, association, by unrestricted, unreserved involvement (total immersion) in the society.[2]

Acknowledging the necessity of Western missionaries learning the Russian language, or at least using competent translators when they do not know the language, Semenchuk adds: "Knowing the cultural language is more important than knowing the spoken language. Yet many well-meaning Westerners find themselves in the CIS culturally isolated. No amount of language study can make up for this handicap."[3]

Second, we must avoid Westernization of the Gospel. Grigori Komendant, president of the Evangelical Christians Baptists of Ukraine, states that "the West needs to be more realistic in recognizing that Russia is not a third world country. The church has been here a long time and we are not interested in the Americanization of our church."[4]

> Russia is not a savage, unexplored territory—ready for our adventuresome, enterprising invasion, conquest, domination and exploitation. Russians—believers or not—will never accept a Western mode of Christianity. . . . When our Western values are projected on the Russian scene, they generate all kinds of tension, offense, negative thoughts and feelings, unhealthy attitudes.[5]

---

[2] Paul Semenchuk, "Western Christians Working in the CIS: Are They in Tune with Russian Evangelical Nationals?" (November 1994) (paper prepared for Trans World Radio, on file with author).

[3] Ibid., 34.

[4] Interview by Peter Deyneka with Grigori Komendant (October 1996), available in Russian Ministries Files, Wheaton, Illinois.

[5] Semenchuk, "Western Christians Working in the CIS," 2.

At a February 1993 consultation on furthering theological education in the CIS[6] sponsored by the Overseas Council on Theological Education, the Institute for East-West Christian Studies, and Russian Ministries, comments by nationals indicated the desire for partnership with the West while at the same time avoiding Westernization:

- We want to know what is going on . . . what is available.
- How can we become part of the loop?
- We are hungry and thirsty for information and fellowship.
- We do not want everything to be given to us, but we must know what is available.
- We do not want ready made Western Christianity to be dumped on us.
- We would love to have the tools, and then we will work it out for ourselves.[7]

Third, we must respect the rights of all religions and cooperate with other Christians whenever possible. Foreign missionaries, increasingly objects of intolerance, must show respect for all religions even when their own legal and religious rights are violated. If national and foreign Evangelicals are to experience true religious liberty, so must all other religious groups whose activities are law-abiding. However, such toleration does not preclude a defense of one's freedoms when they are violated.

Without denying differences or compromising essential beliefs, Russian Orthodox priest Alexander Men advocated not only tolerance, but even an appreciation for the diversity of Christianity:

I hope you may feel that the variety within the church, and still more the contradictions between the denominations—Protestant, Catholic, Orthodox—are not signs of decay and break but rather manifestations of parts of the whole, the united whole which we have to reach at greater depth. . . . It is as if, knowing people's tendency to intolerance, God divided them so that each person in their place . . . the garden . . . would bring forth fruit.[8]

Dr. Mark Elliott, director of the Institute for East-West Christian Studies at Wheaton College, encourages Evangelicals and Orthodox to seek to cooperate whenever possible for the greater good of Russia's religious renewal:

The common ground between Orthodox and Evangelicals has often counted for little as Evangelicals have made their way into territory Orthodox consider to be their exclusive domain. Here the key question is

---

[6] See Manfred Kohl, "Filling the Leadership Void in the Post Communist Church," *Contact* 23 (1994): 45.

[7] Ibid.

[8] Letter from Krister Sairsingh to Anita Deyneka (January 16, 1997).

whether, east of the old Iron Curtain, Evangelicals are interlopers. Many Orthodox Christians, for example, believe that Protestants have no place in Russia. In particular, they view recent Evangelical activity from abroad as an unwelcome and offensive intrusion into a spiritual landscape nourished by a thousand years of Byzantine Christianity. . . .

Western missionaries working in countries with longstanding Orthodox traditions need to apply themselves to a study of history and culture to understand the heritage which has prompted Russian Orthodox to such antagonism to Evangelicals. However, even as Evangelicals come to appreciate Orthodoxy, the exceptional achievements of Russian culture, and the remarkable perseverance of a longsuffering people, they should not feel that they need to apologize for sharing the good news in a Russia without Marx. . . .

Because of Russia's present economic and political travails, and because of Marxism's harvest of moral and spiritual devastation, it would appear that reestablishing Christian moorings and life-changing faith across the land would more than challenge all the resources and efforts of Orthodox, Protestants, and Catholics combined. Proselytism under these circumstances is uncharitable, divisive, and counterproductive, and, by diverting energies into futile interconfessional strife, it diminishes the prospects of reaching the tens of millions of Russian nonbelievers. . . .

Today in Russia, Orthodox-Evangelical relations are strained, with cordial relationships the exception, rather than the rule. But the exceptions can encourage us to hope and work for more fruitful cooperation. One Western ministry new to Russia has quickly established a remarkably productive relationship with a Russian Orthodox diocese. This cooperative effort—as described in the anonymous letter below—deserves to be commended and widely copied:

> "The Lord has helped us to develop good relations with Russian Orthodox Church authorities. We have had repeated consultations with members of the archbishop's cabinet, meetings held with the archbishop's blessing. These have resulted in good mutual understanding and offers of cooperation at some levels. For example, we provide flannel graph materials and training of Orthodox priests to engage in child evangelism. The archbishop has provided Orthodox priests as trainers to help orient our career and short-term missionaries in understanding what the Russian Orthodox Church stands for and is doing in Russia. Orthodox have also participated in a limited way in our summer youth camping programs, and have offered us some of their air time on the government radio station.

> "How has our small Evangelical ministry developed a good relationship with the Orthodox Church and the government? In a number of ways. Perhaps most importantly, we have always taken the initiative to meet with the Orthodox to show respect and ap-

preciation for the good things they are doing and to express our interest in learning from them and being cooperative. Some, perhaps many, leaders of the Russian Orthodox Church are skeptical and hostile toward foreign, Protestant groups because of their fear of what we may be doing. That fear is sometimes validated by the insensitive activities of some groups and the presence of cults which leads people away from biblical truth. Our philosophy has been that what we are actually doing would be reassuring to the Orthodox, compared to what they fear we might do if they had no direct knowledge of our activities. Therefore, we meet with them and communicate with them in person and in writing about our history, our doctrines, our current activities, and our proposed activities. We show them respect as our elder brothers in Russia by asking them for advice about Bible translations, cultural issues, and how to avoid activities which would be needlessly offensive. And we avoid proselytizing Russian Orthodox Christians, directing our ministries instead toward the vast majority of practical atheists. We do our best to stress our common ground, without compromising biblical imperatives. Secondly, we made a matter of high priority the full legal registration of our church, both at the federal level with the Ministry of Justice in Moscow, and at the local levels as needed.

"This full legal compliance for our ministries has opened many doors for us, such as property ownership, visas, and partnerships with government agencies, including youth departments and education departments."[9]

Fourth, we must proclaim the Gospel in word and deed. Humanitarian aid as a part of the Christian mission should be given without coercion to convert to any religious confession. John Bernbaum, president of the Russian American Christian University, observes that "most Russians think Protestants are just worried about finding adherents to their strange theological beliefs; we have to demonstrate that our goals are more significant and beneficial than that."[10]

Paul Semenchuk urges missionaries to cultivate compassion:

If we want to minister in the CIS, our responsibility may be broader than we initially intended or expected. The former Soviet Union is in such severe economic circumstances that it seems "sinful" to go and work there

---

[9] Mark Elliott and Anita Deyneka, "Protestant Missionaries in the Former Soviet Union," *Emory International Law Review* 12 (1998): 361, 383-95 (quoting letter to Mark Elliott [January 7, 1997]).

[10] E-mail from John Bernbaum (July 13, 1996), available in Russian Ministries Files, Wheaton, Illinois.

without providing some sort of practical assistance. If we move among them, how can we let them go hungry? There is a multitude to feed. If anyone in this world is expected to care and share, it is the Christian.[11]

Fifth, we must serve the national church. *Guidelines for Christians Working in Central and Eastern Europe*, prepared by the British-based Evangelical Missionary Alliance, exhorts missionaries to maintain an attitude of servanthood:

Go as a servant to those you will meet. Be willing to accept and respect the Christians you meet as brothers and sisters in the Lord and to serve their needs with compassion and love. . . . Sad to say, some Westerners have shown a superior attitude to Eastern Europeans, many of whom are well educated and resent the paternalistic or imperialistic attitudes they see in some foreign visitors. Share what you have to offer with sensitivity. . . . Look out for things you can learn from the people you visit. . . . If you are going to meet real needs, you need to ask some important questions: Is what you have to offer, in ministry or in aid, really needed? Have you the resources to back up your offer of help? Will you be able to finish the job?[12]

In recommendations resulting from a 1991 consultation convened by the Lausanne Committee, national and Western Christians urge missionaries to "enable the churches and mission organizations in these countries to undertake the work of evangelizing their own people."[13]

Commenting in a 1992 article on finances, one of the most sensitive areas of foreign-national relations, Peter Sautov, director of the Russian Center for Evangelism, noted that it costs twenty times as much to support an American missionary as a Russian worker who knows the culture and language. "It is the Russian believers who should work for Russia," commented Sautov. "I don't want to raise a generation of lazy Russian believers. We need help. But help means teaching us, training us, showing us. Let us be the ones to do it."[14] Sergei Sannikov, president of the Odessa Theological Seminary, declares, "Western missionaries should avoid two extremes: coming and doing everything themselves [and] giving money with no control."[15]

Alexei Melnichuk, administrative director of Donetsk Bible College in the Ukraine, advises Western missionaries on how they can best serve the national church:

---

[11] Semenchuk, "Western Christians Working in the CIS," 4.

[12] Evangelical Missionary Alliance, *Working in Central and Eastern Europe*, 34.

[13] Lausanne Committee for World Evangelization, *Recommendations to Those Working in Eastern Europe and the USSR* (Wheaton, Illinois, 1991).

[14] Randy Frame, "Churches Need Coworkers, Not Tourists," *Christianity Today* (July 20, 1992), 56.

[15] Sergei Sannikov, "Most Pressing Needs of the CIS Church," *East-West Church and Ministry Report* (Summer 1995): 2.

We need Western missionaries in our country. However, we need a very small number who are experienced and well-educated and who can help us prepare our own missionaries. We have many people ready to be missionaries, but they don't have the support. I think Western Christians are ready to spend much money for trips to the former Soviet Union. This is not bad, but if we want to spread Jesus Christ throughout the world, we need a better way not going by our own way, opinions, and visions. American people need to understand the time it takes to [influence] the culture. They need to understand that they don't understand the culture. This is very important. I have met many angry Russian Christians, who say that Western missionaries are causing them problems. The missionaries come and say they will help: Then, after several months, they move on to their own projects, taking the money and many of the best Russian Christian workers with them.[16]

Sixth, there is the rule above all rules—the Golden Rule. Ever since the modern missions crusade to Russia began, foreign missionaries have evidenced considerable concern and care to establish guidelines for their ministries. Numerous Evangelical organizations and institutions have held conferences, consultations, and symposiums in the West to consider how missionaries can best conduct themselves in Russia and the former Soviet Union.[17] Furthermore, the Institute for East-West Christian Studies in the United States publishes a quarterly journal, *East-West Church and Ministry Report*, primarily devoted to this subject.

Foreign missionaries living in Russia also have attempted to establish guidelines through a variety of forums, including the Gathering, a quarterly meeting of foreign missionaries in Moscow. An electronic conference entitled "Gathering" was set up in November 1996 to promote communication among expatriate missionaries working in Russia and to provide a medium to discuss ministry issues.

At a Gathering meeting in May 1996, an all-Russian panel with representatives from both Orthodox and Protestant confessions spoke to foreign missionaries on the topics "What Is Evangelism?" and "What Is the Role of the Culture in Evangelism?"[18] To promote greater understanding, expatriate and national Christians met during a 1995 Gathering and both sides openly voiced their concerns. The Western group challenged themselves to consider some of the following issues:

---

[16] Alexei Melnichuk, "We Asked . . . " *Pulse* (September 23, 1994): 3.

[17] These organizations and institutions include The CoMission, the Evangelical Fellowship of Mission Agencies, the Interdenominational Foreign Mission Association, the Lausanne Committee for World Evangelization, the Overseas Ministries Study Center, and the World Evangelical Fellowship.

[18] Gathering minutes (May 17, 1996), available in Russian Ministries Files, Wheaton, Illinois.

What do our Russian brothers consider to be the proper role of the missionary in Russia? What about Western funding? Some day it will end; how can this be solved? What are the cultural mistakes we make and how can we correct them? Why is it necessary to work through the existing national churches? How can we build mutual trust in spite of differences? Why do national church leaders fear new church paradigms for emerging segments of society? Are Western definitions and models threatening to the national church?[19]

Even when missionaries conscientiously examine their attitudes and activities, specific guidelines are difficult to develop. Many issues are complex and debatable. For example, is it possible for foreigners to be of Christian service in Russia if they do not know the language and culture? Is long-term mission service by foreigners always preferable to short-term? How can nationals and foreigners work most effectively together in missions to Russia? Should foreigners always be subservient to nationals? Should foreign Christians provide financial assistance to national Christians, and, if so, under what circumstances of accountability? Is the greater denominational diversification engendered by foreign missions desirable or does it inevitably promote competition? How should missionaries relate to divisions within national denominations, such as the registered and unregistered schisms in the Evangelical Christian-Baptist movement? With the existence of national evangelists, church-planters, and missionaries, how much of a role exists for Westerners to fulfill these ministries in Russia? How can foreigners learn from the Russians as well as teach and assist them? To what extent should Evangelicals work with confessions and denominations other than their own? When does evangelism become proselytism?

Even the most conscientious missionaries will not find such convoluted considerations easily resolved. In addition, both those missionaries who care deeply and those who appear indifferent to the consequences of their mission will make mistakes. Nevertheless, the accomplishments of missionaries in Russia in the last five years are remarkable. Thousands have left comfort and security to travel to remote regions of Russia, often with families and sometimes intending to remain indefinitely. They have attempted to bring spiritual help and healing to a society scarred by seventy years of Marxist atheism and now suffering political, economic, and social turmoil. During the past six years, missionaries have worked with national Christians to establish as many as six thousand new Protestant fellowships and churches and to expand existing ones. Foreign missionaries also have helped organize an estimated one thousand indigenous parachurch organizations across the former Soviet Union, ministering to even the most neglected sectors of society.[20]

---

[19] Ibid.

[20] Interview by Anita Deyneka with Peter Deyneka and George Law (February 5, 1997), available in Russian Ministries Files, Wheaton, Illinois.

Russian Val Komissarov has analyzed this phenomenon as follows:

Missionary churches dedicated to proclaiming the Gospel all over the world are not a rare thing in the West. Such churches send their members to various parts of the world, support their missionary training and preparation, and regularly pray for their protection, success in ministry, as well as for the salvation of souls in other parts of the world. It seems to me this is the most difficult thing to understand for my compatriots, when they ask, why do they come here? The answer is they come to proclaim the Gospel just as they do in their own countries trying to wake people up from the lethargy of primitive atheism and materialism. Perhaps among missionaries coming to Russia there are some who are interested only in their own benefits. In fact such people cannot be called missionaries; they are businessmen of religion. Does it mean that because of such people, we should demand that all missionary activities in Russia should be stopped and all those who want to come and preach the Gospel should be denied permission to do so? I don't think so. . . . Who can say that thousands and thousands of Western Christians lack love when they continue to collect resources for humanitarian aid, medications, treatments for the terminally ill, and help for education institutions? We believe in one Christ, read one Bible, and pray to one God.[21]

At a February 1995 consultation of Russian and Western Christian workers, when asked what guidelines they would recommend to Westerners wishing to promote church growth in Russia, the nationals urged missionaries to "acculturate, understand, love, accept . . . and be one body with Russian believers, making changes as the Holy Spirit directs."[22] Russian immigrant evangelist Johannes Reimer has urged Western missionaries to be "incarnational rather than organizational" if they wish their mission to succeed; "become one of us and we will listen to you."[23]

Such recommendations appear remarkably similar to the Golden Rule. Although not a detailed description of how missions in Russia should be conducted, Christ's admonition in Matthew 7:12 is the most dependable guide to an enterprise characterized by much uncertainty and controversy: "In everything, do to others what you would have them do to you, for this sums up the Law and the Prophets." In every circumstance, foreign missionaries might be most effective if they were to imagine themselves in the place of the Russian people if the situation were reversed and Russian Christians were arriving en

[21] Val Komissarov, "Missionaries: In and Out of Fashion," *East-West Missionary Report* (Fall 1996): 67.

[22] E-mail from George J. Law, Summary of Afternoon Gathering Sessions (February 15, 1995), available in Russian Ministries Files, Wheaton, Illinois.

[23] Johannes Reimer, "Mission in Post-*Perestroika* Russia," *Missionalia* 24 (1996): 18, 34.

masse to evangelize in America or Great Britain. Such a scenario is not un-imaginable. In the 1980s, a Czechoslovakian physicist was assigned to work at a research institute in the Soviet Union where he also organized clandestine Bible studies among his colleagues. In his own country, he suffered restrictions and repressions but, nevertheless, helped build and lead a church there. In 1984, he remarked, "Communism with the suffering it has brought to believers has swept away corrupt and lukewarm Christianity in our country. It has created a vacuum in millions of people . . . which can be truly filled only with vital Christianity. And that is what is happening—Christianity, purified and revitalized, is spreading throughout our country. Perhaps the day will come when our suffering church will be sending missionaries to your country."[24]

In the meantime, foreign missionaries must cope with a nation repressed by communism and suffering—and yet a nation that has recently passed a law restricting religion.[25] In light of this new situation, Western Christians should pray for and support Russian Evangelicals more than promoting their own missiological program. They should also pray for the Russian Orthodox Church to find its security in spiritual rather than political power. Spiritual interest in Russia is strong, and Russians will continue to turn to their historic church. But sadly, any attempt to strengthen one church at the expense of others is likely to postpone the renewal that could vitalize the Orthodox Church.

In all things, though, the final admonition is that Russia's history reveals a nation attuned to the spiritual—and one that will likely stay that way. In the words of Dostoyevsky: "For real Russians the questions of God's existence and of immortality . . . come first and foremost. . . . For the secret of man's being is not only to live, but to have something to live for."[26] Foreign missionaries must find a way to draw upon and expand this reality embedded within Russian culture while simultaneously recognizing the debt and respect owed to the indigenous Orthodox Church for its role in fostering such an atmosphere.

---

[24] Anita Deyneka and Peter Deyneka Jr., "A Life on the Soviet Precipice," *Christianity Today* (March 1, 1985): 24, 68.

[25] See "Russian Federation Law on Freedom of Conscience and on Religious Associations," trans. Lawrence A. Uzzell as Appendix A, *Emory International Law Review* 12 (1998): 657-80.

[26] Quoted by Deyneka and Deyneka in "A Life on the Soviet Precipice."

CONTRIBUTORS

Donna E. Arzt is Professor of Law at Syracuse University College of Law.

Harold J. Berman is the Robert W. Woodruff Professor of Law at Emory University, Fellow in Russian Studies at the Carter Center of Emory University, and James Barr Ames Professor of Law, emeritus, at Harvard University.

James H. Billington is the thirteenth Librarian of Congress, a former professor at Harvard University and Princeton University, and former director of the Woodrow Wilson International Center for Scholars.

Michael Bourdeaux is Co-founder and Director of Keston Institute, Canon of the Church of England.

Anita Deyneka is Director of Research and Communications for Russian Ministries, Inc., in Wheaton, Illinois, Lecturer at Wheaton College, and Director of Soviet and East-European Studies of the Slavic Gospel Association.

Mark Elliott is Professor of History and Director of the Institute for East-West Studies at Wheaton College, Illinois, and Editor of the *East-West Church and Ministry Report*.

Sergei Filatov is Director of the Sociological Center of the Moscow Public Science Foundation and Senior Researcher of the Institute of Oriental Studies of the Russian Academy of Sciences.

T. Jeremy Gunn is Fellow at the United States Institute of Peace, Washington, D.C., and General Counsel for the National Committee for Public Education and Religious Liberty.

Lauren B. Homer is President of Law and Liberty Trust in the United States and Russia, and Chair of the International Law Group, P.C.

Firuz Kazemzadeh is Professor of History, emeritus, Yale University, Member of the National Spiritual Assembly of the Baha'is in the United States, and Editor of *World Order*.

Metropolitan Kirill is Metropolitan of Smolensk and Kaliningrad of the Russian Orthodox Church and Chairman of the Department of External Relations of the Moscow Patriarchate of the Russian Orthodox Church.

Mikhail M. Kulakov is President of the Russian Division of the Seventh-day Adventist Church and President of Dialogue Foundation, a Russian-based organization promoting religious toleration and Christian education.

Aleksandr Shchipkov is Lecturer in Sociology of Religion at St. Petersburg University, a religious broadcaster for Radio Russia, and a widely published journalist.

Yuriy Tabak is a free-lance journalist for Radio Liberty's "Religion in the Modern World" and Lecturer on Judaism at St. Andrew's Biblical Theological College in Moscow.

Lawrence A. Uzzell is the Moscow representative and Director-Designate for Keston Institute, and Editor of the *Keston News Service.*

Lyudmila Vorontsova is a historian and Senior Fellow of the Sergiev Posad State Museum of History and Art.

Philip Walters is Head of Research at Keston Institute, Oxford, and Editor of *Religion, State, Society.*

John Witte Jr. is the Jonas Robitscher Professor of Law and Ethics and Director of the Law and Religion Program at Emory University in Atlanta.

Index

Davidyuk, Vassily, 209 n.39
Davis, Derek, 17 n.76
Davis, Nathaniel, 32 n.2
Demidov, Valeri, 157 n.16
democracy and democratization (demo-
    kratizatsiia), xi, xii, xiv, 44, 47, 54, 57-
    58, 107, 146-47, 255-56, 318-19
Dennen, Xenia, xiv
Deyneka, Anita, 2, 3 nn.5,6, 5, 5 nn.21,
    23,24, 6 n.29, 7 n.33, 23, 23 nn.95,96,
    24 n.98, 130 n.93, 197-226, 265 n.2,
    266, 331-40
Deyneka, Peter, 202. See also Russian
    Ministries
dialogue, 23, 67, 154, 155, 161-62, 333-
    40
Dikin, Nikolai, 166
Dokuchayev, D., 166 n.4
Dostoyevsky, 38 n.7, 68, 71, 203, 238,
    266, 340
Dudakov, S., 142 n.4
Dunlop, John B., 38 n.7, 131 n.98
Durham, W. Cole, Jr., 10 n.48, 18, 18 n.78,
    24 n.100, 215 n.64, 260 n.82, 276
    n.32, 278 n.39
Dvorkin, Alexander, 7 nn.34,35
Eckhardt, A. Roy, 146 n.18
ecumenism, 44, 46, 69, 72, 74, 148, 153-
    55, 217, 333-40
Eggert, Konstantin, 133 n.104
Eickelman, Dale F., 110 n.6, 113 n.17
Elliott, Mark, 2, 3 n.5, 5 nn.21,23,24, 7
    n.33, 10 nn.44,45, 21 nn.87,88,89, 24
    n.98, 130 n.93, 197-226, 265 n.2, 266,
    333-35
Ellis, Jane, xiv, 8 nn.39,40, 32 n.2, 45 n.18,
    216, 217 n.72
Enlightenment, 20, 26, 27, 34, 39-40
Esposito, John, 110 n.7
Evangelical Apostolic Churches, 86
Evangelicalism and Evangelicals, 5, 7, 21-
    22, 57, 85, 87, 89, 197, 198, 204, 207-
    11, 275 n.10. See also Protestantism
Fairbairn, Don, 21 n.87, 210, 210
    nn.43,44, 211, 211 n.45
Faruqi, Islmail R., 110 n.6
Federov, Vladimir, 44 n.17
Feldbrugge, F.J.M., 256 n.71
Fennell, John, 31 n.2
Filaret, Metropolitan of Minsk, 188

Filatov, Olga, 157 n.18
Filatov, Sergei, 2, 2 n.2, 5 nn.19,21, 6
    nn.27,29, 21 n.88, 24 n.98, 79 n.3, 83
    n.9, 85 n.13, 93-107, 119 n.46, 147
    n.21, 139 n.31, 163-84, 285 n.4, 302
    n.56
Filfei, Abbot, 35
Filipov, David, 276 n.31
Filofei (Philotheus) of Pskov, 231-32
Finley, Mark, 160
Fisher, Doris, 218 n.74
Fletcher, William C., 31 n.2, 213 n.56
Foglesong, David S., 41 n.12
Ford, Annette J., 206 n.32
Fot, Henry, 209 n.39
Francis, Keith A., 151 n.3
Frank, Semen, 41
freedoms. See Law
Friedman, Francine, 133 n.105
Fyodorov, Leonid, 101, 102
Gainutdin, Ravil, Sheikh, 128
Galiev, Mirsaid Sultan, 113
Garadzha, V. I., 79 nn.2,4
Garrett, Paul D., 39 n.8
Gaynudtdin, Ravil, Supreme Mufti, 136
    n.121
Georgian Orthodox Church, 2, 59, 267
glasnost, xiv, 2, 3, 19, 45, 117, 185, 192,
    195, 198, 216
Goble, Paul, 127 n.80
Golabinski, E. E., 228 n.2
Golden Rule, xiii, 24, 337-38
Gogol, Nikolai, 106 n.20, 219
Gorbachev, Mikhail, 2, 3, 4, 6, 26, 27, 45,
    85, 96, 98, 116-18, 127, 172, 185-86,
    189, 196, 198, 268, 271-75
Gorbachev, Raisa, 191
Gorki, 79
Gorodetsky, Nadejda, 38 n.7
Graham, Billy, 164, 186, 300
Graves, Jack, 203 n.20
Great Commission, xiii, 24, 66-67, 294
Great White Brotherhood, 168-71
Greek Catholicism or Greek Catholic, 2,
    6, 37, 43, 91, 100-102
Greek Orthodox Church, 50, 59, 63, 248-
    50
Greenspahn, Frederick, 214, 214 nn.61,
    62, 215 n.63
Gregory X, Pope, 143